Morality Imposed

Morality Imposed

The Rehnquist Court and Liberty in America

Stephen E. Gottlieb

NEW YORK UNIVERSITY PRESS

New York and London

NEW YORK UNIVERSITY PRESS
New York and London

Library of Congress Cataloging-in-Publication Data
Gottlieb, Stephen E.
Morality imposed : the Rehnquist court and liberty in America /
Stephen E. Gottlieb.
p.   cm.
Includes bibliographical references and index.
ISBN 0-8147-3128-7 (cloth : alk. paper)
1. United States. Supreme Court. 2. Rehnquist, William H., 1924– .
3. Law and ethics.   I. Title.
KF8742 .G68 2000
347.73'26'09049—dc21   00-009311

Manufactured in the United States of America
10 9 8 7 6 5 4 3 2 1

*To the generations of lawyers and judges
who dedicated their careers
to a vision of the law
in the service of humankind
and to the teachers
who first introduced me
to the decency and nobility of their work,
Alpheus Mason
and
Walter Murphy*

Contents

Preface

Why and How This Book

Why This Book

Notwithstanding common descriptions of the justices, there is no center on this Court, and there are no moderates. When the Court's "conservatives" find common ground with the Court's "liberals," they have arrived at their conclusions from essentially unrelated premises. Analysis of the Court as if there were a continuum from Rehnquist to Breyer is a serious misunderstanding. This book is intended to clarify the thinking of the nine current members of the Court and the significance of their ways of thinking for the rest of us.

We like to think of judges and justices as deciding cases on the facts and the law. Thus some may find upsetting the suggestion—although it is surely not new—that justices decide cases in line with their own private, preexisting philosophies of law. And more, the suggestion that the justices make specific ideological assumptions. Yet several dramatic recent decisions have underscored the fact that these assertions are as true of the Rehnquist Court as of its predecessors.[1]

To some extent all of the Supreme Court justices decide the cases on the facts and the law. Some cases are simply so clear that all persons of goodwill read the law in the same way. Few cases of that sort reach the Supreme Court of the United States because it has the statutory right to decide which cases it will hear and which it will not. The Court by its own rules and by the inclinations of its members looks for cases where the law is not clear, where there is significant controversy about the meaning of law, where the lower courts are in disagreement. The Supreme Court is the supervisor of the American legal system. It leaves the easy cases to the minions below.

Most of the cases that reach the Supreme Court cannot be decided on the basis of mere logical inference from the language of preexisting legal rules applied to the facts of the cases. They take judgment, choices among different reasonable ways to understand what has been meant. There is disagreement among lawyers and judges about whether that entails going outside the law and applying something that is not law to help make legal decisions, or whether law as it is and has been practiced in the Anglo-American system includes and requires that judges and justices understand the "rules" in light of fundamental American principles of ethics, morality, and humanity. In most of the cases that the Supreme Court considers, the justices have no choice but to allow themselves to be influenced by their understanding of those fundamental principles.

Some scholars and justices argue that where such judgment is necessary there is no "law" and the justices should refuse to extend "law" to such issues. Others hold that such a restricted reading shrinks the reach of the Constitution and statutes, making them both irrelevant just when thinking based on fundamental principles should be most important. They believe that the framers and draftsmen intended that we should never lose sight of those principles in interpreting what they wrote. Even the answer to that basic question, whether we should interpret law in light of fundamental American principles, is not a logical inference from anything the founders told us in the Constitution or that Congress has told us in its statutes. Judgment matters.

But the grounds on which the justices make their judgments have not been easily grasped. Neither liberals nor conservatives have been particularly clear about their own basic philosophical assumptions. Opponents' fundamental principles seem mysterious and opaque. They distort one anothers' views. And they often reason in language shaped by outdated discussions, and focus on critiquing fellow justices rather than explaining their own assumptions. Hence much of the discussion about the Court has been quite misleading.

Adding to the confusion, the members of the conservative bloc hold that ideology should have no place in judging and has no place in their own work. Instead, they are simply guided by the language of the law or the history leading up to its enactment. These are arguments about what lawyers call methods of interpretation. But the discussion turns out to be sterile because these methods rarely yield precise answers in the type of case that reaches the high court.

While the justices contend that they are not driven by ideology, many analysts ascribe a pragmatic or eclectic approach to the justices. Taking for granted that judges are pragmatic or eclectic effectively precludes exploring the central philosophical assumptions driving the work of either the conservative or liberal bloc.

These approaches have created a false picture of the justices because all the members of the Court have strong philosophic convictions that affect their judgments; indeed it could not be otherwise.

The Court until recently was dominated by varieties of functionalists trying to improve society. Utilitarians and liberals, despite important disagreements among themselves, nevertheless share an essential functional or goal-driven outlook. Their objective is a freer or happier society, and they assume that where the Constitution is ambiguous it should be interpreted in a manner consistent with that premise. Utilitarian, functional, cost-benefit modes of thought are so common that the philosophical assumptions of functionalists are often seen as merely pragmatic rather than as structured modes of thought.

The Rehnquist Court represents a far more major revolution in judicial thought in America than is commonly appreciated. It shows little concern for goals, focusing instead on a variety of noninstrumental moral judgments. The conservative bloc has chosen to reject two basic principles of the Anglo-American tradition: the principle that law should be guided by the objective of doing no harm, and the principle of respect for individual moral autonomy where harm to others is not at stake. Those choices are very far-reaching and thoroughly political. This book amplifies the implications of those choices with studies of each of the nine justices on the Court. Chapter 1 provides background on the justices for the lay reader. Chapter 2 opens the discussion of the central elements of this book, describing the gulf that separates the members of the Court's liberal and conservative wings. Chapters 3 through 5 explore the conservative bloc and the divergence between the Court's right wing and its more centrist conservatives. Chapters 6 through 8 explore the more liberal justices, including the contrasts among them and the conservative elements in the thinking of the more liberal justices. Chapter 9 takes a look at Justice Souter. The final chapter returns to the central conflict among the justices.

How This Book Came About

This study grew out of two concurrent projects. I began to teach a course on the justices of the Supreme Court at the same time that I was writing a casebook for use in courses on jurisprudence, the philosophy of law. As I tried to explain the justices to my students, I found myself weighing and testing jurisprudential ideas against the output of the justices. This book gradually emerged from that effort over a period of several years.

The approach taken here differs in four important ways from prior examinations of the Rehnquist Court. First, this book treats judicial rhetoric as a much smaller element in the study of judicial approaches than do those that focus on doctrine. In this respect the book derives from what is known as the "realist" tradition in American law.[2] Second, although the realists were skeptical of philosophy, the contemporary ferment in jurisprudence invites a search for consistent philosophical principles. Third, this book conducts that search by comparing groups of cases with philosophical principles that could account for them. Fourth, by examining all nine justices, it attempts a more accurate placement of each in the proper philosophical traditions, which can be hidden by more narrowly drawn comparisons.

There are several reasons not to be mesmerized by what jurists say about their own views and to explore whether they are accurate, sincere, delusional, or hypocritical. Claims and arguments in individual cases or even long lines of cases are often taken to persuade other justices. They reflect the audience more than the speaker, and they are shaped by the conventions of the legal community. Moreover, few of us have examined carefully the sentiments that move our judgments. One can't simply posit that the justices are entirely aware of their own reasons. Thus the patterns of the justices' conclusions are at least as important as the explanations.

There is considerable evidence that the rhetoric in the opinions of Rehnquist, Scalia, and Thomas does not match their jurisprudential claims.[3] In that respect they appear to be typical justices. They write extensively about being faithful to the law—interpreting it accurately rather than making it. But they and this Court are and will be no more interpretivist than their predecessors, whether or not it were possible.

Instead, all the justices impose their own philosophical convictions on the law. The philosophically conservative assumptions of the conservative jurists are as political as the philosophically liberal assumptions of the relatively liberal justices. What may be different is the degree to which those assumptions seem common or surprising within the American cultural milieu.

The second basic aspect of the method used in this book is the focus on the large philosophical propositions that move the justices. Implicitly, much writing about the justices assumes some degree of pragmatism.[4]

Pragmatism has as a given that the justices have somewhat inchoate biases and respond to diverse factors that influence particular decisions. Consistency is asking too much and is not observed. This book reaches the opposite conclusion. Grand philosophical theories matter even if not completely.[5] Consistency is common and lack of consistency may be described as lack of principle. It is important to understand the philosophical traditions that the justices reflect, however crudely.

It is not my point that all liberals or conservatives believe certain propositions or that liberalism or conservatism are unique philosophies. Quite the contrary. A single conservative-liberal axis for understanding the justices' opinions is seriously misleading because both conservatism and liberalism in America come in many forms.[6] Unfortunately, the bulk of legal scholarship about the members of the Court has ignored these underlying philosophical issues.[7]

The method can be described as putting together the pieces of a puzzle. How do the opinions of any of the justices fit together? Indeed, the first question is whether the justices' opinions fit at all or are just contradictory. The answer to that question depends on whether there is a principle or set of principles that, if applied properly, makes sense of the whole. So, if the opinions fit, how do they fit? What principles make them fit?

By contrast, social scientists trained in statistical analysis have tried to examine the volume of the justices' output using statistical tools.[8] These efforts have the advantage that they do not take the justices at their word. They have made it clear that liberalism and conservatism matter. That is, one can arrange the justices on a liberal-conservative scale or axis and their positions will be relatively constant over time. That helps puncture the notion that justices merely apply the law as given.

But several problems plague these statistical efforts. The statistics are based on categorization or "coding" of the justices' opinions by experts or trained staff. To compare a case not yet before the Court with the cases already decided, a panel of experts is required. For that task, the statistical work represents no significant advance in our knowledge. The statistical work does describe the relative positions of the justices to one another, but we know much about those relative positions without the help of these studies.

More, the universe of cases on which the statistical work is based is itself a skewed universe rather than a random sample of issues. Pivotal issues can come up in isolated cases while the sample responds to multiple cases in narrower areas in which the Court agrees to hear cases. To get at pivotal issues requires a methodology that is more philosophically nuanced and more responsive to cases that play important parts in the logic of ideas rather than to cases that are common because of current disputes.

The basic question is which explanation best explains the observed behavior. If ideology works to explain a justice's behavior, it seems much less likely that he or she is deciding cases on the basis of a theory of interpretation. Thus the philosophic sources of conservative as well as liberal jurisprudence reflect on the debate over whether methods of interpretation matter. On the other hand, if ideological considerations or other predictable regularities are not explanatory, then it may be that the interpretive canons mean a great deal to the justice. In fact, ideology controls this Court.

Thus this book examines many kinds of evidence—looking at the justices' language in part but also exploring contemporary conservatism and the lines of argument that might justify the patterns of conclusions the justices actually reach. Any specific example, of course, is consistent both with the hypothesis that the law was "clear" on the point and the hypothesis that the reason it was "clear" to these justices was a more fundamental antipathy to the object of the laws. That duality is inherent in the problem of identifying causation. In the cases discussed below, the clarity of the law was not obvious to all participants and the philosophical explanation fits a great deal of the data. The issue is much like the famed shift of thought from an earth-centered to a sun-centered vision of the solar system—elliptical orbits are much simpler than the epicycles astronomers once used to describe the relative motion of the heavenly bodies. The question here is whether explanations of the justices' conclusions based on prior rules and decisions are the elliptical orbits or epicycles of law.

I expect the methodological choices in this book to be controversial. Devotees of the traditional doctrinal elaboration of judicial rhetoric have explained and will try to explain opinions quite differently. Many scholars expect a critic, first, to go through the justices' explanations and try to show that they do not account for the decisions, and then, to contend that something else is guiding the justices.

I have not done this for two reasons. First, such a detailed discussion of each case would multiply the size of this book. Perhaps more important, it would muddy the argument. I have a very simple argument to make: that whatever else may steer their opinions, there is a division among the justices that they do not discuss but that is so basic to their thought that it comes out as a set of implicit assumptions that drive a very large proportion of what they do.

The idea that a study such as this one requires a detailed examination of the justices' language is based on an assumption that neither legal scholars nor social scientists actually believe when it is made explicit—the assumption that there is only one factor guiding what a justice does in a case. That is demonstrably false. Competing explanations don't necessarily contradict one another although they do compete in importance. I don't want to argue that nothing else matters. I do want to argue that others have missed one of the most fundamental divisions among the justices. The purpose of this book is to spell out that division.

Acknowledgments

Many wonderful people have read drafts and chapters at various stages of this project and given me the benefit of their comments, criticisms, and encouragement, for which this printed acknowledgment is a very inadequate token of my appreciation. This kind of professional interchange is extremely important to a project such as this. Colleagues who take an interest, both at other institutions and at the schools where one teaches, offer irreplaceable cross-fertilization and not only contribute to the result but relieve what would otherwise be the loneliness of scholarship, especially for a project that has taken most of a decade. To all a great debt of gratitude: Owen M. Fiss, H. Jefferson Powell, Gary J. Simson, Robin L. West, John T. Baker, Martin H. Belsky, Joseph B. Board, Jr., Vincent M. Bonventre, Patrick J. Borchers, David Forte, David Goshien, Joseph D. Kearney, Gregory A. Mark, Bonnie Steinboch, and James G. Wilson. Conversations with Deborah A. Geier, J. Gordon Hylton, and Alan Miles Ruben resulted in some very helpful suggestions. I also want to express my appreciation to participants at faculty seminars at Albany Law School, Cleveland-Marshall College of Law, and Marquette University Law School; to my students in seminars on the Supreme Court at both Albany and Cleveland-Marshall; to my research assistants Michele Ann Baumgartner, Thomas M. Bevilacqua, Christina M. Bookless, David Blumberg, Adam Mark Forman, Paul A. Gomez, Victor Jordan, Shaun R. Knasick, Tonya Melnichenko, Leigh Ann Singleton, and Julie L. Stein at Albany, Jennifer McKeegan at Cleveland, and Terry Radtke at Marquette. David Blumberg and Camille Jobin-Davis also wrote helpful papers under my supervision. Numerous conversations with Patrick Borchers were particularly helpful in trying to analyze the work of Justice Kennedy, though the conclusions are my own. I want to express a special debt to my late colleague Allen Redlich, who enthusiastically helped me isolate difficult-to-find material for this study. Thanks also to Albany Law School for financial support for this project and to my colleagues at Albany, Cleveland-Marshall, and Marquette for their help and encouragement.

Some of the material in this book is drawn from two earlier articles, revised for use here: "The Philosophical Gulf on the Rehnquist Court," 29 *Rutgers Law Journal* 1 (1997); and "Three Justices in Search of a Character: The Moral Agendas of Justices O'Connor, Scalia and Kennedy," 49 *Rutgers Law Review* 219 (1996). My appreciation to the editors of those journals for making it possible to use that material. Portions of this book were delivered as the Joseph C. Hostetler-Baker and Hostetler Lecture at Cleveland-Marshall College of Law, May 1, 1996; the Robert F. Boden Lecture at Marquette University Law School, November 11, 1997; and the Philosophy Forum Spring 1997 at the Sage Colleges—I appreciate those opportunities to explore these ideas.

Finally, my thanks to my wife, Jeanette, who, as always, read, helped, criticized, and endured.

1

Origins

Who is on the Court matters. So also where they came from. Experience provides the background, the challenges, the memories and justifications around which we all build our beliefs. People react in multiple, often unexpected ways to the experiences that "shape" them. Each of the justices tried out conflicting ideas and discarded some. Some have surprised us. Some have "grown" in liberal parlance, "disappointed" or "flipped" in conservative parlance, as they moved from right to left in the course of their service on the Court. Experience is not destiny, but experience matters.

The justices, all of them, come from the edges of the country. Two were brought up in California. Four attended Stanford University as undergraduates and two of them continued as law students. Two of the Stanford graduates left for Phoenix, one stayed in California. Four justices are easterners. Two were brought up in New York City, one spent almost his entire life in New Hampshire, and one came from North Carolina. And one justice, as if to prove the point, moved from the West Coast to Boston. Six justices attended Harvard, one as an undergraduate, one for a master's degree, and five attended law school there. Two justices taught there. Two justices were brought up near the shores of the Great Lakes. One lived his life there until his appointment to the Court. The justices are evenly divided among those who had lengthy careers in private practice, teaching, or government service. Five justices have taught in law school, some at more than one. Two justices have taught at Harvard and two at the University of Chicago, one each at Northwestern, Virginia, Columbia, Rutgers, and McGeorge in California. Three studied in England. There is no heartland on the Court.

William Hubbs Rehnquist is the Chief Justice. He and Justice Stevens are the two members of the Court who were brought up on the shores of

Lake Michigan. They were born four years and a hundred miles apart. In every other respect, their careers have diverged.

Rehnquist was born in 1924, making him one of the oldest members of the Court as well as its Chief. He comes from Milwaukee and was brought up in Shorewood, an aptly named affluent suburb on the shore of Lake Michigan, still full of gorgeous mansions, breathtaking lake views and a few Frank Lloyd Wright houses.[1] His father was in business as a paper wholesaler. His mother was a linguist, fluent in several languages. The family were devoted Republicans who encouraged values of self-reliance and hard work in their children.

When the Japanese bombed Pearl Harbor, Rehnquist was seventeen. In response he organized demonstrations and participated in civil defense. Rehnquist spent one year at the elite Kenyon College in Ohio before enlisting in the army. The army sent him to North Africa, detailed to observe and relay weather patterns. North Africa taught him the joys of warm weather. After the war, instead of going back to Kenyon, he finished his studies at Stanford.

Rehnquist tried Harvard for a master's degree in political science but found that campus far too liberal. So he went back to California to study law at Stanford, where he was much more comfortable. One of his classmates was the future Justice Sandra Day O'Connor. Rehnquist graduated second in his class; O'Connor was next in rank.

His student years show Rehnquist as a fine student who was both restless and independent. Since then he has never been far from controversy.

Rehnquist's first legal position was as law clerk to Supreme Court Justice Robert H. Jackson. Jackson had been the United States prosecutor at the Nuremberg trials called to bring Nazi war criminals to justice. When Rehnquist arrived in Washington, *Brown v. Board of Education*,[2] the school desegregation case, was working its way onto the agenda of the United States Supreme Court. Rehnquist would tell Jackson that segregation should be upheld.

> I realize that it is an unpopular and unhumanitarian position, for which I have been excoriated by "liberal" colleagues, but I think *Plessy v. Ferguson* [the 1896 decision upholding segregation so long as it was "equal"] was right and should be reaffirmed.[3]

Jackson of course voted to overrule *Plessy* and desegregate the country. Rehnquist could have learned from that experience to respect the deep commitment many Americans have to a vision of social justice. He would later assert that his memo was not his own opinion but merely outlined the arguments for Jackson's benefit. But Rehnquist would continue to insist that law should be interpreted without regard to whether it was "humanitarian," that those who wrote the law should not be understood as having meant that the law they wrote should be read to do substantial justice. And in 1964 he opposed passage of an ordinance to bar discrimination in places of public accommodation. In his confirmation hearings, though he would deny it, witnesses would tell the senators that Rehnquist had challenged every black voter he encountered, and threatened blacks to try to prevent them from voting.

Later he told *U.S. News and World Report* that the Warren Court and the justices' clerks showed

> extreme solicitude for the claims of Communists and other criminal defendants, expansion of federal power at the expense of State power, [and] great sympathy toward any government regulation of business.[4]

It sharpens those comments to realize how great the variance was between Rehnquist's description and what the clerks he criticized and their bosses thought they were doing. In the criminal area, for example, the Warren Court was quite explicit that it thought it was making sure that convictions were accurate, that the innocent were not railroaded by abusive procedures into convictions for crimes they had not committed, and that the rest of us are not abused by law enforcement gone out of control.

A little history may put both Rehnquist and the clerks he criticized in perspective. When Rehnquist was too small to remember, a variety of prestigious commissions looked at American police practices and found them little different from what we now condemn in the "Third World." Long before Warren, the Supreme Court had condemned such abusive practices as the "third degree"—the extraction of confessions by force—and trials without minimal protections for the innocent. The Warren Court differed from its predecessors in enforcing constitutional requirements, which by then were uncontroversial, by means of a set of prophylactic rules. Rehnquist would spend a large part of his career working to dismantle those protections.

Both Rehnquist and O'Connor built their careers in Phoenix. Phoenix was home to Barry Goldwater, senator from Arizona, author of *Conscience of a Conservative*, and living conscience of the conservative movement. Rehnquist campaigned for Goldwater. But Rehnquist stayed out of the mainstream-Republican-dominated large law firms representing major corporate clients that are the typical opportunity of former Supreme Court clerks. Instead he engaged in what lawyers call general practice, a mix of wills and other forms of wealth transfer among members of a family and between generations, plus real estate purchases, property disputes, and other fairly routine events.

Rehnquist returned to Washington as assistant attorney general in charge of the Office of Legal Counsel in President Richard Nixon's administration. In that position Rehnquist became anathema to liberals. He argued that the president had the power to order wiretaps without a court order; that police could barge into property without warning or knocking; that people could be held in custody without bail because they were thought to be dangerous; and that relevant constitutional guarantees did not bar those practices. Rehnquist also argued that the writ of habeas corpus should be drastically restricted. The writ of habeas corpus is guaranteed by the Constitution to allow courts to insist that officials not be able to hold people in custody in violation of their rights and to help control the abuse of official power. Rehnquist argued that it should not be available after trial, although the Court had confronted serious abuses of constitutional rights at trials that amounted to little more than kangaroo courts. The Supreme Court had concluded that evidence seized in violation of constitutional rights should not be admissible in court. Its purpose was to discourage law enforcement personnel from employing abusive practices in violation of constitutional provisions. Rehnquist argued that the rule against the admission of such evidence should be abolished.[5]

Perhaps most painful for liberal senators was his participation in the planning for the roundup of demonstrators on May Day in 1971. The nation was caught in an agonizing struggle over the war in Vietnam between those whose patriotism demanded support for the war effort and those whose concern for human life, both of our troops and of innocent civilians caught in conflict, demanded an end to the fighting. Demonstrators themselves split into many competing factions. Some demonstrations were dignified and orderly: carrying candles to a vigil in front of St. Patrick's Cathedral in New York, reading the names of American soldiers killed in Vietnam at demonstrations in front of the White House. Others burned draft cards and ROTC offices, and tried to obstruct munitions factories. Rehnquist argued for surveillance of demonstrators without a warrant or court order. One public demonstration was called for May Day, 1971. Rehnquist worked to suspend reporting rules so that the police could arrest masses of people without documentation. Twelve thousand people were arrested; twelve were convicted. For the others, there was no evidence that they had done anything in violation of the law—demonstrating to show the intensity of one's convictions in opposition to a policy one considers immoral is not, of course, a crime. Among those rounded up and held were many whose presence on the street had nothing to do with the demonstration. Rehnquist defended the roundups and described the demonstrators as "barbarians."[6]

In 1972, Nixon challenged the liberal Senate by nominating William H. Rehnquist to be Associate Justice of the Supreme Court, giving it a nominee whose abilities were clear but whose rejection of liberal principles was equally clear. After a hotly fought contest, Rehnquist took his seat in January 1972. President Reagan nominated him for the position of Chief Justice, to replace Chief Justice Warren E. Burger, in 1986.

In the rarified ideological environment of the United States Supreme Court, justices who are not at the extremes of the Court are often described as pragmatic, unpredictable, or weak, as if they were rolled around by giants in the conference room or by attorneys in the courtroom. Sandra Day O'Connor has a strong will and mind of her own, but it has been shaped by a complex of experience that often leaves others puzzled.

Sandra Day O'Connor's family lived in a remote area of Arizona on the Lazy B Ranch founded by her grandfather Henry Clay Day, named for the great pre–Civil War Whig senator and architect of historic compromises.[7] The area was so remote that the family had to drive to El Paso, Texas, in 1930 so that Sandra Day could be born in a hospital. The ranch still did not have either running water or electricity. O'Connor later described the ranch as a place "where one learns to work and do things for oneself."[8] And she has described the annual cattle roundups as an example of the communal spirit on the frontier where people helped one another.

Though the ranch lacked many of the comforts of modern life, her family was determined that Sandra would be well educated. So she went to El Paso to live with her maternal grandmother, attend an exclusive girls' school, and then attend and graduate from Austin High School at sixteen. Fulfilling her father's frustrated ambition, Sandra Day applied only to Stanford. It took her a mere five years to complete both her undergraduate and law degrees there.

After Stanford she tried to get a job among private firms in California. Not one would hire this star graduate of California's premier law school. At least one major law firm responded to her application by offering her a job as a secretary. Some women, like Justice Ginsburg, a colleague on the Court, would respond to discrimination by becoming a crusader for women's rights, path breakers in the emergence of a new social and economic order. O'Connor's response would be relatively conservative, but the experience continued to rankle her nonetheless. For the moment, Sandra Day O'Connor found employment as a deputy county attorney for San Mateo County, California, while her husband John O'Connor completed his studies, also at Stanford Law School.

A year later, in 1953, she followed her husband to Germany, where John O'Connor served in the army and Sandra Day O'Connor worked as civilian attorney for the Quartermaster Market Center. They moved to Phoenix in 1957, where she did some private practice, gave birth to three sons, and then concentrated her energies on bringing up her children. In 1965 she went back to work as assistant attorney general for Arizona, and four years later she began a political career in the Arizona legislature. She was elected to the Maricopa County Superior Court, and then appointed to the Arizona Court of Appeals in 1979.

Like Rehnquist, Sandra Day O'Connor became active in Republican politics. Senator Goldwater and others urged her to run for governor. It was Democratic Governor Bruce Babbitt who appointed her to the Arizona Court of Appeals. When Reagan appointed her to the Court in 1981, there was reason to believe she would be a different kind of conservative from her classmate and colleague Bill Rehnquist.

Historians have noted that life on the frontier often breeds a very conservative outlook. But O'Connor's background gave her many opportunities to digest competing perspectives, frontier and urban independence, competition and cooperation, ethnic and cosmopolitan values. And she brought to the Court an experience with discrimination more pointed than any of her new colleagues, save, of course, Thurgood Marshall.

Antonin Scalia was born in Trenton, New Jersey, in 1936 but brought up in Queens.[9] Both his parents were educators—his mother taught in grade school and his father became a professor of Romance languages at Brooklyn College. His was a relatively successful family despite the depression raging when he was born. Perhaps it is merely coincidence that Scalia and Rehnquist, two of the Court's archconservatives and advocates of a formal, literalist style, each had a parent who was a specialist in language.

Justice Scalia is one of the Court's most militant textualists. He believes the Court should limit itself to plain language and specific historic examples, omitting historic principles if at all possible. George Kannar has described the influence of Scalia's father and Catholic upbringing as the major influences on his judicial approach.[10] Part of the influence lay in his father's professional work. Eugene Scalia spent his career translating the work of a variety of Italian writers but insisted on literalness and doubted the ability of any translation to convey the original meaning. The text was supreme and its meaning was to be found solely in its language, not in efforts to go "behind" the text and study the author's life and circumstances.

In Kannar's view this was buttressed by Scalia's Catholic upbringing. Antonin, or Nino to his friends, studied at a Catholic military school in Manhattan, then graduated, first in his class, from Georgetown, a Jesuit university, before studying at Harvard Law School and graduating magna cum laude in 1960. Kannar describes Scalia's Catholic upbringing as a constant reference to learned formulae. The result, Kannar asserts, was that Scalia's Catholic training and his father's work in literary criticism led in the same direction—toward a severe textualism.

But Catholic education is also Thomist, demanding adherence to higher law when human law is unjust.[11] Scalia denied the Thomist heritage of his Catholic education. And as Kannar repeatedly points out, Scalia's greatest nemesis on the Court, William Brennan, was also brought up in the Catholic tradition, and Scalia's firmest ally, Chief Justice Rehnquist, was brought up in the Protestant tradition.[12]

Textualists, moreover, come in all stripes. The late Justice Hugo Black was a textualist and a liberal. Perhaps some explanation for Scalia's views may lie in Scalia's ethnic and immigrant experience. There is nothing automatic of course in the immigrant experience and some have reacted quite differently. But Scalia never got over the feeling that since his parents were immigrants and not a source of the racial problems plaguing America, he and his family also had no responsibility to play a part in the solution. "My father came to this country as a teenager. . . . Not only had he never profited from the sweat of any black man's brow, I don't think he had ever seen a black man." According to Scalia, various ethnic groups who had been victims of discrimination were being forced to bear the burden of affirmative action by those at "the top of the social heap where one can speak eloquently (and quite safely) of restorative justice."[13]

Nevertheless, Scalia's rise into the elite of American society was meteoric. When he left law school he practiced with a major commercial law firm in Cleveland, taught at two very prestigious law schools, the University of Virginia and the University of Chicago, and served in the Nixon and Ford administrations. His professional career was largely consumed by working on deregulation of business. President Ronald Reagan nominated him to the United States Court of Appeals for the District of Columbia Circuit in 1982. Then, in 1986, Chief Justice Burger resigned and President Reagan nominated Rehnquist for the chief justiceship and Antonin Scalia to fill Rehnquist's old seat on the Supreme Court. Despite this hugely successful career, Scalia brought with him a sense of hurt, a strong sense of method, and a scholar's knowledge and tools.

Born in 1936, the same year as Antonin Scalia, Justice Anthony Kennedy is one of the Court's Californians.[14] Kennedy's father was a well-connected and very successful lawyer and lobbyist; Kennedy's mother very much involved in community affairs. Kennedy attended Stanford as an undergraduate. Then he came east to study, spent his senior year at the London School of Economics, and studied law at Harvard. After graduating in 1961, Kennedy went back to California to live. He practiced law in San Francisco and then in Sacramento until his appointment to the United States Court of Appeals for the Ninth Circuit in 1975. During much of the time he was in practice and all of the time he served on the Court of Appeals, Kennedy also taught constitutional law at McGeorge School of Law.

When Kennedy's father died in 1963, Kennedy took over his father's practice although he was still a very young lawyer. The practice included major liquor and optical interests, among other significant clients, and young Kennedy became their lobbyist. In the bargain he inherited many of his parents' political contacts. He also inherited much of his parents' skill.

Lobbying took him to "exclusive" country clubs where blacks and women were among those excluded. Kennedy joined anyway and resigned on the eve of his nomination to the Supreme Court. Sacramento was unconcerned with discrimination and, in a 1968 interview, Kennedy told the press that a club should be able to "exclude members as it chooses."[15] The American Bar Association discouraged membership in clubs that discriminated, but Kennedy argued to the Senate Judiciary Committee at his confirmation hearings that his membership was not proscribed because the exclusion was not the "result of ill will" or "intended to impose a stigma," although neither the bar association nor the law excused categorical racial or gender discrimination in that way.[16] On the Ninth Circuit, where he made his own individual selections, five of his thirty-five clerks were women and one was nonwhite.[17] None were black.

Kennedy may have surprised some of his conservative friends by his willingness to drop by at a housewarming for a gay couple who had moved in nearby.[18] "If they can tolerate me, I can sure tolerate them," Kennedy told a friend.[19]

Kennedy won a place in Ronald Reagan's heart with his work as draftsman and major proponent of a 1973 initiative to limit taxes in California. Reagan was governor of California at the time. The voters defeated the measure, but Reagan almost immediately urged President Nixon to appoint Kennedy to the Ninth Circuit, although it was ultimately President Ford who sent his name to the Senate.[20]

On the Ninth Circuit, Kennedy was conservative but avoided sweeping pronouncements and was willing to change his mind. A colleague, Judge Alex Kozinski, described Kennedy's reaction when his clerks found it difficult to draft an opinion according to Kennedy's instructions. "'If the case wouldn't write that way,'" Kennedy would wonder, "'maybe the result was wrong.'"[21]

At the time of his nomination to the Supreme Court, Kennedy still lived in the house in which he grew up, still attended the same Roman Catholic church he attended as a child and in which he served as an altar boy, and still maintained boyhood friendships.

Kennedy was not Ronald Reagan's first choice for the Supreme Court. Rehnquist, O'Connor, and Scalia were all appointed or promoted by Reagan. When Justice Powell retired, Reagan first nominated Robert Bork, whose nomination was defeated in a very contentious Senate battle. Reagan then nominated Douglas Ginsburg. Only after Ginsburg withdrew following revelations about his use of controlled substances at parties was Kennedy nominated.

One focus at the hearings on Kennedy's nomination was a talk he gave at Stanford in which he was very critical of the idea of unenumerated rights but agreed that some had a strong constitutional grounding. Senators and analysts searched his words for a clue to his opinion about *Roe v. Wade*. It would be years before they found out.

At the point of his nomination, one could have described Kennedy as a man from a very traditional white privileged background who rarely saw its moral limits, or one could have described him as skillful, pragmatic, and ready to compromise.

Justice Clarence Thomas, perhaps the Court's angriest justice, was born in Pin Point, Georgia, in 1948, the only sitting justice born after World War II, the Court's only southerner, and only black.[22] Like Sandra Day O'Connor, Thomas was initially raised in a home without indoor plumbing or electricity and then sent to live with grandparents while going to school. But the similarity ends there.

Pin Point was an extremely poor and very conservative rural community, populated by the descendents of slaves who eked out an existence at the fringes of society in segregated Georgia. Thomas's mother married after becoming pregnant with Clarence's older sister. Her husband deserted her and the family when Clarence was an infant. Neither illegitimate births nor desertion were typical of this community and the Thomases were humiliated. To survive, his mother moved into a rotten wooden shack with a sister. She supported her family by shucking oysters and crab for five cents a pound and working as a maid in Savannah.

One day, after their mother left for work, Clarence and his younger brother accidentally set fire to the house. Leola Thomas was greeted in Savannah with the news that the house was gone. Impoverished, she pleaded with her father to take the children in. Her father, Myers Anderson, had abandoned her as a small child when her mother died and her relationship with him was never warm. Anderson and his wife had no children, and he was not interested in taking the children in. But he agreed to take the boys at his wife's urging. Clarence Thomas's sister was left to be brought up in the same miserable conditions that his mother had.

Thomas remembers his childhood as marked by his own hard labor and determination to succeed. He contrasted his success, which he attributed to his own efforts, with his sister's welfare dependency, though she had a family to support when she too had been deserted, and, by the time of Thomas's remarks, was working several jobs in an effort to support their aunt.

In fact, the move to his grandfather's home made a crucial difference. Anderson was a self-employed tradesman who had put together a middle-class life by means of extremely hard work. That hard work reflected a sense of mission for himself and his community. And once he agreed to take them in, he was determined that the boys would succeed. Anderson pushed the boys to work long hours both on their school assignments and on the family business and met any resistance or transgressions with whippings. He was also determined that his grandsons would share his sense of obligation to the black community. Anderson worked with the local NAACP, brought young Thomas to meetings, and bragged about the boy's success as evidence that blacks could make it.

Grandfather Anderson sent the two boys to a Catholic school in Savannah that had opened in the nineteenth century for the purpose of educating black youth and was staffed by a determined group of white Franciscan nuns. Punishment was physically painful, but the children were pushed hard to learn.

Thomas continued at a segregated parochial high school until his grandfather switched him to St. John Vianney Junior Seminary, which had been a white institution. Thomas was one of the first black students at the seminary and he was admitted despite having to repeat the tenth grade. His grandfather then sent him to Immaculate Conception Seminary College in Conception Junction, Missouri, in 1967-68. Again he was one of three black pioneers in a white institution.

In the wake of the assassination of Dr. Martin Luther King, Jr., Holy Cross College, in Worcester, Massachusetts, set up a scholarship in King's honor and stepped up its recruitment of blacks. Grandfather Anderson was incensed at Clarence's decision to abandon study for the ministry. Without his grandfather's support, Thomas received one of the first Holy Cross King scholarships. He graduated in 1971 though he had nearly packed up again in response to the racism he experienced there.

From there Thomas went to Yale to study law. Yale had a long history of admitting and graduating black students, but in small numbers. The faculty at the Yale Law School had long included many who played large parts in the struggles for both civil liberties and civil rights, including work on the pivotal NAACP brief in *Brown v. Board*. No faculty could have been more dedicated to the movement for integration. Nevertheless, when Yale decided to expand its black student population significantly, that decision was very controversial within the faculty. Yale has also been the nation's most selective law school, the result of its small size combined with its high standing in the legal community. Thomas graduated in 1974 but without the top-of-the-class status enjoyed by some of his eventual colleagues on the Court.

For Thomas, his education was a mixed blessing. He benefited from the establishment of a school for blacks by white Catholics in Savannah. He benefited from scholarships to Holy Cross and Yale. And he benefited from special admissions designed to diversify St. John Vianney, Immaculate Conception Seminary, Holy Cross, and Yale Law School. But Thomas grew up lonely and angry. His bookish habits and the rigorous schedule forced on him by his grandfather separated him from his black peers. As a pioneer in white schools, he confronted bald racism and became disillusioned with the church. Eventually, he also became disillusioned with black leadership.

Initially, he was attracted by Malcolm X and other black radicals. But Thomas found Thomas Sowell's brand of black conservatism much more satisfactory. Sowell treated all efforts at integration and assistance as attacks on the black community. White generosity was designed to benefit the white community, not the black. Getting into the white world meant abandoning the black. Somewhat inconsistently, Sowell argued that blacks should devote themselves to personal gain rather than the advancement of the black community. These views undoubtedly resonate with the work ethic that is much stronger in the black community than most whites understand, even while they conflict with the black sense of grievance at both careless and deliberate exclusion and mistreatment by the white world. Thomas took the individualist, self-help, capitalist values and rejected the ethnic politics of his elders. Thomas's views about the place of black men in a white world spelled a troubled relationship to the civil rights revolution—Thomas accepted and insisted on nondiscrimination as a human right but attacked affirmative action as a breach of that right, and defended racially separate institutions.

Thomas's politics also widened the breach with his grandfather, which had opened when he left the seminary. When Thomas joined the Republican Party the breach widened.

When he graduated from Yale, Thomas was offered a job at a firm where he had worked during the summer as a law student. The firm did civil rights work in Georgia. Thomas chose instead to work for Attorney General John Danforth of Missouri, later senator from Missouri. He stayed with Danforth from 1974 to 1977. The Danforth connection became a major source of Thomas's political rise. He left the attorney general's office to work for the Monsanto Company, a major chemical manufacturer, from 1977 to 1979, then rejoined Danforth, now senator, as legislative assistant from 1979 to 1981.

President Reagan appointed Thomas assistant secretary of education for civil rights and then chairman of the Equal Employment Opportunity Commission. As chairman, he reoriented the E.E.O.C. from the prosecution of large class actions affecting many jobs to the prosecution of individual claims. President Bush appointed him to the U.S. Court of Appeals for the District of Columbia, and nominated him for the Supreme Court in 1991.

The nomination of Thomas posed a difficult problem for the black and liberal communities. The NAACP hesitated but eventually opposed Thomas because Thomas had opposed many efforts to redress discrimination against minorities by means of so-called affirmative action plans. White liberals were predictably uncomfortable attacking a black candidate. They hoped Thomas's background would elicit some sympathy for the people he had left behind. The Bush administration relied on Thomas's rags-to-riches story to negotiate the confirmation process in the Democratic Senate. The nomination was moving smoothly until the detailed description by Professor Anita Hill of his sexual remarks to her came to light. The Senate Committee aired those complaints in a set of televised hearings that have been discussed endlessly since and whose legacy has been reshaped through the lens of the subsequent impeachment hearings. Whatever the truth of those events, many senators took the position that they should defer to the president and that a nominee is entitled to the office unless allegations against him can be proven by a clear preponderance of the evidence—a position questioned by many constitutional scholars and not shared by the Republican Senate, which has held up many of President Clinton's nominations for judicial office. Thomas was confirmed in a close vote, 52–48.

Thomas brought with him the sting of segregation and discrimination alternating with the blessings of the white world. He brought anger at the white world coupled with a desire to succeed in that world on its terms. He had toyed with a variety of ideological tools, and never found a comfortable niche.

Justice John Paul Stevens is the oldest member of the Court and its most modern,[23] often telecommuting from his home in Florida.

Stevens was born in Chicago in 1920 and spent most of his life there before his appointment to the Supreme Court. Stevens's father was a well-known Chicago Republican businessman. Stevens himself graduated Phi Beta Kappa from the University of Chicago in 1941. His penchant for a careful examination of the facts became apparent at the university. Before Pearl Harbor, when isolationist sentiment was carried with ideological fervor, he urged restraint, fact-finding, and debate. Editor of the school paper, he published articles by senior faculty on public issues, generating a sophisticated discussion of serious matters.

During World War II, Stevens served as an officer in the navy, earning a Bronze Star. Then he went home. Every justice except Stevens studied out of state, almost all at a considerable distance from home. Stevens went back to the Chicago area to study law at Northwestern. But what Stevens absorbed from law school linked him with national currents.

The reigning intellectual and philosophical cast of elite law schools in this period has been described as a pragmatic, nonideological, and fact-centered approach open to all considerations,[24] but that is not entirely accurate. Law schools in this period focused endless analysis on "public policy," a shorthand for their basic utilitarian approach. Utilitarians simply ask what will accomplish the greatest social benefit. Utilitarianism is neither Republican nor Democratic. It cuts through ideological debates about the proper ends and means, and holds the policies of both up to the light to examine exactly who will benefit and how.

Legal realism supported this outlook. The legal realists wanted to know what actually happened as the result of legal commands, not just what the language decreed. Thus realists' analysis was not "formalistic" or "legalistic" but directed at the goals of law, whether and how they were attained—"public policy" became a focus for the realists as much as the utilitarians.

In this brew, following the rules was understood as a search for the purposes of law rather than stopping with the apparent plain meaning of the language used. Lawyers as least as far back as prerevolutionary England had focused on the objectives of law, its purposes, as an aid to its meaning, although the techniques had changed over the centuries partly in response to the increasing availability of legislative history after the American Revolution.[25] Focusing on purposes allowed the post–World War II legal positivist, whose only concern was with following the rules, to join the realists and utilitarians in the study of public policy enshrined in law.

Much of this critical analysis of law could be summed up in Justice Oliver Wendell Holmes, Jr.'s famous comment that "general propositions do not decide concrete cases." This approach seems to have been quite congenial to John Paul Stevens. It fit the fact-sensitive, careful consideration of issues without prejudgment of means or ends that characterized his work. Of the justices who studied law in this period, only Stevens, and to a lesser extent Ruth Bader Ginsburg and Steven Breyer, seem to have adopted the assumptions and methods of the elite law schools.

Stevens graduated first in his class and magna cum laude after only two years—with the most outstanding record in the history of Northwestern. In 1947 Stevens went to Washington as law clerk to Supreme Court Justice Wiley Rutledge. Rutledge has been called "one of the most liberal justices ever to sit on the Court,"[26] and Stevens wrote about him later with great admiration. But Stevens's career, before joining the judiciary, had little to do with social movements. After a short period in practice in Chicago, Stevens returned to Washington to spend a year as Republican counsel for the House Judiciary Subcommittee on the Study of Monopoly Power, then returned to Chicago to practice law. During the Eisenhower administration, he served on the attorney general's antitrust study committee. Stevens's practice focused on antitrust law, a subject he also taught at both the University of Chicago and Northwestern University schools of law, and he had a reputation as a preeminent attorney in the field. Nominally a Republican, he was not active in partisan politics. Probably more than any other member of the Court, Stevens had been a prominent business lawyer.

In not needing to be active in partisan politics, Stevens was fortunate. His classmate, Charles Percy, had become a Republican senator from Illinois. Percy took judicial quality seriously and asked area bar associations to suggest names for judicial appointments rather than sending the bar prescreened names to approve or disapprove. Stevens was one of three people proposed. Though the men had not met for years, Percy recounts that he had to urge Stevens to allow him to submit his name to the Nixon administration. President Nixon then nominated Stevens for the United States Court of Appeals for the Seventh Circuit, which includes Chicago in its jurisdiction, in 1970.[27]

Stevens's reputation on the appellate bench was superb, and the esteem in which he was held by bench and bar led directly to his appointment to the Supreme Court when Attorney General Edward Levi asked the American Bar Association to screen a short list of people under consideration for appointment to the Court. The bar responded with high praise for Stevens.

Stevens was nominated by President Ford in 1975. It was Ford's one appointment to the Supreme Court and came in the wake of the resignation of President Nixon—the only president ever to resign—to avoid being tried by the United States Senate on impeachment charges voted by the House of Representatives. Ford pardoned Nixon but otherwise tried to shape a presidency largely above narrow partisanship, trying to bring the country back together after the battles over Vietnam, and the impeachment and resignation of Richard Nixon. Ford carefully chose a man who was very well respected for his work. Stevens was known as a conservative judge but was admired on all sides for his intelligence, his legal skill, and judicial temperament on the United States Court of Appeals for the Seventh Circuit.

The corporate bar out of which Stevens came is generally conservative in its policy prescriptions but has been a major supporter of the legal services program. In New York City the Wall Street bar long held the Legal Aid Society Ball and made it one of the major social and fund-raising events of the year. Justice Lewis F. Powell, Jr., when president of the American Bar Association, led that lawyers' group to take its historic position in support of the legal services program as part of the War on Poverty. The point was not to endorse any specific claims that the poor had but that they had the same right as anyone else to justice and to a competent presentation of their claims. There is a studied insistence on fairness and procedural justice in this milieu. While conservative in their instincts, procedural logic compels them to accept some liberal results. By the time Stevens was appointed, the Court had become so polarized that this combination of conservatism with a fundamental insistence on fairness and procedural neutrality led people to describe Stevens as a "maverick," "gadfly," "wild card," "free of preconceived notions," and "the Court's 'least predictable member.'"[28]

Presidents pick their justices for reasons that generally have little to do with satisfying legal faculty and bar association definitions of good lawyering and good judging. Nixon, Reagan, and Bush systematically tried to screen out lawyers who inherited the careful utilitarian cast of mind favored by law faculties and bar associations. Stevens, a star pupil not just in his grades and professional success but in his adoption of the spirit of law as it was then taught and admired, was appointed by a president looking for a man the bar would admire.

Justice David H. Souter also has a reputation as both conservative and independent. He was born in Melrose, Massachusetts, a suburb north of Boston, in 1939.[29] His parents, Joseph Alexander Souter and Helen Adams Hackett Souter had no other children. When David Souter was eleven, the three Souters moved to Weare, New Hampshire, near Concord. He would later continually refer to Weare as his hometown. His classmates at Concord High School voted Souter "most literary," "most sophisticated," and "most likely to succeed."

Other than John Paul Stevens, Souter stayed closest to home of all the justices. Souter attended Harvard College and Harvard Law School, a few miles from his birthplace and just across the border from New Hampshire, where the family had moved. He then lived and worked in New Hampshire for his entire career prior to joining the Court.

As a senior at Harvard, he wrote a thesis about the legal philosophy known as positivism in the work of Supreme Court Justice Oliver Wendell Holmes. As Souter described it, Holmes believed that good judges should not impose their own views on the law. By the time that Justice William Brennan, whose seat Souter would take, resigned from the Court, the view that judges should not impose their own views on the law had in some quarters become a code for hostility to the work of the Warren Court and the abortion decisions of the Burger Court, and in other quarters it had become a code for standing by the precedents of those courts. By then David Souter would have a much more sophisticated notion of what it meant to interpret law.

Souter graduated from Harvard College in 1961, magna cum laude and Phi Beta Kappa. After graduating, he went as a Rhodes scholar to Oxford, where he studied law and philosophy. He was deeply religious and unusual among the students there in attending church and taking communion. He was also unusually studious and ignored the opportunities to travel to the major cities of Europe in order to pursue his studies.

Souter returned to Harvard to study law. Despite his outstanding undergraduate record, Souter did not graduate at the very top of his law school class, as did some of his colleagues on the Court, nor did he make the *Harvard Law Review*, the prime status symbol and sophisticated experience for a law student.

Unlike most law students, David Souter wanted to be a judge. At law school most students study with only practice in mind. From a practical perspective, they want to know "the rules" and the arguments. Law teachers often despair at their students' devotion to ephemeral and illusory "black letter law." Professors would prefer to teach law from the perspective of the jurist, examining the policy behind law, the reasons for shaping and interpreting law in one way rather than another, the consequences of the different choices judges can make. Law school with judging in mind is a completely different experience. So outstanding was this difference that friends called him "Mr. Justice Souter," using the appellation then current for Supreme Court justices. He was considered good company, though then and always, a very private person.

Souter graduated in 1966. Unlike Chief Justice Rehnquist or Justices Stevens and Breyer, who went to Washington after graduation to clerk for a justice of the Supreme Court, or Justice Ginsburg, who clerked for a judge of a United States District Court, and unlike Justice Scalia, who began his practice with a large firm, Souter went home and began his practice with a small firm in Concord, New Hampshire. Private practice did not satisfy the future justice. He stayed just two years and in 1968 joined the New Hampshire attorney general's office.

The descriptions of David Souter as unassuming, quiet, and modest are ubiquitous. He drives small cars, wears drab clothes, and never accumulated any significant assets, unlike several of his colleagues. Back home, Souter became a vestryman at St. Andrew's Episcopal Church in Hikington, New Hampshire, and by the time of his appointment to the high court had settled into a routine of walking the same elderly woman home from church and then visiting his own mother in a nursing home.

When President Bush nominated him in 1990, David Souter's views were virtually unknown. He was a protégé of Senator Warren Rudman of New Hampshire, having worked for him when Rudman was state attorney general, first as assistant attorney general in 1968, then deputy attorney general in 1971. Souter succeeded Rudman as attorney general in 1976. The two developed a strong friendship, and Rudman pushed his friend's career at every opportunity, through every step in the judicial ladder. Souter achieved the first step of his judicial dream in 1978 when he joined the New Hampshire Superior Court. In 1983 Governor John Sununu appointed Souter to the New Hamphire Supreme Court. In 1990 Souter was appointed to the United States Court of Appeals for the First Circuit. At Rudman's urging later the same year, Sununu, as chief of staff for President Bush, suggested Souter for nomination to the United States Supreme Court.

In none of those earlier positions had Souter had to take a position on the controversial questions of the day. Souter was ambitious, and angled for the position of chief justice of the New Hampshire Supreme Court, the one major appointment that eluded him. But he was not a public personality. When Rudman suggested Souter to John Sununu, Souter's very privacy made him attractive.

The struggle over the Bork nomination was still on everyone's mind, and Bush and Sununu were determined to avoid the kind of controversy that scuttled the Bork nomination. Souter had no record—no record to attack and no record to stand on. The liberals were suspicious, but the political wisdom of the period made presidential prerogative almost determinative—instead of demanding that a candidate demonstrate in some way that he or she was one of the most qualified candidates in the country, the senators would have to come up with some explanation for opposition. That there were no grounds to oppose would be sufficient for confirmation. Liberals promptly labeled Souter the "stealth" candidate who would unhinge the most sacred precedents of the Supreme Court like a radar-resistant bomber with curved wings and a teflon skin. But no one knew.

Justice Ginsburg is the most successful litigator on the Court since Justice Thurgood Marshall.[30] She was an almost mythical figure in the women's movement before coming to the Court. She created the women's rights project for the ACLU and won seminal cases insisting on equal treatment for men and women in front of the Supreme Court on which she now sits—five of the six cases she argued there.

In one important victory, Ginsburg won a woman's right to be considered for appointment as the executor of her son's estate without regard for her gender. But many of her pathbreaking Supreme Court victories were forged on behalf of male claimants. Her strategy was simple: if women could not get equality directly, the principle could be established by male plaintiffs' asking for the same benefits—the same rights to social security survivors' benefits, the same right to drink at age eighteen, the same military housing benefits for male dependents that female dependents got. And before she was appointed to the Supreme Court, she had criticized the reasoning, though not the result, of *Roe v. Wade* because it was based on privacy rather than equal protection. Her preferred mode—seeking strict identity of treatment—would stop short of some of the objectives of the current women's movement.

The leaders of the women's movement eventually became unhappy about her treatment of women's issues—for Ginsburg, women are entitled to whatever men are entitled to, but no more, while many feminists moved on to assert rights to meet the special needs of women. For this and other reasons, many old-fashioned liberals regard her as having left the fold and finding common ground on the right.

Ginsburg was born in Brooklyn in 1933 and brought up in Flatbush. She went to James Madison High School, not far from where the author was brought up. Ruth Bader's mother, Celia Bader, died of cancer in 1948 while Ruth was still in high school.

Ethnically, Flatbush was a Jewish ghetto. These were second- and third-generation Americans with little or no trace of the Old World in their speech and even in their attitudes. Their parents came with a strong sense of the injustice of the Old World, escaping from the pograms and feudalism of eastern Europe. They brought with them a strong sense of public spirit. Their public spirit slid over into socialism—the view that we are one for all and all for one in public affairs and in private life. But more than anything this generation wanted to make their children Americans, rejecting with no nostalgia any attachment to the Old World and its ways. The Nazis and the Holocaust changed that somewhat, as it did for Jews all over the world, demanding that some of that public spirit include other Jews in diaspora, much the way that Sinn Fein galvanized the minds of Irish Americans and apartheid African Americans. The second- and third-generation Jews of Flatbush had also escaped from older communities of immigrant Jews. This was a land of comfort, with tree-lined streets and for the most part individual homes that could have been in a Currier and Ives portrait though built four or five decades later. But it was not an area of great wealth. It was where the teachers and the small shopkeepers, the accountants and some attorneys lived, nicely but not ostentatiously.

Ruth Bader went to Cornell, in Ithaca, New York. She graduated, first in her class, and married, in 1954. She entered Harvard Law School in 1956. During her two years there she made law review, cared for an infant daughter, nursed her husband, Martin, back from cancer, and helped him complete his studies. Ruth Ginsburg then followed Martin to New York City and graduated from Columbia Law School in 1959. She was tied for first in her class. It is a record of success that conceals the strong hostility toward women as law students that she encountered constantly.[31] She remembered "wanting to drop through a trapdoor when the dean at Harvard asked her to justify taking up the place where a man could be."[32] When she completed her studies at Columbia after an outstanding two years at Harvard, Harvard refused to grant her a degree, though doing so was traditional for students who had completed two successful years. She holds a degree from Columbia instead. Harvard attempted to rectify the error decades later, but by then she refused.

Like Sandra Day O'Connor on the West Coast, Ginsburg found the traditional opportunities of top law graduates denied to her. She was offered neither a Supreme Court clerkship nor a position with a major law firm. The Wall Street bar was still segregated into white, male, Christian, and Jewish firms although a few token Jews had recently entered some "old-line" firms. All of those barriers—race, religion, and gender—would eventually be lowered, but not for her. The lack of the kind of offers that a male graduate with her credentials could have expected was a slight that still rankles.

Nevertheless, she did have an offer that many law students would have appreciated—after graduating she clerked for U.S. District Court Judge Edmund Palmieri. And after clerking, she worked as a researcher for the Columbia Law School Project on International Procedure. That project sent her to Sweden, where she began to encounter feminist thought. A generation before her birth, Jewish women in New York were forgoing their own education and going to work to put their brothers through school. By 1960, the culture of Flatbush and one of its star daughters were ripe for feminism.

Ginsburg began a teaching career at Rutgers in 1963. While at Rutgers, she became pregnant with her son, her second child. After her experience looking for work as a premier but unwanted law graduate, and in the midst of litigation about the right of pregnant women to remain at work, Ginsburg hid her pregnancy under loose clothes. As fortune would have it, she gave birth before the fall semester began.

During the Rutgers years, Ginsburg started on the path that made her a major player in American law, taking cases for the ACLU, including several early gender-discrimination cases. She spent a year teaching at Harvard, which had finally decided it was time to consider women for the faculty, and then from 1972 to 1980 taught at Columbia, where her appointment made her the first tenured woman on the faculty. In the years she taught at Columbia, Ginsburg directed the Women's Rights Project of the ACLU and served as its general counsel.

Ginsburg was appointed a Judge of the U.S. Court of Appeals for the District of Columbia by Jimmy Carter in 1980 and nominated for the U.S. Supreme Court by President Clinton in 1993. By that time, Ginsburg brought with her substantial experience as a litigator, activist, and scholar who plowed in liberal causes and had come to seem passé in some of just those circles.

Justice Steven Gerald Breyer was supposed to be the playmaker on the Court because of his ability to work with others without regard to their politics. He has been at centers of power for most of his professional career.

Breyer was born in San Francisco in 1938.[33] His father, Irving, was an attorney for the local school board. By the time he had graduated from high school, he had been pegged as most likely of any of his classmates to succeed—and however inaccurate those picks ordinarily are, these kids got it right. Breyer attended Stanford and graduated Phi Beta Kappa in 1959. Like two of his colleagues, Kennedy and Souter, Breyer studied in

England. He went to Oxford as a Marshall scholar, studying philosophy, politics, and economics and left with another bachelor's degree in 1961. He also left with respect for things English. In 1967 he married Joanna Hare, the daughter of Lord John Blankenham, who had been leader of the British Conservative Party. The two met in Washington, D.C., perhaps symbolizing the way Breyer crosses boundaries—political, national, and social.

Breyer studied law at Harvard Law School. He was a member of the *Harvard Law Review*, graduated with high honors in 1964, and went to Washington to clerk for Justice Arthur J. Goldberg. Goldberg was one of the liberal justices who helped to define the Warren Court, but his service on the Court was brief; Goldberg left the Court the summer following Breyer's clerkship to become United States chief delegate to the United Nations. Perhaps most notable among his duties as clerk, Breyer helped Justice Goldberg prepare his opinion in *Griswold v. Connecticut*, the groundbreaking decision that held that doctors could give contraceptive advice to married couples.

After his clerkship, Breyer served as special assistant to the assistant attorney general for antitrust at the U.S. Department of Justice. He returned to Harvard in 1967 to teach law. He was assistant special prosecutor on the Watergate Special Prosecution Force in 1973, served as special counsel of the Senate Judiciary Committee in 1974–75, and returned to Washington as chief counsel of the Senate Judiciary Committee in 1979–80. Teddy Kennedy was his boss, but he had good working relations with the Republicans on the committee. That bipartisan support was crucial in winning Republican support for his later nominations.

Jimmy Carter appointed him to the United States Court of Appeals for the First Circuit. While there, Breyer wrote a pair of books criticizing much economic regulation as anticompetitive and criticized many environmental and health regulations as too restrictive. Breyer argued that government was putting too many resources into achieving the last ounce of benefit and argued that a more intelligent approach to environmental and health problems would be driven more by experts than by popular clamor and would achieve more benefits for less cost, thus attacking liberal politics with technocratic and elitist ideas. During Breyer's confirmation hearings, Ralph Nader attacked him for consistently rejecting the claims of antitrust plaintiffs.

Nevertheless, Breyer's work on the Court of Appeals in the environmental area won him praise from environmentalists, perhaps all the more remarkable because Breyer had made an investment in Lloyd's of London, which made him potentially liable for environmental cleanup costs. That investment, however, could create a conflict of interest, and Breyer told the Senate that he would endeavor to dispose of the investment.[34]

Breyer was also known for his work on the United States Sentencing Commission. Responding to a congressional mandate to establish more uniformity in federal criminal sentences, the commission examined actual judicial practice to determine what usual sentences were and the basic reasons for stricter or more lenient sentencing in individual cases. These were turned into guidelines, and judges were required to explain any deviation from those guidelines in the sentences they imposed. Judges often dislike the guidelines because the guidelines limit their power to dispense individual justice. Breyer had the additional responsibility of explaining the guidelines to federal judges and then interpreting the guidelines as a member of the Court of Appeals and of the Supreme Court.

Looking for a nominee who could be confirmed without a fight, President Clinton nominated Breyer for the Supreme Court in 1994, the first time since 1939 that two Jewish justices would sit on the Court together. As predicted, his confirmation went smoothly.

In the stereotype, people come to Harvard and turn left. Breyer came to Harvard and has been chopping the foundations off the Left's most precious claims ever since. As Kenneth Jost has written, "Breyer's work crossed ideological lines. He played a critical role in enacting airline deregulation in the 1970s and writing federal sentencing guidelines in the 1980s."[35] Such line crossing leads people to think of Breyer as nonideological.

Experience matters, but experience is not destiny. From the opportunities and options available in their experiences each of the justices has inherited a personal set of assumptions that affects the way they react to problems. Their experiences cannot tell us what those assumptions have been. Our relation to our backgrounds is more complex than that. Instead, the justices' experiences invite and require us to find what they have taken from the paths of their lives and placed on the path of the Supreme Court.

2

The Gulf

Once appointed, Justice Rehnquist attacked what he described as the intrusion of liberal ideas into judicial decisions by the Warren Court and those members like Justices Brennan and Marshall who remained on the bench for two decades after Chief Justice Warren's retirement. Justices Scalia and Thomas have joined his campaign. Clearly major changes have been taking place on the Court.

Rehnquist, Scalia, and Thomas steered the argument onto questions of interpretation, questions that are very similar to questions about how to read the Bible. They argued vigorously that judges should read legal rules literally. Where the words of the Constitution are opaque, as they sometimes are, it is appropriate to turn to the original intent of the language, whatever the founding fathers who wrote the language meant to do. The liberal justices countered that changing times made such "interpretation" impossible or unfaithful to the full meaning of the original document and that the Constitution should be understood in light of enduring principles of freedom, democracy, and equality.

The argument over interpretation, however, has had little to do with the substance of the disagreements between the liberal and conservative wings of the Court.[1] The results reached by the liberal and conservative justices are far too patterned to reflect such rules of interpretation. The founders were neither twentieth-century liberals nor twentieth-century conservatives, and decisions made in their name should be neither consistently liberal nor conservative in twentieth-century terms. The arguments about the proper way to interpret the Constitution have been a smoke screen behind which the real changes have been taking place.

In fact, a yawning philosophic gulf divides the members of the Court. Despite considerable ambiguity in each system of thought, the culture wars have come to the Court in the form of a coherent philosophical difference among the justices, not a mere collection of conclusions, and it has little to do with how to interpret law.

The members of the conservative bloc have abandoned two assumptions that have been important and influential parts of the Anglo-American tradition since the eighteenth century. One, sometimes called freedom of conscience or moral autonomy, is that people are entitled to make their own moral choices unless they would injure others.[2] The second is that people and courts should avoid harm to others, should avoid injuring people unnecessarily.[3] Having abandoned those classic propositions deeply etched in historical traditions, the most "conservative" justices on the Court cannot be characterized within the grand philosophical traditions of Western thought sometimes described as the "canon." Instead, they are within much more contemporary post–World War II "traditions" somewhat misnamed conservative.

For the conservative justices, moral autonomy is more aptly called relativism and they reject it categorically. Rejecting relativism gives conservative justices the freedom to define right and wrong. And the liberal principle of avoiding harm to others becomes a casualty of what conservatives then describe as proper behavior.

At the same time the more liberal members of the Court have moved toward the conservatives by accepting more hierarchical assumptions about social welfare, a story we will tell later in the book. But they have pulled away from the conservatives by defending harm avoidance and pushing the legal frontier further in the name of autonomy.

The consequences are enormous. They not only explain the conservative shift across constitutional law in areas like religion, speech, race, abortion, capital punishment, redistricting, eminent domain, and economic regulation but make it clear that the revolution the conservative bloc has been bringing to the law will be restrained only by their political sense—their philosophic views turn much of constitutional law on its head both with respect to basic principles and the resolution of specific controversies.

We start by examining some of the false starts in explaining the divisions on the Court. Then we will describe the fundamental philosophical divide between the Court's more conservative and more liberal justices. Finally, this chapter will explore the implications of this divide for judicial reasoning and the role of the courts, the protection of democratic processes and the substance of constitutional law.

Conservative Counterattack in Liberal Language

The first issue to be confronted is whether the justices are merely "applying" the law properly. If they are merely obeying and applying the law, then it is meaningless or unimportant to ask about their own judicial biases.

Liberals from the Progressive era to the New Deal argued that the justices were misapplying the law. They argued that the Court was substituting its own views for Congress's and the states' policies for regulating the economy. Instead, liberals demanded that the Court restrain itself from imposing its own views and defer to the other branches of government. President Roosevelt attacked the Court, threatening to appoint more justices to change its decisions, and got a judicial revolution. In 1937 the Supreme Court, in a famous about-face, accepted the Progressive/New Deal position and stopped deciding that economic regulation was unconstitutional because the justices thought it was irrational. If there was any connection to any legitimate legislative goal, the Court would henceforth announce that it had a rational basis and leave policy for the legislative branch. That has become known as judicial restraint. The result was a major change in judicial direction, accepting and legitimating the policies of the Progressives and New Deal where prior Courts had declared many of them unconstitutional.

Presidents Nixon, Reagan, and Bush also intended a judicial revolution. They appointed justices to the Supreme Court and judges to the lower courts with the specific intention of changing the law in a more conservative direction. The agendas of these presidents and their appointees included reversing the major decisions of the Warren Court in the areas of civil rights, civil liberties, voting rights, and criminal procedure, giving government more power over criminals and suspects, and reversing affirmative action. That story has often been told. But we need to spend a moment on the explanation these Nixon, Reagan, and Bush appointees have given about what they were doing, for they have denied that their efforts had anything to do with imposing their own ideologies on the law.

Beginning with President Nixon's appointment of Chief Justice Burger to the Court in 1969, several of the conservative appointees on the Burger and Rehnquist Courts appropriated the language of judicial restraint and used it to attack the Warren Court and its remaining members just as the new majority on the 1937 Hughes Court retained the language of the prior era.[4] Following the Nixon, Reagan, and Bush appointments, journalists and commentators seized the conservatives' use of the language of judicial restraint and were fond of describing the new justices as restrained.[5]

The Court's conservatives, asserting greater adherence to judicial restraint, criticize the prior Court for biased decision making and seek to replace its decisions with "neutral" decisions based on "correct" interpretive principles.[6] They urge a "positivist" enterprise in which justices merely apply law they have been given. These conservatives describe that as a model of judicial statesmanship. Conservatives argue that liberals had failed to adhere to precedent, to the law as it had been announced, and had failed to practice judicial restraint.

There are several threads to this attack. First, is the assertion that a "neutral" "strict" interpretation of law is possible in almost all cases and that the judges and justices have no business deciding cases where it is not possible. By "neutral" they mean that judges and justices should be "neutral" about the meaning of the law and simply and accurately give voice to whatever it says. Second, "the need for obedience to legitimated authority . . . drives conservative positivism"[7] and pushes conservatives to insist that "strict" interpretation is possible and appropriate and that judges should defer to coordinate branches. Third, the conservative members of the Court describe their votes as the result of a democratic orientation—they, the unelected judges, are deferring to the elected branches of government.[8] Not only is the authority of the president, Congress, state executives, and legislatures legitimate, they were all elected.

Since this traditional restraint is in favor of government, commentators also began to describe the new conservatives as statists.[9] Indeed, the conservative justices claimed that various public policies overrode the importance of claims of individual rights, and that added yet another way in which conservative rhetoric favored government over the individual.[10] Those early cases could also have supported the view that they saw a degree of mutual responsibility between citizens and government. On the one hand, individuals have responsibilities toward society and its government that sometimes override claims of rights. On the other hand, the reason government cannot honor all claims of individual rights is that it has a still more pressing obligation to protect everyone.

This view of the conservative members of the Court as statist democrats advocating mutual obligations for democratic reasons missed the point entirely; this cohort of justices means something entirely different by its attack. It is not necessarily statist since there are important lines of cases in which the conservative bloc favors individual interests.[11] A commitment to democratic self-government does not explain their decisions because they do not support democratic rights when they are at stake, a position described at length later in this chapter. The Court rejected any significant commitment to mutual obligation in such cases as *DeShaney v. Winnebago County Dept. of Social Servs.*[12] In that case, Joshua DeShaney had been mauled by his father so seriously that he became a virtual vegetable for the rest of his young life. Employees of the County Department of Social Services had been assigned to Joshua and his father and had good evidence that Joshua's father was beating him seriously but did nothing. On one occasion Joshua ran away, and the police actually returned him to his father. The Court could have held that it could not fashion a rule that would distinguish between honest errors and serious derelictions of duty. Instead, it held that the government simply had no responsibility to aid Joshua. In effect, neither a preference for government, nor democracy, nor any attachment to public obligations explains this Court.

The conservative counterattack also proved quite confusing with regard to interpretation. Part of the reason the conservative counterattack on liberal methods of interpretation has proved so confusing has to do with the difficulties of interpretation. Following the intentions of those who wrote parts of the Constitution often conflicts with judicial restraint because the original meaning of the Constitution may, and often does, require judicial activism to protect the rights and powers described in the Constitution.[13] But more important, ascertaining what a clause means is far from a mechanical operation. Without repeating here an old and very complex argument, David Hume,[14] the legal realists,[15] and the critical legal theorists[16] have all told us in different ways that "neutrality" is impossible—we can rarely follow the orders that our lawgivers have left us without taking a stance on the issues we face. Was the clause intended to deal with this situation? Did the draftsmen intend for us to ignore the way that the equities have shifted, new knowledge about human affairs, or technical developments? As we try to bridge the gap between ourselves and the draftsmen, we inevitably make assumptions.

There is another sense in which people define neutrality. It might be called interpretive consistency. According to this approach, a neutral jurist picks a preferred method of deciding cases—such as reading the text according to its plain or common meaning, being guided by the history of a clause and the way it was used in practice, or being guided by the purpose and principles that were the reasons for the provisions, and so on—and sticks to it. Even though interpretive strategies do not yield unambiguous answers, it might still be possible to say that justices reach answers because they think those strategies require them. The point of this theory is to enforce a degree of ideological neutrality. The jurist would have to accept whatever conclusions—liberal or conservative—a rigorous study of the Constitution guided by consistent interpretive principles yielded. On the other hand, it may be possible to conclude that the interpretive strategies function as little more than rationalizations.

One could respond that interpretive consistency is not neutral at all—even though the consistent application of any set of interpretive principles will yield some decisions that are liberal and some that are conservative, choices about what evidence to consider are likely to tilt the results in relatively predictable ways among large groups of cases.[17] I want to respond in a different way: no one is neutral—there are no paragons of interpretive neutrality. All the justices' conclusions are based on politically charged philosophic assumptions, not interpretive canons.

The important question is what those assumptions are. We know in a general sort of way that they are "conservative" or "liberal." But that does not begin to explain what is going on and just how fundamental the changes have been.

The Shift in Fundamental Principles

Individual Moral Autonomy. The belief in individual moral autonomy, the conviction that each individual is entitled to choose his or her own private values, has been central to the classical liberal tradition at least since Bentham and Mill.[18] Though we now describe it as part of the classical liberal tradition, conservatives once shared that tradition.[19] Indeed, libertarian thought has been an important ingredient of twentieth-century conservatism. More moderate conservative readings of that tradition have also played a large role in contemporary American thought. At this point, Justices Stevens, Souter, Ginsburg, and Breyer share the belief in individual moral autonomy; Chief Justice Rehnquist and Justices O'Connor, Scalia, Kennedy, and Thomas do not.[20]

The issue has repeatedly roiled the Court, most obviously in cases regarding sexual relations—testing what we have been calling the rights of privacy. In most of the earlier cases, one could respond that the claimed rights had serious implications for others in society so that privacy and autonomy had to compete with other values. The watershed was *Bowers v. Hardwick.*[21] In *Bowers* that claim was foreclosed.

Hardwick was a homosexual male who was arrested for sodomy with another adult male in the privacy of his home. When the district attorney decided to drop the case contingent on additional evidence, Hardwick sued in federal court to have the Georgia statute declared unconstitutional. But the United States Supreme Court upheld the statute.

Bowers could be dismissed as a case of liberals reaching for too much, trying to extend the earlier privacy decisions too far. But it has a deeper philosophic meaning that reverberates through the fabric of law. The Court refused to recognize any right for adults to engage in consensual homosexual relations and held that it was enough to sustain the statute that Georgia had a reason for banning sodomy that some otherwise reasonable people might accept, even if it was not a good reason—in the jargon of the Court, Georgia had a "rational basis," which is the easiest test for a statute to meet. The Court refused to require that the statute have been necessary to accomplish an overridingly important public purpose—a much stricter test reserved for important rights. The state could restrict or forbid such relationships on grounds that need not be terribly important. Indeed, it could forbid such relationships on the simple ground of disapproval, regardless of whether there was any injury to the rights of others.[22]

Utilitarians and liberals would defer to individual choice in cases not affecting the rights of others, following the classic mid-nineteenth-century argument of John Stuart Mill in *On Liberty.*[23] Blackmun wrote in dissent:

> The statute at issue . . . denies individuals the right to decide for themselves whether to engage in particular forms of private, consensual sexual activity.[24]

Stevens, also in dissent, added:

> [T]he fact that the governing majority in a State has traditionally viewed a particular practice as immoral is not a sufficient reason for upholding a law prohibiting the practice.[25]

The significance of *Bowers* is precisely that it was a private consensual act between adults. The only community injury could be the knowledge of the permissibility of such consensual sexual relations. But that knowledge alone cannot count as an injury without canceling the entire classical liberal project. The only "harm" of the knowledge is that someone else might choose to engage in the behavior on the basis of the information gained. But then to prevent one from gaining the information is to prevent an individual from making an informed choice for himself or herself. There would, then, be no meaning at all to the concept that the state has no business banning consensual relationships that cause no injury to others. In place of the liberal and utilitarian positions that restricted interference with individual choice to those cases in which the rights of other parties are affected, *Bowers* substituted mere disapproval.

To defend the rejection of individual autonomy, conservatives might argue that they do so out of deference to democratic values. Or they could argue that they are adhering to what have been called "traditional" values, though those values are in fact one set of competing traditional American values. Or they could outline some criteria for acceptable personal choices. White wrote the majority opinion and his choice was to refer to democratic values in preference to individual personal rights.[26] The majority rules. It chose to ban sodomy. The Court should respect the majority's wishes. Case closed.

By contrast, that analysis does not work for Rehnquist or O'Connor, who joined the majority in *Bowers*; it does not work for Scalia and Thomas, who have made their support for the result in *Bowers* clear in later opinions; and, as we will see, support for democratic values does not work well for Justice Kennedy, who made his rejection of moral autonomy clear in other cases. The position of these five justices has not been consistent with support for the overriding significance of democratic rights.[27] From apportionment to gerrymandering to voting rights cases, they have been very hostile to the notion that there is enforceable meaning in the constitutional clauses defining participatory democratic rights. Yet without those rights, the majority itself is but a legal fiction. The legitimacy of democratic rule depends on the right to vote and the right to have that vote counted equally and fairly.

The jurisprudence of the conservative justices on the Rehnquist Court is far more consistent with a turn toward traditional values.[28] Rehnquist confirmed this position, speaking also for Justices O'Connor and Kennedy, in *Barnes v. Glen Theatre*.[29] There the state banned nude dancing on moral grounds. Rehnquist treated the state's moral objections as sufficient justification for restraint. In other words, the state was allowed to treat traditional values as more important and as overriding the first First Amendment privilege. Justice Scalia, concurring, was more blunt:

> Perhaps the dissenters believe that "offense to others" ought to be the only reason for restricting nudity in public places generally, but there is no basis

for thinking that our society has ever shared that Thoreauvian "you-may-do-what-you-like-so-long-as-it-does-not-injure-someone-else" beau idea—much less for thinking that it was written into the Constitution.[30]

Scalia put his pen right on the fault line. Justice Souter, concurring, specifically disclaimed reliance on the theory of moral objectionableness.[31] For Justice Souter, it was sufficient for the judgment that there appeared to be significant secondary effects of nude dancing—that is that the nudity of the dancers had an impact on the safety of the neighborhood. That is critical to the utilitarian and classical liberal positions. Regulation is justified by injury to others, not merely distaste; if distaste were enough to justify regulation, there would be no zone of individual autonomy free of whatever regulation society chose to impose. For Souter, there was injury and the important ground of mere distaste did not have to be crossed.

Justice White, joined by Justices Marshall, Blackmun, and Stevens, treated those moral objections as a bias in selecting speech to regulate. Rules that select which speech to ban on the ground of content are particularly disfavored in First Amendment law. Therefore, the four justices argued that the moral standard itself, which selected some speech for regulation based on its content, needed justification according to traditional First Amendment rules.[32]

Chief Justice Rehnquist and Justices Scalia and Thomas reaffirmed their rejection of moral autonomy with respect to private behavior in a recent case in which the Court overruled the antigay amendment to the Colorado Constitution, an amendment that had been adopted by referendum.[33] The provisions of the amendment would have overruled all state legal rules and principles that would have protected homosexuals from discrimination.

Scalia, writing in dissent and joined by Chief Justice Rehnquist and Justice Thomas, argued at length that *Romer v. Evans* was about democratic rights. This is the same argument that Justice White made in *Bowers v. Hardwick*. But the rejection of democratic rights in a multitude of contexts by these three members of the Court makes it an argument that is hard to accept from Justices Scalia and Thomas and from Chief Justice Rehnquist. More to the point is Scalia's constant refrain, albeit under the claim of democratic rights, about "preserv[ing] traditional sexual mores."[34]

The three dissenters also accepted the extremity of the Colorado remedy. The amendment would have allowed discrimination in places of public accommodation, including "hotels, restaurants, hospitals, dental clinics, theaters, banks, common carriers, travel and insurance agencies" and all other shops and stores, and would further have allowed discrimination in all government services, which are otherwise supposed to be available to the general public.[35] This effectively placed homosexuals beyond the pale and protection of law.

Scalia, writing for himself, Chief Justice Rehnquist, and Justice Thomas, argued that the amendment did no more than deny "special protections" and "favored status for *homosexuality*."[36] "Favored status" presumably is different from being treated like everyone else. And that is the central issue: What does it mean to be treated like everyone else? Scalia, Rehnquist, and Thomas adopt a very rough-and-tumble view of being treated like everyone else and apply it not only to homosexuality but to race, gender, and discrimination generally. For them, being treated like everyone else means being subject to the same possibility that one will be discriminated against on the ground of race, gender, or sexual preference that one might experience on a host of other issues.[37] It does not mean that homosexuality will make no difference with respect to jobs, public accommodations, and the like.

The consequences of Scalia, Rehnquist, and Thomas's view are extensive. The statutes repealed by the amendment were themselves designed to cope with preexisting forms of discrimination.[38] The majority pointed out that the statute affected virtually every area of life and "nullifies specific legal protections [for homosexuals] in all transactions in housing, sale of real estate, insurance, health and welfare services, private education, and employment."[39] In other words, in each of those areas homosexuals would have been fair game for exclusion or discriminatory treatment. This would be true wherever anyone, public or private, had any discretion, for then homosexuality could enter in. Gays and lesbians would be "treated like everyone else" in the sense that their sexual preference would be treated as irrelevant only where they could claim some categorical, nondiscretionary entitlement—Scalia gave the example of a pension.[40]

For Stevens, Souter, Ginsburg, and Breyer, *Romer v. Evans* was an easy case. Justice Kennedy, however, wrote the majority opinion, joined also by Justice O'Connor. This case raises the question whether Justices Kennedy and O'Connor should be included in the group that rejects individual moral autonomy. Justices Kennedy and O'Connor stressed, both in their questions during oral argument, and in the opinion of the Court, that the problem with the Colorado amendment was its breadth. Justice Scalia, in dissent, charged the majority with overruling *Bowers* without mentioning it.[41] It is as consistent with what they told us, however, to conclude that Kennedy and O'Connor would treat some sanctions on homosexual activity as appropriate, perhaps as in *Bowers,* but that open season on gays and lesbians, as they understood the Colorado amendment, is insupportable. That is similar to the Eighth Amendment, which allows punishment for crimes but prohibits those so severe that they are cruel and unusual. If that interpretation is correct, Kennedy and O'Connor continue to reject moral autonomy for private behavior but do not share the vindictiveness or severity of the dissenters.[42]

The same difference among the justices was apparent in the recent "right to die" cases.[43] Washington and New York prohibited anyone from assisting another person to commit suicide. In both states, doctors and terminally ill patients challenged the law. If the Court were to accept the principle that there is a right to moral autonomy, it would strongly support one's right to make a decision about ending one's own life. Chief Justice Rehnquist, and Justices Scalia, Kennedy, and Thomas, simply denied that there is any such right. Justices Stevens, Souter, Ginsburg, and Breyer all found it necessary to differentiate their positions from the majority opinion precisely on the ground that they were not prepared to dismiss so quickly the autonomy of individuals near death. They concurred, however, because such a right would not be harmless.[44] People might be misled, misunderstood, or coerced, if not murdered. Thus they recognized the power of the claim but found, in classic liberal and utilitarian terms, that potential injury outweighed the claim. Justice O'Connor found herself drawn to both positions—she agreed with the Court that there was no right to commit suicide, but agreed with the dissenters that the case should be decided on narrower grounds.[45]

This split among the members of the Court, between those who do and those who do not accept the proposition that there is a right to moral autonomy, reverberates throughout almost its entire docket.

The Avoidance of Harm. Moral autonomy is a corollary of another fundamental liberal and utilitarian principle—of doing no harm—a point recognized in Justice Scalia's remark above. For liberals and utilitarians, one is not justified in interfering with individual behavior except to avoid harm, preferably to someone else.[46] Beyond that line, individuals should be treated as autonomous.[47] Interference in that zone is likely to cause harm without justification. Avoidance of harm is fundamental.[48]

These traditions have deep roots in Anglo-American law. The American Revolution was defended in liberal or libertarian terms as the protection of liberty.[49] At approximately the time of the Revolution, Jeremy Bentham, the father of utilitarianism, argued that legal rules should be judged by the pleasures and pains they cause.[50] Later John Stuart Mill explained that keeping government out of individual choices is necessary for human happiness unless there were injury to others.[51] Thus he married the protection of individual liberty to social happiness. Bentham's version can be very statist, overriding individual preferences in favor of general happiness. Mill's version has a more individualistic appearance. Subsequent Anglo-American philosophy has attempted to wrestle with the conflict between the individual and the society at the heart of Bentham's and Mill's descriptions.[52] But all versions unite in attempting to reflect rather than impose individual and social judgments.

Despite much criticism, liberalism, utilitarianism, and their progeny have had a powerful effect on American law. The instrumental premises of the utilitarian system were forcefully echoed by then-judge Benjamin Cardozo: "The final cause of law is the welfare of society."[53] In the language of Rule 1 of the Federal Rules of Civil Procedure, enacted not long after Cardozo's remarks, rules should be interpreted "to secure the just, speedy, and inexpensive determination of every action," or, in the language of Rule 8(f), "to do substantial justice." Law was understood as instrumental. Its goal was a safer, happier world. Law intervened to resolve disputes and relieve unfairness.

The more conservative bloc has rejected that tradition. *Herrera*[54] was the decisive break. Angel Herrera was imprisoned on death row in Texas. Herrera's counsel, after years of hard work, had found evidence that he was innocent. Herrera asked that a court, state or federal, take a look and hold a hearing. Existing rules in Texas did not permit a hearing to consider evidence of innocence discovered more than thirty days after a person had been sentenced. Several justices concluded in dissent that Angel Herrera was probably innocent. For Blackmun, Stevens, and Souter, dissenting, the harm, the possible loss of an innocent life, exceeded the cost of further careful review of the facts of Herrera's case. For a utilitarian, *Herrera* was not a hard case.[55]

The conservative bloc rejected that conclusion. More, they rejected the proposition that a court should take a look. For them, Herrera's death and possible innocence were unrelated to what they described as the separate question of the process due. Herrera had had every procedural protection. No further procedures were required merely because newly discovered evidence might suggest that the existing processes had been insufficient to do substantial justice. Herrera had all he was entitled to. Now the state was entitled to his life. He has since been executed.

No one committed to the avoidance of harm could have taken that position. It would have been enough to save Herrera's life had the Court merely decided that Texas's thirty-day rule denied due process, or that a judge had discretion to review his claim and require a hearing if the evidence warranted. Two years later, when Justice O'Connor joined the liberal group in *Schlup v. Delo,*[56] the Court decided that a judge did have discretion to look at the facts in a narrow class of cases. Chief Justice Rehnquist dissented vigorously in an opinion joined by Justices Scalia, Kennedy, and Thomas.[57] Angel Herrera and Lloyd Schlup could not convince the core of the conservative bloc that strong evidence of innocence gave rise to any rights whatever.[58]

Like the split over moral autonomy, this split over whether law is or is not about the general welfare, about the harms and benefits to the public, reverberates throughout constitutional law.

Rejection of the Liberal Agenda

Now we sketch the way that the justices' acceptance or rejection of these fundamental philosophical propositions of doing no harm and respecting individual autonomy drive their conclusions in a wide variety of areas. The justices' philosophies fit the pattern of their decisions better than their own explanations—obedience to the Constitution or to the popular will, application of proper interpretive strategies, or dedication to federalism. First we map the conservative rejection of the liberal landmarks of prior courts, particularly the familiar understandings of the general welfare, liberty, democracy, and judicial behavior.

Liberty. Moral autonomy and the harm principle are central to the notion of liberty. Liberty, after all, is about choices, about what to do with oneself. The harm principle is about personal safety and the pursuit of happiness, which are at the core of liberty. Thus the conflict over the right to moral autonomy and the harm principle affects virtually every claim of freedom—from property to the right to die, from personal safety and security to privacy and sexual freedom.[59] The Rehnquist Court has been expanding rights to property while narrowing other personal liberties. It does not accept any general libertarian notion of protecting individuals from the state no matter how great the "conservative" distrust of government, and this has been particularly evident in the criminal law.

Some conservatives trace the liberal tradition to John Locke and emphasize his defense of property. That would support the protection of property rights. But Locke, one of the intellectual fathers of the American Revolution, explicitly defined life and liberty as among an individual's property rights.[60] There is a libertarian strand of conservative thought that would take account of Locke's broad account of liberty.[61] That strand is generally hostile to government interference. This is a so-called classical liberal approach, not to be confused with modern American liberalism. The market is much admired by such conservatives because it can operate largely without official intervention.[62] But regardless of their praise for market mechanisms, the current conservative justices are not libertarians. The Court's conservatives are willing to regulate private consensual behavior and insist that no objective social injury is necessary to justify the regulation.[63] Their refusal to shed many tears over the loss of liberty in criminal proceedings that may have gone awry or the possible error involved in capital punishment[64] simply belies any general libertarian notion of protecting individuals from the state. *Bowers, Romer, Barnes*, and *Herrera* should make that amply clear.

Instrumentalism and General Welfare. Initially, as they joined the Court, the conservative justices often argued that the general welfare outranked individual rights.[65] They described their decisions as a judgment among competing constitutional claims. They also argued that rights must be narrowed because rights can be dangerous. Especially if expansively interpreted, rights can subvert established traditions, social order, national or personal security. Therefore, conservatives could attack expansively interpreted rights as merely personal or individual rights and argue that such rights took advantage of society's forbearance. Liberals treat rights as socially constructive and essential, but conservatives argued that society's needs outranked individual rights.

For example, it is not difficult to see the conflict between social and individual rights in what is generally called the "exclusionary rule"—the rule that excludes relevant evidence of an accused's guilt if the police obtained the evidence improperly.[66] There are two competing objectives.

One is to protect ourselves from official abuse of power that is sometimes misdirected at law-abiding citizens. The second is to protect ourselves from those who commit crimes. That creates a balancing act with lots of room for disagreement, still governed by the principle of trying to do as little harm as possible.

This mode of judicial thought is instrumental—interpreting law to achieve the most socially constructive results. Achieving an objective—whether liberty, happiness, or some other socially defined goal—requires looking at consequences. Judges historically have done that; they have interpreted the law in light of what they understood as its objectives.

But Rehnquist, Scalia, and Thomas eventually condemned instrumental thinking in its entirety. Scalia colorfully described balancing as "like judging whether a particular line is longer than a particular rock is heavy."[67] Rehnquist has called for exclusion of all considerations about the impact of law on people.[68] For Rehnquist, Scalia, and Thomas, law is simply and properly a matter of following commands. In turn, the commands are understood directly from the language or from historical examples. There is no need to explore the effect of changed circumstances on how the draftsmen would have reacted—an exploration that would require that the jurist explore the impact of different reasonable ways of construing the law.

Thus one aspect of the move away from the traditional liberal/utilitarian paradigm is a move away from instrumentalism and toward what is often called legal formalism—treating law as a logically deductive system rather than an experiential one. The harms that could be avoided by the recognition of rights are simply irrelevant. The general welfare is no longer part of the thinking of the Court's most conservative justices.

The Rejection of Democratic Values. Still, the conservative justices have described their formal approach as obedience to democratic decision making. That makes their rejection of democratic values all the more surprising. Nevertheless, for reasons soon to be explained, conservative philosophy doesn't provide strong underpinnings for democratic values. And the rejection of democratic values is clear in the decisions of the conservative justices.

Conservative disdain for democracy shows quite starkly in the voting and districting cases where the Court's conservatives have backed away from the Warren Court's insistence on the right to vote, and on equality among voters.[69]

The Constitution provides for reapportionment of representation in the Congress every ten years, after the census. The political consequences of reapportionment are huge. Until the Court outlawed the practice in the 1960s, politicians in power could and did "reapportion" (or refuse to reapportion) representation so that most of the legislators came from whatever part of the state they favored—rural areas, cities, or suburbs—and few came from the others. And since who was in power depended on where a previous generation had allocated legislative seats, power essentially stayed put.

The Supreme Court concluded that whatever else such a system might be called, it was not democratic government. If voting power can be skewed, then elections don't reflect the public will but simply reflect the desires of those who have been handed the power to run the government. The result is the rule of some by others. Since the voting power of some of the people is suppressed, it is probably minority rule—only by pure accident might those with voting power reflect the wishes of the majority of the people.

When the Warren Court decided on the one-person, one-vote principle so that the size of the population in electoral districts must be as close to equal as possible, the resulting power shift was clear, but the country understood the democratic logic of the decisions and embraced the principle. Equality of population in the districts that elect legislators is central to representative government. Without question, the larger point is that the mechanism of voting ought not to be abused in order to manipulate the result. Any manipulation that compromises the equality of the voters compromises democracy. That is indeed the bedrock of democracy.

But the conservatives on the Court have not embraced it. This has been true consistently since each member of the current conservative bloc joined the Court. In *Brown v. Thompson*, Justices Rehnquist and O'Connor agreed that districts can differ from one another by as much two and a half to one, and declined to address the difference of more than three to one in the population of the largest and smallest districts.[70] Indeed, early in their careers on the Court, Rehnquist and O'Connor concluded that voting for representatives to water and power districts could be restricted to landowners in proportion to the land they owned, even though the districts had important control over the lives and livelihoods of the entire public in the area.[71]

Where voters could not be excluded, and when districts had to be equal, politicians revived and mastered the arts of gerrymandering for the same goal of political control. Gerrymandering is a technique of wasting opponents' votes by selectively stuffing or dispersing them in districts where they have little effect on the outcome. It allows those who control the way legislative district lines are drawn to defeat much larger groups of voters. Justice Stevens recently provided an example of the way that gerrymandering has reversed Texans' preferences: a majority of Texans voted for Republican candidates in 1994, but Democrats won nearly two-thirds of the legislative seats; in 1992 Democrats won a small majority of the vote but won twenty-seven of thirty seats.[72] For Chief Justice Rehnquist and Justice O'Connor, political gerrymandering raises no constitutional issue that the Court could address.[73]

The Voting Rights Act prohibits "denial or abridgement" of the right to vote because of race and requires that no changes in voting practices take effect in certain places without approval of the attorney general of the United States or the federal court in the District of Columbia.[74] Under that statute, the attorney general, with the support of the Burger Court, had required many states to design districts more hospitable to the minority communities.

Minority voting strength has been minimized, manipulated, and diluted in several ways. The simplest has been to create districts in which minority groups are always outnumbered and outvoted. In the racial context, where voting is often polarized, this matters much more than it does in other more fluid situations. Normally, victories are created out of complex and unstable electoral coalitions and no group is entirely left out in the cold as politicians struggle to win some votes even among those groups usually opposed. But where voting is polarized, the issue is whether you are for or against the minority group itself and the representatives are disabled from doing anything to win support in that community. The problem with polarized voting is that the losers are unable to exert any influence or to have their needs considered at all. Defeated voters are effectively excluded from the political process and its benefits.

The 1982 amendments to the Voting Rights Act required the courts to judge whether minority votes had been diluted, not by examining the good or bad intentions of those who wrote it but by the results of what they created. At the same time Congress wrote into the act a proviso that declared that the statute established no "right" to proportional representation. In *Thornburg v. Gingles*, the Burger Court concluded that where polarized voting made alternatives useless, and where the minority was "sufficiently large and geographically compact," it would require the creation of an additional district in which the racial minority constituted a voting majority—a so-called majority-minority district. The minority could not then be frozen out as completely. Justice O'Connor responded that the *Gingles* test "comes closer to an absolute requirement of proportional representation than Congress intended when it codified the results test in §2."[75] Plainly, no disproportionate advantage is possible by this method, as Justice O'Connor's attack attested.

But the Rehnquist Court no longer finds districting plans discriminatory when they arrange to outnumber and outvote minorities systematically. And it treats efforts to remedy that situation as violations of the Constitution unless clearly subordinated to other considerations.[76] The Rehnquist Court stressed regularity of district shapes, even though virtually all American jurisdictions had long since abandoned that idea as utterly unworkable.[77] And Justices Thomas and Scalia have gone further in declaring the very fact that a racial minority constitutes a majority of an electoral district makes the districting constitutionally suspect as a racial gerrymander.[78]

The turning point with regard to the Voting Rights Act was in *Shaw v. Reno*.[79] The attorney general had objected that North Carolina designed too few districts that reflected black voting power. The state then developed a revised plan, under which white voters continued to hold power in North Carolina's congressional districts out of proportion to their numbers. The Court held, however, that the revised plan did not violate the rights of blacks, who remained underrepresented, but did violate the rights of white voters because the state had made a conscious effort to cure some of the underrepresentation of black voters.

It is important to ask whether these districting decisions, painful though they may be, are made necessary by a substantial conception of democracy or whether they are evidence that the justices reaching these conclusions are not attached to democratic principles. Justices Scalia and Thomas have expressed a decisive view about the meaning of democracy in the districting context: black voters are a minority, so they should lose. In effect the Voting Rights Act, at least as applied to districting, is wrongheaded. They are unimpressed by the fairness of proportionality in which different groups have electoral majorities in different districts in rough proportion to their share of the population. They have concluded that proportionality is improper as a statutory remedy even in the limited circumstances described by the Burger Court. And going well beyond that, they have also concluded that there is a constitutional right not to suffer minorities to control any districts except by accident.[80] If, say, blacks are a third of the population of a given state but are a majority of the population in a tenth of the electoral districts, according to Scalia and Thomas, that tenth isn't too little, it's too much.

It is hard to argue that such rough and conditional proportionality is not *a* fair system, even though it is *not* the *only* fair system. In fact, where voters are racially polarized so that a racial minority is unable to exert influence by means of any other system, it may be the *only practical* fair system. Whether the disproportion violates the statute depends, according to *Gingles*, on both the feasibility of additional minority districts and on whether the districts are racially polarized.

Scalia and Thomas, however, have also expressed the view that there is no fair definition of democracy, no uniquely right way to do districting.[81] They have objected to the Court's conclusion that the Voting Rights Act protects minorities against the dilution of their votes by the way that district lines are drawn.[82] Essentially, they are skeptics about democracy. Indeed Scalia has written that he is more concerned about tyranny of the majority than tyranny of the elite.[83]

Given their skepticism, and given the obvious fairness of a proportional system, one would have expected them to keep hands off the administration of the Voting Rights Act in accord with that view. Nevertheless, and somewhat inconsistently, Thomas and Scalia have concluded that proportionality alone is inadmissible as an electoral principle. In effect, they would make it impossible to prove discrimination, or the intention to discriminate, against racial minorities by the very techniques that everyone involved in politics knows are the bread and butter of efforts to gain electoral advantage—the drawing of district boundaries. By their standards, it doesn't happen because it can't. That could be described as a rough-and-tumble democratic system for minorities but one in which the majority is protected from the tumbles. It is a version of electoral government in which the common interests of blacks and whites will be systematically subordinated to their differences.

One scholar has argued that Thomas holds an individual theory of democracy.[84] There are two problems with that contention. First, in the absence of apportionment cases since Thomas joined the Court, it is impossible to test Thomas's commitment to such a theory. Second, Thomas's claim that plaintiffs are assuming group behavior is transparently false. In each area, there are investigations and evidence about whether groups divide and how those in control treat the divisions, if any. Polarization and dilution are questions of fact. Hence, Thomas's claim becomes a claim that groups don't count when they act together. That claim challenges the heart of democracy.

Rehnquist, O'Connor, and Kennedy have written many opinions in the districting cases but have yet to describe a theory of democracy. Their argument in the current series of cases has been about a definition of impermissible racial line drawing and therefore the types of majority-minority districts that *cannot* be drawn.[85] The conservative majority has offered only limitations on what can be done to minimize the dilution of black votes, not standards for how their votes should be protected. They have deferred to traditional methods, but those methods are eminently manipulable by those who do the districting. The result has simply been to dismantle districts in which there are black majorities in polarized areas, even though the number of such districts is *less* than proportional to black voting strength.

The question with respect to the conservative bloc—Rehnquist, O'Connor, Scalia, Kennedy, and Thomas—is whether it is the case that their stand on the Voting Rights Act can be ascribed to a positive view of democracy. Such arguments are available. They might argue, for example, that majority-minority districting is a form of gerrymandering by wasting black Democratic votes in favor of Republican electoral success. But the conservative majority has not been willing to examine this larger gerrymandering context either alone or in conjunction with the Voting Rights Act cases.

Simply put, the claim that they are responding to a positive view of democracy seems implausible because white claims against voting in black majority districts are the only kind of "democratic" claim this bloc supports. They do not support claims that voters have been excluded. They do not find it discriminatory or worthy of a remedy where district lines in racially polarized areas are drawn so that minorities lose a disproportionate share of the seats[86] or where the rules are rewritten when blacks threaten political success so that those blacks who are elected cannot exercise the powers that their white counterparts had.[87] They disclaim any procedural theory of democracy that describes any right way of drawing district lines. They are not prepared to protect majorities in the apportionment and gerrymandering cases and they are not willing to protect minorities in the Voting Rights Act cases. It is an interesting question what democracy means to this group.

Another index of their actual refusal to defer to democratic self-government despite their democratic rhetoric is in the lines of cases in which they have taken an activist role and overruled government on constitutional grounds. The conservative justices on the Rehnquist Court describe the Warren Court as undemocratic because, when the Warren Court held legislation unconstitutional, it overruled the people's elected representatives. The conservatives on the Rehnquist Court have, by contrast, claimed to be restraining themselves in deference to democracy when they pared back or reversed Warren Court restraints on the behavior of other public officials. When this Court finds legislation unconstitutional, however, it puts the shoe on the other foot. One strong example is the conservative bloc's treatment of the takings or just compensation clause. Traditionally, the just compensation clause required payment when a government took title to private property or invaded the property as by building a road across it. Generally applicable rules, like zoning rules, did not require compensation. The Rehnquist Court, however, has expanded the meaning of the clause so that it now imposes new costs on generally applicable regulation, particularly environmental regulation. Owners who wanted to build in flood plains or on fragile portions of coastline, have been able to defy state rules or extract compensation for compliance. States that were prepared to offer a variance to allow otherwise prohibited construction in exchange for public access to the beach or other public amenity have been told that they could not use the variance in trade.[88] The justices understood that this view does not rest on the original meaning of the just compensation clause or historical practice.[89] Rather, whatever the merits of their view, it rests on their own conclusion that the clause should control state regulation, and it overrules self-government in favor of government by judiciary.

Still more recently, they dropped a bombshell on almost all of the states in the country, holding that the way that legal services for the poor is financed may amount to a taking of private property.[90] Lawyers' escrow accounts are often too small to pay any interest; the interest is eaten by a variety of bank charges. Federal banking and tax regulations were changed so that lawyers could pool many accounts that individually were too small to pay interest, into a large interest-bearing account, the interest from which could then be used for the support of legal aid programs. In such an account, the cost of separating the interest on each client's account would be prohibitive. Hence, the value of those accounts for each client was zero but the banks ended up with the money. The laws, generally known as Interest on Lawyers' Trust Accounts or IOLTA statutes, sent that interest to state funds to support legal services programs. When the Court looked at the practice, forty-nine states and the District of Columbia had employed this method to generate income for legal aid programs. The conservative majority said it did not matter that there was nothing of value to the client at stake; it was still the client's money. Therefore, it might be a taking. Since there are still some difficult questions—What is the appropriate compensation for taking nothing of value? for example—it might be a tempest in a teapot. But then one wonders why they bothered.

The conclusion that the takings cases reflect an activist court rejecting democratic premises is further buttressed by other areas in which this has been a conservatively activist court. It has, for example, overruled both federal and state efforts to deal with the consequences of discrimination, sharply limited congressional power over firearms, the environment, and national power to require state compliance with federal rules.[91] Thus, it is more accurate to say that the Court has changed the areas in which it is activist and restrained; it is no longer activist in protecting democracy but is now activist in protecting economic rights. That exchange does not reflect any greater deference to democratic decision making than prior Courts', and the Court's unwillingness to insist on participatory rights shows less concern with democracy.

Some would claim recent cases limiting national power indicate a conservative dedication to federalism and that federalism, that is, a preference for state and local control over national decision making, is a theory of democracy. This is a preference for a geographically defined minority over a larger geographically defined majority, on the ground that the local community works better to reflect popular will. There are, of course, constitutional provisions that define the extent of local independence and national democratic rights. Beyond that, in the absence of any theory or standards about how states and localities must honor their democratic commitments, the federalism claim reduces to the claim that whatever states and localities do is democratic. That claim is clearly barred by the republican government clause. Stripped down in that way, federalism is a theory of power equally consistent with entrenched hierarchical power as it is with democracy. As a result, federalism cannot stand on its own as a theory of democracy without a theory of how states and localities must honor the commitment to democratic government. In any event, there is no evidence that this group of conservative justices is wedded to federalism except when states and localities take positions the group supports on other grounds.[92]

The right of free expression is a second crucial area of democratic values. From the Hughes Court in the 1930s to the Burger Court in the 1970s, there were certain staples of First Amendment law. The Court carefully protected the "poor man's free speech"—his opportunity to speak or pass out literature in public. It protected demonstrators against vague discretionary rules that allowed public officials to let those they favored march, picket, or demonstrate, but provided a screen behind which local officials could prevent demonstrations by people like the Reverend Martin Luther King, Jr., and groups like the NAACP, labor unions, and others whose message was locally unpopular and could imprison their leaders if they tried.[93]

The conservative bloc on both the Burger and Rehnquist Courts has been hostile to effective opportunities to engage the public in public. Public airports and the sidewalks in front of post offices are off-limits for solicitation, and Justices Rehnquist, Scalia, and Thomas would also have barred passing out literature in those places. Shopping centers are available only at the discretion of the owners except in states like California that have created a state right to their use, although the Warren Court had started to open them for peaceful demonstrations. Posters can be barred from all public places if they clash with official aesthetics.[94] Many Americans therefore never go anyplace where people might be asking for signatures on a petition or urging a point of view not seen on the media.

In a 1992 decision, several members of the conservative bloc voted to weaken the protection against discretionary, potentially discriminatory administration of parade and demonstration rules.[95] The point of trying to eliminate discretion in controlling speech was to protect unpopular groups or groups that opposed official policies from being targeted for restraint under the cover of vaguely worded conditions and restrictions. One of the groups that prior Courts had in mind was the NAACP Legal Defense and Education Fund that fought to end segregation in *Brown v. Board*. With the Rehnquist Court's blessing that very organization was barred from participating in the joint solicitation of federal employees for charitable contributions.[96]

In a world in which many otherwise private organizations participate in public programs, several members of the Court have been urging that government can use public funding of private organizations to favor or control the speech of others. They have approved tax exemptions for favored speakers that were not available to others. They voted to bar public television stations from editorializing. They barred some publicly funded doctors from advising patients about remedies some of the patients would have wanted.[97] The consequences of that support for official financial favoritism for points of view are extensive.

Some, like Justice Scalia, claim a firm attachment to the principle that government rules about speech, press, and religion must not discriminate among viewpoints but must, instead, be "neutral" with respect to those differences among the public.[98] They have treated neutrality as a convenient bright-line rule. The conservative bloc protects little else, however, and little neutrality in the bargain.[99] In fact, most of the conservative bloc on the Court have treated speech rights as relatively unimportant. For them, trivial benefits are sufficient excuse to limit speech.[100]

Conservatives' rejection of autonomy and harm avoidance helps explain their view of democratic values. Respect for individual moral autonomy supports the traditional values of a free society—liberty of speech and conscience, and democracy. If there is no absolute answer, then there is no objective ground on which to refuse to honor self-determination of either the individual or the society. Rehnquist himself has made that point. Moreover, liberty of speech and conscience become the engines by which society undertakes to figure out what it wants to do and should do. Respect for the individual also implies the right to participate in decision making—self-determination by means of the democratic process. Those process rights are sacred.

There are conflicts among those rights, of course. The underlying participatory rights may conflict with the self-determination of the society. Under the liberal paradigm, society has no right to deny participatory rights to its members. If enforcing participatory rights to education, voting, and similar fundamentals imposes significant changes on the society, those changes are nevertheless necessary in the name of self-determination itself, for there is no self-determination if portions of the society are not permitted to take part in the democratic process. Whatever the justification, the philosophy of liberalism leads directly to many of the changes undertaken by the Warren Court. Theory mattered.

Theory matters to conservatives too. Conservatives repeatedly charge liberals and utilitarians with relativism. Liberals and utilitarians cannot be neutral about the core values of freedom of conscience, speech, democracy, and universalism. Therefore, their relativism is only partial. But it is strong nonetheless, often expressed as tolerance for other people's views and practices.

For those who reject this partial relativism, more absolute moral values would interfere with or limit what it might be proper for the people to express or decide. For those who reject this partial relativism, the values in their separate traditions war with other traditions of freedom, democracy, and judicial restraint. Many choices no longer seem reasonable in the light of a variety of traditional values. Without moral autonomy as a fundamental principle, all views are not equal and there is no principled reason that society should treat them so. In fact, deference to democracy is somewhat hard to explain without respect for individual autonomy.

It makes considerable sense, therefore, for democratic values to play a smaller role for these justices, in light of their fundamental rejection of the historic autonomy principle. Of course, democratic values are themselves traditional in this country, so one can abandon a belief in moral autonomy and still believe in democratic values. But without the underlying organizing principle, democracy is just another tradition in conflict with other values. From time to time those competing values may seem more important. Inevitably, the pattern of decisions about the consent and participation of the governed loses its coherence and becomes more erratic.

The Role of Judges. Having explored the culture war over liberty, democracy, and the general welfare, we are in a position to examine the battle over the role of judges. The conservative justices have attacked the liberal distinction between judicial restraint and judicial activism. Therein lies a very important story of the impact of the fundamental conservative rejection of the autonomy and harm-avoidance principles.

The partial relativism of classical liberal thought and the respect for democracy that it fosters led directly to the classic definition of judicial role spelled out in *United States v. Carolene Products Co.*[101] In that 1938 decision, the Hughes Court decided that the courts should be particularly alert to denials of rights to participate in democratic governance and to racial, ethnic, and religious distinctions that resulted from the absence of participatory rights and that were likely in turn to corrupt the democratic process. Democratic theory in this pure version does not honor rules that would exclude other people in the community from the governing process—such rules are understood as contrary to democracy.

Liberal partial relativism requires activism in support of liberty and democracy. Those are the basic core values of the liberal state. Liberalism requires restraint regarding all else. Thus, judges must be active in defense of liberty and democracy—judicial activism but in its proper sphere. Otherwise judges must be respectful of society's decisions—judicial restraint in its proper sphere. Except in those fundamental areas, to disregard society's wishes is to substitute judicial politics for public politics and individual choice—judicial activism where it does not belong. *Carolene Products* spells these relationships out and, despite difficulties in application, that scheme is integral to the entire liberal and utilitarian project. It built a theory of the job of judges from the principle of respect for democracy.[102]

The question becomes, What happens to judicial activism and judicial restraint when they are not guided by a liberal or utilitarian philosophy? Other values, of course, may conflict with what a democratic society wants to do.[103] If a justice accepts democracy as the root value, then those other values may have to take a back seat. If a justice does not accept democratic theory as the standard for judicial behavior, it is less clear what would restrain the justice from imposing his or her personal values. The conservatives on the Court have rejected *Carolene Products.*[104] They can still derive judicial restraint from tradition. The imperative of judicial self-restraint, however, will seem increasingly irrelevant as the justice is drawn toward different solutions to constitutional issues. Restraint is likely to be governed by the strength of judicial convictions—the more attractive, the more reasonable, a justice finds a particular interpretation, the less significant restraint will seem. Ultimately restraint will have to rest on the apparent reasonableness of the policy chosen. In that way the conservative rejection of relativism defines both activism (against apparently unreasonable choices) and restraint (where lawgivers are trusted or the policies seem reasonable).[105]

There is a way of describing judicial restraint that depends on tradition or personal judgment rather than fundamental democratic principles and that is therefore much more congenial to conservative instincts. That vision is described by *Muller v. Oregon,*[106] decided in 1908, instead of *Carolene Products*, decided thirty years later. *Muller* was the Progressives' challenge to a slightly earlier and quite infamous decision. In *Lochner v. New York,*[107] decided in 1905, the Court denied that reasonable men could believe that it was appropriate to regulate the hours of work of bakers to protect their health or otherwise. *Lochner* has become almost synonymous with improper judicial activism, with a court substituting its judgment for the legislature, which ought to be deciding the terms on which we live and work together. In *Muller* a similar issue arose with respect to working women. The future Justice Brandeis and his wife, a social worker, developed an extensive brief showing the Court the extent of current sentiment in support of special protections for working women. The Court accepted their argument. It seemed reasonable to those justices that the legislature would try to protect women because they seemed so much more vulnerable. Judicial restraint in *Muller*, as in *Lochner*, was based on what reasonable men believed, defined in part by what was traditional. *Muller v. Oregon* replaces *Carolene Products* as the seminal case for conservative judicial restraint because *Muller* restraint was defined by tradition and rationality while *Carolene* restraint was founded on principles of democratic access to the political system.[108] Rejecting special protection for democratic rights, the Court has returned to traditionalism, now understood in a contemporary conservative version, as the ground of restraint.

In that sense *Bowers*,[109] which bowed to public sentiment for regulating the private consensual behavior of a closeted gay and lesbian minority, is the modern *Muller*. The roots of the conservatives' restraint in *Bowers* are in the traditionalism of the condemnation of homosexuality rather than gays' access to the political process.[110] Justice White's opinion in *Bowers* argued for deference to Georgia's treatment of sodomy on democratic grounds: the legislature should be trusted. But his conservative colleagues' rejection of democratic rights in other contexts undercuts that explanation of their judicial role and makes traditionalism a much more likely explanation of their understanding of judicial restraint.[111]

In each case—liberty, instrumentalism, democracy, and judicial role— conservatives have rejected not merely the twigs and branches of liberal thought but the most basic and historic liberal assumptions and values. The converse is also true. Conservatives have substituted values of their own.

The Conservative Agenda

Now we sketch the way the conservative rejection of moral autonomy and the harm principle drive the conservative agenda—specifically the kind of conservatism that represents the Court's right wing.

To reject moral autonomy and the harm principle because of the degree of relativism involved is to be more absolutist in one's moral judgments. Morality, then, is not a matter of choice but is independent, absolute, and controlling regardless of individual desires or beliefs. Many of us believe that to some degree. The issue is the extent to which we are prepared to defer to the judgment of others with respect to how they live their lives. For liberals and utilitarians, the harm principle is the fundamental dividing line: do what you want so long as you injure no one else in any significant or unjustified way. Moral absolutists do not make that distinction.

As explored above, deference to the views of others, individually or collectively through legislatures, makes less sense to moral absolutists, to people who reject moral autonomy. A moral absolutist, therefore, may feel freer than liberals to espouse substantive values that are not rooted in liberty or democracy as part of constitutional law. Values rooted in liberty and democracy are often called process values; they protect an individual's and society's ability to make decisions by appropriate means. Values not rooted in liberty and democracy are often called nonprocess values; they protect particular outcomes regardless of individual and social choices.

Many modern conservatives who reject individual moral autonomy and harm avoidance substitute a vision of moral character for protection of process values.[112] For them, moral character may be understood as the foundation of the republic. They perceive liberal respect for process values of individual choice and collective decision making as nihilism, that is, as the absence of values. They ignore, of course, the insistent liberal humanism reflected both in respect for individual choice and the harm principle as values. Those principles, particularly respect for individual choice and collective decision making, are perceived instead as the enemies of conservatism.

Consistent with this approach, the Court's conservatives have realigned constitutional law in accord with conservative ideas about moral character. What follows is a survey relating how this plays out on some of the major issues of the conservative agenda and a prelude to the descriptions of the positions of individual justices, which is the subject of the remainder of the book.

Character and Religion. The view that individuals are morally autonomous supports a strong position in favor of separation of church and state. People are entitled to choose what to believe and what not to believe without public pressure. Conversely, a rejection of moral autonomy and an emphasis on character are more consistent with state support of religion. In this view, religion is critical for the health of the society and needs to be supported. Religion builds character. Moreover, conflict among different believers may be less important if one disregards their moral autonomy. De-emphasis of the harm principle also allows the justices to minimize the significance of the discomfort inflicted on religious minorities and dissenters.

Each member of the conservative coalition on the Court has a slightly different view of the religion clauses, but O'Connor's view of those clauses is nevertheless a good example of how the conservatives' absolutism and their emphasis on moral character shape the religion clauses. O'Connor's views make religion more prominent. She supports, for example, displays of religious symbols on public property so long as government does not appear to "endorse" a particular faith, but she's not terribly fussy about that constitutional limitation.[113] So she was happy with the display of a Nativity scene on public property because there were also a number of "secular" symbols related to Christmas—trees, Santas, and the like. Non-Christians would view the entire Christmas display from creche to tree as intimately associated with Christmas and take Christmas as a celebration of Christ and Christianity. Many Christians view the tree and other ornaments as purely secular, as they may have been used in Rome before the Christian era. For O'Connor, the presence of the tree neutralizes the religious message for Christians—even though it deepens it for non-Christians. Effectively, the autonomy of minority faiths is less important than the propagation of religion.

In *Employment Division v. Smith*,[114] the Court, with O'Connor concurring, concluded that Native Americans could constitutionally be prevented from using peyote at a religious ceremony. For the majority, it was enough that the regulation of peyote was "neutral"—that is, it applied generally without reference to religious use. The use of alcohol as an accepted part of the ceremonies of other faiths presses the question whether the Court's approach is "neutral" or "discriminatory." O'Connor agreed with the suppression of peyote but did not like the ground on which the Court decided the case. She argued that religious practices should be accommodated unless the state had a particularly strong reason for refusing. Following the peyote decision, Congress adopted O'Connor's reasoning in the Religious Freedom Restoration Act (RFRA), requiring efforts to accommodate religious practices. Her colleagues struck the act down in *City of Boerne v. Flores*, a decision upholding a local zoning law in conflict with the expansion plans of a Catholic church.

Both *Boerne* and *Smith*, however, are largely hostile to nonmajority faiths since one expects the majority to write its laws in ways that are consistent with its religious practices. Alcohol, which is part of the secular and religious traditions of most Americans, is not a problem; peyote, which is not part of common American traditions, is a problem. The same might be said for Sunday closing laws. Catholics still see themselves as a minority faith discriminated against in the law and in many parts of the country they clearly are in a minority. *Boerne* and *Smith* will by no means relieve that discrimination.[115]

The liberal and conservatives justices approach *Boerne* and *Smith* quite differently. The liberals easily accommodated the Indians' different religious practices in *Smith* but split over whether RFRA would lead to religious establishment in *Boerne*. They feared that RFRA could transfer too much power to religious groups. The conservatives have been transferring power to religious groups but balked at doing that for minority faiths. That, apparently, could lead to disorder unless subordinated to rules of general applicability as in *Smith*. O'Connor dissented in *Boerne*, but in the peyote decision as in the cases involving religious displays on public property, she supported minority faiths in theory while looking askance at them in practice.

O'Connor would also break down much of what has been known as the "wall of separation" between church and state. For example, she believes government schools must make their facilities available to religious groups.[116] In effect, O'Connor not only believes that religion is important to the state, she also does not treat the state as a threat to religion—except when it excludes religion from public places and functions or endorses a faith or practice, religion is a public good.

In the earlier American experience, there were quite serious battles over government interference with religious doctrine. The use of the Bible as a text for the learning of English resulted in a lengthy battle among Christians because of differences in the texts used in Protestant and Catholic editions.[117] The creation of local school boards was in part a reaction to the opportunity of school authorities to interfere in religious belief and practice.[118] By early in this century, it had seemed that the best solution was to build a "wall" separating church and state. The Court later endorsed the "wall of separation," as Jefferson had called it a century and a half earlier.[119]

Chief Justice Burger wrote a lengthy history of Christmas celebrations in his opinion in *Lynch v. Donnelly*.[120] As Burger explained, the Christmas celebration changed radically in the nineteenth century. Christian clergy tried to downplay what was developing as a folk religious celebration of the story of Christ in favor of a focus on the teachings of God in both testaments. In that context, state acceptance of Christian symbols tilts a lengthy religious debate—one that traditional Christian clergy may long since have lost.

The Creationists and other fundamentalists have made the wall itself the problem. Without religion, they argue, schools promote secular humanism.[121] The possibility that school authorities might meddle in religious matters is not lost on them.[122] But they apparently believe that the opportunity to control the religious practices in the schools is more important than the danger that those whose religious practices are not fundamentalist would define the religious content in an unacceptable way.

O'Connor's resolution of the religious issues suggests less a fully consistent approach than a belief in the importance of state encouragement of religion. The state may not endorse any faith but may become much more involved in religious matters and promote and affect them all substantially through displays that are internally secular but obviously loaded to outsiders.[123] The import of supporting religious institutions and allowing religious displays overrides the protests about partiality. In other words, morality outweighs autonomy.

Roe. Morality is at the heart of the controversy over *Roe v. Wade,*[124] the abortion rights case. *Roe* can be approached from either a utilitarian or an absolutist perspective. It can simply be an overriding moral issue in which autonomy is irrelevant. In that guise, there is nothing to balance—abortion is bad. Or it can be an issue in which the unborn are innocent victims and thus dealt with within the traditional liberal/utilitarian paradigm. In that guise, abortion may be bad to the extent its harms are unjustified. In the courts, the issue of abortion has been fought on largely liberal terrain in which the harms to the fetus and to the women are at issue. We have women's rights arrayed against public interests in protecting both the woman and the fetus. But it obviously can be fought from conservative premises in which these issues are irrelevant. From that perspective, there may be no justification for an abortion. The views of the conservative minority dissenting in *Casey* are quite consistent with that perspective.[125] There is no right to abort because it involves terminating potential life, and, therefore, there is nothing to balance. In other words, abortion should be unprotected because it is categorically a moral wrong, not because on balance the harms exceed the benefits.

Character and Intent. The role of intent in law may seem quite arcane but, in fact, it has had a shattering effect on large areas of law and once again it reflects the substitution of a conservative moral view for a liberal/utilitarian view.

When Justice White defined the denial of equal protection as intentional discrimination,[126] it was immediately apparent that intent would be used as a brake on the meaning of discrimination. Decisions that had a significant and negative impact on minorities would not be treated as discriminatory if they were not "intended" to be. An example was a decision to screen job applicants by tests whose relevance to the jobs open was questionable but nevertheless tests that minorities tended to fail in much greater numbers.[127] It would not be found discriminatory unless one concluded that responsible officials instituted the tests because the tests would exclude minorities.

That was in sharp contrast from Title VII of the Civil Rights Act of 1964. If that act applied, a discriminatory job qualification would violate the statute unless there were a good business purpose. So for example, a company had been employing whites without high school diplomas for many years in a particular job but then decided to require diplomas before the equal employment provisions of the act went into effect. The diploma requirement had the effect of excluding blacks from moving up or moving in to that department, although it said nothing about color. Interpreting the Civil Rights Act, the Court concluded that one couldn't argue that it was OK to impose a job qualification that excluded minorities needlessly as long as "I didn't mean it." As the Court pointed out, there are historical, economic, and educational reasons that, for example, blacks were much less likely to have a high school diploma, reasons that have little to do with ability. If there were a good business purpose, a "bona fide occupational qualification," the requirement would be fine; otherwise, not.[128]

The intent standard did not need to work out negatively for minorities. Indeed, it is also possible to find intent in situations where the act and the decision makers make no explicit mention of race. An early example was the closure of a Jackson, Mississippi, swimming pool in response to a desegregation order.[129] The action affected everyone without discrimination—no pools would remain open. But the purpose was clear and, indeed, Justice White argued that the closure should have been held unconstitutional for that reason. So it was possible to make the intent standard into a rule that would separate discriminatory from nondiscriminatory actions in a reasonable way.

Liberals and conservatives, however, meant very different things by intent. Justice Stevens and several colleagues argued that consequences are powerful evidence of intentions but were rebuffed.[130] So for liberals, both the irrelevant job test and the swimming pool closure could be understood as discriminatory because both actions were unreasonable for any proper purpose.

Liberals had already been largely persuaded by the realist movement. Not all liberals were active realists looking to get to the empirical bottom of every idea. But realist insights came naturally. For liberals, intent easily had an objective flavor, an observability about it. They were cynics about intent. Talk about improper intent was fine for liberals because they discerned bad intentions in the behavior they despised, both from speeches and by inferences from actual behavior, so that for them an intent standard need not have constricted discrimination law and might actually have broadened it.[131]

The Court conservatives confined intent to conscious purpose, excluding states of mind like indifference to or even conscious disregard of the impact on racial minorities. Repeatedly, they refused to find that segregation and disadvantage were motivated by race. For the conservatives, it was possible to see neither the irrelevant job test nor the swimming pool closure as discriminatory because both could be "explained" without reference to race.

It turns out that intent has a very special resonance for conservative moralists. First, connecting intent with notions of moral responsibility, intent is the moral element of behavior. Thus, rules about intentions do not merely encourage, discourage, or engineer social results; they judge character. Second, making intent the standard allowed the substitution of permanent moral standards for contextual instrumentalism. Conservatives define intent by conscious purpose and measure it by conformity to rules. To worry about consequences would treat morality as contextual rather than absolute. One must do the right thing, not bring about the right results. One is entitled, indeed required, to do the right thing regardless of the consequences. The consequences will take care of themselves. So conservatives sharply differentiate wanting a result from awareness that it will occur in the wake of one's behavior. Conscious purpose allows conservatives to separate the morality of judgment from calculations about consequences. Thus, in conservative minds, conscious intent lost any significant connection to obviously discriminatory consequences of behavior, and actions with powerful discriminatory effects were treated as flowing from pure motives.[132] Indeed, that may be the third conservative advantage of the intent standard: it functions as a screen behind which to stanch the inexorable march of disfavored rules.

When, in First Amendment law, Justice Marshall held that it was un-constitutional censorship to regulate speech in a way that was biased to-ward some speech and against other speech, he, too, saw the bias idea in a liberal mode.[133] Bias was not merely conscious purpose. Nor was it simply explicit bias. In earlier cases, the Court had concluded that free speech properly puts burdens on the state, like collecting trash in the wake of people passing out handbills or providing police protection to demonstra-tors.[134] To claim trivial excuses like that would not satisfactorily explain censorship, and therefore the Court would easily be able to find that the real reason for censorship was distaste for the speech.

But for conservatives, speech could be excluded as long as it was done without bias among viewpoints. One consequence is that speech could be restricted "across the board," for then there would be no bias. So everyone could be excluded from distributing handbills, soliciting contri-butions, or putting up posters on some sidewalks, airports, street poles, and other public places. A second consequence of the bias focus of the Court's treatment of the First Amendment was that favoritism was OK as long as it was unintended. For example, it was all right to provide a de-duction for lobbying by some not-for-profit organizations and by busi-ness entities but to withdraw a charitable deduction from nonprofit orga-nizations if they lobbied, even though that meant that the law discrimi-nated among Americans in their assertion of the First Amendment right to petition their government. But any effect on the viewpoint urged in all this lobbying could be treated as totally accidental and unintended. First Amendment law narrowed accordingly.[135]

This substitution of personal morality for earthly results plays a signifi-cant role in free speech, racial, and gender discrimination cases. Justice O'Connor has worked to moderate the impact of the intent standard on the gender discrimination cases. In the speech and racial areas, however, the conservatives have used the intent standard to substitute conservative notions of personal morality for an instrumental standard, which would have judged actions by their often predictable effects.

Race. Initially, it must be made clear that there is no single conservative ap-proach to race. There are several strains of thought "out there," and it is important to explore what they are. The consistency of the conservatives' position in the race cases makes it difficult both to test which rationale they have been following and to discern the limits they would put on it. So the point here is to identify the stakes—what the shift to a moral perspective on law can mean—and leave to subsequent chapters a more precise description of the positions of each of the justices.

The conservative justices themselves have been writing in the language of formal equality. That approach could even be consistent with the historic assumptions we have been exploring, of individual moral autonomy and avoidance of harm, because it tries to respect and provide opportunity for all individuals. One need only conclude, as many justices have expressed it, that formal equality is the best road to the equal and fair treatment of all. Thus, one might argue that the conservative bloc's rejection of affirmative action flows from an insistence on equality. The problem with that hypothesis is that the conservative bloc has also resisted claims of discrimination—so much so that the Civil Rights Act of 1991 was largely devoted to reversing a number of this Court's statutory decisions on discrimination.[136] It seems unlikely, then, that the bloc's objective is real equality.

Thomas has expressed views that suggest a radical multiculturalism or an insistence on freedom of association.[137] But that is also hard to take at face value because nothing else in his jurisprudence suggests either a multicultural or libertarian view.

On the other hand, rejecting moral autonomy and the harm principle opens the door to imposing a moral order on society. That can include the formal and procedural terms on which the races should interact. The significance of that open door is indicated by one of the ideas about diversity circulating in the conservative community. The more seriously one takes the import of a detailed moral code, the more concerned one may become about the difficulty of establishing morality in a diverse community. Such communities tend to be tolerant rather than what conservatives understand as moralist.[138] This is the intercultural corollary of the conservative attack on what they term liberal nihilism. Peace in the community requires acceptance of differences and therefore the loosening of various moral convictions. Strong community voices reinforce that imperative toward coexistence. Thus, for social conservatives, diversity, especially at the community level, creates a problem. It tends to undercut morality and promote relativism. Conservative expressions of support for federalism and localism lends some credence to the view that homogeneous moral communities are attractive to the conservative bloc. And the fact that the Court's conservatives do not allow local communities to adopt policies that encourage racial diversity supports the conclusion that it is the homogeneity, not the federalism, that is important to them.

Those conservatives who take that approach to race relations pose a fundamental challenge to the entire diversity project, not merely its "extreme" manifestations. Eighteenth-century American republican thought used by the Anti-Federalists in opposition to the adoption of the Constitution, worried that democracy was impossible amid diversity.[139] For modern conservative moralists, concern about decency and order are most important locally, where homogeneity is most critical.[140] For liberals, pluralism is the solution to the diversity of both nation and world.[141] It avoids harm: the conflict over racial, ethnic, and religious rivalries. To this branch of conservatives, by contrast, pluralism is the evil to be fought.[142] In other words, integration promotes moral autonomy. Rejection of integration as a goal permits the imposition of moral order. Thus the logic of a moral view of constitutional law threatens to play havoc with the integrationist idea, including not merely affirmative action but nondiscrimination.

None of the justices have explicitly advocated such a position, but their consistency in rejecting not merely integration and affirmative action but also charges of discrimination as well[143] makes it hard to tell what drives them. And nothing they have told us explains the pattern of their decisions. So one cannot reject the possibility that any or perhaps all of them are pulled by this vision of a moral order in locally homogeneous worlds, that this vision plays a role in their thought at least subconsciously, even if other factors also affect their legal judgment.[144] If moral autonomy is objectionable, so too are the real-world conditions that produce it.

The Market. The free market, espoused by many conservatives,[145] has no inherent morality. Nevertheless, abandonment of liberal assumptions about moral autonomy and protection against harm allows conservatives to bend the market to their purposes.

An economist should be able to describe, on the basis of expert knowledge, the consequences of decisions that might be made about the structure or regulation of a market. But markets can achieve many quite conflicting goals, so economics as a science cannot prescribe goals or predetermine the best form of market structure or regulation. In turn, that requires that we be careful about the goals and conclusions ascribed to free marketeers.

An initial impetus for free market economics was connected with the utilitarians. The market in a utilitarian framework could be defended, and managed, as a way to achieve the greatest benefit for the society. It allows the individual to register personal preferences in the marketplace. That improves the value he or she receives over many kinds of planned allocation. But utilitarian free-marketeers are very conscious of what are described as the market's failures. Some of those failures are distributive—some people start and end with inappropriately small shares. Redistribution can increase utility because a dollar in the hands of an impoverished person may be worth much more than the same single bill in the hands of a millionaire. Thus for the utilitarian, commitment to a free market is not ideological but empirical and conditional.[146]

The same is true in some liberal and libertarian traditions. John Rawls's work is in this liberal empirical and conditional tradition. He recognized important limits to the value of redistribution, reflected in his "difference principle." That is, starting with a preference for equality, he pointed out that some differences in wealth and resources are constructive and beneficial for society. They should be retained.[147] Thus even an egalitarian can embrace capitalism, but only conditionally; everything depends on the actual results.

This tradition requires tinkering with the market to make it work better. Rules are not sacrosanct. They can work well or badly. The fundamental consideration in regulating the market is whether the public will benefit from the regulation. That depends.

Judge Posner has suggested another way to see the free market—as an institution designed to maximize wealth.[148] Posnerians measure performance in currency, dollars or the equivalent. Policies or regulations should be undertaken if they produce more dollars than they cost, regardless of how those dollars are distributed. It does not measure the effect on people individually or on the majority of people. Posner allowed $1,000,000 in the hands of a single individual to count as much as $10,000 each in the hands of one hundred people. Wealth, not social benefit, becomes the objective. For Bentham's insistence that all people are equal, Posnerians substitute Mammon's command that all dollars are equal. Thus his approach abandons the objectives of a utilitarian system. It also abandons the objectives of a liberal system because Posner's criterion justifies government imposition of nonconsensual solutions to individual conflict, overriding freedom of choice, and does so not for the purpose of increasing other freedoms, a liberal goal, but for money, which has only instrumental functions in liberal thought.

One concerned with harm would have to prefer human happiness to the aggregate of wealth. One concerned with individual moral autonomy could not impose the financial criterion of wealth maximization. Rejecting moral autonomy, the conservative bloc is free to decide what economic measures should produce.[149]

The Court's treatment of explicitly economic issues appears to follow the path of wealth maximization. Marking a sharp break from the jurisprudence of the Warren and even Burger Courts, the Rehnquist Court has been activist in defining when government has "taken" private property and owes its owner compensation. Most dramatically, it has treated environmental regulation as takings, as public benefits that the state and local governments were extorting from private property owners and therefore required compensation. Quite explicitly, the Court's decisions do not interpret the Constitution on the basis of tradition, precedent, community values, or utility.[150] It did not respect changing definitions of property rights, as one who defers to the community might have.[151] Nor did it evaluate definitions of property on the basis of community benefit, as a utilitarian judge might have, reserving constitutional barriers for cases that pass the bounds of reasonably expected behavior and threaten to unsettle the business climate.[152] Instead, the Court has focused on the economic loss to investors. The social cost of requiring the public to compensate property owners whenever they threaten what the society treats as antisocial behavior entered the Court's calculus only to the extent of traditional judge-made nuisance rules. A utilitarian could complain that the Court's eminent domain rules reward private extortion from the public, rewarding private entrepreneurs who threaten to alter and damage the environment, and a utilitarian could also complain that the Court's eminent domain rules undervalue environmental concerns, concerns that are difficult to define in monetary values. Wealth, not social value, controls.

Perhaps no case could have shown as dramatically the difference between a utilitarian and a wealth-maximization treatment of the takings clause as *Phillips v. Washington Legal Foundation*,[153] in which the Court held that it may have been an unconstitutional taking to fund legal aid for the poor by pooling interest on individual accounts that were so small that the banks did not bother calculating interest or paying it out to the owners of the accounts and had no usable value to them. From a utilitarian perspective, any taking of such unpayable interest could only be theoretical and no compensation could be required for an injury that never took place, especially by comparison with the very useful project of funding legal aid for people who could not afford counsel to defend their legal rights. But for Posnerians, such transfers take money in the hands of banks, though the banks are its keepers only by default, and place it in much less economically productive hands.

The Court's pension cases also follow this wealth-maximization model.[154] The federal ERISA statute regulates private pension and benefit plans. The states tried to protect workers from being dismissed by employers seeking to cut off their pension rights, and from other similar abuses. The Court used the ERISA statute to preempt the states from enforcing these rules even though an instrumental view of Congress's social goals might have dictated a very different calculus. In a wealth-maximization model, aggregated wealth in the hands of large pension funds can be used effectively. Payouts are potentially unproductive. Let the pensioners make other arrangements.

Conclusions—Divergent Paths

Moral autonomy or relativism is a major divide for the conservative members of the Court. The core members of the conservative bloc have rejected moral autonomy and substituted more personal views of a just world. The centrists and liberals on the Court retain faith in the moral autonomy concept. In turn, acceptance or rejection of that fundamental assumption has important implications for the work of the Court. In religion, speech, race, economics, and other areas, the abandonment of the traditional Anglo-American principle of respect for individual moral autonomy in favor of an absolutist view of values has significant impact on the Court's decisions about substantive claims.

Given the impact of conservative views about moral autonomy in each area, conservative jurists' protests about support for judicial restraint, originalism, and democracy cannot ring true. Theirs is not a system committed to democratic governance. Instead, they replace the requirements of the democratic system with substantive conservative values. Clearly, it is no more true of the conservative justices than it was of the liberal justices that their decisions are based "solely" on the Constitution, if that were possible. All the justices bring important values, assumptions, and dispositions to their work.

Moral values need not have a single meaning for the justices. Some justices might treat moral character as meriting reward; they might be very concerned about accuracy in capital verdicts or rewarding those who have been discriminated against. Some may see the law as so many hurdles that test the tough. Some visions of a moral legal order are humanistic, judging law by the consequences for people. Other visions of a moral legal order are draconian, judging people without regard to the conditions under which they labor. Diversity and community lie in the balance. In some degree this is a battle between the cosmopolitan city and the homogeneous countryside. Even truth has no universal importance; it is important for those who would reward good character or behavior. The Court's capital cases have made clear the rejection of truth as a fundamental goal, as well as the rejection of a humanist notion of law.

The Rehnquist Court has worked a revolution with respect to the underlying jurisprudence of American law, "substantive" versus democratic values, and judicial restraint. It remains to be seen whether we can, will, or will want to live with it.

3

Eclectic or Unprincipled?

We all talk about whether judges inject their own views into their decisions and whether they are result oriented. Both of these ideas are understood negatively. Judges should follow the law rather than their own muse. They should react to the facts rather than implement some preconceived result they like.

That language, however, is very careless. Was Justice Blackmun result oriented when he cried, "Poor Joshua," as a prelude to his dissent in *De-Shaney v. Winnebago County*,[1] a case in which young Joshua literally had his brains scrambled in a beating by his father? Blackmun wanted to hold the state responsible for not reacting to signs that Joshua was in danger—indeed, the state had returned Joshua to his father when the boy ran away from home. Is it result oriented because Blackmun was sympathetic? Or is sympathy part of the philosophy of law, that law should be for the benefit of human beings, and that the damage our interpretations can do should be part of the calculus about what law means? That is the understanding we inherited from Justice Cardozo.[2] Or is sympathy part of a philosophy Justice Blackmun brought to a body of law that should be read to exclude such considerations?

What we mean by being result oriented and injecting our own views into the law is in fact a very complex issue. More than complex, it defines what we mean by law. Are judges and justices entitled or required, discouraged or forbidden from looking at the consequences of their decisions and the human pleasure or suffering that will result? If law requires judgment, so that judges and justices inevitably do insert some views, should those views be eclectic, ad hoc, what we lawyers often call "case-by-case"? Or should those views themselves be principled?[3] Is the proper question whether the justices should bring a personal philosophy of law to bear on their work, or is the proper question what philosophical views they ought to bring?

These questions define what we mean by both law and good law, judging and judging well. I would like to explore part of that in connection with Chief Justice Rehnquist, who, after nearly three decades on the Court, has given us a great deal of information about what he does and does not believe.

Chief Justice Rehnquist and other conservative jurists have done much to develop a notion of judicial role in which the application of principles is the very antithesis of neutral, unbiased decision making.[4] He has criticized the Warren Court for bringing its own principles to bear in the interpretation of the Constitution.[5] The result, in Rehnquist's view, is political rather than constitutional. Justices should be above such principles and should simply apply whatever the Constitution requires without resort to political or philosophical principles.

Rehnquist's approach can be and has been described as positivist. It is a notion of obedience to text and to the intentions of the draftsmen. We lay the statute or order down against the Constitution and compare and then we do what the Constitution says. The desires of the justices are irrelevant. Everyone should see and reach the same conclusions if he or she is acting honorably.

Many critics argue that vision is simply impossible.[6] No judge or justice can do what Chief Justice Rehnquist's version of positivism demands. Language isn't that clear. More, the Constitution is written in majestic open-ended phrases—due process, equal protection, freedom of speech. And the passage of time and changes in circumstances make it difficult to apply ancient ideas to current problems. It is hard to recapture the full meaning of old ideas and even if we could, the founders did not think about our problems, did not work out how to balance their competing policies in our circumstances. And still more, it seems unlikely that the founders wanted us to surrender the insights of subsequent history to recreate the postcolonial world.[7]

On some issues we can figure out with some clarity what was meant or expected by constitutional language. Interpretation is possible—sometimes. But the more interesting issues are usually interesting because the meaning isn't so plain. Some argue that the Court should solve these interpretive problems by deferring to other branches of government when the meaning of the Constitution isn't clear.[8] Over time that makes the Court a smaller and smaller player in constitutional interpretation. It is not clear the delegates to the Philadelphia Convention or the ratifying conventions expected or wanted that either.[9] So once again there is no real escape from the necessity of factoring in some decisions of our own.

Rehnquist also has many critics who argue that he is not true to that positivist vision. He has proven quite willing to overrule precedent,[10] ignore text,[11] and flout original intentions[12] when it suited his purposes. And his arguments are no more often positivist, originalist, or textual than those he criticizes.[13] In short, Rehnquist's willingness to constrain his own preferences is more like other justices' willingness to do so than he would have us believe.

I want to make a completely different criticism. I want to argue that this vision of neutral, nonphilosophical judging is not desirable, that justices who abandon principles when they try to interpret the Constitution or other law are no more faithful and may be less just than those who stick to their principles. "Neutrality" may not be advanced by a "middle-of-the-road," eclectic, ad hoc, or "case-by-case" approach. The lack of apparent principle may not be an index of political neutrality but of political bias.

Therefore, I want to explore the possibility that Chief Justice Rehnquist has actually done what he proposed, that beyond the bare outline of the moralist conservative position we explored in the last chapter, he hasn't filled the gaps by sticking to any moral or philosophic principles, liberal or conservative; that his actual behavior on the bench can be described either as eclectic or as unprincipled depending on the commentators' reactions to his opinions; that he has not substituted any consistent principles for those, described in the last chapter, that he rejected. And I want to argue that's a poor way to describe neutral, unbiased judging and a poor recipe for deciding cases.

Some principles stink, of course, and we'd be better off without them. So I don't want to argue that any principle is better than none. If it is the case, for example, that Rehnquist's views could be described in the language of social Darwinism, which we will consider later, it is not clear that our judgment of his work would differ or be more positive. But some principles are better than none. I want to argue that the important issue is not whether justices bring their own views to constitutional interpretation but what principles are legitimate.

The first step is to look at the principles Rehnquist might be applying and see if he sticks to them. Step two will be to look at the consequences and ask whether we would describe the consequences as good, open-minded, eclectic judging, or as bad, unprincipled, biased judging.

To explore whether there are principles that might explain his work, I will begin with his own self-description of his constitutional philosophy and then add some hypotheses developed by other scholars for principles that might explain his work. I will of course deny that any of these explanations work. Strictly speaking, of course, that will not prove my point. There might be some better explanation that I haven't discussed or considered or understood. But showing that Rehnquist has not applied such principles consistently is at least evidence for my propositions. If it really turns out that Rehnquist does have and apply principles in his decision making, we would still be entitled to ask whether it would be better, whether he would be a better justice, if he abandoned them in favor of the model of "neutral" judging he espouses.

I am going to argue that, beyond rejection of the principles described in the last chapter, and the substitution of a moralist approach, no principles fill out that moralist posture in Rehnquist's thought, and I am going to argue that the result is bias based largely on race, class, and wealth.

Self-Description

Chief Justice Rehnquist has described his principles as positivism, democracy, and relativism, and many admiring commentators have taken him at his word.[14] The point of deference to democracy, as Rehnquist describes it, is partly that the Court should defer to the popular will as expressed in the Constitution. Deference to democracy supports Rehnquist's positivism because it explains why judges should keep their own ideas out of their work—in order to let the people make the rules. His point is also that the Court, as an appointed body, should defer to the elected branches of the government. He presents himself as a small "d" democrat devoted to popular choice.[15] That's closely related to moral relativity; if there is no ground on which to overrule the popular will, then a democrat should respect the popular will. Rehnquist has argued, in an article in the *Texas Law Review*, that no such subordinating ground exists: "Beyond the Constitution and the laws in our society, there simply is no basis other than the individual conscience of the citizen that may serve as a platform for the launching of moral judgments."[16] There are two problems with this self-description. First, it is hard to find support for democratic rights in his decisions. And second, it is hard to find support for moral relativism in his decisions.

With respect to democracy, Rehnquist has opposed applications of the one-person, one-vote principle.[17] He has voted against efforts to give blacks an equal voice in voting,[18] voted for devices that gerrymandered them out of any influence on public affairs,[19] and he has been unable to bring himself to find that white majorities have ever tried to do that since 1901.[20] He has voted to permit water and power districts to restrict the vote to property owners, thereby excluding many from participation in those important areas of government altogether.[21] One can see in this a deference to the powers that be, but it is a little confusing to call it democratic.[22] Nor does he show any particular deference to democratic decision making; his explanation that he is a democrat devoted to popular will does not account well for decisions in which Rehnquist overturns legislation, as he does, for example, in the eminent domain or takings cases[23] and the race cases.[24] So much for democracy.

Rehnquist's self-description as a moral relativist is quite extraordinary because relativism not only is the bane of many, perhaps most conservatives, but also is precisely contrary to his behavior as a justice. To clarify Rehnquist's rejection of moral relativism, let us return briefly to some of the cases we discussed in the previous chapter because his positions in *Bowers*,[25] *Barnes*,[26] *Roe*,[27] and the religion cases[28] strongly indicate that Rehnquist has, in fact, rejected moral relativism.

Bowers was the case about homosexual sodomy in Georgia. The Court, with Rehnquist's vote, held that Georgia could prohibit the private behavior of two consenting adults even without pointing to any harm to anyone else. For a moral relativist that is the paradigm case. Government has a proper role to play regulating what we do to others. If the acts of the Georgia homosexuals had been in public, if they had made someone else watch, or if someone had not consented, a moral relativist would agree that there would have been a proper reason to regulate. Of course, other people may have been aware from public discussion of homosexuality that people might do such things in Georgia and that does have effects on others, but because of the First Amendment, the Court understandably avoided any talk about the consequences of mere knowledge or discussion of the possibility of homosexual behavior. So the point was not the harm that might have been done to others by this private behavior. The point was whether this behavior could be condemned on moral grounds without regard to the harm to others.[29]

Barnes was a Rehnquist opinion involving more consensual adult behavior, this time nude dancing in a go-go bar. What was extraordinary was not the result—upholding the ban against nudity—but Rehnquist's reasoning, that the community's moral condemnation was enough to overcome the First Amendment claim that the dancing was protected expression.[30] Justice Souter highlighted the philosophical issue by arguing that it was not necessary for the Court to have reached out to state the moral point because it could simply have held that the nude dancing did have an effect on nonconsenting people.[31]

Roe, of course, was the abortion rights case and although Rehnquist wrote his dissent in dry historical terms, in light of the subsequent controversy it is difficult not to find moral outrage in his reactions.[32] The state should be allowed to protect fetal life. And in the religion cases, Rehnquist has argued that the state should be able to promote religion.[33] Thus he wrote, dissenting in *Wallace v. Jaffrey*: "The Establishment Clause did not require government neutrality between religion and irreligion nor did it prohibit the Federal Government from providing nondiscriminatory aid to religion."[34]

One could reach those results on democratic grounds. That was the path Justice White took in his opinion in *Bowers*. The people are entitled to make those decisions because this is a democratic society. But that path is not open to Rehnquist. He doesn't require democratic procedures and he doesn't believe that the people are entitled to do whatever they want; he votes to overrule the popular view in many areas.[35] Thus the moral relativist position is not one that Rehnquist has adopted in the crucial cases on the Court. One might think of him as a moralist on the basis of these decisions, but I will argue later that one must qualify that conclusion to the extent that his judgments are ad hoc and that principled moral judgments do not explain his behavior either.

In effect, Rehnquist has adopted a rhetorical stance aimed at what he perceived as liberal vulnerability. Liberal justices applied liberal principles. Rehnquist and many conservatives objected to the Warren Court's conclusions and blamed its principles.[36] Therefore, they argued, justices should not apply their own moral or philosophic judgments. It is not, however, a stance that accurately describes Rehnquist's own work.

Shapiro's Hypotheses

David Shapiro's interpretation of Rehnquist has been widely cited and quoted. He suggested three basic propositions for understanding Rehnquist:

(1) Conflicts between an individual and the government should, whenever possible, be resolved against the individual (The same holds for conflicts between an individual and an employer, for example, under civil rights legislation.);

(2) Conflicts between state and federal authority should, whenever possible, be resolved in favor of the states;

(3) Questions of the exercise of federal jurisdiction should, whenever possible, be resolved against such exercise.[37]

Early in his judicial career, Rehnquist questioned the doctrine that the Fourteenth Amendment incorporates the Bill of Rights,[38] thereby giving considerable support to Shapiro's hypotheses. The incorporation doctrine goes back to a takings case in 1897 and has been developed and extended in numerous decisions.[39] Overturning that doctrine would, in a single stroke, eliminate the vast majority of federal guarantees that restrict state government power. So it would, in a single stroke, make the Constitution much less helpful to individuals and much more supportive of the states and would make the courts much less open to litigation—thus validating all of Shapiro's hypotheses. In fact, incorporation of the Bill of Rights in the Fourteenth Amendment is most significant in the speech, religion, and criminal areas, all of which involve protections that Rehnquist construes quite narrowly.

Rehnquist's position on the Eleventh Amendment has a similar effect on federalism. The Eleventh Amendment bars suits by a citizen against another state in federal courts. The language was carefully crafted to negate what has been called "diversity" jurisdiction: the power of the federal courts to hear cases that are between citizens of different states or between states and citizens of other states. The Supreme Court, however, decided some time ago that it was illogical to allow citizens to sue their own states under federal law. The Eleventh Amendment then became a barrier not just to diversity jurisdiction but, where a state is the defendant, also to what is known as federal question jurisdiction, that is, the power of the federal courts to hear cases that are based on federal law. That ruling is somewhat inconsistent with the very precise language of the amendment. As a result, the Court almost immediately created a legal fiction to get around some of the harshest consequences of its reading of the Eleventh Amendment. The Court decided that a suit to enjoin a state official is, in many circumstances, not a suit against the state and therefore not a violation of the Eleventh Amendment. As a result of that and several other long-standing doctrines, it remained possible to enforce federal law in federal courts against state efforts to defeat federal requirements.

Nevertheless, Rehnquist has turned the Eleventh Amendment into a means of significantly narrowing national power. First, shortly after his appointment as Associate Justice, he read the Eleventh Amendment to protect state sovereign immunity in any case brought to enforce an act of Congress authorized by the Fourteenth Amendment, unless Congress is explicit about abrogating the doctrine of state sovereign immunity for that purpose.[40] Second, in several recent decisions he has interpreted the Eleventh Amendment to prevent federal courts from entertaining any suits against states for damages under federal statutes drawn under the commerce clause.[41] Third, he tried to narrow considerably the major legal fiction the Court constructed around its own nontextual enlargement of the Eleventh Amendment barrier to enforce federal law against recalcitrant states.[42] The result of his positions in those and several still more recent decisions is to leave the states largely immune to federal law except in their own courts and with their own consent and to raise significant questions about the uniform enforcement of federal law.

Rehnquist has also tried to keep litigation against the government out of court by means of the legal requirement of standing. Essentially, in a long series of opinions he has held that the plaintiff did not have a sufficient stake in the outcome of government behavior (or misbehavior) to permit the courts to adjudicate the controversy. Standing requirements have been directed against plaintiffs who objected to government support of religious institutions, environmental degradation, and other liberal causes.[43] In an interesting recent decision he expanded the standing of commercial banks to challenge regulations whose effects on them were indirect through competitors.[44] So Rehnquist's hostility toward standing in cases involving government action seems limited to a subset of claimants.

Shapiro's hypotheses have not held up well in other areas, however. His hypotheses have not held true, for example, for race[45] or property[46] cases in which Rehnquist overturns or narrows both federal and state legislation in favor of his preferred version of individual rights. Nor does Shapiro's hypothesis that Rehnquist favors the states over the federal government hold true for the extraordinary series of "preemption" decisions in which he voted that the silence of a federal statute withdrew considerable power of the states to protect their citizens from discriminatory dismissal of workers whose pensions were about to vest, and from discrimination by health insurance plans not covered by federal law.[47]

Conservative Principles

It is apparent that Rehnquist's self-description and a variety of commentators haven't got it right. It is time to try some conservative hypotheses. There are many possible conservative approaches, some quite contradictory with others. Some that have been suggested are legal, organic, and moral traditionalism and economic conservatism, which is more radical than traditional. Let's take a look.

Economic Conservatism. Free market conservatives have been quite prominent recently. Economic conservatives believe the market best solves most problems.[48] There are aspects of Rehnquist's work that appear to borrow from an economic perspective. Rehnquist sometimes seems to work for what he understands as efficient resource management by means of property rights subject only to market constraints.[49]

This economic perspective is a tempting explanation of Rehnquist's conclusion that government can keep people out of airports and, with some exceptions for tradition, off of sidewalks just the same as if it were a merely private owner of property with no special responsibility under the First Amendment toward people who want to speak, or leaflet, or try to raise funds for their favorite cause.[50] Moreover, as Rehnquist and this Court conceives the First Amendment, government need not require the owners of private property to make their property available for speakers even when the private property, like shopping malls, performs the functions street corners once did. Only when government regulates the property of others would it be subject to the restrictions of the First Amendment. Government could organize the use of public spaces to maximize convenience and comfort. That looks like market economics—property is king.

An economic efficiency hypothesis also could explain Rehnquist's willingness, in a RICO case, to support wholesale seizure of inoffensive books and pictures from a bookseller whose stock included some obscene material because such seizure would improve the effectiveness of law enforcement.[51] Efficient, though, at the sacrifice of some speech and press values.[52] And it was the efficiency of government regulatory efforts that Rehnquist seemed anxious to protect.

But economists do not agree about which economic goals to pursue and that choice has a tremendous impact on conclusions from an economic model. Some economic systems are based on the very moral relativism that Rehnquist abandons.[53] To the extent that Rehnquist's opinions fit the pattern of an economic view, his view is closer to wealth maximization in a Posnerian fashion[54] than to other economic standards.

We will return shortly to the plight of Angel Herrera, convicted of murder and sentenced to death, who told the Court that the state courts were barred from considering newly discovered evidence that showed his innocence because the time limit had passed long before the evidence was discovered.[55] Herrera petitioned the federal courts to review the evidence through what has been known as the writ of habeas corpus. The Supreme Court, in an opinion by Chief Justice Rehnquist, refused to hear the evidence. One can illustrate how a wealth maximization approach might have worked. Rehnquist might have treated habeas corpus as inefficient in economic terms—government may be wrong but it is better to be wrong cheaply.[56] One trial is enough. Looking at evidence found years later takes time, money, and effort. But how cheap is the loss of an innocent life? Very cheap if one takes account only of financial matters. And if all one is concerned about is the totality of wealth, not its distribution, that view has momentous distributive consequences; great losses to a few people like Angel Herrera—his life—are acceptable for smaller but more generalized financial benefits through reduced government expenses.

Treating those Rehnquist conclusions as driven by efficiency, however, implies that a public agency best regulates the activity. Many conservatives are quite distrustful of government. It seems to them that government would be inefficient. Rehnquist denies that—selectively. He has decided that government can be quite efficient in the First Amendment cases and therefore can appropriately regulate speech,[57] and he has decided that government can be quite efficient in the habeas corpus cases, particularly those where there are lives at stake, and that government can proceed without the trouble of careful review of capital convictions.[58] The selectivity of his acceptance of government efficiency cautions against too facile an embrace of the efficiency theory. Moreover, to the extent that these cases have anything to do with efficiency, competing efficiency arguments can be made in most. If one believes with the words of Jesus Christ that "you will know the truth and the truth will set you free,"[59] then many government restrictions of speech are inefficient.

A preference for an economic free market theory does not account well for cases in which Rehnquist supports regulation.[60] It is apparently not very important to Rehnquist that government regulation be unintrusive.[61] Rather than a generalized economic attack on regulation, he often accepts regulation as an appropriate given, not as a disruptive intrusion into the market. And whether or not regulation is efficient in some areas, Rehnquist is hardly consistent in espousing an efficiency model.[62] Efficiency alone cannot explain Rehnquist's choices.

Chief Justice Rehnquist is not Alan Greenspan.

Legal Traditionalism. Legal traditionalism would involve adherence to precedent.[63] The point here is continuity with the past, not a radical readjudication of the meaning of the Constitution. Conservatism in the sense of traditionalism is about continuity. Rehnquist has quite clearly been doing his best to rewrite the judicial slate, not follow it.[64] Legal traditionalism is not a good explanation of what he does as a justice. Chief Justice Rehnquist is not Justice David Souter.

Organic Conservatism. Organic conservatism involves deference to the variety of existing institutions in society.[65] What exists should not be tampered with lightly. Human beings have limited ability to re-create the world intelligently and should respect the world as we have acquired it. A related variation is deference to what have been called intermediate institutions. The point here is that institutions that are more removed from the people and that by their nature have to deal very broadly with issues are less likely to succeed than more local ones. Human beings are better at dealing with smaller problems than larger ones. Rehnquist and his conservative colleagues have often spoken and written about such intermediate institutions as states (in a federal system)[66] and have consistently supported religious institutions, particularly of majority groups.[67] He does not seem to embrace the notion that national power should be respected just because we have inherited it—national power is now both traditional and organic but does not reflect a preference for an intermediate institution that many conservatives believe can handle problems better. The states are important existing institutions intermediate between the national government and the people and they should be respected. Religious organizations are also intermediate organizations close to the people and perform crucial functions of training and indoctrination.

But Rehnquist is less deferential to intermediate institutions than that characterization would lead one to expect.[68] It is significant that Rehnquist overturns or narrows state legislation and state court rulings on issues of particular importance to states and local communities, like the cases dealing with state affirmative action plans, cases dealing with state environmental regulations and alleging that the government regulation takes private property without just compensation,[69] and cases dealing with state regulation of business.[70] Similarly, Rehnquist has been prepared to restrict the speech rights of political parties[71] and corporations[72] that also function as intermediate organizations. It may be that Rehnquist doesn't actually support intermediate institutions, like states, as such, but supports them only when they pursue goals of which he approves.

Intermediate organizations are often important to conservatives because of their relationship to local, homogeneous communities. We introduced the question in the previous chapter whether any of the conservatives on the Court were concerned about diversity itself. To examine the possibility that Rehnquist is an organic conservative, it is necessary to recall that issue briefly. In some conservative theory, community and homogeneity are important and integration is problematic because, in these conservative views, it is harder to establish morality in a diverse community. Such communities tend to be tolerant rather than what conservatives understand as moralist.[73] Applying that approach to race relations poses a fundamental challenge to the entire diversity project, not merely its "extreme" manifestations. Many eighteenth-century Americans, especially Anti-Federalists opposed to the adoption of the Constitution, worried that the diversity of the nation would undermine democracy at the national level.[74] For some modern organic conservatives, the advantage of deferring to states and localities is their relative homogeneity, which promotes decency and order.[75] Liberals, on the other hand, seek pluralism, including integration, elimination of discrimination, and the celebration of diversity, as the solution to the diversity of both nation and world.[76] To some organic conservatives, however, pluralism is the problem.[77]

When the attorneys for the NAACP were preparing their legal strategy for the assault on segregation, they decided to bring and did bring a number of lawsuits challenging segregation in higher education as a way of breaking the ground for later cases challenging segregation in elementary and secondary education.[78] They reasoned that objections in the South were stronger with respect to younger children and they could have more success with graduate students.[79] Part of the opposition they discerned was opposition to interracial marriage.[80] That left the attorneys somewhat puzzled. They understood that interracial marriage was a much more likely consequence of desegregation at the graduate level than in kindergarten. Nevertheless, they based their strategy on this facet of southern beliefs.

But there is a logic to the idea that integration is more threatening in kindergarten than in graduate school, a logic quite important to the strand of conservative theory that seeks morality through homogeneity. Group identity, community hierarchies, and internalized standards of morality are all formed at younger ages. Thus the earlier grades are crucial to those who seek to use schooling to instill group identity and a group perspective on morality. And for many conservatives, diversity just creates chaos in the education of the young.

Rehnquist may have other reasons, but his treatment of the race cases is consistent with this hypothesis. Jerome McCristal Culp, who teaches at Duke, has described Rehnquist's singular record in opposition to efforts to end racial discrimination and segregation and opposition to affirmative action.[81] The consistency of Rehnquist's record in this connection makes it difficult to see the limits he would put on segregation and to know where he would find that discrimination and segregation were unacceptable. Culp found only a pair of voting cases, in one of which Rehnquist accepted the conclusion that an old southern statute had been intentionally discriminatory, and in the other of which he partly bowed to the congressional definition of voting discrimination.[82] Some indication of the limits Rehnquist is willing to place on homogenous segregation of communities may also be evident in *United States v. Fordice*.[83] In *Fordice* Rehnquist joined the majority, which held that applying the proper legal rule to the lower court's findings of fact required the conclusion that the system of higher education was still segregated in Mississippi and not in compliance with the Constitution. That ruling is consistent with the insight of the NAACP attorneys that integrated higher education raised less opposition than integrated elementary and secondary education. On the other side of that comparison, Rehnquist has voted to terminate desegregation orders and send students into segregated neighborhood schools.[84] In other words, some integration in higher education is permissible for Rehnquist, but it is still unclear after his quarter century on the Court what the circumstances might be in which he would order relief from segregation at the elementary or secondary level. It is possible, in other words, that

Rehnquist is driven by that model of homogeneous communities improving the socialization and morality of the young. Desegregation, integration, and pluralism would then be his (unstated) targets.

Rehnquist can't tell us that, however. To say that pluralism should be avoided, that diversity is bad and segregation good, flies directly in the face of *Brown v. Board of Education.*[85] In fact, Rehnquist had earlier opposed *Brown* and efforts to desegregate schools, public accommodations, and political parties.[86] But to make his nomination possible, he had to announce his support for *Brown* in a letter to Senator Eastland, then chairman of the Senate Judiciary Committee.[87]

Nevertheless, it seems clear that Rehnquist rejects diversity. The more important question for our purposes here is whether Rehnquist has found a principle with which to fill that void or he is acting instead in an unprincipled and particularistic manner, simply preferring whatever group he finds most congenial. One way to get at that issue is to ask how Rehnquist treats other groups. If he extends the principle that homogeneity is good and that deference to local homogeneous groups strengthens the moral fabric, then he ought to support the authority of the Indian tribes, the other major area where local autonomy is an issue. But Rehnquist does not. And his hostility is palpable.[88]

Rehnquist is not Edmund Burke.

Moral Conservatism. Could we, then, describe Rehnquist as a moral conservative?[89] Is it the point that Rehnquist thinks that white society is moral and black and Indian society is immoral? It would be tempting to treat Rehnquist as a moralist in view of his position in the quartet of areas I mentioned before: homosexuality, nudity, abortion, and religion. But his role in the habeas corpus cases makes that a very difficult proposition to accept.[90]

Some background will be helpful. Prior to the Warren Court, habeas corpus (a prisoner's plea to the courts for relief from illegal imprisonment) had relatively little bite because the Court had given little meaning to the Bill of Rights and other constitutional restrictions on how someone could be incarcerated—including the behavior of the police, the prosecutors, and the courts.[91] The Court's recognition that the Constitution requires that the state actually provide counsel for poor people accused of a crime dates from *Powell v. Alabama,*[92] which came out of the struggle to free the innocent Scottsboro boys from a racially charged conviction and death sentence in the 1930s. The Warren Court built on this legacy, trying to stanch the stream of abusive cases coming before it with a set of rules.[93] Throughout this period there were no restrictions on petitions for habeas corpus except that they present to the Court a claim that the prisoner was held because of the violation of a constitutional right.[94]

The Burger Court's conservatives attacked habeas corpus in *Stone v. Powell*,[95] arguing within the premises of the Warren Court that the restrictions the Court imposed in *Stone* would not significantly undercut the accomplishments of its *habeas* cases. But the Rehnquist Court has been far bolder. In a series of opinions it concluded that the Court need not be concerned about police behavior. Forget procedural technicalities. The Court need concern itself only with cases in which innocent people may have been convicted.[96] Substantive justice counts.

Then Angel Herrera petitioned for relief, claiming that the Texas courts would not even give him a hearing on newly discovered evidence of his innocence because of a rule that cut off the opportunity thirty days after being sentenced for murder.[97] At the time of his petition to the Supreme Court, Herrera was on death row awaiting execution. If substantive justice counts, Herrera had a strong case. The Court could simply have ruled that Texas's thirty-day rule impermissibly risked the lives of innocent people. The Court could have followed its own precedents and reached a result in his favor.[98] Instead, Rehnquist wrote for the Court that Texas's refusal to offer Herrera a forum to review his newly discovered evidence of innocence is not a constitutional violation and that the Court sits only to review procedural violations.[99] Whether or not he committed the murder for which he had been convicted, Herrera could constitutionally swing. Substantive justice doesn't count; only procedural justice does.

Herrera tested the outer limits of the conservative bloc's claim to a principled form of conservatism. No universal principles treat life itself as less than basic. The conservative devotion to the antiabortion cause is after all a "Right-to-Life" cause. No dedication to human welfare can treat the taking of life as trivial.[100] In *Herrera,* Rehnquist, O'Connor, Scalia, Kennedy, and Thomas made it clear that the possibility of executing an innocent person was not as important to them as finality of the judgment.[101] That was expressed most forcefully by Scalia and Thomas,[102] but it clearly formed a large part of the Rehnquist opinion.[103] No doubts, however strong, not even a probability of innocence as Blackmun, Stevens, and Souter urged,[104] would save one from the chair. In an obvious effort to hold onto Justices O'Connor and Kennedy, Rehnquist reserved a small hole for the possibility that relief might be granted if there were overwhelming evidence,[105] but he closed even that small loophole later in another case, known as *Schlup v. Delo*,[106] in which he concluded, this time in dissent, that the district court did not have jurisdiction to examine the issue of actual innocence brought out in evidence acquired after the trial. Justices O'Connor and Kennedy took pains to argue in Angel Herrera's case that the issue of executing an innocent person was not closed for them but they concurred on the facts.[107] Justice O'Connor then split with her more conservative brethren when they voted to allow the execution of Lloyd Schlup despite even stronger evidence.[108]

The prior development of the actual innocence exception to the Rehnquist Court barriers against *habeas corpus* makes it difficult to credit an explanation of the need to obey precedent or stand by the decisions of the state courts. Rehnquist's willingness to overrule precedent[109] and even original intent[110] in other areas as well supports the conclusion that deference to preexisting rules was not what drove his conclusions in this pair of cases.

In fact, the Court conservatives have themselves in something of a box. Rehnquist, Justice Scalia,[111] Judge Bork,[112] and other ideological conservatives[113] fashioned that box by arguing that other justices were misinterpreting the Constitution and that a neutral jurisprudence of text and history should be substituted.[114] Thus Rehnquist, Scalia, and Thomas, particularly, have been forced to write about the application of rules rather than about which choices seemed preferable to them among available alternatives.[115]

But rules don't work either as jurisprudence or as explanation.[116] Rehnquist's use of rules is plainly selective. And because of his public commitment to neutrality, if not for other reasons, he can't tell us what he really thinks.

Instead of rules, one might conclude that what Rehnquist, Scalia, and Thomas have actually decided is that lives would be saved and welfare improved by finality in the face of miscarriages of justice. Indeed, their somewhat ambiguous discussion of finality suggests as much.[117] That conclusion is hardly neutral and is very controversial—political to its core.

It is very hard to distinguish tired justices shirking work from principled justices drawing the conclusion that it's better that way. The benefits of the finality of judgments are somewhat theoretical in the face of the extremity and finality of the loss of life. It is certainly inconsistent with both conservative and liberal distrust of government, and it does not seem consistent with the more activist jurisprudence of this group of conservative justices in other areas of law.

Rehnquist's harsh treatment of the innocence issue, coupled with his refusal to subordinate his conclusions to any interpretive principles, makes it difficult to ascribe any moral principle to Rehnquist, despite his stance in favor of a version of traditional morality in the abortion, homosexuality, nudity and religion cases.[118]

Would a consistent application of moral principles offend us? Would a consistent support for the right to life distress us? It would have saved Angel Herrera's life—quite likely an innocent life. Herrera's death makes Rehnquist's objections to *Roe* hollow, and that cannot be satisfying. A consistent application of moral principles might produce some results we would find hard to live with but it would produce many of which we would be justly proud. The consistent application of moral views or of the right to life might spell good news for the homeless and needy as well. What is troubling here is not the consistent application of moral or philosophic principles but their selective omission.

Instead of Principle—Biased or Open-Minded?

So Rehnquist cannot be described as a traditionalist, either legal or organic. It is not accurate to describe him as a moral conservative or an economic free-marketeer. Perhaps there is another and better way to describe him. The question is, does it matter? If you like Rehnquist, is it because you believe that he does have principles and sticks to them, or do you like him because you believe he is "open-minded"?

Rehnquist has attacked the void for vagueness,[119] overbreadth,[120] and chilling effect[121] rules that were staples of First Amendment analysis before he joined the Court. Those rules were designed to prevent public officials from enforcing the law with bias. Without clearly defined restrictions, the Court, from Chief Justice Hughes to Chief Justice Burger, was unable to tell whether restrictions were being enforced because the defendants were affiliated with the civil rights movement or other embattled group. The Court in this lengthy era refused to accept the risk of such bias.[122] Indeed, Justice Scalia has argued in favor of a law of rules rather than standards precisely because its greater clarity holds the judges in check.[123]

Thus one definition of bias is attention to the identity of the parties rather than the nature of the legal issues. Lack of principle, like the absence of rules, invites that result. It is a risk Rehnquist is plainly prepared to take. Indeed, Rehnquist recently attacked the majority for finding unconstitutional a discretionary fee for a parade permit.[124] A discretionary fee would have made it easier for local authorities to decide to encourage or discourage a march or parade on the ground of personal or political favoritism. It is not clear that Rehnquist should be let off the hook of bias. The Warren Court looks neutral by comparison.

There are several ways to describe the judgments about the parties that run through Rehnquist's work. One of those, social Darwinism, follows a set of principles, though they are judgments about people, not behavior. But it can be very difficult to distinguish the conclusions of social Darwinism from the conclusions generated by stereotypes or a preference for the kind of people with whom Rehnquist identifies. Perhaps the easiest way to look at these possibilities is to look first at the individual judgments and then see how they add up.

Some commentators have reached the conclusion that Rehnquist has more faith in large, presumably efficient, organizations.[125] The converse is distrust of individuals. Institutions work; people don't. Perhaps he has more confidence in courts, so *habeas* is unnecessary. Judges, juries, and district attorneys merit his faith. Similarly, executives are OK but legislatures cannot be trusted. The problem is with groups. Groups that meet his apparent displeasure include legislatures,[126] unions,[127] workers,[128] political associations,[129] Native Americans,[130] and blacks.[131]

Conservatives tend to trust institutions that have "proven themselves" and to distrust people who have not. All theories, of course, liberal and conservative, have their risks. The risks of deferring to proven institutions are hierarchical, and somewhat anticompetitive and inefficient, since deference to proven institutions could protect outmoded ones from competition. As any decision theorist can explain, decision rules can be either efficient by saving us from the necessity of thought or inefficient by employing outworn means to solve new problems.[132] Proven institutions may not be proven for current or future problems.

But conservatives differ widely on the extent of their distrust. Expressions of trust and distrust can be found side by side in Madison and many thoughtful jurists. Only a fool would trust everyone all the time. For most conservatives, therefore, and liberals as well, concern about the risks posed by people and institutions is contextual, not categorical.

Rehnquist's distrust appears far more extreme than most of his colleagues'. But distrust of groups is also not entirely consistent with Rehnquist's respect for corporations.[133] Corporations are no more trustworthy than other organizations and human institutions. Many conservatives explain their distrust of governmental institutions by reference to what has become known as social choice theory. A consistent application of social choice theory, however, reveals many problems of inefficient and untrustworthy corporate behavior. Social choice theory is not nearly as consistently condemnatory of liberal positions.[134] Rehnquist's trust is particularistic, not explainable by general principles about who is truthful or trustworthy.

Social choice theory is a faceless theory of group behavior. Rehnquist's reactions may not be faceless at all. His reactions may simply be driven by a view of workers, blacks, and other minorities as failures, unworthy of protection and undeserving of respect or trust.[135] Most of his colleagues on the bench, liberal and conservative, have been far more realist, nuanced, and discerning in their judgments. Much as Rehnquist's economic instincts are political to the core, so too are his judgments about whom to trust. All judgments are refracted through the lens of his own identification and trust of various social groups. This of course is not blind justice. Indeed, it is the very opposite.

These judgments can be described as rules about whom to favor. Whether they can be defined as social Darwinism depends on Rehnquist's intentions. If he wants to create or promote an "improved" race, we would describe him in Darwinistic terms. The usual Darwinian devices are systems that weed and crush "losers": capitalism, a voracious penal system, eugenics and euthanasia, and hostility to redistributive systems (such as affirmative action and welfare programs), unions, and similar "conspiracies" of the weak. He might just despise losers without caring what happens to them.

But what is gained by calling any of these explanations "principles"? Or lost if they are described as eclectic or particularistic? The problem, either way, is that equal justice under law is inconsistent with both rule-based "principles" and *ad hoc* judgments that focus on the identity of the parties rather than their behavior.

It is not clear that describing Rehnquist's views in those terms would make him more or less biased, or make the pattern more or less admirable. The same would be true of Justices Scalia and Thomas, whose patterns are similar, as will be described below.

Conclusion

The absence of principle leaves judges as open to charges of biased judg-ing as the presence of identifiable principles. Judges without identifiable principles may be open to bias on the basis of the litigant's identity or other inappropriate considerations. In that light, principles can look bet-ter. If many of the critics are correct that judges cannot avoid applying their own personal principles, the issue cannot be whether judges bring standards and values to their positions. They all do. The issue must be which standards are appropriate. And much of what seems morally eclectic may be described by a morally contested defense of social hierarchy, a principle but not a universally accepted one.

The Left and Right often describe each other as nihilistic, and there is a sense in which their nihilism meets at the extremes. There is a strong deference to individual moral judgment on the left. In many, this is lim-ited by principles of mutual respect and happiness. For those on the left who become skeptical about those limitations, nihilism beckons. On the right, skepticism about change can become exaggerated into a prefer-ence for order in defiance of other principles. The nature of order, the particular form of order among many possibilities, is happenstance, and the choice among possible orders therefore is amoral if just happen-stance. Thus the Right appears nihilistic to the Left, much as the Left appears nihilistic to the Right, and on the extremes these conclusions are certainly accurate. Thus to the extent that Rehnquist cannot be de-scribed by any principle except order, he appears unprincipled to the Left. Social Darwinism is a justification for order without regard to other moral principles, and it too can appear nihilistic to those on the Left for the same reason.

I think we are misled in asking for justices without philosophy. What we get instead are unconscious biases at best, hidden agendas or philo-sophical approaches that border on nihilism. That's not to say we should be seeking ideologues. James Fishkin has demonstrated that no theory of right, carried to extremes produces justice—not democracy, not equality, not liberty.[136] And Dahl and Lindblom, in a study too little remembered, have done a similar job with capitalism, socialism, and regulation.[137] We need justices who are reflective enough to see the limits of ideas. We need justices whose theories of justice are humane. We do not need justices who can look on with equanimity while innocent men are executed with the full warrant of the law, attested by their own signatures.

4

Three Justices in Search of
a Character

The rejection of the autonomy and harm principles and substitution of a moralist approach as described in chapter 2 makes it easier
for conservative justices to delve into conservative philosophy and allows,
although it certainly does not require, them to produce principled forms
of conservative jurisprudence. In fact, a set of views about character that
resonate in historic strands of American conservatism are fundamental to
the treatment that Justices O'Connor, Scalia, and Kennedy give to the
complex issues before them. Those views have a powerful impact on many
issues not normally characterized as issues of morality.

O'Connor, Scalia, and Kennedy agree on a core set of propositions, implicitly if not explicitly. That core set of assumptions, however inarticulate,
drives a good deal of their decision making. They agree, first, as we explored in chapter 2, that relativism is not acceptable, even in the absence of
harm to others. On this point the entire conservative bloc is united. That
view opens them to a variety of substantive commitments. O'Connor,
Scalia, and Kennedy agree, second, that virtue, values, and character,
though with somewhat differing definitions, must be a major goal of
Supreme Court jurisprudence. They agree, third, that those propositions
are relevant to their understanding of a number of the major controversies
that reach the Court, including civil rights, abortion, free exercise and religious establishment, criminal law, and, less clearly, issues surrounding democratic government. Fourth, but most important, these conclusions
mean that the liberal diversity project is anathema. Diversity invites relativism and threatens the development of character. On this point too,
though not for the same reasons, the entire conservative bloc is united.

The three justices have very different views, however, of what character
means. A shorthand portrait of the characters that O'Connor, Scalia, and
Kennedy promote would be, respectively, an irreproachable individual, a

Darwinian survivor or winner, and a thinker. O'Connor's irreproachable character has applied for every job, spoken only in turn, and prayed in the right pew. Scalia's more brutish character has simply come out ahead. His view is closest to Rehnquist's and hardest to describe as a moral perspective. Kennedy's thinker has remained pure of heart and innocent of the consequences. The standards that Justices O'Connor and Kennedy set for their visions of character help to explain why they have been swing justices. Justice Scalia's social Darwinism suggests why he has not. The divergent images of character these three Justices hold also help to explain the issues on which they are likely to vote with either wing of the Court.

Character and Conservativism

Character is a conception of what makes an individual good, admirable, or worthy. In conservative thought, a number of different ideas about character compete. One strand of conservative concern about character is instrumental because character has an impact on the way society functions, especially in a democracy. Another strand of conservative concern with character is hierarchical because character describes a way of showing deference and recognition to distinguished individuals. In addition, conservatives are more likely to think of character as independent right thinking, rather than contextual or pressured. Good characters with good thoughts will distinguish themselves and exalt the country. For still other conservatives, character is a naive idea. What counts are order and stability. So to understand O'Connor, Scalia, and Kennedy, we will have to untangle these ideas a bit.

Democracy Rests on Character. An important part of the anxiety that led to the American Revolution stemmed from the colonists' perception that the British were behaving in immoral ways and that their immorality sapped the crucial self-restraint of a democratic people.[1] The founders' emphasis on education stemmed in part from the same source. A free people had to learn how to use their freedom wisely and well. For the founders, democracy could function only if the people had "virtue," which they understood as placing the interests of the society ahead of those of the individual.[2] Property helped to encourage virtue because property bound one's personal fortunes to the fortunes of the republic. The founding generation called it a "stake" in society.[3] De Tocqueville termed that stake in society "self-interest rightly understood."[4] Individuals without property could not be trusted.[5] We have come to describe this respect for the needs of the larger society as a part of character.

Modern conservativism is somewhat schizophrenic about what the founders called virtue and we now include as a part of character. Many conservatives insist that inculcating virtue is the fundamental aim of the republic.[6] Others insist that the opportunity for individual gain is the wellspring of a healthy society.[7] In that sense, modern conservatism is divided between those who stress public-minded values and those who emphasize values that are self-centered.

Conservative Admiration for Character. An individualistic and hierarchical way to think about character is as a recognition of distinction. Conservatives often have particular admiration for great men. Social grace reflects character; social position honors and defers to character.[8] Wealth may create, reflect, or reward character. Thus, character can be individualistic when it is an accolade ascribed to people with wealth or power. Or it can be social when character makes systems run right. In both guises, character puts the emphasis on individual traits and behavior rather than on systems. Systems reflect and depend on character.

Intent. If we have free will, then character guides our intentions. And our intentions define the quality of our character. So intentions matter—in the law and in our evaluation of one another—although our intentions always do a complex dance with our behavior.

The importance of free will is actually common ground to liberals, libertarians, and conservatives, but they treat it differently. Libertarians support restraint of official power. They resist imposing legal standards on what they see as private behavior. They insist on strong limits on government, including the behavior of law enforcement agencies. Their objective is to protect free will.

Modern political liberals are less likely than libertarians to assume that the will can be unconstrained, and they tend to see intentions as part of a complex web of factors. As constraints on people multiply, the line dividing personal responsibility from coercion becomes harder to discern.[9] Indeed, liberals recognize that the will is always constrained in some degree and that the state has a large impact on individual choices. They want that influence to push in the "proper" directions.[10]

The way liberals judge intentions derives from the fact that liberals are likely to be consequentialists—their moral standards have to do with outcomes rather than unvarying rules of behavior. When things go predictably wrong, they are likely to be skeptical of expressed good intentions. Like the "legal realists," when liberals try to understand what people were "really" trying to do, they tend to judge intent by the consequences of behavior.[11] Indeed, much of modern accident law is based on the concept of foreseeability: we are generally responsible for the consequences that we can foresee. So for liberals, our intentions include what we bring about knowingly, recklessly, or unreasonably.[12]

For conservatives who reject this liberal consequentialism, intentions look very different. These conservatives seek to differentiate intrinsic intentions from extrinsic consequences. They argue that good consequences flow from moral decisions, but morality is not defined by the consequences. For such conservatives, treating consequences as probative of intent is very unsettling.[13] Character may be good for the republic, but specific moral decisions are based on more absolute standards.

These conservatives are also more likely to discount the pressures government places on people; they are more likely to assume that people should be able to reach independent decisions despite government pressures.[14] It is almost as if these conservatives decided to treat intent as if the will were free, with some cutoff for "coercion". Intentions are free at both ends—free of pressure and free from consequences—so that people can be held to clear, permanent, "bright line" rules.

From a liberal perspective, this conservative moral prescription is less moral and much easier to satisfy than a consequentialist prescription.[15] It evades responsibility. People could, for example, discriminate unintentionally when they refuse to be held accountable for the consequences of their decisions.[16] Conservatives respond that when some people take responsibility for others, they weaken the latters' sense of responsibility.[17] But the two groups are talking past each other with respect to responsibility. Conservatives accept responsibility for teaching morality but not for the decisions other people make or the material consequences of their decisions. To them, the world is too complex to base morality on consequences to any large degree.[18] From this conservative perspective, morality is intrinsic to rules rather than functional. Liberals are "bleeding hearts," improperly judging their moral obligations by material and behavioral consequences rather than prescriptions.

In the conservative view, the rejection of moral autonomy establishes common ground in the conservative approach to character. Individuals are not free to decide what is right and wrong, even in those situations where no one appears to be injured. Conservatives attack such relativism most vehemently. Character, in turn, reflects enduring rather than contextual values—albeit in competing varieties.

Overview of the Justices' Outlook

Concern with character is only one branch of conservative thought, but it fits a good deal of the work of Justices O'Connor, Scalia, and Kennedy while many other well-known branches of conservative thought do not.

Justices O'Connor, Scalia, and Kennedy should not be mistaken for legal economists, even though they have supported property and efficiency interests in many important decisions. In one set of decisions, for example, they helped to redefine the law of eminent domain and have expressed themselves on economic values like "investment backed expectations."[19] Nevertheless, economic conservatism does not sufficiently explain the patterns of these three justices. Many of the issues presented to the courts, of course, are not economic in nature. Moreover, economic questions are never separable from choices about more fundamental values.[20] Classical economics developed in tandem with and was dependent on basic assumptions about moral neutrality.[21] But O'Connor, Scalia, and Kennedy do not accept that position.[22] Therefore, we have to go deeper into their personal value choices than purely economic assumptions about the mix of desires distributed among a population.

Despite the bow to tradition that Justices O'Connor and Kennedy took in *Planned Parenthood v. Casey*,[23] neither they nor Justice Scalia have often been mistaken for traditionalists. Indeed, even were they inclined to be traditionalists, adherence to tradition would explain little because tradition itself is complex.[24] Although the justices hesitated to make sharp breaks with the past in *Casey*, they had to choose among competing traditions. All three have demonstrated a willingness to distance themselves from the past.[25]

These are not Burkean justices. Organic conservatism, as we have noted, emphasizes the value of institutions that are intermediaries between the state and the individual. Commentators and Justice O'Connor, herself, have stressed her support of federalism.[26] Federalism would localize power, bring it closer to the people, and mediate between the populace and the national government.

Nevertheless, the commitment of these justices to intermediate institutions varies considerably with the congeniality of the policies those institutions adopt. Federalism is a good example because, despite their rhetoric, they often restrain states in accord with their own policy and philosophic preferences. State court decisions offering greater liberties now have to make their reliance on state law clear and explicit according to *Michigan v. Long.*[27] These justices have used federal preemption of state law to void state attempts to protect the economic well-being of workers.[28] They helped to jettison local attempts to redress a century of discrimination.[29] And they have been nationalist or antilocal in a number of other areas.[30] Their attack on state environmental regulation is notorious.[31] Religious institutions are another example of intermediate institutions but, even here, the support of the three justices is conditional on religious traditionalism.[32] Plausible arguments may be made in favor of all these decisions, though the conclusions certainly were not "clear" or correct for other members of the Court. Whatever value intermediate institutions have for these justices is outranked by other values, either doctrinal or philosophical in nature. Thus organic conservatism is, at best, only a partial explanation of the positions of these justices.

Commentators have been impressed by Justice O'Connor's textualism and the feminine voice in her opinions.[33] To claim that she is a textualist means that she sticks to a literal meaning of the language she is interpreting. Sometimes, but quite often, she does the opposite. In fact, the balancing of competing policy considerations is pervasive in her work.[34] No one should mistake her for Scalia or Thomas.

The idea that she displays a feminine voice, of course, is just the reverse of the claim that she is a textualist. It is a notion that she incorporates lots of competing interests in her thinking. It is sometimes true but often not. She frequently prefers hard-edged, "bright lines" legal rules. With the exception of a few cases that involve issues of particular importance to women, any feminine voice in her opinions is more a matter of style than substance, revealing more how she writes her opinions than what conclusions she reaches.

It is more helpful to see the pattern of Justice O'Connor's opinions as reflecting a consistent emphasis on moral character, related to self-reliance, propriety, and merit. Her opinions stress that individuals must earn what they have and use it in what she regards as the public interest. O'Connor's view of the public interest, however, is confined by a narrow perspective that leads her to understand and trust voices of the establishment far more than those outside it.[35] But within the constraints of that view of the facts, she consistently wants to reward virtue in the rules adopted.[36]

Before continuing with the discussion of Justice O'Connor, let's take a look at the very different approach of Justice Scalia. Then a comparison of the two will make the views of both stand out much more clearly.

Justice Scalia claims to be devoted to textualism.[37] He has argued repeatedly that one should read legal texts literally and, if literalism is impossible, one should resort to historic examples, but without the principles people thought they were living. He claims that he brings no social vision to his work as a justice. George Kannar argues that Justice Scalia does have a social vision, that it is a vision of moral character based on self-discipline, stability, and objectivity.[38] These are the same virtues Scalia requires of judges. In effect, Kannar has melded his description of Scalia's social vision with Scalia's arguments about the right way to interpret law.

Textualism can't explain Scalia for three reasons. Language is too ambiguous to explain very much in the kind of cases that reach the Supreme Court. Interpretation of the original meaning of constitutional language written one and two centuries ago is simply too hard. So arguments about literal meaning and historic examples tend to boil down to arguable assertions about what the language must have meant because Scalia or his colleagues would mean that. And Scalia himself is not consistently devoted to his theories about the interpretation of law, abandoning them when it is inconvenient.[39]

Moreover, it is somewhat difficult to understand Scalia's position as a set of judgments about the ethical position of the people involved, whether they demonstrate self-discipline, stability, and objectivity, or otherwise. As Kannar also pointed out, Scalia seems oblivious to the personal characteristics and even the behavior of the parties in many of his opinions.[40] Scalia could therefore be attacked as amoral by both liberals and conservatives.

Having just rejected Scalia's self-description much as we rejected Rehnquist's in the previous chapter, we might try describing Scalia in terms of a philosophy that he has rejected.[41] My hypothesis is that Scalia is moved by a vision of social Darwinism.[42] The point of social Darwinism is survival of the fittest. Law is designed to eliminate or subordinate the weakest members of the society.[43] That resonates with some conservative views of the good society.[44] The point of law in this Darwinist view is based on character. What becomes of people is much less important than what people themselves become.[45]

The point of O'Connor's vision is ethical behavior. The point of Scalia's is survival; virtue is superfluous. Whatever he may believe about the impact of the struggle for survival, his decisions do not differentiate among those consequences. Scalia is unconcerned if neutral rules result in the execution of the innocent,[46] burden a religious group,[47] leave the victims of discrimination without a remedy,[48] or exclude speakers entirely from a forum.[49] Only society's entrepreneurs and its fortunate need to be compensated.[50] Whatever the struggle produces is what Scalia's opinions support. That is Darwinian regardless of what one may believe about the victors. By contrast, politics is a social Darwinist's enemy. Politics threatens to allow society's "losers" to overwhelm its winners. Thus, Scalia defers toward society's subordination of its underdogs[51] but not its entrepreneurs.[52]

Although they vote together often, the fundamental philosophical gulf between O'Connor's ethical view and Scalia's Darwinian outlook is apparent in large areas of decision.[53] O'Connor has tried to differentiate herself from the harshest results of Scalia's position in cases related to capital punishment,[54] religion,[55] discrimination,[56] and speech.[57] For O'Connor, even welfare claimants have procedural rights.[58] O'Connor believes that appropriate behavior entitles people to defined rewards. Thus she has eloquently argued the claims of those most vulnerable, but honest, claimants. By contrast, Scalia conceives that poor people, virtuous or not, have few, if any, substantive or procedural rights.[59]

Whatever role virtue may play in Scalia's mind, it is not helpful in differentiating his decisions. What does matter is his Darwinian view of the world. The rules that Scalia defines reflect that tough-minded view of the world. Rules don't make things easy or reward virtue but instead are hurdles to be overcome.

Like both O'Connor and Scalia, Justice Kennedy has not spelled out his moral or constitutional theory explicitly. Nevertheless, like them, he rejects individual moral relativism in areas where no one can be described as injured.[60] Kennedy shares their keen concern with the issue of moral character.[61] Like Justice O'Connor's, Kennedy's conclusions are consistent with the desire to inculcate proper values. He shares the conservative insistence on moral responsibility. The pattern of Kennedy's opinions is defined by a strong emphasis on molding character through religion and public affairs, respecting free will, and affording it protection from coercion and excessive pressure.[62] Coercion is objectionable because it subordinates the will.[63]

Kennedy's and O'Connor's emphasis on character fits well the Court's use of intent tests.[64] Intent tests character.[65] Moreover and most important, their concern with character leads both of them to distance themselves somewhat from Scalia's indifference to the consequences of legal rules.[66]

Character as Applied

Race. For the founders, race conveyed both threat and status. Racial divisions threatened the good order of a democratic society because they were chasms that prevented people from thinking about the general welfare.[67] The movement for the abolition of slavery is older than the republic.[68] The desire for a republic in which skin and other surface qualities would prove fundamentally irrelevant animated many of those who fought the Civil War. Thaddeus Stevens dreamed that "no distinction would be tolerated in this purified republic but what arose from merit and conduct."[69]

But many people also found in race a confirmation of their own social superiority. Race became the basis not just of an economic but also a social hierarchy. Masters could make choices. They were admired for their independence and resources.[70] Power and independence were treated as if they were the basis of character and worthy of deference.

Modern conservatism has struggled with the relation between race, character, and socioeconomic position. Some conservatives treat socioeconomic position as a reflection of underlying character.[71] Character can act as gatekeeper, holding off the unfamiliar hordes until and unless they have bowed to the standards and mores of the host community. Character is a standard.

Some conservatives insist that the progress of the republic depends on ignoring race in order to instill values and character that are healthier for the country. Some favor withdrawing public safety nets and insist that people rely on themselves. They assume that self-reliance breeds the "character" necessary to deal with life's challenges.[72] Character is an objective.

From these perspectives, there is no concept of group racial justice, only of individual justice. Most significantly, there is no dream of material racial equality. Conservatives who adopt these positions would describe their vision as treating people as equals. Operationally, however, their vision simply refers to the consistent application of rules.[73] Equality in this conservative view is formal and legal; it has nothing to do with opportunities and resources.[74]

The hypothesis that the conservatives on the Court prefer to treat discrimination as a parable of character is embodied in the pattern of their opinions. Concluding that good people of all races can succeed, this Court's conservatives virtually never find that discrimination has taken place. Justice O'Connor argued that there had been one notable exception.[75] In apparent conflict with that statement, however, Justice O'Connor, Chief Justice Rehnquist, and Justices White and Scalia found the race-based remedy in that case unacceptable because its effort to redress official discrimination would have promoted blacks at a rate considerably faster than their proportion in the department. On the facts, these justices can't see it.

The Rehnquist Court has decided that racial and gender discrimination by counsel in the selection of jurors is not permissible.[76] That judgment was on the theoretical question. But when *Hernandez v. New York* (in which a prosecutor had explicitly excluded potential jurors who could speak and understand Spanish) came to the Court, Chief Justice Rehnquist and Justices O'Connor, Scalia, and Kennedy concluded that the prosecutor's action was not indicative of prejudice against Hispanic jurors.[77] *Hernandez* is part of a pattern. The conservative justices on this Court have been spared the necessity of finding discrimination in the educational environment by other courts that had long since done that for them, and they have done little more than reaffirm the 1968 ruling of the Court that it was not enough to repeal statutes requiring segregation without dismantling the system of segregation and its bitter fruits.[78] Nor have the conservatives on the Court found discrimination against minorities in the construction of election districts or in the employment context despite many opportunities. They write as if they find the American dream alive and well and treat challenges to that assumption as damaging.[79] Indeed, Justice Scalia has been explicit in challenging the assumption that official discrimination is at the base of socioeconomic differences.[80]

For many conservatives, race cases are about the character of the minorities instead of the bias of the decision makers. The central question is whether the party complaining about discrimination behaved honorably.[81] In that respect, the white job applicant or contractor stands in the same position as the minority applicant or contractor.[82] Race is irrelevant. The issue is not whether the system remains biased or builds on earlier biases. Instead, concerns are individual, focused on the applicants for the job or contract. Hiring and contracting decisions should be based on personal characteristics, including one's quality, ability, and resources for the job.

In this regard, Justice Scalia takes one of the most extreme positions within the Court's conservative bloc. Scalia would permit no governmental action except that necessary to eliminate its own de jure discrimination.[83] Discrimination is just a social fact.[84] Scalia's position is consistent with a survival-of-the-fittest perspective. Thus, difficulties serve only as challenges, not injustices. Character is required to surmount those challenges.

Justice O'Connor also seeks to individualize the issues. Her view of character, however, would require reward and punishment based on the justice of individual treatment. In the race cases, she has consistently argued that compensation of victims of discrimination should follow familiar tort principles, either where the victims are individually identified or where it can be determined that the victims are a precise proportion of a minority. But she consistently distinguishes black plaintiffs from black "victims" and "innocent" whites.[85] According to O'Connor, merely struggling against generalized discrimination does not suffice to label one innocent or deserving.[86] Given her descriptions of bystanders and victims, it is almost superfluous that she insists that compensation of a racial group on the basis of an imprecise and arbitrary approximation is unjustified.[87] Without denying that discrimination may have changed the position of racial classes, O'Connor argues that it is impossible to quantify discrimination and that remedial measures disproportionate to the precise extent of harm are unfair to those persons forced to take a back seat.[88] She argues that what she calls "societal discrimination" cannot be precisely defined and therefore cannot be remedied. Her position implies that what we all have a right to is the status quo, not a level playing field,[89] and that departures from that status quo have to be justified, even if they would result in a more just world, closer to a level playing field. What justifies a departure from the status quo is the correction of individual misbehavior. Justice is individual and retail. The issue is behavior, not equal starting points or opportunities. Character is promoted by that limited role for government, and character counts only with respect to behavior.

Justice O'Connor does not argue, however, that we have no obligation for one another. Some people object to supporting a welfare system, for example, because they argue that they have no obligation to help anyone else. Most decidedly, Justice O'Connor does not object to some proportionate burdens.[90] Consider O'Connor's eloquent objections to denial of certiorari in *Gregory v. Town of Pittsfield*:

> The conclusion of the Supreme Judicial Court [of Maine] that an applicant for general assistance does not have an interest protected by the Due

Process Clause is unsettling in its implication that less fortunate persons in our society may arbitrarily be denied benefits that a State has granted as a matter of right.[91]

Hers, therefore, is not a Darwinian world and she cannot join Scalia's categorical indifference. Discrimination law as a recognition and compensation of individual effort is appropriate; discrimination law as social engineering is not. O'Connor has waged a long crusade to define remedies for discrimination by the damage that can be demonstrated.[92] That view clearly implies drastic limitations on efforts to end discrimination, but it nevertheless recognizes the justice of some claims against past misconduct.

The interaction of race and character has a slightly different cast in Kennedy's jurisprudence. In discrimination cases, Kennedy subscribes to the conservative focus on the perpetrator's intent. The Court defined discrimination in terms of intentions in *Washington v. Davis.*[93] As we have noted, Justice White and the more liberal justices were prepared to evaluate intentions critically, taking consequences into account,[94] but intentions have long had a special resonance for conservatives. For them, character is manifest in a person's intentions. The conservative bloc tends to accept explanations of intent, even where many would regard the explanation as a pretext. They do so by focusing on the decision maker's conscious reasoning,[95] not the decision maker's apparently selective indifference to the concerns of other groups.

Hernandez v. New York was the case in which the prosecutor excluded bilingual individuals from a jury.[96] It was Kennedy who had written one of the decisions breaking new ground by holding that the courts have an obligation to prevent counsel from excluding jurors on the basis of race.[97] Nonetheless, Kennedy, joined by his conservative colleagues, accepted the prosecutor's explanation that the jurors were excluded because they would not rely on the translator but, instead, on their own interpretations of testimony. He concluded that their ability to understand the witnesses without the aid of a translator was a nonpretextual, nonracial ground for the exclusion of bilingual jurors. The ability to understand witnesses without benefit of translators is a rather ordinary characteristic of jurors and can certainly seem advantageous.[98] Hence Kennedy's and the conservative majority's acceptance of this explanation reflects minimal skepticism— comparable to what lawyers call minimum scrutiny or the rational-basis test and not the kind of careful scrutiny that the Court is supposed to exercise with respect to racial or ethnic discrimination. A realist would respond that an objection to Hispanics and an objection to those who understand Spanish are almost identical. In the realist's view, people of one ethnic or racial group were being singled out for different treatment in publicly obvious ways. But the majority conveniently "explained" the behavior in a decorous way. It is noticeable, however, that where discrimination favors a minority (and is called "affirmative action") instead of the majority (where the Court concludes it was "not racially motived"), Kennedy and his colleagues demand stricter examination of the purposes. A rational explanation does not suffice.[99] They apparently do not see the inconsistency.

Nevertheless, Kennedy is more prepared to examine intent than his more conservative colleagues.[100] Even in *Hernandez,* Kennedy noted the possibility that excluding bilingual jurors might reflect a possible pretext for discrimination, although he ultimately rejected this premise on the facts.[101] By contrast, Justice O'Connor was concerned even about that theoretical concession. Only conscious intent counted for her.[102] O'Connor found it dangerous to base the definition of motivation on "reality" or "pretext."[103] Kennedy is prepared to explore pretext on the basis of reality but insists on preserving the difference between intention and consequences. Intent is what counts.

Kennedy frequently breaks ranks with his conservative colleagues on racial issues.[104] But Kennedy's focus on character apparently leads him to make free will central to his understanding of race, largely to the exclusion of other considerations. It is the perpetrator's will and character, not the victim's deserts that generally seems to concern him. No perpetrator of discrimination was identified in *Richmond v. J.A. Croson Co.*, in which O'Connor had expressed disdain for providing compensation for merely societal discrimination. Therefore, it was consistent for Justice Kennedy to join most of O'Connor's opinion for the Court and express his preference, if he could have written on a clean slate, for Justice Scalia's proposal to "strike down all preferences which are not necessary remedies to victims of unlawful discrimination."[105] In such ways, Kennedy's treatment of character and free will sometimes make him sympathetic to racial claims and, at other times, make his treatment of race share the more draconian cast of Scalia's approach.

These views of character among Justices O'Connor, Scalia, and Kennedy are very different. The differences have only marginally affected their treatment of the Court's racial docket, however, because of the way the legal issues have been framed and the Court's choice of cases to review. As it is, their common elevation of issues of character over issues of bias has been far more powerful than their disagreements about how character should be reflected in their judgments.

Religion. Much of the argument about the interpretation of the Constitution's religion clauses has involved arcane discussions of text and history.[106] But the issue is far more fundamental and reflects a continuing divide between liberal and conservative views of the role of religion in American society.

Religion is integral to character both as a test of individual mettle and as a crucial building block to good character and ultimately to a stable society. During the Enlightenment, theology increasingly emphasized the opportunity to exercise free will in a godly way. In turn, the emphasis on free will led to a liberalization of Western religious views.[107] Religion in liberal theological systems requires freedom so one can choose to perform one's religious obligations.[108] Religion makes character important because it judges one's choices.[109]

At the same time, the fundamental conservative view is that religion is important and that it must be inculcated.[110] The state should not merely be a bystander on the basic issues of religious participation. Instead, the state should promote religious practices, preferably in Western or Christian denominations, in order to preserve American society.

This view of religious activism took hold in the early American republic alongside more liberal conceptions and has never completely retreated. The states in the early republic maintained religious establishments. Historically, American "republican" ideology emphasized the importance of encouraging character and the role of religion in accomplishing that objective. Without character, democracy would be unsupportable and would descend into a Hobbesian anarchy.[111]

State religious establishments ultimately crumbled, partly from theological concerns about free will, partly from concern for the liberty of individuals, and partly from distrust of the impact of the state on religious practice.[112] Although the creation of local school boards was in part a reaction to a fear that school authorities would interfere in religious belief and practice,[113] the emerging public school system immediately adopted the Bible as the basic text. The use of the Bible as a text for the learning of English resulted in a lengthy battle among Christians because of differences in the texts used in Protestant and Catholic editions.[114] By early in this century, the "wall of separation" had become the apparent resolution of that long-running controversy, later endorsed by the Court.[115]

Current advocates of that "wall" argue that state involvement inevitably takes sides in religious controversy. So, for example, the continuing controversy over the public display of religious icons reflects a popular interpretation of a historic dispute about the meaning of Christianity. Indeed, the public display of those icons reflects what many Christians today regard as the secularization of their faith and what nineteenth-century Christians would have regarded as substitution of the story of Christianity for its teachings. The legal issue of public display, and other arguments over the "wall" of separation, therefore, have intra- as well as interfaith consequences. For advocates of the wall, this symbolism is precisely what government should avoid.

The wall of separation between church and state harbors many internal contradictions.[116] The interesting question, of course, is how to revise it. From the perspective of the conservative justices, the major flaw of the wall of separation can be described, depending on where one draws the baseline, as hostility toward religion or failure to endorse religious practice.[117] The wall contradicts the objectives of public religion.

Creationists and other fundamentalists have made the "wall of separation" itself the problem. Without religion, they argue, schools promote secular humanism.[118] There is some disagreement about the proper role of religion in the schools, perhaps because some fear that school authorities might meddle in religious matters.[119] But creationists apparently believe that the opportunity to control religious practices in the schools outweighs the danger that those whose religious practices are not fundamentalist would define the religious content in an unacceptable way.

Viewed from the perspective of an advocate of the importance of inculcating religion to build character, the unexplainable becomes obvious. It is not possible to explain why creches embedded in holiday exhibits, other Christmas displays, and menorahs in similar surroundings are not religious. They clearly are, despite the Supreme Court's ruling that they are not.[120] These symbols may not be sufficiently pious to some and may seem intuitively secular to the unreflective, but a Supreme Court Justice, whose job is to analyze events, can hardly miss the inherently religious character of symbols that uniquely define religious traditions. No explanation of why they may be secular can make any sense analytically. If the conservatives on the Court, however, recognized the nonsecular and religious character of these displays, they would undermine precisely what they seek to support, that is, public guidance toward religion. Religion instills character.

The Court's conservative bloc has made a critical shift in its interpretation of the religion clauses in line with its view of character. The issue for these justices is not the protection of individual rights to practice religious views. Although they have adopted a formal doctrine of neutrality in cases such as *Employment Division v. Smith*,[121] which requires that legislation define permitted and proscribed practices without reference to religion, the justices have not been willing to endorse a position that requires equivalent treatment of different faiths.[122] Indeed, in *Smith*, the justices declined to review majoritarian refusals to accommodate minority religious practices, although they have frequently accepted accommodation to majority practices.[123]

Congress attempted to overrule *Smith* by passing the Religious Freedom Restoration Act (RFRA). RFRA would have required accommodation for minority faiths like the Native Americans' in *Smith*. The Court overturned RFRA in *City of Boerne v. Flores*.[124]

Instead, the conservatives emphasize the importance of encouraging belief.[125] Justice Kennedy has been quite outspoken about the importance of religion. In his view, the Court's establishment clause jurisprudence "reflects an unjustified hostility toward religion."[126] Kennedy would condone much public, governmental religious activity. He treats religion as an important source of values and appears dedicated to maximizing its role. Kennedy makes no fetish about neutrality: "Whatever test we choose to apply must permit not only legitimate practices two centuries old but also any other practices with no greater potential for an establishment of religion."[127]

Justices Kennedy and O'Connor have waged a lengthy paper war about the kinds of religious symbolism, prayer, and text that government can display on public premises or in public meetings or ceremonies. O'Connor treats nonendorsement of a religion as the objective of the establishment clause. Justice Kennedy objects. The endorsement test that O'Connor espouses outlaws too much.[128]

> [A]s I understand that test, the touchstone of an Establishment Clause violation is whether nonadherents would be made to feel like "outsiders" by government recognition or accommodation of religion. Few of our traditional practices recognizing the part religion plays in our society can withstand scrutiny under a faithful application of this formula.[129]

In other words, having seen the problem, Kennedy prefers not to deal with it. The endorsement test is vague and could compound the problem.

More to the point, it could sanction hostility toward government religious practices.[130]

But one should not make too much of their dispute. Despite her effort to reconcile those views with the injunction of "neutrality" or "nonendorsement" language,[131] the pattern of Justice O'Connor's conclusions promote religion,[132] especially majority faith. She condones the public display of a form of popular Christian symbolism. Indeed, for O'Connor, explicitly religious symbols are "neutralized" by the presence of other symbols that she views as secular but that, nevertheless, are now uniquely attached to Christianity and are viewed as "secular" only by some Christians.[133] Similarly, Christians and Jews can use wine in their services but Native Americans cannot use peyote.[134] Nor has O'Connor been terribly concerned about the effects of the government's nose in the religious tent. Religious organizations are entitled to use the schools and to be funded by them, despite the risks created by government involvement.[135] Government can send public school teachers into private religious schools to help out.[136] Her opinions are consistent with the hypothesis that she finds the major threat to be the exclusion of religion from the public domain. Thus, like Kennedy, O'Connor's treatment of the religion clauses fits the conservative emphasis on moral character.

This is not to suggest that these justices place no limits on religious establishment. Kennedy's limit reflects his respect for character: strong people can, and should, resist the pressures of everyday life, including unwelcome religious ones, but coercion is improper.[137]

In *County of Allegheny v. ACLU,*[138] Kennedy wrote:

> Our cases disclose two limiting principles: government may not coerce anyone to support or participate in any religion or its exercise; and it may not, in the guise of avoiding hostility or callous indifference, give direct benefits to religion in such a degree that it in fact "establishes a [state] religion or religious faith, or tends to do so." *Lynch v. Donnelly.*[139]

Coercion is unacceptable to Kennedy because it subordinates free will. Kennedy, however, wants some latitude to recognize faith.

Kennedy's coercion test does not rubber-stamp religious ceremonies. In *Lee v. Weisman,*[140] Kennedy wrote for the Court that "at a minimum, the Constitution guarantees that government may not coerce anyone to support or participate in religion or its exercise."[141] In *Lee*, the school decided what should be done and included in a graduation ceremony,[142] and "[t]he degree of school involvement here made it clear that the graduation prayers bore the imprint of the State."[143] The problem was that social pressures orchestrated by the school gave the government's involvement a coercive impact.[144] Justice O'Connor joined Kennedy's majority opinion. Justice Scalia dissented, joined by Chief Justice Rehnquist and Justices White and Thomas, arguing that such ceremonies were traditional and did not therefore have to be subjected to the rule of neutrality or to the ban against bias or coercion.

In *Church of Lukumi Babalu Aye v. City of Hialeah,*[145] the city banned ritual slaughter of animals. Kennedy wrote for the Court that the ordinance, which interfered with the religious practice of a minority faith, was not neutral,[146] and was intended to discriminate.[147] The willfullness of the city was blatant. Though Scalia supported the Court's outcome, he was not concerned about the city's motive for passing the ordinance;[148] formal neutrality would have been enough.[149] In *Hialeah,* their two approaches led to identical results.

Justices O'Connor, Kennedy, and Scalia all disagreed with one another in *Board of Education v. Grumet.*[150] There the majority objected that the school district, which was drawn for the Hasidim of the town of Kiryas Joel, was a singular legislative event rather than part of a rule of general application.[151] The Court feared that New York's legislature would not be as generous to other similarly situated groups and had no way to tell if it would.[152] Scalia, joined by Chief Justice Rehnquist and Justice Thomas, gasped that the majority apparently thought the Hasidim must be the special favorites of the New York legislature.[153] Both O'Connor and Kennedy, however, objected that this was an improper way to accommodate a religious community. O'Connor, joining most of the majority's opinion, concluded that the legislation was improper because it was for a single religious group rather than generic legislation. Kennedy took issue with all his colleagues. He was concerned that the majority opinion would make religious accommodation difficult because it would "need-less[ly] restrict[] the legislature's ability to respond to the unique problems of a particular religious group." He argued that "[t]he real vice of the school district . . . is that New York created it by drawing political boundaries on the basis of religion."[154] He explained that position by writing:

> There is more than a fine line, however, between the voluntary association that leads to a political community comprised of people who share a common religious faith, and the forced separation that occurs when the government draws explicit political boundaries on the basis of people's faith.[155]

Thus, racial or religious lines are permissible if they result from neutral laws such as those providing for a village formation,[156] or, alternatively, if they are drawn unconsciously, are merely historical, or if the racial content is not otherwise noticed. But racial or religious lines are unacceptable if they are "forced . . . government . . . [or] explicit."[157] Coercion is bad because it subordinates free will. Government action is detrimental if it forces the behavior. Rules that provide for voluntary village incorporation are also governmental but the decision to shape and incorporate the village is not.[158]

Free will also fits Kennedy's conclusions requiring government accommodation toward religious practice. Kennedy agreed, for example, that it is permissible for government to pay for a sign-language interpreter in a sectarian school if the provision of the interpreter was based upon parental choice and a neutral rule, one that made no reference to religion.[159] Free will requires respect for choice. Parental choice was private, neither governmental nor coerced, and therefore permissible.[160] This position represented a significant relaxation of prior standards, which had sought to avoid government entanglement in religious practice and religious decisions—entanglement which would take place if government employees taught in sectarian schools or government money were used to support teaching in sectarian schools. More recently, he and the Court have expanded that approach to allow the public to send its teachers into religious schools to teach important subjects at government expense, thus significantly changing the financial structure of sectarian education in the United States.[161]

Allowing publicly supported teachers to teach secular subjects in religious schools appears neutral as well as noncoercive to those who believe that the educational system should leave parents financially indifferent between public, private, and religious schools for their children, and nearly accomplishes under a different legal doctrine what Kennedy and the Court refused to allow the Hasidim of Kiryas Joel—a publicly funded school of their own. But it does not look neutral to those who believe religion is threatened and diluted when it is supported by government. Nor does it look neutral to those who see public support of secular public schools as the neutral baseline for people of all faiths, leaving everyone to study religious questions at their own expense. It should be said that terms like "coercion" and "neutrality" are somewhat inadequate because, despite competing rhetoric, one can describe situations in which both visions tend to coerce different groups of people. Regardless of perspective, using parental choice as the constitutional baseline of neutrality has the effect of permitting the use of public dollars to facilitate religious indoctrination to a greater extent than using public support for secular public schools as the constitutional baseline of neutrality. Indeed, the Court's tilt toward parental choice has raised both hopes and fears that the Court will bring about the voucher program that the political branches have not.

O'Connor's concept of nonendorsement is similar to Kennedy's concept of coercion. Indeed, it is almost the flip side since endorsement can be coercive. It is at least as ambiguous as his test. Nevertheless, doctrinally, Justice O'Connor starts from a very different position than Kennedy's. She is more concerned with applying what the Court had previously laid down as the "bedrock principles" of the establishment clause.[162] Her nonendorsement principle turns on whether there was what she considers apparent official approval.[163] For O'Connor, appearance of official partiality and pressure on dissenters is unethical and constitutionally impermissible. Nevertheless, her conclusions rarely differ from those of her conservative colleagues, and she has been much more hospitable to religious claims than justices on prior courts. Despite their argument, parental choice has almost exactly the same impact on O'Connor as it does on Kennedy. For both it meant that the state had not established religion by sending public teachers into religious schools. For O'Connor, there was no endorsement because the religious decision belonged to the parents, not the state. For Kennedy there was no coercion because the parents had made the decisions.

While Kennedy, like Rehnquist, explicitly welcomes the encouragement of religion, and O'Connor explicitly chastens it, Scalia adopts a tough-guy stance: people should be able to look out for themselves. So the invocation and benediction at Deborah Weisman's graduation was merely traditional, and he agreed with Justice Kennedy that the creche in the county courthouse in Pittsburgh was not coercive. Scalia promises no one a level playing field. Statutes have to be neutral on the surface but neither evenhanded nor fair in reality. In the peyote case, he wrote an opinion that changed the law and held for a 5–4 majority that it was not necessary for the Court to find that the state had important reasons to refuse to accommodate the Native American religious practice. In the case overturning the federal Religious Freedom Restoration Act, he joined another 5–4 majority confirming that no important reason would be necessary when government refuses to accommodate a religious practice. Some religions will get and exercise power and the weak will lose out. As long as no one is forced, such is the way of the world. An occasional act of tolerance is fine but not required. It's a Darwinian world.

Speech. The speech cases also reflect this trio's conservative views of character. A sense of character limits what it's permissible to say and why. Possession of character also describes those with the strength and resources to reach the public.

Although she has been somewhat inconsistent doctrinally,[164] O'Connor has little fear of speech or speakers.[165] She stands ready to defend proper speech against government bias,[166] interference,[167] or prior restraint.[168] Government, like the speakers it regulates, must behave ethically and observe proper social rules.[169] Thus, more than some of her conservative colleagues, O'Connor is quite prepared to protect speech from intrusive regulation.[170]

Justice O'Connor's support for speech, however, is sharply bounded: decorum must be observed. She and Justice Kennedy objected to solicitation, not speech or leafleting, when political activists set up a table on a sidewalk in front of a post office in *United States v. Kokinda*[171] and religious alms seekers solicited contributions in an airport in *International Society for Krishna Consciousness v. Lee.*[172] Justice Scalia objected to both the leafleting and the solicitations.[173] As O'Connor observed, those who solicit contributions often not only follow and harass people in ways that speakers rarely do but also compel people to make difficult on-the-spot decisions that mere speech does not.[174] Thus, her view can be described either as valuing the privacy of passers-by more than the organizational opportunities of countercultural groups, or as a reaction to the decorum of public interaction. Decorum can also describe her objection to allowing advertisers to place newsracks on streetcorners or candidates to put flyers on utility poles.[175]

Similarly, she believes that professional codes should be able to control the behavior of lawyers and accountants to preserve the dignity and good standing of the professions in preference to First Amendment claims.[176] Decorum again defeats speech rights.

Justice O'Connor's treatment of speech as defined by proprieties of communication resonates with a traditional understanding of speech as a reasoning process. The much-discussed Meiklejohn interpretation of the Constitution proposed that government should undertake the role of moderator at a town meeting to bring order to the discussion and see that all are heard.[177] The Meiklejohn interpretation focused on speech as a reasoning process in which all ideas could be heard and considered. O'Connor rejects, however, the paternalism that played a part in the Meiklejohn interpretation. She maintains a principled and consistent protection for speech that excludes the government as the arbiter of who gets to say what even for purposes of improving the content of the debate.[178]

Justice O'Connor's speech principle, however, does not protect what others would treat as core speech. As Justice Harlan pointed out in *Cohen v. California*,[179] and as Justice Brennan emphasized in *FCC v. Pacifica Foundation*,[180] an insistence on proprieties tends to discriminate precisely against groups that protest against unfairness or mistreatment by those in power. Requiring what the majority regards as proper decorum has the potential to inflict significant damage on disfavored groups or individuals. *Gentile v. State Bar* is a good example.[181] In the underlying litigation the prosecutor engaged in extensive pretrial publicity suggesting defendant's guilt. Defense counsel responded with allegations of public misconduct, but the bar sought to censure counsel for those statements, although they had far less impact on the trial than the publicity occasioned by the prosecutor. As Justice Kennedy wrote, the allegations of public misconduct for which the attorney in *Gentile* was being censured were core political speech.[182] Moreover, in his view, attorneys were in the best position to perceive and complain about the issues being raised. Nevertheless, O'Connor believed that it is harmful for lawyers to engage in pretrial publicity about a case coming before the courts.[183]

Justice Scalia is far more willing than Chief Justice Rehnquist to defend speech he abhors,[184] but like Rehnquist, and unlike Justices O'Connor and Kennedy, Scalia is quite prepared to exclude speech from many areas entirely—no soliciting, no leaflets, no problem. Scalia merely requires the exclusion be achieved by formally neutral rules.[185] The requirement of neutrality applies only when government regulates; he would not restrict government favoritism by taxes or grants[186] or control over its own property.[187] Speech rules are not for weaklings. A good example is his opinion in *Rutan v. Republican Party*,[188] in which he argued that patronage in government service is appropriate despite its coercive impact.[189] Speech is just a battle of the titans in which only the fit survive and the weak are not entitled to be coddled.

Kennedy, by contrast, has become one of the staunchest defenders of free speech on the Court, writing lively opinions with ringing rhetoric in its defense, both for the Court and in dissent.[190] Kennedy's strong support of speech rights suggests a view of character that values civic involvement and mutual deliberation. That view would be consistent with his emphasis on will and intent, but builds on it to develop public virtues. Kennedy reserves his most vigorous defense for political speech. His defense of the censured attorney in *Gentile* did not conceive of First Amendment protection as a personal right or privilege of the attorney but, rather, as a reflection of his public duty to air the facts of possible official malfeasance.[191] In *Masson v. New Yorker Magazine, Inc.*, Kennedy defended the writer's alteration or "cleaning up" of quoted material as necessary to make the material more intelligible for "reasonable reader[s]."[192] In Kennedy's view, the values of the First Amendment are better served by allowing writers to correct errors and reconstruct conversations to clarify, but not to change, meaning.[193] Thus, the character Kennedy honors in the speech cases is more involved and less prissy than the character O'Connor esteems and, at the same time, more honored and less tested than the character Scalia respects.

Abortion. The right-to-life movement comes out of a very different tradition than the forms of conservatism we've been considering, but modern conservatism has worked hard to accommodate and domesticate it. There is nothing inherently liberal or conservative about any of the religious movements involved.[194] Indeed, each of the religious denominations involved in the right-to-life movement have been historically aligned, at times, with liberal, progressive, or reform movements and, on other occasions, with conservatism.[195] But modern conservatism has made abortion a parable of bad character. For example, bad characters become pregnant when they should not and "solve" the problem of pregnancy by means of abortions. In the modern conservative's view, abortion licenses people to have bad character.[196] Thus, abortion is both a cause and a symptom of the breakdown of "values" in American society. Women of good character do not need abortions and would refuse them. Abortion allows women to stray from the requirements of conscience. In turn, and in contrast to conservative thought about hedonism in economic affairs, hedonism in the sexual context leads to strains that undermine society.

Abortion is plainly an area in which the Court's conservative bloc has shown significant cracks. Nevertheless, it is important to highlight the conservative justices' fundamental agreement that abortion is an evil.[197] This is not an agreement that would have come from economic conservatism. Nor is it an agreement that would have come from many traditionalists.[198] What unites the conservative bloc on the abortion issue nec-

essarily derives either from views about religion or character or both. Religious views are an obvious hypothesis in this area. Each of these justices
is obviously promoting the public inculcation of religious values, and their
positions on abortion could be driven by their religious views.[199] Kannar
has argued that Scalia's work is driven in general by his religious training.[200] If that were true, however, it doesn't explain his divergence from
the more "liberal" aspects of Catholic teaching in other areas. In any case,
beyond their support for religious indoctrination and their support for
Western religion in general, little of the work of these justices outside the
free exercise and establishment clause cases has any plain relationship to
specific religious views. So it is worth exploring the hypothesis that their
views on abortion can be partially explained by their views on the import
of individual character, whether or not those views were to some extent
also shaped within religious communities.

Justice O'Connor's attitude toward *Roe* can be understood as exempli-
fying her insistence on public spirit. In O'Connor's view, a woman is not
entitled to make decisions even about intimate matters without taking account of competing interests.[201] For Justice O'Connor, restrictions on
abortion seem to stem from the need to consider competing public and
private interests.[202] Indeed, public needs and interests generally play a large
part in her jurisprudence.[203] In O'Connor's view, the abortion cases appear to be about the proper decision or proper scope of decision-making
authority.

Justice Scalia's view, however, is not about public interests. He rejects
both the concept of fundamental rights on which the woman's claim of
right to abort a pregnancy is based,[204] and the predicate that there exist
competing public interests.[205] The problem is to discern what led Scalia to
his conclusions about abortion. Scalia's arguments in the abortion cases do
not parse the substantive values. His arguments rest on the text and do not
investigate the social meaning of abortion. His textual argument leaves a
vacuum of indeterminacy that makes it necessary to try to understand the
impulse that leaves him so sure that the right to govern the use of one's
own body is not a protected liberty. Such a right, however, would give
women a second chance. Insurance, that is, protection against the worst
consequences of one's mistakes, foils the Darwinian plan by protecting the
condition of the unfit. Only privilege merits protection. As with blacks,
whom he would leave to scramble for their place in the sun regardless of
the odds and hurdles, so with women.[206] Abortion is just a break they
don't deserve.

Justice Kennedy has not detailed his objections to abortion in his own voice. The legal community anticipated that Kennedy would vote to overrule *Roe* on the basis of an opinion written by Chief Justice Rehnquist.[207] Kennedy's opinion in *Planned Parenthood v. Casey*,[208] affirmed *Roe,* though gutting it, and was written jointly with O'Connor and Souter.[209] As with Justices O'Connor and Scalia, the best one can do is to try to determine what likely hypotheses are consistent with his conclusions. Kennedy does not share Justice Scalia's Darwinian view of human life. Nevertheless, his focus on free will may lead him to share the condemnation of the women as well as the act. The opposition to abortion in the conservative movement is not merely religious; it is also social. Abortion represents weakness, both in becoming pregnant and in dealing with pregnancy. Abortion reflects a failure of character as much as a religious transgression. Kennedy's treatment of abortion easily fits a pattern dominated by a vision of character. It would be quite consistent with his treatment of other areas of law if he simply concluded that he would not protect these women from their own decisions.

Criminal Law. In the criminal cases, an emphasis on moral culpability could lead Kennedy to the conclusion that bad guys should get nothing because they exercised their free will—badly. An emphasis on moral culpability, however, should function as a shield around the innocent, ensuring that procedures are followed to determine that the accused are in fact guilty. In *Herrera v. Collins*,[210] Kennedy and O'Connor left open for decision in a later case where the record might be more persuasive, whether a person on death row awaiting execution could obtain relief in federal court on the ground that state courts refused to consider newly discovered evidence of innocence.[211] Thus, it has been somewhat surprising that Kennedy's insistence that the significance of innocence that remained open in *Herrera* did not mature into the conclusion that a district judge could consider the powerful evidence of innocence in a later case.[212] Instead, Kennedy stuck to the conclusion that the district court had no discretion to consider newly discovered evidence. O'Connor, more concerned with accurate and proportional justice, broke with her conservative colleagues on precisely that point. Although O'Connor is disinclined to believe that the system has gone wrong, she is also less apt to ignore the error if it has.[213]

In *County of Riverside v. McLaughlin*,[214] Justice Scalia argued eloquently that the point of constitutional guarantees regarding criminal procedure was to protect the innocent.[215]

One hears the complaint, nowadays, that the Fourth Amendment has become constitutional law for the guilty; that it benefits the career criminal (through the exclusionary rule) often and directly, but the ordinary citizen remotely if at all. . . . The common-law rule of *prompt* hearing had as its primary beneficiaries the innocent—not those whose fully justified convictions must be overturned to scold the police. . . . Hereafter a law–abiding citizen wrongfully arrested may be compelled to await the grace of a Dickensian bureaucratic machine, as it churns its cycle for up to two days—never once given the opportunity to show a judge that there is absolutely no reason to hold him, that a mistake has been made. In my view, this is the image of a system of justice that has lost its ancient sense of priority, a system that few Americans would recognize as our own.[216]

The suggestion that Scalia intended substantive values, particularly concerning the rights of the innocent, to take precedence over procedural ones, such as finality, was dispelled, however, in *Herrera*.[217] *Herrera* tested Scalia's position because it was an extreme case. A man about to be executed developed substantial evidence of his actual innocence of the crime.[218] Justice Scalia, nonetheless, announced that he believed even substantial evidence that the condemned man was probably innocent raised no constitutional obligation to provide a hearing on newly discovered evidence.[219] It was a view he confirmed on even stronger evidence in *Schlup v. Delo*.[220] Scalia's Darwinian world easily sacrifices those whose legal representation fails to exonerate them under the given rules.

Democracy. For conservatives, democracy is a less important value than it is for liberals. Their substantive commitments conflict with democratic ones to a greater extent than does the partial relativism of liberal thought.[221] O'Connor has been reasonably explicit in rejecting *Carolene Products*,[222] the democratic credo of the liberal view.[223] In addition, the conservative bloc has been relatively united in rejecting challenges to allegedly undemocratic procedures.[224]

The conservative stance on democratic government has deeper roots than conservative visions of character and is grounded in a rejection of moral autonomy.[225] Perhaps reflecting the fact that democratic values are less important to conservatives, democratic values are not clearly worked out in the jurisprudence of these justices except to the extent that they are subordinated to other values.

Conservative visions of character, however, may modify this stance in different ways. For Scalia, there is no external standard to judge procedure.[226]

Procedure is whatever tradition establishes, given that the fittest survive. This view could explain his support for political parties, which encompasses both the system of party patronage and regulations to protect the parties from independent voters.[227] In effect, parties are proven and fit and, therefore, measures that protect them are proper.

O'Connor's participation in the relaxation of reapportionment law[228] suggests a detachment from the political process. Nonetheless, she has recently attempted to compromise the districting cases in a manner that may reflect both her belief that virtue deserves a reward and some underlying view about what democracy ought to be.[229]

Kennedy has joined some of O'Connor's efforts in the redistricting area[230] and also expressed support for democratic institutions.[231] Both joined Scalia's dissent in *Rutan v. Republican Party*,[232] concluding that political organization is more important than popular control. Kennedy and O'Connor subsequently abandoned their positions in the *Rutan* case and now assert that one has a democratic right not to suffer official coercion of one's political attachments.[233] Beyond these recent cases, neither has marked out any significant set of democratic rights worthy of the Court's protection or any description of the meaning of democracy.

Federalism. Their views of character make some sense of the conservative justices' treatment of federalism. Commentators have described the three justices as supporting federalism.[234] Nevertheless, the justices themselves have been much more eclectic, overruling local preferences in areas such as integration and civil liberties.[235] Thus, the claim that federalism is a basic conservative value is not a universal truth.

Federalism, however, plays an instrumental role in conservative thought, as we have noted before.[236] Local communities can be effective agents for instilling values and developing character. Local communities often enforce a more extensive moral code than does the more pluralist nation.[237] When these communities perform this function, as by banning sex and abortion and by authorizing school boards to weed school libraries of books they find objectionable, the conservative justices support federalism.[238] When the local community opts for diversity or liberty, as by implementing affirmative action or regulating the police, the character of the citizenry might be undermined and the conservative justices object.[239] In contrast, for the more liberal justices, the point of federalism is liberty.[240] When local communities attempt to impose a moral order, the liberal justices object.[241]

That brings us back to the decision on the Religious Freedom Restoration Act. Justices Kennedy and O'Connor both wrote about the powers of Congress under the Fourteenth Amendment. The decision, known as *Boerne v. Flores*, could therefore be understood as evidence that the justices in fact care a great deal about federalism, contrary to the views I have expressed here. Commentators have followed their lead.[242]

Nevertheless, there is another way to understand this case. Congress in RFRA relied on section 5 of the Fourteenth Amendment. Section 5 gives Congress the power to enforce the provisions of section 1 of the Fourteenth Amendment, the section that guarantees to all of us the privileges and immunities of American citizens, due process and equal protection of law. Although the Court got there in a way that differs from the original expectations of those who drafted the amendment, the Fourteenth Amendment was intended and for much of this century has been interpreted to "incorporate" most of the provisions of the Bill of Rights and therefore to require that the states act in line with the provisions of the Bill of Rights. That, of course, includes the First Amendment, which guarantees free exercise of religion and prohibits religious establishment, among other provisions. Congress in RFRA was trying to enforce the free exercise clause of the First Amendment by means of its powers under section 5 of the Fourteenth.

In writing the Religious Freedom Restoration Act, however, Congress went further than what the Court said the free exercise clause required. Since the power under section 5 is merely a power to enforce, the majority concluded that Congress did not have the power to expand the protections of the free exercise clause under the guise of enforcing it.

This problem, however, had come up before, and on the preceding occasions the Court had found that Congress could prevent violations by writing legislation somewhat stricter than what the Constitution requires. After all, there are many problems in proving violations of constitutional rights and sometimes it is easier to avoid those problems by creating clear rules and hard lines. There are a number of other statutes that are nearly indistinguishable from RFRA in the constitutional structure we have been describing.[243] For example, the Court had said literacy tests for voter registration were permissible. But Congress forbade literacy tests where there was a risk that they would be used to discriminate, regardless of the absence of any finding that the tests had been used to discriminate, or even a finding, by a lower court, that they had not. The Court approved. For a second example, where discrimination had existed in the past, Congress has required states and local governments to submit to the attorney general any changes in their electoral system, even if the new rules were perfectly consistent with the Constitution—because there was a risk of designing new rules in ways that would discriminate. The Court approved. For a third example, the Supreme Court's definition of discrimination has been intentional discrimination. Congress wrote a statute that forbade rules about elections that had the effect of discriminating against minorities whether or not a court might find the procedures were intended to discriminate. Again the Court approved. The Supreme Court agreed that there was a risk of discrimination even where there was no evidence that could be introduced in a court to show that the discriminatory result was intended, and that Congress could, by expanding the constitutional prohibition, ensure against that risk. In each case, the constitutional authority was to enforce the provisions of § 1 of the Fourteenth Amendment. In each case, Congress had prohibited behavior the Court found constitutional. In each case, the Court held that preventing such a risk was a way of enforcing the Constitution. And the means were identical: substituting an effects for an intent standard.

The Supreme Court's decision might still be about federalism, but it might be about those prior cases, all of which were aspects of the enforcement of the civil rights laws. Justice Kennedy understood that relationship and specifically wrote about those prior cases, arguing that they were different from the RFRA case. They were different because there was a record supporting Congress's action in the civil rights area, but he argued that there was no record in the case of the religion statute. That is troubling on both fronts. It is troubling with respect to the civil rights laws because they and their supporting record are getting older. It is troubling with respect to the religious freedom statute because there is plenty of reason to believe that decisions are not made without regard to religious affiliations, whether with respect to funding or zoning or other privileges. It seems much more likely that the conservative members of the majority were simply drawing the blinds over the kinds of discrimination that can be wielded, with all apparent innocence, against religious minorities.

So maybe they were writing about federalism, and maybe they were writing about legislative records, and maybe they were telling us a great deal about the substance of their views on civil rights and what the Court will accept from majority faiths imposing their views on those who disagree.

Conclusions

Justices O'Connor, Scalia, and Kennedy start from the proposition that relativism, at least as understood by more liberal jurists, is not acceptable. Instead, they agree, despite much rhetoric to the contrary, that some substantive views should play a large part in their constitutional jurisprudence. Their substantive commitments involve what they see as the virtues and values of good character, and they agree those considerations have a large role to play in the Court's work, including areas as disparate as criminal law and religious establishment cases.

The liberal diversity project challenges the views of the conservative justices, particularly in the areas of equal protection of minorities and religious establishment. They start from a fundamentally different assumption. What liberals cherish, they fear.

Nevertheless, there are significant philosophical gaps between Justices O'Connor, Scalia, and Kennedy. Scalia's survival-of-the-fittest approach to legal analysis is quite different from the more fully communitiarian views of Justice O'Connor. Kennedy's intentionalism borrows from both, without mimicking either. Given a legal culture in which many of the cases arise as a reaction to liberal policies, the differences among the three justices have proven less important than their common ground. Their differences, nevertheless, have generated splits within the conservative bloc that have produced some surprisingly liberal results.

Justice O'Connor's view of character moderates her views in many areas and disposes her to vote with the liberals, on occasion, in such areas as the death penalty. The same view drives her approach to speech and federalism. In a similar way, Kennedy's view of character moderates his views of race and fuels his views of speech and religion. In contrast, Scalia's view of character is not responsible for his occasional votes with the more liberal bloc. Instead, Scalia's social Darwinism holds him firmly to the conservative camp.

None of this, of course, bears any relationship to Justice Scalia's claim of a neutral, technical jurisprudence in which courts merely find constitutional law embedded in the text, the history of the document or elsewhere.[244] Conservative principles are no less real and significant in their decision-making than the liberal principles they condemn had been on prior Courts.

5

Between Two Worlds

Thomas's originalism has tantalized his critics but, inevitably, it is inconsistent. As Gerber[1] has forcefully shown, Thomas resorts to what he believes are historical principles in the race area but confines himself to specific historic examples elsewhere. Plainly history is not the point. When we turn to Thomas's substantive choices we confront a similar inconsistency. He resoundingly rejects libertarianism and privacy except that his writing in the area of race suggests that he values an individual right of association and he appears to support a strong right to property. Other factors are at work.

The rejection of the autonomy and harm principles, which conservatives understand as relativism, dominates Thomas's jurisprudence as it does his conservative colleagues'. Beyond that, the deep structure of Justice Thomas's views is identity politics. He seeks respect for African Americans by means of assimilation. If blacks are seen as liberal New Dealers, then Thomas will seek the respectable Republican "mainstream." If blacks are seen as pleading for special advantages, Thomas will bend over backwards to be a lawyer's lawyer, proposing to ignore all consequences and focusing only on rules. Indeed, instead of seeing blackness at all, he proposes to see individuals. When white conservatives reject affirmative action, whether from a preference for their own crowd or for moral conformity, Thomas worries about respect for black institutions.

Lawyer's Lawyer

Like Justice Scalia, Justice Thomas has adopted a formal methodology.[2] He seems to share with his conservative colleagues a great respect for the common law. We will describe some of those cases as we consider Thomas's work in various specific fields of law. But some introductory comments are in order. The common law has very long historical roots both here and in England and is generally understood as judge-made law. Historically, the judiciary adopted the rule that changes in the common law by the legislature were disfavored unless they were clearly spelled out. Gradually, the courts accepted the principle that legislation is superior to the common law, that the proper judicial role is to defer to the legislative branch when it legislates on an issue previously covered by the common law, and that the proper way to determine whether the legislature intended to amend or replace the common law was to examine the purpose of the legislation. Reverting to the common law in the late twentieth century provides judges at once with a lawyers' tool that keeps their noses in the books and that disregards most of the twentieth century.[3] It is a tool that can be used to roll back elements of the social welfare state without regard to any explicit discussion of the comparative wisdom of the various alternatives or the justices' preferences.

Conservative Fundamentals

It is of course well known that Justice Thomas's voting record closely parallels Justice Scalia's,[4] and, indeed, that of Rehnquist as well. Like Chief Justice Rehnquist and Justices O'Connor, Scalia, and Kennedy, Justice Thomas rejects individual moral autonomy. Also in common with the conservative wing of the Court, he appears to reject the post-1937 *Carolene Products* paradigm of judicial role. Thomas also reaches the same conclusions as Rehnquist and Scalia on race and democracy. His conclusions may be described, therefore, in the philosophically eclectic, hierarchical, and Darwinian terms that fit their views. He may differ from some fellow conservatives in being more willing to attack discrimination[5] but also more willing to accept single-race institutions.[6] Thomas does not generalize that view, however, into support for ethnic self-determination, as he makes clear by his consistent denial of Indian claims.[7]

Thomas announced his rejection of moral independence in *Swanner v. Anchorage Equal Rights Commission*.[8] That case involved a statute that prohibited discrimination on the basis of marital status in the rental of an apartment. Thomas made it clear that the privacy of unmarried couples was of the very lowest order for him and could not be protected against contrary claims even by a state statute. Thus this was not merely a case of one moral right (to free exercise of religion) overpowering another (to privacy) but, rather, a categorical rejection of the claimed right to privacy in that most private sphere of housing arrangements.[9] He confirmed his rejection of a right to privacy in *Romer v. Evans*, the case reviewing the Colorado antigay amendment.[10]

Thomas backs up his rejection of relativism by supporting a larger role for government support for and involvement in religion. Thomas argues that the establishment clause does not require that government keep its nose out of the religious tent. He supported the Court's conclusion that public schools can, and in some circumstances must, make their funds and facilities available to religious groups on nondiscriminatory terms.[11] Further, he has suggested that he may support the notion of nonpreferentialism that would permit government support for religion over nonbelief so long as it did not favor one religion over another.[12]

Consistent with that rejection of moral independence, Thomas is not particularly dedicated to freedom of speech or to democratic rights. Thomas did support the requirement of neutrality among viewpoints in *R.A.V. v. St. Paul*.[13] He concurred in *McIntyre v. Ohio Elections Commission*[14] to support anonymous pamphlets, on the ground that the founders did it. And he has argued that commercial speech should be treated as well as other forms of speech.[15] On the other hand, he has not supported access for speakers either to public or employer property.[16] He joined Rehnquist's attack on the majority's condemnation of a discretionary fee for a parade permit.[17] And he has joined Scalia in concluding that denials of subsidies are not suppression of speech and so are not restricted by the First Amendment.[18]

Further, he appears to share the conservative rejection of the classic paradigm of judicial restraint. As discussed more fully below, his views about voting rights criticize the existing jurisprudence without suggesting that Thomas takes seriously the need to replace it with another more satisfying approach toward curbing the abuse of the election system to subordinate some groups in favor of others. While rejecting a special judicial role in cases dealing with democratic rights, he asserts an active judicial role in cases dealing with property rights.

Thomas's moral absolutism affects a large area of his jurisprudence, allowing him to pick and choose the freedoms he will support, like freedom of association and free markets, while rejecting others at least as important. Thomas is not libertarian. He will not protect individuals from the state, even from gigantic errors.[19]

Much of those positions are affected by his treatment of federalism. Thomas has taken a strong position in favor of devolving power toward the states and limiting national power.[20] One of his claims has been that the original meaning of the terms of the commerce clause requires that interpretation. The commerce clause is the provision of the Constitution that gives Congress the power to regulate commerce among the states. The claim that he is deferring to the original meaning of the language of the Constitution will not work for Thomas's participation in the Court's Eleventh Amendment decisions, which are in direct contradiction to the language of the clause.[21] The language of the clause does not in any way prohibit federal courts from hearing cases asserting claims against the states under federal law, but the Court has interpreted the Eleventh Amendment to mean that federal courts cannot hear most such suits. That conclusion is plainly its preferred result, immunizing the states from many suits in federal courts over compliance with federal law and partially gutting the federal enforcement machinery. Since the conservative majority, Thomas included, has not taken originalism seriously in the context of the Eleventh Amendment but has simply reached its preferred result on other grounds, it is hard to take its originalist claim seriously in the case of the commerce clause. What does have to be taken seriously are the implications of Thomas's interpretation of the meaning of the clause. The language as he reads it would not give Congress power to regulate manufacturing, agriculture, insurance, or most of the myriad transactions of modern business. And it would eliminate the power that Congress has exercised under the commerce clause to eliminate segregation in public accommodations and at least some of the discrimination in employment. Whether the Court would find that Congress would have the power to prohibit segregation in public accommodations under section 5 of the Fourteenth Amendment is questionable because most of those facilities are private. Under a momentous nineteenth-century decision, state failure to eliminate segregation in such private facilities would not give Congress power to step in.[22] As a result, Thomas's view of the commerce clause and the Court's view of the Fourteenth Amendment would terminate the public accommodations provisions of the Civil Rights Act of 1964, and narrow the scope of the employment provisions. Like Rehnquist's attack on the incorporation of the Bill of Rights through the Fourteenth Amendment, it is a strike at the very heart of contemporary national law.

Thus federalism as Thomas wields it fits his conservative objectives. He does not defer to states when they do not reach the same conclusions that he would on such matters as affirmative action or takings.[23] But his interpretation of federalism would diminish procedural protections in the criminal process, minimize the enforcement of civil rights law, and minimize federal regulation of the national economy.

With a Difference—Higher Law

Unlike the others, Thomas has explicitly avowed his belief in higher law.[24] But the more interesting problem is the content and implications of that law as Thomas sees it.

For Neither Liberty nor Privacy. Clearly, for Thomas, higher law is not a privacy right and it is not an endorsement of moral independence.[25] Perhaps more surprisingly, his higher-law instincts are not defined by or in defense of a right to freedom from government abuse, a stance clearly reflected in his treatment of the habeas cases. Thomas is so consistent in this area that one looks almost in vain for the criminal defense claim that he would sustain,[26] a position more consistently exteme than Scalia's though Thomas is often alleged to be his clone. Thomas's position is too consistent for some kind of interpretive explanation based on the text or history of the Constitution. Since most of these cases dealt with mitigating factors in death penalty cases and other sentencing issues, it is possible that he simply doesn't care about what happens to those convicted of felonies. Indeed, he votes to protect guards from suits for even the most outrageous behavior[27] and wrote an opinion for the Court permitting the states to use the civil commitment process to lengthen an individual's confinement, even if no treatment is provided.[28]

More disturbing, however, is his posture of not caring about innocence, joining both Rehnquist and Scalia in *Herrera v. Collins*[29] and *Schlup v. Delo.*[30] In *Wright v. West*,[31] he questioned the whole enterprise of federal oversight of state imprisonment through habeas corpus.[32]

Equality in Education. Thomas has given some clues about what he believes natural law implies. Some relate to equality and discrimination; others to economic issues. Although he reached the same conclusions as Rehnquist and Scalia in the various cases that have come before the Court regarding racial relations, it is probable that they reached those conclusions for different reasons. Rehnquist appears uncomfortable with the integrated world of the late twentieth century. Thomas and Scalia do not share that aversion but they defend freedom of association. Scalia appears to defend it as part of his attachment to a Darwinian world—racial problems are just facts of social life with which strong people have to deal with no special protections. His view is detached; the cookie crumbles as it will. Thomas's view is engaged—he appears attached to competing visions—the freedom to assimilate and the freedom to segregate.

Thomas has written, without a great deal of elaboration, that the first Justice John Marshall Harlan's understanding of the rights of citizens in the privileges and immunities clause and the Declaration of Independence as expressed in Harlan's dissent in *Plessy v. Ferguson*,[33] would have solved the problems of *Brown v. Board of Education*.[34] And according to Thomas in an earlier article, *Brown* would be different if it were based on a discussion of slavery rather than of badges of inferiority.[35] He contrasted reason, justice, and freedom, in what he treated as the founders' vision, with sentiment, sensitivity, and dependence, in what he treated as the error of *Brown*.[36] He infers that reason, justice, and freedom led to the earlier Harlan's insistence on a "color-blind" Constitution.[37]

The NAACP Legal Defense and Education Fund believed Thomas intended to endorse freedom of choice plans in denouncing the line of enforcement cases that includes *Swann v. Charlotte-Mecklenburg Board of Education*[38] and *Green v. County School Board of New Kent County*,[39] as "'disastrous'" and requiring not only "'desegregation'" but "'integregation.'"[40] In 1968 the Supreme Court in the *Green* case unanimously held that a southern community that had previously required segregation by law could not desegregate by simply declaring that everyone had the right to choose whatever school he or she preferred to attend.[41] The problem with such "freedom of choice" plans was that they perpetuated the official segregation that had been the previous rule. The traditions, stereotypes, and fears that lingered from the prior regime of segregation led both races to refuse to cross the color line—whites chose the "white" schools and blacks the "black" ones—and the schools remained segregated. Thomas commented that resistance to *Brown* made *Green* understandable and suggested that the problem with the remedies used following *Green* was that they "should have been temporary and used only to overcome the widespread resistance to the dictates of the Constitution."[42] Instead he seems to be defending line drawing without racial considerations and without efforts to equalize races in schools.

For liberals, these issues about freedom of choice are complicated by the complicity of government agencies. The federal government facilitated white flight to suburbs by building highways and then compounded the segregation of metropolitan areas by redlining the suburbs against blacks through the Federal Housing Administration, which refused to underwrite loans there for blacks. Thomas makes no mention of these issues or how they might affect his views about freedom of choice and association.

Thomas provided another glimpse into his thinking in his concurring opinion in *United States v. Fordice*,[43] in which the Court held that the lower court's findings of fact required the conclusion that Mississippi continued to maintain a segregated system of universities in conflict with the equal protection clause of the Fourteenth Amendment. Thomas agreed with the Court that "adopting race-neutral policies for the future administration of the system" did not suffice "to dismantle a dual system of higher education."[44] What Thomas wanted to make clear was that this standard

> does not compel the elimination of all observed racial imbalance, . . . [and] portends neither the destruction of historically black colleges nor the severing of those institutions from their distinctive histories and traditions.[45]

Thomas believes the courts should not focus on the imbalance itself but rather the justification for policies that produce it.[46] He elaborated:

> [W]e do not foreclose the possibility that there exists "sound educational justification" for maintaining historically black colleges *as such.* . . . Obviously a State cannot maintain such traditions by closing particular institutions, historically white or historically black, to particular racial groups. Nonetheless, it hardly follows that a State cannot operate a diverse assortment of institutions—including historically black institutions—open to all on a race-neutral basis, but with established traditions and programs that might disproportionately appeal to one race or another.[47]

More recently, in *Missouri v. Jenkins,* Thomas objected to the creation of a magnet school for the purpose of drawing whites into a black district, saying this rests on the presumption of black inferiority.[48] De facto residential segregation is not, according to Thomas, a constitutional injury;[49] whether or not it causes psychological injuries is irrelevant to its constitutional status;[50] unconstitutional discrimination is about distinctions, not about effects.[51] Integration, moreover, has not produced any great leap forward.[52]

Thomas's signals are somewhat mixed between liberty and color blindness. He may have been urging a liberty of association, including a right to segregate oneself. He may have meant that eliminating segregation "root and branch"[53] encourages dependence.[54] Whatever Thomas's views about freedom of association, he is clearly selective in the liberties he supports; freedom of association does not include the moral independence a libertarian or utilitarian would have supported, or offer the most historic liberty to move about with bodily security against unjust incarceration or execution.

He may instead have meant only that the Constitution should be color-blind.[55] A color-blind Constitution would still have to distinguish those classifications that, like race, deserve strict scrutiny from those that don't.[56] In Thomas's view those distinctions would be based largely on impact and history, especially the history of slavery; it is not clear what classifications other than race fit his view.[57] A color-blind Constitution presumably would forbid distinctions based on race for all reasons—no Jim Crow, no affirmative action, presumably no compelling interests or deliberate integration.[58]

But with or without Jim Crow, freedom of association could not be fully protected. Indeed, *Brown* itself was attacked as an infringement of the right of association. There is overlap but not identity between color blindness and freedom of association. The desire of some to segregate themselves is not entirely consistent with the desire of others to integrate or assimilate. The legal system can compromise but cannot protect both fully at the same time. Freedom of association is one of those liberties that cannot be absolute for everyone. A color-blind Constitution, in turn, will protect the status quo at the expense of some of those who seek to segregate themselves and some of those who seek to integrate themselves.

Despite the limits and differences, Thomas seems to put some stock in both color blindness and freedom of association.

Equality in Employment. Thomas has been critical of affirmative action in the area of equal rights to employment, preferring only individual antidiscrimination claims.[59] Although Justice Thomas made it sound easy, in fact identifying exactly how any individuals would have been treated, hired, fired, promoted, or disciplined is very difficult. The difficulty many experienced in deciding between Anita Hill and Clarence Thomas is a good example. Individual cases permit and require all sorts of complex and expensive inquiries into personal characteristics and motives; they allow for and invite character assassination in the effort to elaborate reasons that one might have acted. These are bruising battles. The facts of the individual applicants have no absolute significance; discrimination claims can be determined only by comparison to the treatment of others. Moreover, relief addressed only to identifiable applicants and employees does not address the damage created by incentives not to apply, for example, the awareness that the workforce is hostile and has few if any minorities.

Thomas makes an interesting point that injunctive relief—typical of affirmative action, and providing for the hiring or retention of minorities in specific positions—is paid for by the rejected applicants and may do little to compensate the victims of prior discrimination, while, by contrast, compensating victims financially is paid for by the corporations that discriminated.[60] Perhaps Thomas will try to refocus on more precise explanations for discriminatory behavior and on the remedies for it. It may be significant that he joined the majority in *ABF Freight System, Inc. v. N.L.R.B.*,[61] which found that the NLRB was entitled to provide relief to an employee who had been discriminated against for union activities despite his own misbehavior since it did not actually motivate the employer's discriminatory conduct. The majority, Thomas included, found the NLRB policy appropriate to its mission of controlling employer discrimination for pro-union activity. Scalia, in a separate concurrence, agreed that the board had discretion but attacked the board policy nevertheless. Thomas did not join him.

But Thomas has not broken from his conservative fellows in other race cases and the *ABF Freight System* case is a slender reed on which to build the conclusion that Thomas would, in appropriate circumstances, be more aggressive in rooting out discrimination.

Inequality in Voting Rights. Whatever support he may lend for equality in education and employment, Thomas has not found a description of equality in apportionment or districting that he can support or that allows him to provide relief for minority voters.[62] In a series of vote dilution cases, the Supreme Court had held that drawing district lines in ways that minimized the likelihood that minority voters would be able to elect representatives violated § 2 of the Voting Rights Act. That can be done, for example, by dividing black voters among a variety of majority-white districts rather than allowing blacks one or more districts in which they are in the majority. Thomas took the opportunity to expound his views at length in *Holder v. Hall*.[63] The Court had to decide whether pegging the size of a local governing commission at a single person had the effect of diluting black votes. Under this voting scheme the likelihood that there would be any black elected official was minimized. Thomas argued that the language of the Voting Rights Act, § 2 (prohibiting any discriminatory "voting qualification or prerequisite to voting or standard, practice, or procedure") does not include either the size of a governing body, specifically, or vote dilution generally.[64] More important for our purposes, however, is his treatment of political theory:

> A review of the current state of our cases shows that by construing the Act to cover potentially dilutive electoral mechanisms, we have immersed the federal courts in a hopeless project of weighing questions of political theory—questions judges must confront to establish a benchmark concept of an "undiluted" vote. Worse, in pursuing the ideal measure of voting strength, we have devised a remedial mechanism that encourages federal courts to segregate voters into racially designated districts to ensure minority electoral success. In doing so, we have collaborated in what may aptly be termed the racial "balkaniz[ation]" of the Nation.[65]

Justice Thomas correctly refers to Justice Harlan's objections that it was not clear that

> a group's votes should be considered to be more "effective" when they provide *influence* over a greater number of seats, or *control* over a lesser number of seats.[66]

Harlan had written: "Under one system . . . minority groups have *more* influence in the selection of *fewer* officers."[67] At-large districting, for example, does not produce anything like proportionality in any given election, but it does produce a system in which people on both sides have likelihoods of winning and of influencing the candidates in proportion to their strength.[68]

The choice of proportionality in seats rather than influence is a political choice. In homogeneous districting each group will have little chance to exert influence in each other's districts but will have elected representatives in rough proportion to their numbers.

The consequence of the Burger Court's approach had been to create safe seats for a politically balkanized public.[69] Thomas quotes Justice Douglas in support of his position:

> When racial or religious lines are drawn by the State, . . . antagonisms that relate to race or to religion rather than to political issues are generated; communities seek not the best representative but the best racial or religious partisan.[70]

It is difficult to tell from a case testing the outer reaches of doctrine what Thomas would have done with the initial line of cases stemming from *Baker v. Carr*.[71] Although Thomas quotes Frankfurter's dissenting opinion in *Baker* with approval,[72] he does so in support of Thomas's claim in *Holder* that it was improper for the Court to extend the reach of the vote dilution cases from equal apportionment of population to racial gerrymandering. Also suggestive, however, is his sweeping conclusion:

> [U]nder our constitutional system, this Court is not a centralized politburo appointed for life to dictate to the provinces the "correct" theories of democratic representation, the "best" electoral systems for securing truly "representative" government, the "fairest" proportions of minority political influence, or, as respondents would have us hold today, the "proper" sizes for local governing bodies.[73]

The thrust of his opinion suggests, though somewhat inconclusively, that he has rejected the entirety of the *Carolene Products* approach. One looks in vain for the voting rights that he would protect with the exception of what Thomas treats as the right not to have race count in the way that election district lines are drawn. There is no support for proportionality, randomness, equality of influence (what political scientists refer to as "symmetry") or any principle of the fair distribution of political power through the electoral process. His argument, most fully developed in *Holder v. Hall*, is that there is no standard for deriving such a principle. As we suggested in chapter 2, the rejection of moral autonomy results in a very ambiguous relationship toward democracy itself. Thomas's views support that inference.

Property and Economic Rights. Thomas has suggested that unenumerated rights might attack arbitrary government, particularly congressional arbitrariness, in a way that conservatives would like.[74] It is still somewhat early to understand the reach of that idea for Justice Thomas. Nevertheless, he has taken several suggestive steps, generally without discussing his ideas about natural law but by reverting instead to notions of the common law that accomplish many of the same goals.

Thomas joined the majority in several decisions expanding the takings concept in constitutional law and asserting judicial power over regulations of property through the common law.[75] Thomas has also written several decisions with respect to economic legislation that define rights in common law terms. One example is *Consolidated Rail Corp. v. Gottshall* (*Con-*

rail).[76] In *Conrail* one worker was chewed out for trying to resuscitate a colleague who had collapsed and died during a work detail in ninety-seven-degree heat, and a supervisor was consistently ordered to ignore safety concerns and was required to work extended overtime without days off. Both sued for emotional harm. Thomas wrote for the majority denying that Conrail had any liability to one plaintiff and ordered the court of appeals to reconsider its decision to send the other case to trial.

Thomas and the Court held that Conrail's liability under the Federal Employers' Liability Act was defined by the common law, and then picked a minority position within the common law to hold that liability is limited by the zone-of-danger test.[77] That test limits recovery for emotional injury to those plaintiffs whose emotional injury stemmed from events that could have happened to them though in fact it happened to the coworker whose injury they witnessed.[78] The Court remanded Gottshall's claim since the same conditions that killed his partner might have killed him, but it dismissed the claim of the supervisor who was not within the zone of danger of the risks he was being forced to impose on others. The Court expressed concern with unlimited liability. The dissent pointed out that employer liability to railroad employees does not pose the extended risk of liability to a broad class of plaintiffs. Nevertheless, the Court feared for the railroads:

> [C]haracterizing a rule limiting liability as "unprincipled" or "arbitrary" is often the result of overemphasizing the policy considerations favoring imposition of liability, while at the same time failing to acknowledge any countervailing policies and the necessary compromise between competing and inconsistent policies informing the rule.[79]

The Court then listed

> the potential for a flood of trivial suits, the possibility of fraudulent claims that are difficult for judges and juries to detect, and the specter of unlimited and unpredictable liability[80]

and concluded,

> We believe the concerns that underlie the common-law tests, and particularly the fear of unlmited liability, to be well-founded.[81]

Thus, fundamental to this line of reasoning is the view that statutory objectives do not define law; common law does.

One must always be cautious about the implicit assumptions behind apparently positivist versions of law; there are simply too many choices.

But one has to be careful with the alternatives as well. So, for example, Thomas's conclusions have nothing to do with being either for or against government power or expense. In *Thomas Jefferson University v. Shalala*, Thomas argued that the secretary's regulations improperly denied the teaching university reimbursement by shifting the allocation of some eligible costs to medical education instead of patient care under Medicaid.[82] And economic explanations for his conclusions are equally unsatisfactory. His conclusions in *Conrail* and similar economic cases have a very ambiguous connection to economic thought. Most economists, free market and otherwise, conclude that enterprises must accept responsibility for the harms they cause. The market is not being efficient if it ignores a set of costs or places the burden on other activities. The free market explains the *Conrail* decision only if the harm to the employees does not count.

Another example of Thomas's deference to common law standards or baselines is *Heck v. Humphrey*.[83] Here he agreed with Justice Scalia that the common law defined the extent of liability for improper imprisonment, under the federal statute known as § 1983. Thomas and Souter squared off about the proper use of common law analogies. For our purposes here, it is not important to determine whether Thomas or Souter had the better of the argument. But their argument illustrates, first, Thomas's reliance on the common law, and second, the way that the use of the common law requires the justices to make choices, not merely apply an existing body of law. The very use of the common law was a choice because the Court was interpreting a federal statute and therefore common law does not and cannot directly apply. But the majority proceeded by analogy to the tort of malicious prosecution, while ignoring the analogy to the tort of abuse of process. Justice Souter argued that the common law tort of abuse of process might have been a better analogy.[84] Nor did Thomas take account of the shape of the common law tort at the time § 1983 was enacted, as he might have chosen to do.[85] In fact, Thomas was using the common law to exclude a group of cases from the federal courts. Malicious prosecution, but not abuse of process, requires a favorable termination of the underlying action.[86] By insisting on a favorable termination of the underlying state prosecution before the federal courts can look at the claim of improper imprisonment, the Court effectively precluded a federal court from reviewing the lawfulness of state proceedings under § 1983. The state immunized itself against federal review by the act of wrongfully finding against the claimant. As Justice Souter points out, the formal use of the common law as a baseline introduced limitations that had no appropriate relationship to the problem at bar.[87] Thus, the dispute between Scalia, Rehnquist, Kennedy, Ginsburg, and Thomas on the one side, and Souter, Blackmun, Stevens, and O'Connor on the other is a debate not merely about "following the law," about functional versus formal jurisprudence, or about whether purposes matter but also about the selection of a baseline, here the common law. Since the common law did not protect liberty, neither will Thomas or the majority. Indeed, the very age of the common law means that there are always bodies of historic legal principles available that are a predictably poor substitute for modern statutes.

Conclusions

Several aspects of Thomas's views fit the essential conservative paradigm. He joins their rejection of *Carolene Products* and substitutes a view of law that emphasizes a more absolute individual morality,[88] except that, with respect to race, he insists on a combination of color blindness and freedom of association.

Thomas has taken bits and pieces of a libertarian stand. His property positions suggested some sort of libertarian stance in the economic area—owners versus government. He suggested in an article that conservatives would like the use of unenumerated rights to limit arbitrary government. And his treatment of discrimination also looks libertarian; it avoids considering social consequences and leaves room for considerable freedom of choice. All of that suggests a very libertarian frame of mind, limited however to economic and associational issues. In common with other conservative colleagues, his treatment of discrimination as recompense only for specific injuries is consistent with his treatment of the common law in other areas. But Thomas's views on moral autonomy and the criminal law make it very clear that Thomas is not a libertarian. A traditionally libertarian stance would have based sentencing on the defendants' blameworthiness and protected people from the state run amok. Thomas does not.

Thomas reaches many of the same conclusions as Rehnquist and Scalia do. But the springs of his view appear to be quite different. Thomas's work appears to be a form of identity politics. His acceptance of a black nationalist position appears quite inconsistent with the ethnocentric views of his conservative colleagues. That difference has yet to make itself felt in their conclusions.

6

Consensus on the Left

Origins of the Liberal Consensus

We have touched on the springs of liberal and utilitarian thought in several places in order to compare it with conservative thought. Now we need to expand that discussion of liberal and utilitarian thinking in order to understand both where the liberal justices come together and where they come apart.

For the liberals on the Court between 1937 and 1986, the touchstone of their judicial philosophy was democracy. Their jurisprudence emerged from the Progressive movement and the New Deal. These movements were organized around majoritarian concerns. The rights of workers spawned a great deal of effort in both political movements. Although unions never represented a majority of Americans, workers certainly were a majority and their interests were the interests of most Americans. Concern for the rights and interests of workers was understood in a very majoritarian way. Many of the major free speech issues of the period involved union-busting activities.[1] The Court was criticized in the early part of the century for holding back what the majority wanted to do for the working population, vetoing labor laws, commercial regulations, and tax rules. The Court switched in 1937 and accepted the Progressive/New Deal legislative climate.

The judicial statement of this approach came in 1938 in *United States v. Carolene Products Co.,* a case we have had occasion to discuss before. The Court wrote in a footnote that courts had a special role to play when those in power attempted to block the channels of political change.[2] The people were entitled to control their government free of the machinations of those in power to rig the system in their favor. The Court also stated that instances of prejudices against racial and religious minorities may be the result of a failure of democracy. For most of us, democracy is horse trading—that is, we have learned to take one another's needs into account, and we or our representatives agree to support one another on issues of greatest concern to one another and compromise as we trade. But those excluded from the marketplace of legislative and political trading are denied the benefits of democracy. If democracy not only refuses to respect their preferences on specific issues but refuses to consider their needs as people for all purposes, that is effectively the same as exclusion from the ballot box itself. They lose on all issues. Compromise and influence are blocked.

This understanding of democratic principles effectively described the Warren Court. It was an understanding retained by one of the last remaining members of the Warren Court, Justice Byron White. Although in many respects a conservative, White remained true to the premises of democratic self-governance, deferring to the legislature, especially Congress, as the voice of the majority of the American people but willing to intervene on behalf of racial minorities and in support of voting rights where individuals or groups were excluded from the democratic process.[3] When White rejected claims of fundamental rights like abortion or private consensual sexual activities, he did it from the foundation of a strong belief in democratic rights.[4] What the people condemned, they had a right to outlaw.

The Warren Court, in the privacy cases of its later years, and the Burger Court, which created *Roe v. Wade*,[5] began to diverge from that understanding in their development of the concept of fundamental rights. *Bowers v. Hardwick*[6] was one of the Burger Court's final cases, and it brought to light the major changes taking place on the Court. White rejected the claim of homosexual rights on the basis of democratic self-government.[7] Rehnquist and other conservatives rejected the claim on the basis of moral absolutism.[8] The liberals on the Court embraced the claim, and their embrace was as much of a change as the conservative's embrace of absolutism.[9]

The liberal position could be defended on the basis that prejudice confined gays and lesbians to the closet and therefore excluded them from effective participation in the political process. That defense would fit within the traditional *Carolene Products* paradigm. The homosexual claim also pointed in another direction: a limitation of society's right to control individual behavior because it's nobody else's business. That was also the point of *Roe v. Wade*: not that women are politically underrepresented but that their sexual and reproductive decisions are nobody else's business.[10] One might have argued for reproductive rights on the ground that men are not legally subjected to comparable demands on their bodies, except historically in wartime.[11] Whether or not that argument would have been persuasive, it was not the course the liberals took. The point from *Roe* to *Bowers* to *Casey* was privacy.

The issue of privacy, while newly expanded, was not new to Western philosophy. It has several sources. In the utilitarian tradition of Bentham and Mill, the state just does not have a good chance of legislating for people's self-interest better than they can decide for themselves.[12] As long as people do not harm one another, their decisions are none of the state's business because the state will probably make things worse. In the libertarian tradition of John Locke and Tom Paine, the issue is the sacredness of the individual and the respect due to each person, most particularly including rights of conscience.[13]

Utilitarianism is crudely defined by the preference for policies that bring the "greatest good for the greatest number."[14] Utilitarians try to compare the advantages and disadvantages people receive from different courses of action and take the direction that creates the most happiness, or what they would call utility.

Strictly speaking, utilitarian philosophy is dead. It was killed by Hitler and Stalin and is constantly reinterred by the genocidal rampages in Southeast Asia, the former Yugoslavia, and Africa, as well as the attacks on the remnants of the Indian populations in various parts of the Americas. It is simply no longer possible to believe that the people are entitled to whatever they want enough or that we can just compare the desires of different people and do whatever shows the weight of desire among the population. Some desires are simply unacceptable. In that sense we are all now libertarians.

There are many more subtle criticisms of utilitarianism, and they are very important to a close examination of utilitarianism. In fact, the charge that utilitarianism countenances genocide if only enough people will it is not entirely a fair one and would quite clearly have been rejected on utilitarian grounds by the founders and leaders of the movement.[15] Justifying why that should be so has been a difficulty of utilitarianism and the events of this century have led philosophers to come up with or return to systems of thought that are more clearly and explicitly individualistic in the sense that the dignity and protection of individuals is an irreducible minimum.[16]

In another sense we are all also utilitarians, making just those comparisons instinctively when the issues are not ones of such basic rights. Utilitarianism is agnostic about most values, which is why conservatives refer to utilitarianism as relativist. The issue is not what values we hold but what makes people happy. Essentially, the one built-in value of utilitarianism is happiness—subject now in this popular utilitarianism only to the caveat that no one has the right to benefit from great injury to others.

The fact that privacy is embedded in both the libertarian and utilitarian traditions makes the various positions on *Roe* and *Bowers* tremendously significant. The rejection of the right to be let alone where others are unharmed is fundamentally a rejection of the underlying liberal and utilitarian traditions. As we have shown, that different foundation for conservative thought matters.

The acceptance of the right to be let alone where others are unharmed is an embrace of some combination of those liberal and utilitarian traditions. That too matters, as we are about to explore. There are two parts to this liberal approach. One part is a continuing embrace of democratic rights as described in *United States v. Carolene Products Co.*[17] but limited now by a larger notion of individual autonomy and dignity. Equality, voting and political rights, and protection of people from erroneous execution and incarceration remain central to this liberal prong of the more liberal justices' thought. The other part is more frankly utilitarian, weighing choices by the goods and happiness they create when these fundamental libertarian and democratic values are not involved. In assessing the impact of the utilitarianism of the apparently liberal justices, it becomes critical to discern the assumptions they make about what creates happiness.

Fundamental Propositions—Universalism, Political Rights, and Equal Treatment

For liberals, equality is the basis for the entire structure of their thought, including libertarianism and utilitarianism. Universalism is a major contribution of Western philosophy.[18] Universalism requires that everyone be treated equally according to a set of rules largely without regard to forebears or station in life. This can be very conservative, as illustrated in Anatole France's famous quip: "The law, in its majestic equality, forbids the rich as well as the poor to sleep under bridges, to beg in the streets, and to steal bread."[19] It can also be radical as it empowers the beggars no less than the titans to share in national decision making about the structure of property and economic rights.

On the Court, the conservatives have been arguing for the equal application of rules to blacks and whites and across other similar social divisions, thus staying apparently consistent with a formal interpretation of universalism, as in the Anatole France quip. They have, however, been attacking efforts made to equalize voting power or to allow majority control of property and environmental rights.

The liberals on the Court have drawn their line in the sand on the issues of actual innocence, voting rights, and equality of treatment. As described below, each of these positions is rooted in the notion of equality. The liberals, drawing on the Lockean libertarian tradition, are closely united on these issues. Their differences emerge on more utilitarian issues, stemming from differences in convictions about what works.

Protecting the Innocent. Concern to avoid the punishment or execution of innocent people is unavoidable in liberal thought. It flows directly from concern for the dignity and welfare of each person in the utilitarian tradition, and from libertarian insistence that some values, especially life and liberty, in its most basic sense of the ability to move about freely, cannot be sacrificed for the ease or convenience of government.

Herrera[20] was an easy case for liberals. Herrera offered strong evidence that he was innocent of the murders of which he had been convicted. The evidence was discovered long after his conviction, however, and, because of the delay, Texas law would not permit a court to consider it.[21] The conservative majority concluded that Texas violated no constitutional requirement and allowed the state to execute him.[22] The liberals then on the Court, Justices Blackmun, Stevens, and Souter, dissented from the decision to permit this execution;[23] they could not have justified any other conclusion.

For the liberals, *Herrera* was an easy case. Respect for the equality of all human beings required respect for Herrera's life and freedom. To execute him if he was probably innocent would treat his life as unimportant. Liberals could not do that.

Later, in *Schlup v. Delo,* after Justices Blackmun and White retired, Justices O'Connor, Ginsburg, and Breyer joined Stevens and Souter to conclude that a lower court had the power to review evidence acquired long after trial to determine whether there was ground for *habeas corpus* review.[24] Again it was an easy case for the liberals, though a hard one for O'Connor, who concurred to explain the narrowness of her decision to join the liberal bloc.[25] Again there was strong evidence that Lloyd Schlup had not committed the crime for which he was to be executed. The liberals could not justify looking the other way.

The liberal bloc is not nearly as united where procedural protections do not impair the courts' ability to protect the innocent from unwarranted conviction—questions about whether we can be searched or otherwise bothered in the process of law enforcement.[26] Those procedural questions are much less stark. They invite the justices to examine what will result in the least damage to society collectively and to the rights of people who might otherwise be the victims of criminal behavior as well as of official misbehavior. Executing an innocent person raises no such problems.

Voting Rights. The voting rights cases are also part of the liberal consensus.[27] These come up in several different contexts. One concerns whether a smaller population in one legislative district can have as much representation in the legislature as the larger population in another district. These are the apportionment cases. A second context is where the district lines are drawn in order that one party will control the legislature or a house of the legislature almost regardless of how many people vote for the other party. This is done by a variety of methods of "wasting" opposition votes. These are the gerrymandering cases. A third context involves the use of a variety of devices to suppress a racial minority. This can be done by drawing boundaries that submerge such minorities, the traditional tools of gerrymandering, or by changing the rules for candidacy or the mechanics of voting or the authority of officials.

Respect for the dignity and humanity of every individual as the starting point for law prohibits picking and choosing who can vote and who can't.[28] To pick and choose who votes is to decide whose interests to consider and whose to ignore. Again the liberals are united in attacking any tactic that smacks of such endeavors to stack the game.

Many of the recent legal battles over voting rights have involved the issue whether districts should be drawn along racial boundaries so that minorities have representation proportional to their strength in the population. If the lines are drawn strictly according to race, neither majority nor minority can be seriously overrepresented. That is a consequence of the one-person, one-vote rules: the districts have to have the same number of people to be as close to mathematical equality as possible.[29] The result is that the proportion of people who are members of minority groups in the population and the proportion of districts that are inhabited by people who are members of minority groups would have to be roughly the same. Only if the lines are drawn partly across racial boundaries can racial gerrymandering take place.

Political gerrymandering can accompany racial line drawing neverthe-less. If minority votes are concentrated into minority districts, they may be, in the parlance of those who draw district lines, wasted. If nonminor-ity voters who support the goals of minority voters are then scattered, they too are wasted. The result may be proportional to race but not to politics.[30]

In fact, the districting cases pose some very difficult factual issues, and it is not always clear that the racial line drawing that liberals have typically favored will accomplish liberal ends of equal representation.[31] Such line drawing may, in some instances, result in ghettoization and diminution of influence. In areas where voting is racially polarized, however, minorities have no influence except in districts of their own. Racial polarization is a requirement for relief under the Voting Rights Act as the Court has inter-preted it, although the judicial definition of polarization allows for some white support. Sometimes, therefore, racial districting is necessary to give minority voters a fair role in democratic governance. The result is a com-plex factual issue.

Because of those complexities, none of the doctrines adopted by any of the participants on the Court will always require the districting that is racially either most homogeneous or most mixed. Despite these complex-ities, the liberal–conservative divide on these issues is significant.

The liberals complained, first, that instead of actual injury to a vulnera-ble group, the Court has focused on whether the districting seemed to make race important, which, conservatives argue, injures the dignity of racial groups. The conservative Court has not focused on whether blacks were over- or underrepresented in legislative bodies but whether race counted in the districting process. To the liberals, that concern about the effects of government districting on attitudes about race is precious at best.[32] Given the fact that racial districting is called for only when voters are racially polarized in their views, such districting simply reflects the ob-vious.[33] For liberals, that "tenuous" risk to attitudes is certainly secondary to whether minorities have the opportunity to select or at least influence representatives who will support their objectives.[34]

The liberals objected, second, that the Court has denied minorities any avenues for treatment equivalent to whites.[35] There are several pieces to this problem. In some of the cases the majority rejected district lines that seemed to them to be drawn in a way that would divide black from white voters.[36] To understand the position of the liberal dissent, it is important to recall that racial line drawing produces proportional representation and therefore to

understand that the majority's position makes proportional representation almost impossible. In none of the cases is there or could there have been concern about the overrepresentation of minorities. In each case the problem is the underrepresentation of minorities and the right of nonmajority voters to object to efforts to cure that underrepresentation.

Adding to this difficulty, the majority objected when the districts had a majority of people who were members of racial minorities even when the districts were in fact multiracial. Three members of the majority objected that districts with black majorities were probably drawn with race in mind, and two members of the majority objected that such districts were improper in any case unless largely accidental.[37] They made no objection, however, to districts that have a majority of white persons.[38] For the dissenters, therefore, the result was to require the subordination of minority voices—a consequence not visited on other ethnic groups that are a minority of the statewide population but a majority in smaller areas, and certainly not a consequence visited on majority whites.[39] In areas where voting is polarized, this does not result in influence on the eventual winner but in total defeat.

A still greater difficulty for minority voters is created by the majority's conclusion that some racial districting is permissible where the minority group is compact, large, and united and the district accidentally coincides with their community, or where the racial considerations are otherwise not used "'too much.'"[40] That has the effect of wasting some minority voters by packing them tightly into one district and then leaving the rest as an even smaller minority in hostile districts. That effectively amounts to an antiblack gerrymander.[41] It is the traditional use of inconsistent principles in districting to make the most of one's supporters and make the least of the opposition's. That is gerrymandering at its most basic. Each of these conclusions by the conservative majority—their objections to homogeneous districts and to some black districts while accepting others—has the result of denying to blacks the benefit of forms of districting that are available to whites, and each of these conclusions results in the subordination of black to white voters.

The liberals objected, third, that the Court had no standard for political gerrymandering. In fact, without any standard for political gerrymandering, minority voters would be not only denied representation in their own right but also denied potential allegiance with sympathetic whites. Justice Stevens pointed out that Texas's delegation had been so thoroughly gerrymandered that the statewide popular vote had little relation to the shape of the legislative delegation.[42] To bar racial districting while still allowing partisan gerrymandering doubles the injury.

Finally, the liberals objected to the way the majority read the evidence to show the existence of racial intent. In effect, unlike many cases in which the majority of the justices refused to draw inferences of racial discrimination by the majority of the people in the electoral jurisdiction against local minorities, the Court strained every piece of evidence to fit the conclusion of racial bias in favor of the minority.[43]

Thus, for the dissenters, the issue has been the equivalent treatment of minority and majority voters, equivalent opportunities to elect representatives by the same means that majority voters have long used. It was about whether minority voters had been deliberately gerrymandered into oblivion and whether federal and state officials could use traditional techniques to counter that history.

The objective on the part of the liberals is evident in the consistency of their approach to these issues. They have been consistent in their insistence on the one-person, one-vote principle and their support of meaningful enforcement of the Voting Rights Act. The liberal position on the Voting Rights Act will not, in fact, produce the maximum political gains for minorities. That would require a definition of political gerrymandering.[44] Nevertheless, the liberal position is aimed at equal voting rights and is more likely to approximate that objective than the majority position, which rejects both a stringent definition of political gerrymandering and the use of racial line drawing in the enforcement of the Voting Rights Act.

Similarly, the liberal justices have objected when the Court permitted communities covered by the Voting Rights Act to reshape government offices so that elected blacks would not hold the power their predecessors did[45] or to rearrange the size of governing bodies so that large electoral districts would overwhelm black voters who would have been able to participate in government were the districts smaller.[46] None of these liberal conclusions would give blacks more power than their numbers permit. The liberal justices insist instead on voting systems that allow the expression of minority voting power on the same terms that white voting power has been expressed in the past.

Freedom of Speech. Free speech is essential to democracy. Democracy and associated speech rights come in many guises. Most essentially, democracy requires a choice among competing aspirants to power.[47] Democracy here and in England existed first for aristocrats before it was broadened to include the general public. For conservatives, it may have been sufficient to allow a voice to major political institutions.[48] For liberals, democracy and associated speech rights had and have a much broader meaning. Democracy must include all the people, and speech rights must reflect that.

On the other hand, democracy has at times governed aspects of society we no longer find appropriate.[49] The founders withdrew religious matters from popular control partly because it was necessary for the public peace, partly out of a variety of skeptical views, and partly because rights of conscience were too personal and private. Liberals have extended that understanding to other behavior that causes no harm to nonconsenting others. Speech rights for liberals broadened, not to aid democracy but to respect the autonomy of individual choices.

The liberal bloc has been almost solid on free speech cases.[50] Quite recently Justice Stevens wrote for all members of the Court except Justice O'Connor and Chief Justice Rehnquist, striking down some of the provisions of the statute regulating inclusion of material that is "indecent" but not "obscene" on the Internet.[51] It was an easy case for liberals unwilling to confine adults to materials deemed acceptable for children according to a fastidious Congress and whoever would enforce the statute.

There have been exceptions. In one, Justice Breyer was willing to subordinate speech values to protect accident victims from solicitations by lawyers for a month (though the statute did not prohibit or delay contact by insurance agents) and Justices Stevens, Souter, and Ginsburg were not. Breyer, utilitarian in his instincts, balanced what may have been conflicting desires for information and privacy.[52]

Another exception involved a challenge to the rules that required that cable companies carry certain television signals. The Court has objected particularly strenuously when regulation differentiated among speech on the ground of the viewpoint of the speech. This has been known as the requirement of viewpoint neutrality. The Court has also objected, though a bit less consistently, where regulation differentiated among speech, not on the basis of its viewpoint but on the basis of subject matter. That has been known as the requirement of content neutrality. Viewpoint neutrality was not in issue in *Turner Broadcasting System v. F.C.C.,*[53] and the Court, including some of the liberal justices, concluded that the regulations were acceptable because they were content-neutral, that is, the regulations did not say anything about subject matter. Of the liberals on the Court, only Justice Ginsburg advocated the traditional free speech position in this case. She concluded that content neutrality requires "close scrutiny" and that the must-carry provisions were not neutral with respect to content.[54] Instead, they were created to preserve local programming. She added that over-the-air broadcast television does not appear to be at risk, and that protecting broadcast television is not entirely independent of Congress's content preferences or even necessarily more important. Ginsburg also joined a partial dissenting opinion written by Justice O'Connor, who identified rules regarding educational television, diversity, news, and public affairs, all as content preferences.[55] O'Connor and Ginsburg argued that there are legitimate ways that Congress can advance those objectives, but not by restriction on what cable operators may carry.

Market structure cases like *Turner* can be difficult for liberals because they see competing objectives. On the one hand, they firmly resist censorship, concerns embodied in the Court's neutrality rules. On the other hand, they seek to improve the marketplace of ideas so that people have maximum accurate information and analysis. That appears to be consistent with the purposes of the First Amendment. There is no clear understanding, however, of what principles would do that. So liberals are somewhat at sea with the rest of us examining the structural decisions of Congress and the Federal Communications Commission.

Another interesting case that initially looks like an exception involved government assessments from fruit growers that were in turn used for government speech on behalf of the fruit grown.[56] Some of the growers objected, however. Here three liberals (Stevens, Ginsburg, and Breyer) plus Justices O'Connor and Kennedy thought the requirements were fine, but three conservatives (Rehnquist, Scalia, and, in part, Thomas) joined Justice Souter in dissent.

The historic liberal position, however, has been to see both the opportunity for collective speech (here the governmentally required marketing collective on behalf of the growers) and the opportunity for dissent as speech rights. For different reasons, both liberals and conservatives have supported collective speech and opportunities for dissent in other situations. Their positions have been quite different, however, on who gets what. Liberals have been much more concerned than conservatives about the coercive effect of tax rules and government speech; conservatives have been much more concerned than liberals about the coercive effect of union speech. In this case, all the fruit growers would have benefited from the collective advertising and those who refused to contribute would have reaped the benefits without paying their fair share of the costs. Many union activities have that effect: the benefits of collective bargaining and public relations in support of a strike and related activities benefit all members of the bargaining unit regardless of their own position about the union. Looking at the situation in that way, the liberals can see theirs as a decision in favor of freedom of collective speech and they can see themselves as careful to protect dissent nonetheless.[57]

Group Equality. From a utilitarian standpoint, the pleasures and pains of all people count in precisely the same way. Equality therefore means much more than apparently neutral rules. Utilitarianism, after all, is about the consequences for people, their happiness and their pain. Inequality always implies that there may be a better distribution of resources that produces more happiness because utilitarians expect a declining value of goods and services as people's wealth increases and greater happiness from those goods and services as people's wealth decreases. The utilitarian question therefore is whether inequality improves the position of those less well off.[58] It well may because of efficiencies or incentives, and similar reasons, but it is hardly automatic.[59]

Neutral rules—rules that make no mention of race, class, and other family and group characteristics—have value if and because they are acceptable and accepted as fair, prevent destructive kinds of conflict, and allow people to thrive without regard to their parentage. But not all rules are created equal. Rules that are apparently neutral may yet be adopted with an understanding of what will happen. Fairness doesn't stop at the edge of "neutral" rules when we can look at those rules and evaluate them. The equality of formal rules can look very empty and indefensible, as it did to Anatole France when he quipped about the prohibition against sleeping under bridges.

More important, from a liberal perspective, is defining a fair starting point, putting guiltless infants in reasonable positions to approach the world. Some would go further, noting that "failure" at economically defined enterprise is not equivalent to failure or worthlessness as individuals. There is a limit on the harms that are appropriate—a notion embedded in the criminal context in the Eighth Amendment's prohibition of cruel and unusual punishments. Even guilty persons are not simply fair game for whatever gore that people might want to extract. There is ultimately a sense of human dignity that everyone, equally, is entitled to.

Thus the liberal/utilitarian bloc has been fairly consistent in its support for affirmative action[60] and quite critical of claims that people are treated equally by neutral rules with plainly divergent results.[61]

Affirmative action is about strategy. The liberal goal is a world in which racial, gender, and ancestral matters do not determine one's success in life. Everyone is entitled to the same opportunities, the same liberty and autonomy. Some conservatives argue that government should treat people without regard to those characteristics regardless of consequence. Liberals, however, refuse to ignore the fact that the world acts on its prejudices. Worse, if government refuses to act, its "neutrality" will simply aggravate the prejudice of the world, rewarding credentials and successes and punishing failures that are themselves reflections of discrimination. In Justice Blackmun's famous words, "In order to get beyond racism, we must first take account of race. There is no other way."[62]

Stevens resisted that position. His resistance was based on the view that affirmative action would be counterproductive. That his views were not mere window dressing for a deeper hostility was made clear by his objection to the Court's inability to see discrimination in many of the cases before it. More recently, in *Adarand Constructors, Inc.* Stevens joined the rest of the liberal bloc supporting racial set-asides. The set-asides were rebuttable and the federal program was directed against demonstrable discrimination in construction contracts. He commented that the Court could not tell "the difference between a 'No Trespassing' sign and a welcome mat."[63]

There are similar issues of group versus individual rights and of practical consequences versus formal rules in the gender context. Ginsburg for her part helped to create the ACLU Women's Rights Project and served as its director. In her view, men and women get the same rights; consideration of differences and different needs is dangerous.[64] Thus pregnancy requires protection as a disability, just like male disabilities of various sorts, not because women have special needs. Some feminists argue that women are not just entitled to whatever men have, or whatever is equivalent to what men have, but that they are entitled to what they specially need. Ginsburg's view is less far-reaching. Her view of sexual equality is significant, nevertheless, because of the breadth of her appreciation of the causes and consequences of gendered inequality.

Ginsburg stunned portions of the feminist community with her views about procreative rights. She has argued, repeatedly, that the Burger Court should not have dealt with the Texas abortion statute at issue in *Roe v. Wade* by creating a set of medical categories—all it needed to have done was to find the Texas statute too extreme and let state legislatures continue to grapple with the problem.[65] That point is partly political, a view of judicial restraint that is informed by the Court's political weakness.[66] It would allow legislatures to take into account the view that women are not the only people affected in these decisions. Thus a less extreme law than Texas's might be permissible.

At the same time she has argued that academic criticism could have been muted had the Court focused on gender equality rather than sexual autonomy. Her point essentially is that the consequences of reproduction are very different for women than for men, in very stressful ways and in ways that cut off and restrict women's life choices. She argues that this is not because of anatomy but because of the way that society handles the consequences in a gender-specific way.[67] The logic of her position leads to the conclusion that if the burdens and stigma of pregnancy were shared by men equally, then it might be constitutionally permissible not to protect a right to abort. In other words, she does support protection for abortion rights, but as a consequence and limited by the existence of gendered inequalities. She might also agree with Guido Calabresi that if there were general obligations to permit the use of our "extra" organs like kidneys and bone marrow that applied to both genders, then the pregnancy issue might not have to be seen as so special.[68] What Ginsburg finds is pervasive inequality. If the inequality were rooted out, society might have a greater right to make decisions about issues like procreation and birth control.

The conservative conception of equality has very different roots from hers; free will, social Darwinism, and adherence to formal rules are central to conservatives' understanding of equal protection. As Ginsburg's treatment of abortion makes clear, her view is not aimed at the will or even narrowly at the state but at pressure and society. Equality is not a matter of equal application of formal rules but of equal life chances, limited by the practical requirements of an imperfect world.

Religion. Religious autonomy is central to liberalism. Although conservatives charge liberals with supporting "secular humanism," that is a fundamental misdescription. Liberals are quite committed to individual autonomy—that is the essence, the core of liberalism. Nothing is more central than freedom of belief and freedom to believe. Liberalism is not anti-God; it is against official constraint or interference. Faith is between an individual and his or her maker and religious institution. It is not a matter for official guidance. That would inevitably take sides among religious choices. Government would be a particularly untrustworthy religious leader. It would channel prejudices toward people who hold different, though not harmful, religious views.

Even conservatives like O'Connor and Kennedy feel the pull of this brand of liberalism. O'Connor argues that government must not endorse any religious view or practice. Her nonendorsement test is a kind of neutrality test. Kennedy draws the line at coercion of individual views or practices, but he too has argued for official neutrality among faiths at least with respect to the state's regulatory authority.

The liberal position does not force the state to leave divinity out of school; schools can teach about religion and religious beliefs if they do not adopt any. Still, liberals permit schools to remain silent, viewing religious institutions as adequate and more appropriate to define relationships between religious and secular subjects.

Moreover, liberalism is not neutral about multiculturalism, including religious multiculturalism. Exposure to different peoples and practices expands the horizons, understanding, and ultimately choices of all. Ben Franklin expressed a liberal view in his autobiography when he praised the Dunkers for their refusal to treat any set of religious views as final Truth but insisted on continual search for better understanding.[69]

For those reasons, state-run education can, inexplicitly, encourage secular humanism. To that extent it is not entirely neutral. It cannot condemn religion because that would violate autonomy, but it can teach without examining religious perspectives. In order to avoid coercion among faiths, it is permitted to act as if faith does not matter. A liberal's response is that any other official posture would be more, not less, coercive. Ultimately, complete neutrality is impossible and liberals opt for diversity.[70]

Their objective, whether or not successfully pursued, is to take the state out of religious wars. These conflicts are evident in *Kiryas Joel*,[71] a case we discussed briefly in an earlier chapter but that deserves a fuller discussion in this context. A community of Hasidic Jews had settled in the Monroe-Woodbury school district. Most of the children were educated in parochial schools. Education of handicapped children is expensive, however, and the community was unable to afford it. The existing school district tried a variety of solutions to work with the Hasidic community, but the Hasidim eventually decided that the ridicule to which their children were being subjected required a school of their own. First they petitioned the legislature to create a new village. That was done under preexisting New York law and was legally unobjectionable, although the village created by this petition followed the lines of the religious community precisely. Any community, if it desired, could have done the same. The second step, however, was to ask the legislature to create a school district that followed the boundaries of the village.

One could easily argue that the Hasidic community of Kiryas Joel was merely being allowed to do what all other communities have done—resettle, incorporate, and create a school district. Many American towns have been created by religious groups and run public schools. Many more are essentially monolithic. The Hasidim wanted to emulate that world. As a public school, moreover, it would have had to exclude religious teaching or do it comparatively, objectively, and evenhandedly—the same requirements that apply to all public schools, though often honored in the breach. The legislature had to consider the Hasidim's claim. Should this be treated as giving them what other groups have or as giving them a special favor, as removing discrimination or as discriminating in their favor?

The Court used the statutory trend rather than the history or distribution of faiths among school communities as its starting point and found the statute unconstitutional. In an opinion by Justice Souter, the Court found that the creation of the district was not constitutional because it was not done according to a law that would allow any village to qualify and was not the result of a general policy of the legislature. Instead, this was done specifically for this village. Of course, the claim against the school district was a claim of religious establishment, and it is hard to think of this minority sect of self-segregated Jews as an established religion regardless of the school district, a point Justice Scalia made in dissent.[72] For the Court, the problem was the lack of neutral, secular definitions of the districting policy.[73]

For liberals committed to autonomy and equality, *Kiryas Joel* is very troubling. On the one hand, this could easily, with considerable justification, be viewed as an accommodation to protect a discrete and insular minority, to give it a measure of equality rather than to prefer, exalt, or damage it. This is leveling up to a standard of functional equality. On the other hand, it threatened a relationship between states and religion that liberals fear. Even if the Hasidim were treated less well than others in fact, the principle of state neutrality is crucial for liberals.

This is the converse of affirmative action. Instead of looking at the map and seeking equality, they looked at the principle and sought neutrality. Liberals seem less concerned about the substance of equality here. They may have bought into the common belief that Jews are no longer at risk, even though this sect of Jews is hardly accepted. They may have concluded that there was no principle on which they could measure equal treatment other than tearing down the "wall" between church and state, a wall they are committed to preserving.

Ginsburg joined Stevens's concurring opinion in *Board of Education of Kiryas Joel Village School District v. Grumet*.[74] The state, the local school district, and the people of the village of Kiryas Joel tried in a number of ways to ease the cultural clash among the disabled Hasidic schoolchildren of Kiryas Joel and the children of the Monroe-Woodbury school district in which they had been included by creating a separate school district limited to the town of Kiryas Joel. Nevertheless, Stevens's opinion concluded that teaching tolerance could have solved the problems posed by integrating the groups in a single school, and he expressed concern that the state, instead, isolated the groups and thereby increased the likelihood that members of each group would stay within the fold.[75] With Ginsburg in agreement, he found that to be a religious establishment. Multiculturalism is the one true liberal faith, supporting autonomy, and combating prejudice.

Property Rights. The positions of liberals and conservatives on the Court have somewhat reversed in the last decade. In a set of cases the conservative justices then on the Court argued that due process rights should be assimilated to property rights and limited to whatever the states provided. If the states said one had a right to a job and might be dismissed only for cause, but the state nevertheless created a very arbitrary procedure that left public employees at the whim of their superiors, the conservatives said people must take the "bitter with the sweet" and had no right to appeal.[76] Stevens, writing for the Court, supported then by the Court's conservative justices, was very explicit: property rights are designed by the state; they are not prepolitical, overriding positive law.[77] The liberal members then on the Court defended a right to careful procedures for a broad range of property interests.[78]

The conservatives now treat property rights as beyond state control. The majority—Rehnquist, O'Connor, Scalia, Kennedy, and Thomas—have concluded that the states could not bar all building on coastal plains without compensating some of the property owners,[79] could not offer variances from zoning or other property restrictions in exchange for public access to the shoreline or for other public amenities, even though the property owner took advantage of the variance as better than the preexisting situation or had the option to turn it down if it were not.[80]

Mirroring the conservative shift, the entire liberal bloc has rejected the conservative majority's effort to limit the power of the state through the just compensation requirement of the Fifth Amendment. Stevens, however, has been consistent in this respect, perhaps because he has migrated from a position once closer to the conservatives to a position now closer to the liberals. He has stuck to the position that property rights are defined by the states, not by the Constitution. As a result, he has dissented from the recent line of takings cases, along with Ginsburg, Souter, Blackmun, and later, Breyer, who replaced Justice Blackmun. Their position is much more consistent with the outlook on property cases that prevailed from 1937 to 1987, in which the Court deferred to legislative judgment on economic matters.[81]

Once again the liberals spoke from a utilitarian rather than a libertarian position. Rights are not simply inalienable as the Declaration of Independence put it. Instead, they are defined by their usefulness. Property rights that inhibit the ability of the public to provide for the population at large and for future generations are therefore not supported.[82]

In this respect, as the conservatives realized, the utilitarians on the Court are faithful to the founders' design.[83] The founders would not have used and did not use the eminent domain clause to limit the regulation of property, believing that would work a drastic limitation on the legislative ability to provide for the general welfare.[84] In related discussions, some members of the Constitutional Convention expressed the view that restraints on changing laws that apply to property would work an unacceptable limitation on government for the general welfare. They were careful not to limit the federal government's ability to change law, except that they prohibited ex post facto laws, which criminalize behavior after the fact. They also imposed on the states, but not the federal government, a limited restriction on altering contracts that people have already made.[85] The eminent domain clause was designed for narrower circumstances in which the government sought a specific piece of property. Nor did the founders have in mind a requirement that government could pay for land with only some kinds of concessions in return—those the conservatives find relevant and proportional to the use the public seeks.[86]

The founders' thought is not identical to modern utilitarianism but their notion of the general welfare has much in common with it nevertheless. A utilitarian judge would interfere only if allowing the regulation would damage general welfare in a way the legislature was unlikely to have considered.[87] In respect to the environmental regulations in these cases, that is an unlikely proposition.[88]

The "liberals" on the Court could have reached their position from historically liberal premises as easily as utilitarian ones. To do that, they would merely have had to understand as inalienable not only the property right in material goods but one's property in liberty. That in fact fits John Locke's seventeenth-century understanding of property. But the liberals are in the habit of talking about society's rights. Their brand of "liberalism" is very utilitarian.

Liberal Rights—Utilitarian Premises

So the "liberals" on the Court do coalesce around historically "liberal" positions. As we shall see more and more clearly below, it is not fully appropriate to describe their principles as liberal.

7

Calculus

Stevens, Ginsburg, and Breyer share a utilitarian outlook. Nevertheless, the three weigh cases quite differently. Stevens is far more focused on fairness; Ginsburg, on the social value of rules but also alert to intense personal sacrifice; and Breyer, on efficiency. Despite Stevens's strong conservative credentials, those differences are enough to make him stand out as the Court's liberal beacon.

Balancing, Comparisons, and Rules

The utilitarian foundation of the elements of liberal consensus is also the starting point for disagreement among the liberal justices. Utilitarians compare benefits and burdens for different people and whole communities. Such comparisons are very problematic, imprecise matters of judgment. It is not truly possible to compare the benefits and burdens to different people.

Utilitarians try to ignore this problem, partly by counting everyone as equal and generally, but not always, counting the effects of identical benefits and burdens as equal in their effects on different people. The exceptions are circumstances where one may expect diminishing returns, such as dollars for the rich and the poor, medicine for the sick and the healthy, and so on. Economics also developed in part to try to ignore the comparison problem by assuming that even if we couldn't measure the benefits and burdens of goods, services, and policies to different people, we could at least tell the best distribution by means of markets. It has turned out that markets don't do that either, partly because they are very sensitive to the initial distribution of resources.[1]

Therefore, many modern liberals have tried to avoid the comparability problem altogether.[2] Rawls developed what he called the veil of ignorance, in which he tried to imagine what people would do if they did not know what their actual life situations would be.[3] Ronald Dworkin has tried to examine what an individual would do if he or she were making decisions about his or her life at birth without knowing the actual circumstances of his or her life.[4] In this way he has examined the health care debate without having to compare babies with the elderly. Instead, he examines what any single individual would do in arranging for lifelong insurance.

A third approach has been to abandon comparability for some purposes and retain it for others. Thus in *United States v. Carolene Products*,[5] the Supreme Court held that for most issues it simply would not examine the benefits and burdens. Those issues were for the democratically elected branches of state and federal governments. Only on issues of basic democratic liberties would the Court intervene.[6]

Even with respect to basic liberties a major debate took place. One wing of the Warren Court, led by Justice Hugo Black, thought about rights in a more inalienable way and argued that there was nothing to compare on the basic constitutional protections; the Constitution did the balancing and if it said government could not do something, there was nothing to balance. Another wing of the Court, led by Justice Felix Frankfurter, thought about rights in a more utilitarian way and said that rights had to be balanced either with other rights or with other necessities of government. It turns out that some, but not all, of what the Court has described as compelling government interests that justify limitations of rights can be traced to the same constitutionally recognized values protected in the Bill of Rights and other constitutional protections.[7] Ultimately, in a sense, both Black and Frankfurter won—and lost. Black's conclusions about the proper results in the cases have been far more enduring, but Frankfurter's balancing model for thinking about problems has been much more enduring.

Utilitarians can, and many do, believe that it is better for everybody to treat certain individual rights as inalienable, as not up for grabs, almost regardless of the circumstances. They may, for example, despise certain things that people say but believe that it is much better to have a rule that government has no right to decide whether what people say is okay. They may believe that there is a slippery slope, so that allowing government to regulate some speech risks allowing government to regulate much more important speech. They may believe that some personal rights and needs are too important to allow intrusion and interference.

We call this group rule utilitarians because they want to work on the basis of rules rather than evaluate each new situation independently. Hostage taking is a good example although not one likely to confront the justices. Paying ransom may be utilitarian if one looks only at the current situation but may not be utilitarian if one believes that a rule against such payment would discourage hostage takers.[8] Whether one looks at the rule or the system or looks only at the current facts is itself dependent on one's empirical beliefs. For rule utilitarians, a good deal of what is in the Bill of Rights works as inalienable rights, as rights that should not be treated as up for grabs even when they create problems in individual circumstances. In fact, some of the liberals on the Court have attacked other liberals on the Court on the ground that they compare and balance the interests of different people when they should not.[9]

Stevens, Souter, Ginsburg, and Breyer are most certainly rule utilitarians to a degree. They support a group of fundamental rights as largely inalienable and not up for grabs. They are not willing to force some individuals to make large sacrifices so that others can make small gains. With that qualification, and particularly among claims of important rights, all the liberals on the Court are willing to engage in some interpersonal comparison, comparisons between different people so that the happiness of one counts against the pain of another. To that extent, they are all utilitarian or share that important facet of utilitarianism.

It is no small matter to figure out what rule will cause how much pain and to whom, or how many people will be affected by it. Thus, utilitarians differ enormously on the basis of their assessment of causal relationships in the real world. At that point they are very much affected by the great debates among the proponents of the major twentieth-century worldviews. From those different worldviews about the appropriate ways to improve the national welfare, or the general welfare, flow very different answers to the major issues that confront the Court—structural questions like federalism, the extent of national power, the use of regulatory or market-based mechanisms, and questions of social justice, the role of unions, and the proper way to show concern for workers and the poor.

A utilitarian could also simply assume that the legislature has it right. Judgments about cause and effect are not the peculiar province of the courts, and legislatures are much better positioned to determine what it is that people want, what they think will make them happiest.

Stevens

Stevens is now often being called the most liberal justice on the Court.[10] There are some senses in which that is true. A simplistic view of liberalism, however, obscures as much as a simplistic view of conservatism, and in fact obscures the conservatism of John Paul Stevens.

The most insightful study of Stevens's work to date attempted to explain the differences between Stevens and both wings of the Court by characterizing Stevens as a liberal follower of John Stuart Mill, emphasizing dignity and an antipaternalist view.[11] If that were true, it is not clear why Stevens began his tenure nearly as close to Rehnquist, O'Connor, Scalia, and Kennedy as to Brennan and Marshall and long remained not much more distant from the radically conservative justices.[12] Indeed, when liberal justices had a major presence on the Court, Stevens reached very different conclusions from theirs.[13]

Commentary on Justice Stevens has also identified him as a "balancer," a common law lawyer who likes to examine all factors involved in decision making.[14] Balancing has deeper jurisprudential implications. A preference for balancing factors instead of reaching categorical conclusions tells us nothing about how much the items in the scale will be deemed to weigh or who will assign the weights. Balancing requires a judicial philosophy in order to make the comparisons balancing involves.

Stevens himself made the connection to John Stuart Mill as the source of some of his thoughts about the meaning of dignity, independence, and equality.[15] Mill began as a disciple of Jeremy Bentham, the first great apostle of utilitarianism, and went on to publish the tract *On Liberty*, which many would identify as the foundation of a modern libertarian view that people have rights that government may not invade. If we treat the inalienability of rights as the core of a liberal view (*liberal* is the classic term, but I often call the view libertarian to emphasize the distinction between this defense of rights and political liberalism), *On Liberty* is not particularly liberal. *On Liberty* is, in fact, quite utilitarian in many of its arguments, based not on individual rights but social benefits. Its foundation is in the independence of each person and the foolishness of believing paternalistically that the government knows better what might be good for any individual. Thus, Mill argued for individual freedom to choose unless that freedom interfered with the liberty of others. The First Amendment is central to that project because free speech and conscience are the foundations of individual judgment.[16] Liberty in Mill's analysis, however, is logically conditional, not absolute or inalienable.

History has not been terribly kind to Mill. It turns out to be very hard to identify where the freedom of one interferes with the liberty of another. It also turns out to be very hard to identify what individual independence means; the critical legal studies movement has zeroed in on the interrelatedness of each individual so that we all reflect the cultures in which we were socialized, making the independence at the core of liberalism hard to define or defend.[17] Liberty and utility have come to seem at cross-purposes as well.[18] Although some have tried to describe the objective of law as human dignity,[19] that too is sufficiently ambiguous that, without further specification, it could easily lead to positions on either the liberal or conservative wing of the Court.

Sounding more like a liberal than a utilitarian, Stevens defended the concept that the Court should protect fundamental rights that are not explicitly labeled in the Constitution:

> [S]ome of the values found in the Constitution that the Court has found appropriate to protect based on examination of the history of the country and a feeling for the traditions that have motivated people throughout the two hundred years that we have had the Constitution are totally legitimate even though the Court has had to rely on nothing more specific than a vague reference to the word liberty in the fourteenth amendment of the Constitution.[20]

His explanations of the fundamental rights he identified, however—rights to travel, marry, and raise a family—were based on traditions, not philosophy.[21] Stevens's judgments about the meaning of law are clearly geared less to his understanding of individual rights than of the general welfare. He is often willing to sacrifice individual claims to what he understands as the general welfare.[22] He made that very clear in the flag-burning case.[23] That was an easy call for anyone steeped in libertarian traditions. Texas wanted to protect the flag because of its symbolic value. The prosecutor didn't care about the danger of fire in a public place; other statutes regulate that risk. Nor was he concerned about private property; other statutes regulated theft and damage to property. Instead, the point of Texas's statute and of the prosecutor was that Johnson was expressing contempt for the flag as a way to underscore his anger at the Reagan administration and certain Dallas corporations.[24] The state and the prosecutor were happy to have people use the flag to show pride in the country and its policies and traditions. Johnson's speech was on the wrong side of the patriotism issue. For civil libertarians, that is not even a close call. The First Amendment prohibits government from suppressing speech because of its point of view. The Court had been quite consistent in taking that position over several decades. Given that record, what was astonishing was that four justices, Stevens included, dissented. Stevens balanced and decided patriotism mattered more than the freedom to attack the flag as a symbol of American policy. There is little reason to see Stevens as a Rawlsian or Dworkinian justice, redefining individual rights for an egalitarian age.

Stevens's conception of the general welfare is best understood as utilitarian. For example, *City of Richmond v. J.A. Croson Co.*[25] concerned the legitimacy of set-asides for minority businesses in public contracts being let by the City of Richmond, Virginia. Many treat this affirmative action issue as one of inalienable rights: either a right to be treated without regard to race or a right to some form of compensatory treatment. Stevens's concurring opinion emphasized "the legitimacy of race-based decisions that may produce tangible and fully justified future benefits."[26] In other words, affirmative action might, sometimes, do more good than harm and then it might be constitutionally acceptable. Stevens decided, however, that Richmond's race-based remedy would indeed produce more harm than good. His language was instrumental rather than categorical. Not all instrumentalists are utilitarians, but Stevens's opinion compares the benefits and costs for different people in a way that is typical of utilitarian thinking. Stevens pointed to the benefits of an integrated faculty for students or an integrated police force for the community as examples that might justify a race-based remedy. In each case the benefits flow to a community or a portion of it, like schoolchildren, while the costs, lost jobs, are borne by a very different group of people. By contrast, he commented that it would prove almost impossible to figure out who might have been injured by the discrimination in Richmond so that nothing should be done on that score. Stevens did not mention his philosophy in those comments, but the juxtaposition of utilitarianism to liberalism could not have been more pointed; he was concerned about welfare, not rights.

Utilitarians, of course, want rules that maximize human happiness.[27] All human conditions and arrangements are measured against that standard. For that reason, utilitarians share with liberals a fundamental agnosticism about what will be best. They want to know what people want. They are not paternalistic because they do not assume, and to the extent that they do not assume, that they can better choose for people than people can choose for themselves.[28] They are also agnostic about the economic market. Sometimes markets work for the benefit of the public; sometimes they don't. Whether they do is a question of fact, not ideology or principle.[29] Stevens wants to know how badly people are being injured and what the alternatives are.[30] That has been read methodologically as balancing. The underlying jurisprudence is utilitarian or very much like it.

If utilitarian judges believe that a legislature is pursuing the same goal—trying to maximize the public welfare—then utilitarian judges may be quite deferential toward the legislature.[31] Stevens shows considerable deference toward legislatures.[32] Indeed, many of Stevens's efforts are directed toward understanding what the legislature seeks. In this, he seems to fill in the blanks with the assumption that the legislature was concerned about the welfare of all the individuals involved. Thus Stevens frequently differs from his conservative colleagues with respect to the meaning of legislation.

If the legislature has allowed great harm to develop, however, a utilitarian may believe that the legislature has miscalculated and step in. That has been clear in cases like *Herrera*,[33] where the rules did not permit a hearing to consider evidence discovered years after the original conviction. For Stevens, the harm, the possible loss of an innocent life, exceeded the cost of further careful review of the facts of Herrera's case.[34] For a utilitarian, *Herrera* was not a hard case.

It is useful here to take a digression to Stevens's left. For liberals like Brennan and Marshall, the answers to many claims of right were as obvious as Herrera's was to Stevens. Brennan and Marshall might simply have been utilitarians who had such firm prior convictions about the consequences of denials of rights that they no longer had any serious balancing to do. They might have seen rights as important for society, acting as the basis of a successful, peaceful, and productive society.[35]

Brennan's and Marshall's more categorical approach could have been the result of a Kantian or fundamental rights jurisprudence instead of a utilitarian one. In a Kantian jurisprudence, rights are treated as virtually inviolable regardless of social benefit. Kant argued that people should be treated as ends in themselves, not as means to the ends of others.[36] The central weakness of utilitarianism is that it permits the sacrifice of the interests of some people for the benefit of others.[37] That sacrifice conflicts with many philosophical systems. Where fundamental individual rights are sacrificed, that is a particularly oppressive result.[38] Hitler posed a not unanticipated theoretical challenge to utilitarians. Mill had argued a century earlier that sacrificing individuals for the sake of the multitude would have disastrous results.[39] It does not matter, in fact, for most utilitarians how many Nazis would have taken how much pleasure in exterminating Jews, Gypsies, and other "non-Aryans." Still, utilitarian theory struggles for explanations about why that should be so.

Thus liberals learned to "take rights seriously," in Dworkin's phrase, either as rule utilitarians or by jumping off the utilitarian wagon entirely in favor of Kantian, categorical, liberal systems.[40] The Bill of Rights exists not as weights in a scale but as trumps that are "the supreme law of the Land."[41] In effect, many of us take rights seriously in the face of genocide and other atrocities. That can be reflected in Brennan's and Marshall's more categorical conclusions.

We need to go a step further because both liberals and conservatives can argue from either utilitarian or categorical nonbalancing premises. Indeed, in a recent example all nine justices joined opinions in a balancing mode. Stevens, O'Connor, Kennedy, Souter, Thomas, Ginsburg, and Breyer balanced the value of greater mental health by protecting privacy against the value of the testimony that mental health professionals might provide about their patients, and concluded that communications with one's mental health professional deserved a legal privilege.[42] Scalia and Rehnquist responded in a balancing mode that psychotherapists are not so important. Conservatives can be utilitarians who, inverting the position of Marshall and Brennan, have such firm prior convictions about the consequences of the rights themselves that they no longer have any serious balancing to do. In effect, rights can be dangerous, especially if expansively interpreted; they may subvert established traditions, social order, national or personal security. Rights could be seen as merely personal, taking advantage of society's forbearance, precisely contrary to the more liberal option of treating rights as socially constructive and essential. Conservatives need not, however, read the Constitution in a utilitarian manner. Instead, conservatives can adopt a categorical position hostile toward rights, in which conservative values like security, order, or tradition cannot be balanced. Finally, conservatives may simply impose their own "traditionalist" values on the text or history of the Constitution. In effect, both liberals and conservatives come in different flavors, and the flavors matter: they change the method of analysis, the issues treated seriously, and some of the results.

So Stevens's utilitarianism needs considerable fleshing out. Nevertheless, it should be clear already that Stevens's approach differs from both the conservative wing of the Court, and the liberal wing when there was one. His balancing methodology reflects a fundamentally utilitarian attitude that differs considerably from the moralizing approach of the conservatives and the categorical approach of his late liberal colleagues. He takes his values largely as he believes society defines them and implements them largely without strong assumptions about the importance of rights or governmental power. This is not to say that Stevens is apolitical or neutral; his crucial and quite political assumption is that society should be understood in a utilitarian manner, as trying to maximize the general welfare, and not imposing private moralizing on one another.

Stevens's utilitarianism is pervasive. It may come as a surprise to some, for example, that Stevens claims to believe in federalism. He wants states to have "the maximum freedom to experiment with new ideas and new approaches to problems that arise throughout society."[43] But his support for the states is conditional. He finds it hard to credit interpretations that do not serve what he understands as the general welfare—indeed, a populist thread seems to run through his opinions in areas that involve economic issues.[44]

Stevens's balancing and utilitarian approach is reinforced by another aspect of Stevens's thought, his realism. He wants to examine the consequences of legal rules or opinions and prefers not to take those consequences on faith or to accept logical implications alone.[45] In *Croson*, for example, he insisted that it was important to compare and distinguish the impact that affirmative action would have in education from that in public contracts. Realism requires that one look at impact because legal rules are designed to cause consequences. The proper interpretation is the interpretation that causes the intended or desired consequence.[46] Similarly, Stevens has struggled for years to introduce a fairly realistic assessment of motive by inferring motive from the natural and probable consequences of the actions taken.[47]

This realism may account for Stevens's opposition to giving police and public officials immunity from liability for their official misbehavior and his preference for leaving the door open to proof of abusive behavior.[48] For example, Stevens attacked the Court's decision in *California v. Hodari D.* because it invited intimidating and coercive behavior.[49] The Court had decided that when police officers give chase they have not seized the person they are chasing. That decision had the legal result that the Fourth Amendment, which requires that the officers behave reasonably, does not apply to police chases. Stevens worried about "the protections that undergird our adversarial system" when the Court allowed law officers to interrogate a defendant without counsel even though the defendant did have counsel in another pending case.[50] He worried about the possibility of convicting the innocent because of the harshness of a procedural rule designed to even the gender balance in court but that nevertheless excluded possibly significant evidence from a criminal trial.[51] He was concerned about jury bias because bilingual jurors were excluded in *Hernandez v. New York*.[52] He continually worried about the factual accuracy of criminal verdicts as opposed to merely procedural concerns.[53] Procedural concerns where guilt is not an issue may be counterproductive—certainly a hotly contested view because of competing considerations, but niceties that interfere with accurate verdicts in criminal cases do threaten important values. Similarly, in a First Amendment case, it was inevitable that a realistic justice would join Blackmun's majority opinion in expressing the fear that discretion in setting fees for parades would lead to abuse.[54]

Stevens's balancing and his realism serve the deeper utilitarianism of the justice. Indeed his utilitarianism both provides a rationale for his interpretive method and helps to explain what he puts on the scales. It is a philosophy so deeply ingrained in the culture that it is easy to miss its presence, but it is a powerful worldview nonetheless.

The Newer Members of the Liberal Bloc: Ginsburg

Justice Ginsburg came to the Court from a strong, almost mythic position in the civil liberties and gender movements. Thus, it is easy to assume that she should be placed squarely in the liberal tradition. Ginsburg, however, is plainly willing to make the comparisons that typify a utilitarian approach to law. There is also a strong formalist pull in Justice Ginsburg's work, an effort to mask the choices and make legal decisions appear inevitable. In fact, Justice Ginsburg has been touted as an individual who tries to adhere to law as it has been handed down, respecting precedent and deciding cases in a technical way. One aspect of that technical side of Justice Ginsburg is extensive use of the common law to explain the meaning of later legal rules. As we noted in the chapter on Justice Thomas, that can transform judicial activism and restraint, but Ginsburg disagrees with more conservative colleagues about the meaning of the common law tradition.

One can see Justice Ginsburg's formalism in a case like *International Union, UMWA v. Bagwell*.[55] In that case, a lower court judge had imposed a fine of $52 million against a union for breach of an injunction order. The Supreme Court reversed on the ground that this was a criminal contempt order and that a criminal contempt order required a jury trial. In reaching that decision, Justice Blackmun's majority opinion concluded that criminal contempt was more appropriate to these events that took place outside the court because of the more stringent rules about fact-finding and the procedural protections in the criminal contempt process. Ginsburg, however, refused to join that portion of his opinion. She argued simply that the Court had consistently used the distinction and that the parties presented their arguments based on it. Chief Justice Rehnquist joined her opinion. Such cases illustrate her concern with "rule of law virtues of consistency, predictability, clarity, and stability."[56]

Her acceptance of the controlling authority of the common law is evident in cases like *Heck v. Humphrey*.[57] There Justice Scalia wrote for the Court that the common law defines the extent of official liability for improper imprisonment under the federal statute known as § 1983 and should be determined by analogy or reference to the common law tort of malicious prosecution.[58] Justice Souter attacked the use of the common law as an appropriate analogy. Ginsburg joined the majority opinion. In *Honda Motor Co., Ltd. v. Oberg*,[59] Honda challenged a punitive damage award of $5 million, more than five times the amount that the jury had awarded plaintiff for actual injuries. The Court examined Oregon's procedure in cases in which juries are permitted to award punitive damages and found it insufficient. Justice Scalia concurred briefly to explain that Oregon had always allowed judges to review awards of punitive damages at common law, so as a matter of his historical view of due process, it was not now entitled to deprive defendants of that procedural protection.[60] The Court also treated that history as instructive, although in a more flexible inquiry.[61] Justice Ginsburg argued that the Court's examination of history, and implicitly Scalia's as well, was incomplete because it omitted the power of juries in the early republic.[62] She seemed to accept the reference to the common law as the appropriate baseline, however. Indeed, she joined the majority opinion in *American Dredging Co. v. Miller*,[63] which explicitly followed the Court's infamous opinion in *Southern Pacific Co. v. Jensen*,[64] infamous as the case in which Justice Oliver Wendell Holmes eloquently objected that the Court treated the common law as if it were a "brooding omnipresence in the sky."[65]

Nevertheless, Ginsburg also writes eloquently about individual facts.[66] Her approach to the meaning of constitutional provisions includes a strong endorsement of the belief that the meaning of the Constitution, the real, actual, proper meaning of the Constitution, changes. That meaning is not confined to the outlook of the founders but has "growth potential."[67] She treats gender equality as without a historical foundation "deliberately set" in the amendment process,[68] yet she treats it as firmly grounded in the Constitution nevertheless. How do those square?

She would surely argue that she is quite faithful to the Constitution. A view of the Constitution that is based on principles rather than historical examples inevitably produces an equal protection clause with changing consequences. We have changed our understanding of which people are in the same situation as one another, changed our understanding of what people are capable of, and changed our understanding of the consequences of sex roles. Women are now pushed to do much of what they were excluded from in the nineteenth century. Under those circumstances, with significant alterations in the social pressures and other conditions of women's lives and in our understanding of those realities, there is a good argument that the nineteenth-century treatment of appropriate gender differences is not true to the equal protection clause in the twentieth because the nineteenth-century understanding would now result in treating men and women who are similarly situated as if they were situated differently.

Hers is a view of constitutional interpretation that sees the draftsmen as creating principles, not sets of examples; standards, not precedents.[69] It is not just the existence of change. Life changes constantly. These changes are on point, as we often say. They change the impact of equality and inequality. They change the perception, the felt harm, and the real harm.

Thus Ginsburg's technical, rule-following, "legalistic" common-law instincts turn out to be influenced by her assessment of contemporary reality. As we shall see, those twin poles of her jurisprudence lead her to outcomes that cannot be consistently defined as either liberal or conservative.

Breyer

Justice Breyer taught at Harvard before joining the Court and wrote considerably about federal regulatory efforts. His academic writing suggests, and his judicial writing confirms, that he is best described in the realist and utilitarian traditions and their twentieth-century offshoots. Thus he shares a great deal in his fundamental philosophical approach with the work of Justices Stevens and Ginsburg. Their analyses of individual issues often differ, however, based on different instrumental views of what works and what doesn't.

Justice Breyer believes the justification for economic regulation is market failure: "Through lengthy argument, it should be possible to persuade those who advance other justifications that 'market defects' . . . lie at the bottom of their claims."[70] Economic regulation is only part of the story, however. According to Breyer, many regulations have noneconomic goals and, therefore, have to be analyzed in a very different way.[71]

Even with respect to regulation with economic objectives, there are different perspectives from which one might judge economic concepts. The point is that economics tells us about outcomes, but as Justice Breyer is careful to point out, we have to pick the type of outcomes we like.[72]

Breyer's economics is not based on libertarian thinking. He makes clear at the outset that although he is very critical of some regulation, he is not opposed to regulation in general. In fact, he believes some regulation very appropriate and well executed.[73] Nor does Breyer categorically reject the idea that at least in some circumstances government knows best, as John Stuart Mill, one of the fathers of libertarian thought, would have. Instead, it is just one form of market failure that has to be analyzed; there may be reasons, in the specific area under consideration, why people might not be able to evaluate their own self-interest properly and why, in that specific area, it is reasonable to believe that government could do it better.[74]

There are several alternatives to a libertarian approach to economics. Judge Posner, for example, once advocated treating the goal of economics as the maximization of wealth, an approach that is very seductive in light of gross national statistical measurements available. Utilitarians, however, are not interested in maximizing values that can be reduced to dollars; they seek to maximize human happiness.

It is worth a moment to compare Justice Breyer's utilitarian calculus to Posner's wealth maximization for the insights it can afford into Breyer's thinking.[75] For the wealth maximizer, the distribution of wealth is not important. A dollar is a dollar regardless of whose hands hold it. One consequence is that it may seem inappropriate to undertake expensive judicial or administrative procedures to identify who is responsible for what even if there is considerable predictable injustice. Misallocated dollars may not affect total wealth at all except to the extent that they scare people into avoiding otherwise efficient ventures. The dollars are just in different hands. Even the lives or freedom of people unjustly convicted may not justify much in the way of administrative expense if measured simply by the effect on total wealth.

To a utilitarian, by contrast, and those who adopt other consequentialist approaches based on equality and individual rights, the sense of injustice is a cost, a decrease of utility. The lives and freedom of innocent individuals have value, perhaps not economic value but great value nevertheless. Injustice toward those who have little may matter even more than injustice toward those who have much. A dollar doesn't have the same value in everyone's hands.

Justice Breyer's work makes him appear much closer to the utilitarians than the wealth maximizers for several reasons. First, Breyer is very sensitive to noneconomic values. For example, he describes the different values that people might quite reasonably place on the risk of death in different circumstances even where the percentage chance of dying is identical.[76] The economic value of life hasn't changed but people care differently about the various possibilities. Wealth isn't the whole of his thinking. Second, Breyer is sensitive to differences in affected populations. Children and the aged, for example, might rationally be treated differently.[77] The value of expenditures for the young may be greater because of their longer future; protecting the health of those in middle years may be more important because of their greater responsibilities. Dollars are not identical in different hands; we can't just add them up. Third, he does not believe that those with financial power should be able to determine what regulation is allowed. Instead, he adopts a much more egalitarian approach.[78] People, not dollars, count. Fourth, Breyer argues for the maximization of health and, implicitly, other values across the population, trading small risks in one area for easier to reach risks in another. The underlying goods that people seek, not the wealth with which they seek them, matter. The end result of Breyer's thinking is not simply the maximization of wealth but its distribution.

His apparently utilitarian approach is strongly affected by a realistic view of politics that identifies many shortcomings in standard political communication and political pressure. Thus, Breyer is inclined to try to be a sophisticated social engineer—not sophisticated in the sense of trying to design complex solutions but sophisticated in the sense of trying to determine precisely what evil is being addressed and how it interacts with other social objectives before determining how best to respond.

All Together Now

Because they are balancing all the costs and benefits, utilitarians compare the interests of the mass of society with the individual interests at stake. Generally, therefore, utilitarians are likely to put the interests of society ahead of individual interests, except where the individual interests are particularly important or the social interests particularly unimportant. For a utilitarian, environmental concerns pit the rights of the mass of society against the claims of individual property owners, a contest in which social interests will often outweigh individual ones. Thus Stevens, Souter, Ginsburg, and Breyer joined in interpreting the Endangered Species Act broadly.[79] Federalism pits national interests against partial ones.[80] Thus Stevens, Souter, Ginsburg, and Breyer dissented in *United States v. Lopez*,[81] arguing that the collective impact of the Gun-Free Schools Act on commerce established Congress's power under the commerce clause.[82] In fact, they have voted fairly consistently on the side of national power.[83] They opposed interpreting the Eleventh Amendment as a barrier that protects states from suits against them to vindicate rights under federal law—so-called federal question litigation.[84]

All this works out differently for someone with an economic mind-set like Breyer than it does for Stevens, Ginsburg, or Souter. For the four justices, cases about the Federal Employees Liability Act, securities regulation, bankruptcy, immigration, and seamen's injuries added up in very different ways. For Justice Breyer, the cases make it clear that he treats the point of utilitarianism not merely as a choice between society and individuals but as a choice about efficiency. Economic regulation pits social interests against individual burdens. Breyer looks for an efficient path among competing interests. What Breyer means by efficiency is that he prefers to accommodate social and individual interests where large benefits can be obtained for small costs. He is afraid of trying to maximize any policy, social or individual, if that last ounce of protection comes at great cost. His view of utility, therefore, is driven by the law of declining returns; he believes in precise but easy solutions.[85] Thus Breyer is comfortable with extensive securities regulation.[86] He is comfortable with giving bankruptcy judges extensive power.[87] But he is uncomfortable with unreviewable discretion.[88] He is uncomfortable with interpretations of law that leave individuals vulnerable to grievous and uncompensated losses that could more easily be spread among and borne by a group, a company, or an institution.[89] Each of Breyer's liberal colleagues cut those cases uniquely. Stevens could be described as lining up for the "little guy" in every one of those cases. Ginsburg and Souter seemed to be neither bothered by efficiency issues nor consistently concerned about ordinary people in dire straits, but they disagree on all but one of the cases!

A common framework yields very different answers. We will expand on the ways that utilitarian justices can diverge quite extensively from one another in the next chapter.

8

Where Utilitarians Diverge

The "liberals" on the Court are not committed to individual liberty. They are utilitarians in outlook, showing very centrist American assumptions. Yet they are also very different from one another. Part of the difference among the justices has already been suggested: their different emphases on fairness, efficiency, and rules. Utilitarianism is relatively open-ended. It is a balancing process that says relatively little about how to weigh whatever is in the scales. It tries to look objective by weighing everyone's happiness or utility as it seems to each. In the vast majority of situations, we have no accurate way to do that. So each of us almost inevitably generalizes from the ways that we ourselves evaluate harms and benefits to ways that we expect that other people evaluate them, thus masking or ignoring enormous differences among us. Differences about both the value of social goals and the means to get there are fair game for utilitarians. Thus, it is necessary to probe further to do justice to these jurists.

Consent, Choice, and the Ability to Structure Risk

One of the strands of thought that is central to utilitarian thinking regards the way that consent is treated. We all recognize the importance of consent in such phrases as "the consent of the governed." The idea of consent affects many legal issues, and utilitarians can treat it differently. A good place to start is by exploring what are known as ex post facto laws. Ex post facto laws penalize things that were done before the laws were passed. That is often difficult to avoid.[1] For example, changes in the tax code affect the investments and other assets that you have already acquired, perhaps some length of time past. Changes in the regulations relating to a business or profession affect activities that we are committed to because of the time, effort, and money already invested in those areas. Nevertheless, changes in taxes and regulation are essential for good government. To avoid hamstringing governments, the prohibition against ex post facto laws is generally confined to a prohibition against criminalizing past behavior.[2]

There are two fundamental reasons to prohibit ex post facto laws. One of those reasons has to do with the possibility that they allow legislatures to single out people whom they dislike for special penalties while avoiding any chance that the legislation would injure those they like. You could tailor a statute to imprison political opponents, blacks, Serbs, or Kosovars, for example. That is an instrumental reason for the prohibition: it protects something else, in this example, political rights, racial status, or national origin. The instrumental reason for the prohibition against ex post facto laws is not that it is an intrinsically basic right but that it is necessary to protect other rights, a distinction James Madison made when he introduced the Bill of Rights in the first Congress.[3] Justice Stevens was sensitive to that reasoning in his opinion in *Morales,* though his point may seem misplaced in context. In *California Department of Corrections v. Morales,*[4] the Court held that new legislation could delay parole hearings of multiple murderers whose crimes took place before the change in law. Stevens pointed out that hostility to those affected and their lack of representation could result in unfairness.

The second reason is in some ways more basic but has come to seem somewhat less convincing than it did in the founding era. Classic liberalism was about liberty. The fundamental demand of libertarian thinking is that law be arranged so that individuals could choose what would happen to them without coercion. Criminal law therefore had to be set out in advance. People who chose to do a criminal act implicitly consented to their punishment. If their penalty is changed later, they have not consented to the change. We do limit that idea by doctrines about what people ought to have known were terribly wrong. There are aspects of the Nuremberg trials that exemplify that idea—that the Nazis could be punished for their crimes against humanity because they should have known how wrong their behavior was. The continued resistance to the legitimacy of the Nuremberg trials, and even whether they stand for the proposition that people could be punished for crimes against humanity, evidences the continued power of the idea of consent to the laws under which one is punished—though of course that objection ignores the significance of consent with respect to the Nazis' victims.

In any case, consent is fundamental for utilitarians and liberals. Requiring individual consent is one way to respect each individual equally. In the

Revolutionary period, consent was the touchstone of liberty: there could be no just government without the consent of the governed. The consent of the governed initially meant only consent to the society in which we chose to live, but then over time the idea expanded so that we required consent to the governmental system under which we lived, consent to the people who became our elected representatives, and consent to the policies undertaken by the government.[5]

Consent, in fact, is a very complex concept. It is constructed as much by the society as by the individual. Society distinguishes consent from coercion based on its evaluation of which pressures it is fair for individuals to confront and which it is not.[6] There are virtually no choices any of us make that are completely unconstrained. Choices made under pressures society deems fair are treated as voluntary or consensual. Thus for modern liberals who are influenced by the analyses of consent undertaken by the legal realists early in this century and by the critical legal studies movement more recently, the idea of consent solves very little. What is important is the fairness of the constraints that limit our actual choices.

For all these reasons, issues touching consent are often deeply disturbing for liberals. Arguments based on consent often seem insufficient and unpersuasive. When someone kills others, it is not clear why that person's consent to his or her own punishment should be respected. In fact, none of these justices is a pure libertarian in that classic sense. None of them are convinced that law cannot legitimately be applied to people who have not agreed to be bound by its provisions or to invoke their legal fate by their own acts. In that sense, none of them are classic liberals, and their thinking is not tied to liberty in the sense of a generalized freedom to do as one wishes and to be penalized only as one chooses to act with known consequences.

Utilitarianism gets around liberalism's insistence on consent but at the cost of creating another difficulty, the difficulty of comparing the pains and pleasures of different people. Utilitarianism does not require that all people consent to whatever consequences may befall them. Instead, it tries to maximize pleasures while minimizing pains. It is therefore grounded in individual choices and respects them, but it requires that decision makers try to calculate the best options based on those choices. Decision makers are public officials, rather than individuals at liberty.

Utilitarians recognize that unconsented impositions are one cause of unhappiness. There are others. Thus one crucial issue for utilitarians is what assumptions they make about what is likely to bother people and how much. These considerations appear to be at the base of several recent opinions of members of the liberal bloc. Of the four, Justice Ginsburg appears more willing to dispense with the requirement of consent and thus is less libertarian than her colleagues, though not necessarily less politically "liberal."

The recent decision limiting punitive damages raises these problems for liberals. Punitive damages have long been available, premised on fairly egregious conduct, and are designed to deter potential wrongdoers since they ought to know what they are getting into. In some highly publicized cases, punitive damages have been awarded against corporations whose greed has harmed the public interest. One might expect liberals to line up to protect the award of punitive damages. Yet only Justice Ginsburg did that. More, her argument had nothing to do with that issue. She argued that judges have no standards for deciding when juries have awarded punitive damages that are too large, and that the Supreme Court will have no help from lower federal courts in defining the limits. She was joined by Chief Justice Rehnquist. They stuck to traditional doctrine, finding it unnecessary to alter long-standing rules.

The other justices in the liberal bloc voted to limit punitive damages considerably. That decision could have come out of two aspects of the utilitarian tradition. They might have decided that punitives were not utilitarian where they caused companies to be too risk averse and to stop or cut back socially productive activities for fear of lawsuits. From Breyer's perspective, that would be inefficient. So it was quite consistent with this concern for individual autonomy and consent when Justices Stevens, Souter, and Breyer, joined by Justices O'Connor and Kennedy argued that the need to respect individual autonomy required fair notice of the extent of liability and the size of the penalty before punitive damages can constitutionally be awarded. Notice gives the wrongdoer a chance to calculate the benefits of the risky behavior in accord with the actual financial risks.[7]

For similar reasons, it is troubling for liberals to allow government to seize private property from people who have done nothing wrong. In *Bennis v. Michigan,*[8] the Court, with Justice Ginsburg's vote, held that the state need not pay a woman and co-owner of a car for her share of the value of the car seized because her husband had a tryst with a prostitute in it. We will return to *Bennis* later when we discuss the quartet's handling of gender issues. Just note here the implicit judgments about consent this quartet made. Justice Stevens, joined by Justices Souter and Breyer, concluded that Mrs. Bennis should be compensated because she was not culpable and not in control of her husband's behavior. Her property was being taken against her will, without an opportunity to stay clear of the law by acting properly.

The liberal, consensual basis for the conclusion that Stevens, Souter, and Breyer reached is direct: Mrs. Bennis should not be punished because she had done nothing punishable. The utilitarian basis for their conclusion is that punishment for events out of one's control is not useful. Thus, individual moral responsibility matters both ways. Absolute liability for damages caused by a vehicle or other property may affect the behavior of whoever has the property so long as that person has some control. The majority may have thought such control irrelevant in the context of a family vehicle; it is not likely that husband and wife would have discussed this particular use. The majority, including Justice Ginsburg, perhaps drawing on different utilitarian traditions, may simply have concluded that the benefits weighed more than the costs because the seizure was so likely to deter the misbehavior.

Intoxication also affects the fundamental liberal value of choice. If people do not have the capacity for choice, they are, in liberal terms, less blameworthy. Those stressing individual liberty and choice might insist on retaining a defense that alcohol interferes with one's capacity for choice. The blameworthy act is the murder, car crash, or assault. Penalties have less influence on persons under the influence of alcohol; they have less capacity to avoid risk. Despite those quite traditional considerations, the Court, in *Montana v. Egelhoff*,[9] held that Montana could withdraw intoxication as a defense. The liberals found this issue troubling. Intoxication is relevant to voluntariness and voluntariness has been an essential element of criminal behavior, so Stevens, Souter, and Breyer joined O'Connor in dissent. Ginsburg and Souter, however, agreed that the state could redefine the intent element of the crime, and Breyer and Stevens refused to resolve that issue. In fact, seven members of the Court concluded that states could redefine the mental element of crimes.[10] In effect, the act of drinking can become the legally blameworthy event.

Deference to individual autonomy may also have influenced the conclusion of Stevens, Souter, Ginsburg, and Breyer, joined also by O'Connor, Kennedy, and Thomas, that statements to a psychotherapist may be privileged. They balanced the value of mental health against the value of the evidence that mental health professionals might provide.[11] Mental health is fundamental to the ability to act voluntarily, to consent or to refuse, and to be responsible for the results.

Intrusion

Another area in which utilitarians may diverge is in the value that they place on freedom from state intrusions. Ideally, utilitarians want to know what value people put on intrusions into their own lives. It is not always possible to know or to translate those feelings. So utilitarians have to make assumptions about how important specific intrusions really are.

The state may bother people by taking their time or restricting their freedom. Justice Stevens is very sensitive to the imposition of state intrusions on individual time and freedom in such encounters as mass searches and preventable errors in law enforcement. Stevens and Souter broke from Ginsburg and Breyer regarding drug testing. For Stevens and Souter, mass searches were not worth the cost.[12] Where Ginsburg and Breyer saw only minimal inconvenience, Stevens and Souter found an unjustified intrusion. But Ginsburg joined Stevens in objecting to the damage from inaccurate criminal records, errors that could result in temporary incarceration or humiliation. Stevens and Ginsburg saw considerable personal risk well worth preventing, while Breyer and Souter were less troubled.[13] Thus Breyer could be described as striving for efficiency. Ginsburg appears to put much more weight on the humiliation or incarceration that inaccurate records might bring. Souter, despite his concern for the inconvenience of searches, apparently valued the protection of record keepers more than the still greater intrusions their mistakes cause. Stevens seemingly put a greater value on liberty and worried about the invasions in both these cases. There is no party line on these issues; it depends on one's view of the consequences.

Accuracy of Justice

Clerical errors may cause temporary mistakes, but wrong judgments may do irrevocable harm. Judicial mistakes can impose very high individual costs in the form of fines and imprisonment, as well as the cost of defense. The liberal justices are much less likely to believe that efficiency justifies ignoring such errors. Hence the clear contrast between the unity of the liberal bloc in insisting that the courts look at evidence found after trial that indicates that death row inmates awaiting execution are actually innocent; the relative unity of the conservative bloc in denying that courts have even the power to look; and the ambivalence of Justice O'Connor.

For the liberals, this reflects an enormous potential harm. For the conservatives, there are other far more important matters than the life or death of an individual inmate.

Factual judgments, however, easily divide the liberal bloc. In *Tome v. United States*,[14] Stevens, Souter, and Ginsburg joined Kennedy and Scalia, unwilling to trust an out-of-court statement made when the person making the statement had a motive to fabricate, but Breyer dissented, joined by Rehnquist, O'Connor, and Thomas. Some of the "liberals" are much more sensitive to risks to accurate judgments than others. Stevens and Ginsburg seemed relatively complacent in *Stone v. Immigration and Naturalization Service*.[15] Stone filed an appeal after the lower court denied a motion to reconsider an earlier ruling. That raised a procedural issue with significant consequences. The Supreme Court, in an opinion by Justice Kennedy, was guided by the federal policy to expedite the deportation of illegal aliens. The justices decided that it would be better and faster to require that appeals be filed within a set length of time from the original judgment of the lower court, not the subsequent denial of the motion to reconsider. Justice Breyer, joined by Justices O'Connor and Souter, feared that the Court's ruling creates a trap for the unwary because it created an exception from the usual rule that parties would be expected to follow. Complexity seemed inefficient and unnecessary.

Plea bargaining might seem either to promote or to hinder accurate decision making. It might promote accuracy by simplifying the prosecutor's tasks, and facilitate inevitable conclusions with minimal time and resources. Plea bargaining might conflict with accuracy because, regardless of the facts, defendants may agree to plead guilty to avoid the risk of a much harsher penalty.[16] Prosecutors may agree to light sentences to save time and money. Normally, the discussions are confidential in order to encourage the bargaining process. In one case that reached the Court, the prosecutor had gotten the defendant to agree that anything said in the negotiations could be used at trial. At trial, prosecutor questioned defendant, over counsel's objections, about some of those statements. The majority decided that the defendant could waive the confidentiality of plea bargaining discussions. Ginsburg and Breyer agreed, perhaps because confidentiality can conflict with accurate fact-finding.[17] Souter and Stevens objected that Congress saw confidentiality as a necessary part of a bargaining process that gives defendants some protection against abuse by prosecutors.

Even though utilitarians are likely to resist strongly any procedures that result in the incarceration or execution of innocent people or otherwise punish people unjustly, they are also likely to support extensive efforts to put criminals behind bars. Consistent with those goals, the liberal justices find that lower courts have jurisdiction to examine whether a prisoner convicted of murder was probably innocent of the crime,[18] and they must grant relief if they have "grave doubt" about whether a constitutional error was harmless at trial,[19] and the more liberal justices also concluded that disciplinary segregation should trigger procedures likely to result in an accurate determination of misbehavior.[20] But over Stevens's objections in each case, Breyer showed little concern about the weight judges may place on the sentencing recommendations of advisory juries in capital cases,[21] or about the exclusion of evidence improperly seized because of clerical errors;[22] he saw little problem with allowing defendants to waive objections to statements made during plea negotiations[23] and supported enforcement of drug laws by means of random methods, which pose a burden on many innocent people.[24] Each of those poses what are often described as procedural problems. Procedural problems can have large impacts. They determine the likelihood that people who are uninvolved in criminal activity will be burdened by the criminal process, stopped, taken to the station, required to provide samples of anything from urine to hair; the likelihood that police and other public officials can abuse their authority, stop people for all the wrong reasons, such as "driving while black"; or the likelihood that departments will take proper care of the rest of us. There are benefits to a stricter enforcement of procedural regularity. But Breyer sees declining benefits and concludes the trade-offs must be inefficient. Ginsburg and Souter drew a line that diverged from both Stevens and Breyer.

Procedural issues, like the exclusionary rule and plea bargaining, pose rights on both sides. The exclusionary rule in the context of mass searches threatens to release some guilty persons in order to protect innocent ones in other cases—it could be thought of as victims of criminals versus victims of police abuse. Thus Ginsburg's and Breyer's acceptance of the searches and resulting evidence does not necessarily show a balancing away of individual rights for lesser goods.[25] It does show a different evaluation of the benefits to be gained by enforcing procedural rules. Despite Stevens's conservative origins, it is rare to find either Ginsburg or Breyer, let alone any other justice, to his left. When they disagree, generally Stevens supports the individual and those he opposes support the government.[26]

Minorities

While equality is presumptively preferable for utilitarians, there is no fixed set of rules about the best arrangements. It all depends on the consequent benefits and costs. More, there are differences in the evaluation of the treatment of various groups among the "liberal" justices.

The liberal justices are least unified with respect to aliens and Native Americans. All four—Stevens, Souter, Ginsburg, and Breyer—would have held that no state is immune from suit in federal courts by tribes or others for violating federal requirements.[27] On other issues, Justice Breyer has seemed more sensitive to the costs to aliens and native peoples than his colleagues, and conversely, Justices Stevens and Ginsburg have seen somewhat more value in government controls. Thus Breyer with O'Connor and Souter objected to a trap for aliens in deportation proceedings created by confusion about the date to appeal, but Stevens and Ginsburg supported the rule that created the difficulty.[28] Breyer, Stevens, O'Connor, and Souter would have denied states the power to tax income of Indians living off the reservation but working for the tribe on the reservation, but Justice Ginsburg voted to give states that power and in a series of succeeding cases most of the quartet voted for state taxing authority and against Indian claims.[29]

The group is much more unified with respect to gender issues, but even there significant differences arise. On the unified side, Stevens, Souter, Ginsburg, and Breyer, the entire liberal bloc, joined Kennedy and O'Connor in *Romer v. Evans*,[30] holding that Colorado had gone too far in prohibiting all measures to require equal treatment of gays and lesbians.

Bennis v. Michigan was more divisive. That was the case in which the Court held that the state need not pay a woman and co-owner of a car for her share of the value of the car that was seized because her husband had a tryst with a prostitute in the car.[31] Ginsburg joined the majority, writing that the burden in this case was very small because the car had minimal value. For Justice Ginsburg, an unstated premise may have been that this case raised an equal protection issue: making the men pay, as well as the women prostitutes. Another important factor was that placing ownership of family assets in the hands of different family members can thwart a good deal of law enforcement, including the enforcement of antiprostitution laws against the male customers. If that interpretation is right, then individual choice was less important to Ginsburg than gender equality.

Souter and Breyer joined Stevens's dissent, weighing the benefits differently. Perhaps they too saw it in gender terms. For them, women ought not to be treated as mere appendages of their husbands, forced to cough up their assets when their spouses misbehaved. They wrote about Tina Bennis as an "innocent third party," not simply as a spouse, as well as arguing that she should not have been penalized because she was not responsible for her husband's behavior.[32] Even starting with a concern for gender equality does not provide a unique way to evaluate the consequences. One could put more or less value on penalizing men for using women as prostitutes, holding women responsible only for their own fault or just simplifying law enforcement, positions that respond to feminism in different ways.

The group is united with respect to the importance of racial equality but not with respect to the identification of racial discrimination or the best means for combating it. Justices Souter, Ginsburg, and Breyer concluded that the existence of many federal prosecutions of blacks on crack charges in San Diego and the absence of any such charges against whites for the same period might simply be the result of black criminal behavior. Thus, they would not allow a district judge to require the prosecutor to provide information on their treatment of black and white offenders unless defendants first made a showing that there were white offenders who were treated differently. Although many professionals would agree with him, on the Court only Stevens found it hard to accept the conclusion that whites did not engage in the crack trade in San Diego and thought the exclusive prosecution of blacks for crack in federal court raised a presumption of different treatment.[33] Some have suggested that Ginsburg sets out strict criteria for proof in discrimination cases but does so with a clarity that allows easier victories later. The evidence may be sufficiently available that courts need not bear the burden of assumptions in the area of selective prosecution. Another possible way to understand the Court's treatment of the racial disparity in crack prosecutions is that "they did it"; Souter, Ginsburg, and Breyer had no sympathy for crooks and dealers. The conclusions these justices reached can be understood in utilitarianism terms based on their estimate of reality (who participates in the crack trade) or their estimate of the disutility of investigating the possibility that blacks were the victims of selective prosecution (because the remedy could involve absolving actual criminals of these prosecutions).

Where Resources Matter Most—The General Welfare

Equality is fundamental to utilitarianism, and the welfare that utilitarians seek clearly means mass welfare, not specific advantages for a favored few. Welfare is defined in humanist rather than moralist terms. Utilitarians can take many views of economic relationships. They can regard the society at large as benefited by what are variously described as efficiency, supply-side economics, or trickle-down economics. This is the complacent liberalism of some ivory tower liberals. Utilitarians can believe that the general welfare is better based on strong protections for workers and lower economic classes whose demand for services spurs the economy and whose productive employment improves the safety of all. There is not, in other words, a utilitarian choice of models for the best socioeconomic engine for society, only a utilitarian argument about how to measure the results.

The liberal justices' conclusions about economic regulation are often consistent with respect both for the health of significant institutions and substantial justice for those they serve.[34] In *Consolidated Rail Corp. v. Gottshall,* Ginsburg, joined by Blackmun and Stevens, eloquently expressed concern for injured railroad workers and would have required railroads to take responsibility for the emotional injuries caused by lax safety practices.[35] In *ABF Freight System, Inc. v. N.L.R.B.,*[36] Stevens, joined by the relatively liberal Blackmun, Souter, and Ginsburg, but also by the relatively conservative Rehnquist, Kennedy, and Thomas, supported the responsible federal agency's decision to protect workers against corporate abuse despite employee misbehavior. In what may have been a similar vein, Ginsburg would not exempt railroads from a tax merely because others were exempted under the federal statute.[37]

The liberals are not united on these issues. Recently, for example, Stevens and Breyer showed more concern for the rights of seamen than Ginsburg or Souter.[38] The issue there was whether an employee on duty at sea was covered by the protections of the federal statute known as the Jones Act. For Stevens and Breyer, if the employee was on duty at sea, he was covered. Stevens wrote his concurrence in the language of textual analysis and picked up Thomas's vote. The majority, including Ginsburg, sent the case back to find out whether the employee's duties so regularly required him to be on duty at sea that he could be termed a seaman, a much narrower category. Only if the employee could be called a seaman would his injuries be covered, even though they occurred while on duty at sea.

Ginsburg's stand on punitive damages, which we discussed above, fits a pattern of insistence on corporate responsibility, but the position of her liberal colleagues seems more driven by considerations of efficiency or consent. Although all the opinions described the punitive damage issue in procedural terms, driven by the text of the due process clause, they can also be evaluated as expressing an underlying substantive judgment about corporate responsibility.[39]

For liberals, the environment represents rights to clean surroundings and abundant natural endowments versus a claim of an individual right to treat the environment as one wishes. Given rights in conflict, a liberal can arrive at a calculus not much different from the one that would motivate a utilitarian. With rights in conflict, a liberal might want to accommodate both, but where that is not possible, the greater right defeats the lesser. For utilitarians, the solution is much more direct: interpretation of the law, where possible, to produce the best environment for most people over the long run. The liberal bloc, joined by O'Connor and Kennedy, united behind Stevens's majority opinion in *Babbitt v. Sweet Home Chapter of Communities for a Greater Oregon,*[40] interpreting the Endangered Species Act to prohibit damage to the habitat of wild animals, as well as direct damage to the animals themselves. Their decision treated the act as important for long-run welfare and interpreted it generously.

Another example of Stevens's concern for the little guys and underdogs was his defense of farmers' rights to sell patented seed to neighbors, but Souter, Ginsburg, and Breyer did not join him.[41] The majority might have treated this as values or rights in conflict between the farmers and the seed companies and simply decided that the overall benefit of the additional patent protection was worth the cost to the farmers.

The contrast was somewhat more stark in a case involving a group of marginal pro-football players. The players' union bargains with a multiemployer owners' union. The owners declared that the bargaining had reached an impasse and unilaterally imposed the terms they preferred on this marginal group of players. Unless the labor laws exempted the owners, this collaboration among them would have been a violation of the antitrust laws. Only Stevens defended the players and their union. Stevens described what he was doing as applying the assumptions of the broad liberal era that was responsible for the statutes involved and the congressional desire to shift some power toward unions, rather than as an instance of his own views.[42]

Consistent with the assumption that wealth in the hands of those without it produces more happiness than wealth in the hands of those with it, one would expect a utilitarian to be more concerned with the rights of underdogs, especially economic claims, unless the utilitarian also believed that some form of trickle-down benefit operated. In fact, there is considerable divergence. Among the liberal group, Stevens seems most concerned with underdogs. The others are far more erratic: sometimes protective, sometimes concerned with efficiency, sometimes convinced that law is protective, sometimes convinced that it is not.[43]

Organizational Assumptions

Separation of Powers. Traditionalists in the eighteenth century thought the legislative, executive, and judicial branches of government each had its own unique tasks that should not be interfered with by the others. Government functioned best when each branch minded its own business. By 1787 that picture had been destroyed by practice. Legislatures took over the government of the new country and the new states, appointing executives and deciding cases as if they were courts. The Federalists who wrote the Constitution would have neither approach to the separation of powers, and they were fairly clear about it in their classic statement in *The Federalist*. For them, government functioned best when the branches were arrayed against one another, competing for power over identical issues. We have called this checks and balances. Madison called it blended powers.[44]

We seem to be doomed to refight the battles among the traditionalists, the proponents of legislative power, and the Federalists, as if the Federalists had not settled the issue.

Modern conservatives sometimes have a stake in executive power when it seems to promote order. Modern liberals have sometimes had a stake in executive power when the executive seemed prepared to control private industry and economic power. In fact, neither has a unique and consistent theory of the separation of powers.

The separation of powers matters to the utilitarians on the Court and they are often supportive of coordinate branches, but it is not clear whether for liberty or efficiency. Souter and Breyer opposed Congress's attempt to restore rights cut off by a surprising Supreme Court interpretation of a statute of limitations, but Stevens and Ginsburg dissented.[45] That seems to have pitted social justice against concern for judicial prerogative and split the liberal camp. Stevens, dissenting alone, supported the right of the Federal Election Commission to handle cases in the Court without approval of the attorney general in order to secure the independence of the elections watchdog body, but this time Souter and Breyer preferred to honor the power at the top of the hierarchy of a coordinate branch.[46] Most of them opposed the line-item veto, but Breyer saw no problem with the shift of power to the executive.[47] It seems that Breyer reads the separation of powers with hierarchy and efficiency in mind while Stevens reads them with substantial justice foremost in his thoughts.

Federalism. Federalism has a very different role in liberal than in conservative thought. Conservatives dote on that part of Madison's message that identified the value of localities in defending against a distant national government. They have overlaid that idea with the notion that small communities are more moral because they can oversee the morality of their members. Liberals stress the part of Madison's message that identified the potential unfairness of smaller communities, and the benefits of large communities in meliorating the effects of faction.[48] The national resolution of the civil rights struggle over sectional objections is a modern example of that side of Madison's insight. Chief Justice Marshall understood the nationalism of Madison's argument when he wrote, in *McCulloch v. Maryland*, that the part must not be allowed to govern the whole.[49] Thus, for liberals like Justice White, Congress was the supreme American lawgiver.[50] For liberals like Justice Blackmun, the point of federalism was its protection of liberty, not conformity or community morality, and federalism was valuable if and only when it accomplished that goal.[51] Thus jurists in the liberal and utilitarian traditions can view federalism either as a problem or as a blessing depending on whether they believe it advances liberal goals of independence and liberty. Or they can remain agnostic and treat federalism as relatively unimportant to the major goals of the liberal project.

Consistent with this liberal approach, Stevens, Souter, Ginsburg, and Breyer are far more nationalist than their conservative brethren. They voted in favor of provisions of the well-known "Brady Bill" to support federal authority over gun control and, specifically, to impose requirements on state officials, sheriffs included.[52] They voted against state immunity from suits in federal courts by Indian tribes and others complaining about violations of federal law.[53] The nation may be the repository of more fair rules than the states and the judiciary should be able to enforce those federal rules.

Stevens, Souter, and Breyer, joined by O'Connor and Kennedy, ignored or overrode concern about state prerogatives to hold that state law on punitive damages requires fair notice of liability and penalty.[54] Ginsburg responded that the federal courts are no more competent than the state courts in this respect, having no standards to override them, and the Supreme Court will have no help.

The four treat federalism as a subordinate issue and in most respects Justice Ginsburg's positions reflect the quartet reasonably closely. She finds no automatic relationship between federalism and either liberal or utilitarian goals. On the one hand, she has been fairly consistent in prohibiting state discrimination against interstate commerce,[55] as well as other burdens on interstate commerce.[56] Ginsburg opposed giving the states constitutional immunity from suit for violation of federal law regulating commerce among the states or with the Indian tribes.[57] She supported national power to protect a workman's recovery,[58] to protect women and others in the abortion context,[59] and to prohibit guns in schools,[60] and she held that airline deregulation law preempted state antifraud laws.[61] On the other hand, she has interpreted federal law to favor state taxation,[62] supported state law in favor of a whistle blower,[63] and generally to accomplish substantial justice.[64] Ginsburg has been somewhat inclined toward supporting the states in the area of habeas corpus.[65] There is good reason, in other words, to see the views about federalism of the quartet of relatively liberal justices to be subordinated to their views on the underlying issues, and on substantial justice to the parties.

Planning for Happiness. The members of the liberal coalition, especially the newer members, often appear to treat resource aggregation as very useful. Breyer, Souter, and Stevens protected corporate wealth against punitive damages, for example. That avoided what one could see as squandering corporate assets inefficiently.[66] Reading the labor and antitrust laws to protect professional football owners against labor unions could be understood the same way.[67] Ginsburg's partial support of the employer position against liability to an employee in *Chandris, Inc. v. Latsis*[68] may also be an example of a sympathetic view of protecting corporate finances, though, with a somewhat opposite effect, both Ginsburg and Breyer would have allowed punishment of oral misrepresentation under the securities laws regulating prospectuses.[69]

Agency Assumptions. Utilitarians have to decide whether they trust authority. Will a public agency live up to its task? Will it act in the public interest or will its management pursue self-aggrandizing strategies? Will public officials be truthful in courts or will they distort or even create facts to achieve their goals? Most judges have become quite jaded about the trustworthiness of the police, for example, regularly telling counsel informally that the police tell the truth no more than half the time. Those judges must then decide how to react to their doubts—whether to honor what the police seek even though the judges realize they very likely have no legal right to their object, or to force the police to prove the issue more convincingly. Generally, the more a justice is willing to trust or defer to authority, the more politically conservative we describe him or her; the less trustful, the more liberal we describe them.

Liberal justices generally trust authority much less than conservative justices do. They resisted allowing the state to institutionalize people for "dangerousness" who do not have a defined mental disorder and argued that states should be required to provide treatment where those institutionalized have disorders that are treatable.[70] Joined by Justice O'Connor, they refused to rely on the market to protect inmates of private prisons and concluded that private prison guards do not have immunity from suit.[71] They are not clones in this regard, however. Souter and Breyer often trust authority or are less concerned about political abuse of power.[72] Of the four, only Breyer voted to trust juries to sort out unreliable self-interested statements.[73] By contrast, Ginsburg and Stevens appear considerably more distrustful of authority. Stevens's attack on the control of the FEC by the political branches is one example of many that could be mentioned.[74]

Conclusions

Utilitarianism is a very broad tent. These justices are "liberal" only by comparison to the others on the Supreme Court. Still both their liberalism and their utilitarianism make a difference. Their ideological framework leads them to ask different questions than their conservative colleagues and results in consensus on a broad range of issues. Utilitarian thought does not, however, resolve instrumental questions. Judgments about how to promote general welfare are open. These justices do not make typically "liberal" assumptions about those issues. Their framework is historically liberal. Their instincts are often quite conservative. Utilitarian judgments are largely based on opinions about facts, about what is going on in the real world. As factual judgments, their conclusions are also relatively open to argument and persuasion.

9

Coda

Alone among his conservative brethren, David Souter sees conservatism largely as trying to maintain continuity rather than as making or justifying large changes of principle. As we have noted many times above, however, tradition only partly explains one's conclusions because there are so many competing traditions and because traditions must be interpreted to provide answers to problems that are not traditional. Philosophically, Souter may best be described as pragmatic, not in the everyday sense of that term as practical but in a technical sense of the term as seeking one's goals from similar situations, accepting contradictions, and not trying to rationalize one's entire system of values. In that sense, like Chief Justice Rehnquist, who reaches very different results, Souter can be described as eclectic. It is eclecticism in a very different form, however, since Souter starts by trying to understand the moral principles of the society and interpret constitutional law in light of those principles. The result is that one finds principles in Souter's work that are very familiar if not entirely consistent.

Everyone discusses Souter in connection with *Casey*,[1] and *Lee v. Weisman*.[2] In these well-publicized decisions Souter declared his adherence to precedent and his willingness to explore history at great length. *Casey* may be a poor example precisely because of the way it was politicized. In addition, Souter's methodological views don't identify for us what he will likely find in the history he studies. It is useful to know that he feels strongly about adherence to precedent, but that view cannot tell us what he will understand precedent to mean. For Souter in *Casey,* precedent meant the symbol of *Roe,* but did not incorporate all of its substance. Therefore, as with his colleagues, it is important to search for the guiding instincts in Souter's jurisprudence.

Still, it is an important part of Souter's self-definition that he sees his job as maximizing continuity, not change. Souter does not describe a vision of a new world order but, rather, an old one. He tries hard to discern what society thinks and does not see his role as changing its laws. When Thomas turned to the second Justice Harlan, he pointed to a very specific Harlan criticism of a very specific result.[3] When Souter turned to the same Justice Harlan, he pointed to a method.[4] That seems very accurate. Harlan was a legal conservative, trying to be faithful to the law as he found it, to its principles as well as its limits.

Souter's voting record has moved sufficiently toward the position of Blackmun, Stevens, Ginsburg, and Breyer that many conservatives will find any distinction between Souter and the "liberals" purely imaginary.[5] Moreover, Souter often takes on a major role in writing for the liberal group. His opinions are substantial, well researched, and intellectually well crafted. Quiet and diminutive, he often looks like the liberals' point man to the conservatives.

Conflating the views of Souter with Blackmun, Stevens, Ginsburg, and Breyer, however, misses much that divides Souter from his colleagues and mischaracterizes them all. In *Consolidated Rail Corp. v. Gottshall*,[6] Ginsburg, dissenting with Blackmun and Stevens, described Conrail's driving a short-staffed crew of men in their fifties and sixties in ninety-seven-degree heat to replace a section of track. Even when one of the men keeled over, the supervisor reprimanded another for trying to administer cardiac pulmonary resuscitation, and drove the men to continue at a faster pace after their coworker was laid out in a body bag by the side of the tracks. A close friend of the deceased had a well-documented nervous breakdown. Ginsburg also documented the way pressure on supervisors to ignore safety regulations, coupled with twelve-to-fifteen-hour shifts and work without weekend breaks, drove one of the supervisors to a similarly well documented nervous breakdown.[7] For the dissenters, the jury was well within its province in concluding that Conrail had breached its duty to the workers and should be held responsible. For Justice Souter, the Court's refusal to permit recovery was "a faithful exercise of [the] duty" to expound the federal law of responsibility toward employees covered by the FELA and to "'provide [a] liberal recovery for injured workers.'"[8] Whatever Souter's virtues, and whatever the virtues of his position in *Gottshall* may be, liberals will hardly treat his analysis of Conrail's obligations as "liberal."

Nevertheless, there are important philosophical points of contact or agreement between Souter and more liberal members of the Court. Souter apparently accepts individual moral autonomy. In *Barnes v. Glen Theatre, Inc.*,[9] he concurred in the judgment but argued that it was not necessary to face the issue whether pasties and a G-string could be required simply because of moral sentiments. It was important to him to discern whether there is any actual injury to others that might justify the restriction.[10]

For a conservative who accepts individual moral autonomy, there are several possible choices about basic values. One might be a libertarian, simply defending the individual against the state, though I think there are no examples on this Court. One might be a utilitarian, as I believe Stevens, Ginsburg, and Breyer are, viewing the best results for the community in light of a set of conservative assumptions about consequences for order and security. One might simply prefer adherence to precedent and slow, careful movement, though, as noted above, that would require additional fallback principles to explain the pattern of decision. Or one might be an organic conservative who looks to social rather than legal traditions.[11] Sullivan sees such an organicism or Burkeanism in Souter, O'Connor, and Kennedy.[12] Indeed, Burkeanism is much like the pragmatism described above. Regardless of terminology, and as we have repeatedly noted, both legal and social traditions are somewhat unsatisfactory explanations of judicial decisions because of the different and competing ways traditions can be understood. Hence we repeatedly try to search for other explanations. Nevertheless, Justice Souter appears to be trying very hard to be faithful to his conception of judicial role. That conception of judicial role is to be faithful to existing traditions, and it often overpowers the somewhat different and not altogether consistent conservative, and liberal, visions he harbors. The other explanations just don't work very well.

He is not a libertarian. In a somewhat proindividual vein, accurate criminal judgments are important to Souter. He would give a death row inmate the chance to get counsel to petition for habeas corpus,[13] and he joined Kennedy's majority opinion requiring notice and hearing before forfeiture of property.[14] One ought not to make too much out of these individualistic decisions on Souter's part. In other criminal cases he places a high value on law enforcement by contrast to other values.[15] His apparent acceptance of individual moral autonomy does not lead him to a libertarian position, and one should not misunderstand his championing of the rights of the individual in several important cases in this way. The habeas cases in his first term made it clear that Souter is not a libertarian.[16] They reflected a strong communal, anti-individual rights streak in Souter that could be utilitarian or organic conservatism. The question would become when, as a utilitarian, he thinks the protections of individual rights are not worth the cost, or when, as an organic conservative, he thinks claims of right are not supported by history.

Utilitarianism is a tempting explanation of Souter's work because it is a common framework for decision making by balancing considerations, a mode that often seems typical of Souter's work.[17] Moreover, he often explores the purposes of legal rules, not satisfying himself with recitations of formal precedents.[18] His opinions often have an instrumental cast, typical of utilitarianism. An organicist, viewing history in complex continuously unfolding contexts, however, could appear to be going through a similar balancing process as a multitude of considerations are explored.[19]

Nevertheless, utilitarianism is a less satisfactory explanation of his work than it is of his colleagues'. *Davis v. United States,*[20] for example, was a case in which Justice O'Connor wrote for the majority that the police need not stop questioning if a person in custody makes an ambiguous statement about the need for an attorney. Scalia wrote that only voluntariness should count—if the statement is voluntary it does not matter what the police did—though, of course, the procedural restrictions were designed to protect voluntariness and avoid somewhat unanswerable questions about voluntariness in individual cases. Souter concurred in the judgment because he concluded that the police acted properly when they took the trouble to ask some questions to determine whether the prisoner actually wanted to consult counsel. He disagreed with the Court's conclusion that the police need not have been so fastidious. He wrote that it is better to require law enforcement personnel to clarify whether an attorney has been requested. Souter's approach was not utilitarian. He did not explore the costs and benefits to society of the rule he urged except to admit that it would impose a cost in lost confessions. He urges no social benefits although arguments of that type are available. He might have argued, for example, that the public would benefit because clearer availability of counsel would reduce coercive behavior toward those improperly detained. He might have argued that society would benefit because clearer standards would prevent arguments that undermine convictions. Ambiguous procedures could cause more confessions to be thrown out than a rule that appears more sympathetic to the accused. Rather, he accepted the benefit of counsel for a prisoner who felt the need as worth the cost of interrupting the interrogation. Prisoners could not be expected to contend with a plain statement rule. Precedent and the ease with which the police could check and clarify the request also supported the rule.[21] Souter's fundamental point was that the individual's right to choose to have counsel must be protected.[22] That analysis stemmed from tradition, practice, and a sense of fairness rather than a calculus of costs and benefits.

Another objection to treating utilitarianism as an explanation is that the pattern of Souter's judgments does not fit utilitarianism easily. He did not find the exclusionary rule helpful in preventing significant intrusions on personal liberty, although he insisted on preventing less damaging intrusions.[23] His uncertainty about the environmental takings cases hardly squares with a utilitarian approach.[24]

Justice Souter is clearly drawn to some very conservative nonutilitarian ideas. Recently, the Court decided a case against a fruit packer who objected to being forced to contribute to an industry marketing fund. The Court treated the case as if it were not a free speech case at all but merely a case of commercial regulation. Justice Souter dissented. His opinion could seem like a very unexceptional opinion in favor of freedom of speech. But Souter turned to a discussion of "rent-seeking" in politics to explain why the regulation should be overturned.[25] The idea is that people use politics to gain personal advantages and the public loses. Political scientists used to describe this as pluralism and were confident that on the whole it got the people what they should have, full of inconsistencies and compromises that accomplished a distribution of resources more equitable than any principle would have allowed.[26] Public choice theory has turned this notion on its head and now describes these political efforts as rent-seeking that destroys fairness.[27] In turn, public choice theory is very corrosive of democratic theory and has, appropriately enough, been subjected to a scathing attack.[28] Souter's use of these ideas is hard to treat as minimal or utilitarian. Instead, it appears that regardless of how faithful Souter wishes to be to a vision of impartial judging, he too is unable to avoid revealing the ideological assumptions that give direction to his conclusions.

It may be instructive that Souter and Stevens did not share opinions very often, at least in their first few years together on the Court.[29] Part, but not all, of the explanation for that difference is that Stevens writes quite often, almost twice as often as Souter and nearly half again as much as the next-most-vocal justice. Part of the difference is that Souter's premises are usually rooted in traditions as he understands them, and in interpretations of those traditions that are not utilitarian. Stevens understands the country in a much more utilitarian way.

Accepting individual moral autonomy should lead in the direction of a *Carolene Products* approach to judicial role. That certainly fits Souter's activist approach to the First Amendment.[30] Similarly, Souter retains concern for a wall of separation between government and religion, preserving individual autonomy over religious exercise.[31] He has also taken a fairly strong position on democratic rights in the districting cases. He applied § 2 of the Voting Rights Act to vote dilution claims in *Johnson v. De-Grandy*.[32] He agreed with Justice Blackmun, dissenting in *Holder v. Hall*,[33] that the Voting Rights Act governs the number of seats on a municipal government. The locality wanted to exclude minority participation by leaving government in the hands of a single official elected at large. Whatever the merits of the counterarguments, Blackmun's and Souter's position is not intelligible if they are not strongly committed to democratic and equal rights.[34] In his dissent in *Bush v. Vera*, Souter rejected the Court's attempt to develop a constitutional cause of action for racial districting by challengers who have not suffered vote dilution or other inequality. He argued that the Court had failed "to provide a coherent concept of equal protection injury" and that the ironic result of the line of cases was to reverse the progress made in overcoming the dilution of black voting strength. Equal protection, for Souter, was not merely a matter of ideological or expressive statements but of practical political self-protection.[35] Souter has demonstrated a commitment to equal rights in many other cases as well.[36] The protective role of *Carolene Products* with respect to democratic rights and equal social participation fits Souter's jurisprudence.

Nevertheless, his participation in the proproperty decisions is still somewhat unclear[37] and may lean the other way. In *Dolan v. City of Tigard*,[38] Souter dissented and accepted the position the Court marked out in *Nollan v. California Coastal Commission*,[39] that rules requiring property owners to trade valuable privileges for a variance had to be related to the injury caused by the proposed development—in the Court's language there had to be a "nexus" between the two. Souter argued, however, that the *Tigard* majority addressed a different question: the proportionality of the privileges. That issue, he wrote, was not involved in the case and the Court should not have reached out to deal with it. He did not make his own position clear on how that issue should be decided if and when it arose. He did say that the burden of proof in cases under the "police power" should favor the government. Since the property owner offered no proof on the nexus issue, the government should have won.[40]

That reads very much like the position of the first Justice Harlan in *Lochner v. New York*.[41] Justice Harlan measured the constitutionality of the regulation by the reasonableness of the government's behavior. He differed from the majority in *Lochner* by finding the regulation reasonable. Like him, Souter would give the government the benefit of the doubt.

By contrast, Stevens, Blackmun, and Ginsburg took a stronger position much more consistent with the outlook on property cases that prevailed from 1937 to 1987. The locality merely offered the owner a trade—a variance in exchange for dedication of a portion of land for a greenway and a bikeway—that's capitalism; there's nothing to evaluate.[42] In effect, they argued that the majority had shifted from compensating for a loss gauged by the value of the private rights at a time prior to the transaction, to a loss gauged by the value of the private rights as they would be without the concessions demanded by the locality. The Stevens-Blackmun-Ginsburg approach is more consistent with the judicial role outlined by *Carolene Products* because it allows the society to define property rights through the political process subject only to the most deferential review. Judicial oversight would largely be reserved to protect property owners against selective enforcement. The approach that the Stevens dissent ascribed to the majority is not consistent with the *Carolene Products* definition of judicial role because it substitutes a judicial definition of property rights for a social and political one, enforcing something other than community standards and traditions.

Souter ended his dissent by pointing out that "the right case for the enunciation of takings doctrine seems hard to spot," citing his statement in *Lucas v. South Carolina Coastal Council*.[43] He may have decided that it was not necessary to raise the fundamental issues raised in Justice Stevens's dissent. He may have decided that his adherence to precedent required him to accept *Nollan* regardless of his own personal sentiments. That will require us to wait and find out how he interprets precedent, what leads him to read it one way rather than another. Or he may have simply decided that *Dolan* was premature because the facts did not present the issues the Court addressed. Nevertheless, his opinion raises questions about his understanding of judicial restraint. What clearly mattered for Souter were the burden of proof and the reasonableness of governmental behavior, not the definition of property rights.[44]

A subsequent decision that may have gutted the funding of legal services programs may, by its extremity, serve to push Souter to the left on the issue.[45] To review briefly, Congress and the states had arranged to permit or, in some states require, the pooling of lawyers' escrow accounts that otherwise would yield no interest at all because of the small size of the accounts. The pooling would not make it possible to pay interest to each of the owners of the pooled funds because the accounting would be more costly than the payments. In the past the banks had just kept the funds. By pooling the amounts, it became possible to create a fund that could be used for provision of legal services. The majority, in an opinion by Chief Justice Rehnquist, held that the interest belonged to the owners of the principal and that the plans that took the interest for the funding of legal services programs may have been a taking of property in violation of the Constitution. Souter wrote a dissent and joined both Steven's and Breyer's dissents as well. Stevens wrote that there was no taking where there was no money that the owners could collect. Breyer argued that the funds were not in fact the clients' private property because the funds existed only as the result of the rules under attack. Souter's own dissent criticized the Court for deciding an abstract proposition. He argued that the Court should not have decided the case until the implications of the lower court's holding about property had been fleshed out. Since no money would ever have passed to the owners of the principal, there were still a number of questions to decide, including, for example, what the damages might be since the Constitution does not prohibit taking private property but merely requires compensation if and when it is taken. At this moment the decision, known as the I.O.L.T.A. decision for Interest on Lawyers' Trust Accounts, is a source of considerable worry but no practical consequences until subsequent decisions flesh out the meaning of the decision. From the liberals' perspective, fussing about taking nothing is going a good bit too far. Whether that moves Souter more firmly into the liberal camp on takings law is yet to be seen.

Given the ambiguity of his positions and his writings, perhaps most telling is the example of his constant effort not to develop a principle but to identify traditions. In the suit over the constitutionality of the "Brady Bill" restricting the sale of guns, Souter brushed off Stevens's arguments about the history of federal-state relations and the advisability of this kind of partnership between the national and state governments as correct but insufficient. Instead, he wrote, his vote was determined by a passage in *The Federalist* that others quite reasonably see as ambiguous.[46] Writing in the case testing the "right to die," Souter rejected sweeping statements about personal liberties and sought to identify a method that examined carefully circumscribed historic public values and concluded that, as this case was framed, there was no sufficiently important liberty involved to defeat the states' interests.[47] Again in the case testing the line-item veto, Souter rejected the majority's hard line refusing to allow members of Congress to sue in most cases, and looked for a narrower treatment balancing competing considerations.[48] In the case testing whether publicly funded teachers could be sent into religious schools, Souter refused to go along with a change in doctrine, preferring to treat intervening cases as narrowing but not overturning prior doctrine.[49] He refused to sanction the overturning of a historic rule that allowed private plaintiffs to sue states in federal courts for violation of federal law.[50] On the ground that it was an innovation in free exercise law, Souter expressed doubts about the Court's rule that neutral rules of general applicability do not violate the free exercise clause even if the burden on religious freedom is unnecessary, and he refused, on the current state of the record, to overturn the Religious Freedom Restoration Act.[51] Souter remains cautious, determined to restrict his opinions to the situations before him, sensitive to principles but unwilling to announce sweeping judgments or make an attempt to deflect the course of law.

The philosophical stance of this book, indeed, is probably anathema to Justice Souter. Although some of Souter's colleagues specify nonphilosophical approaches to decision making, their own philosophical stances are not deeply buried. Justice Souter, however, argues at length for traditionalism, intelligently applied, in a way that is hospitable to competing traditions, and he crosses ideological boundaries in his opinions, expressing greatest doubts and finding avenues of compromise at the intersection of strong competing views. In *Casey*, the "right to die" cases, or the "Brady Bill" case, strong philosophical views would have required a clearer statement or position than he took. In each, he found justifications in positions that were not merely at cross purposes but thoroughly antithetical. The *Casey* resolution, for example, is a compromise that cannot be described in a principled way. The right to abort and the states' interests in preventing abortion were wholly in conflict. Souter wrote about precedent. The right to control fundamental aspects of life, which were the basis of the privacy cases including *Roe* and *Casey*, would have controlled the "right to die" cases. Souter wrote at length about common law method. The gun law case involved a fundamental conflict of irreconcilable views about national power, but Souter found it closer than he expected and wrote about constitutional history. In that way Souter's eclecticism is also very different from Rehnquist's, which lurches among positions rather than threads among considerations.

At this point, caution, legal precedent, and Burkean organicism remain viable hypotheses for Souter's organizing principles. Liberalism, in the

A room
without books
is as a body
without
a soul.
Cicero

Book House of
Stuyvesant Plaza
Albany, NY 12203
(518) 489-4761
www.bhny.com

MADE IN U.S.A.

sense of general support for individual rights, is not a viable hypothesis. Souter's conservatism, like Stevens's, emphasizes the distance between the wings of the Court. Both are conservatives who yet feel strongly the pull of the humanist canons of Western philosophy, partly, but not exclusively, because they think it is their job to feel those canons.

10

Ideological Canons

Academics have been writing extensively about what philosophical approach courts should take to interpretation and substantive judgment.[1] The justices categorically denied that they were listening. The Senate grilled nominees to make sure that they approached the bench with open minds, unencumbered by the grand theories of academics.[2] Justices with theories were perceived as biased. Members of the Supreme Court had to be pure. So they argued about the definition of purity. Rehnquist, Scalia, and Thomas argued that they were faithful to the original meaning of the Constitution through what they determined from text and history. There was one true way to understand the Constitution through proper interpretive methods. The framers said such and such and therefore this is what we must do. Brennan and Marshall advocated what sounded like contemporary judicial revision of the Constitution in terms of what they deemed enduring values.[3]

The debate has been misleading. As Brennan and Souter took their colleagues on historically, it has become clear that history solves some but not all of the disagreements and that it sometimes points to resolutions that are not congenial to Rehnquist, Scalia, and Thomas on the Court, and to Robert Bork and others off the Court.[4] Similarly, it has become clear that the text is rarely able to resolve the difficult issues that find their way to the Supreme Court.

The culture war over the Constitution is not about fidelity. Though the conservative justices have argued about fidelity to the original intent of the founders of the Constitution, in the area of individual rights, they have also insisted on interpreting the Constitution in line with the most specific examples of historical practice.[5] As a result, they will not even allow the founders' principles into the discussion. No such interpretation can be faithful to the constitutional tradition. The founders after all believed in principles, believed they stood and worked for principles for the betterment of humankind.[6] In the area of federalism, the battle lines are reversed. There the conservatives infer principles and ignore very precise constitutional language.

In the affirmative action context, the liberals have been much more faithful to the intent of those who drafted and ratified the equal protection clause.[7] Their notion of the right of privacy, however, would likely surprise the founders, who lived in a world not of the conservatives' mythic hands-off style of government but instead of very heavy-handed government that intervened in virtually every important aspect of life.[8]

The ink spilled over text and history leads astray. These are battles of convenience. The more significant battles are for philosophic, not interpretive, principles. In part, the culture war over the Constitution is a war about fidelity to the principles of the Enlightenment that put civilized, humane values ahead of parochial, clannish ones, ahead of values that lead to conflict and the subjugation of one group by another.[9] Above all else the founders valued peace. They wanted to ensure "domestic tranquillity."[10] They wanted Congress to have the powers necessary for harmony among the states.[11] They wanted to keep government out of religious wars that had been the scourge of Europe—Article VI barred religious tests; the First Amendment barred a religious establishment. Those clauses having done their jobs and gradually having been emulated by the states, the Thirty-Ninth Congress incorporated the Bill of Rights into the first section of the Fourteenth Amendment. Henceforth everyone had a right to equal treatment and consideration under the national tent.

The Need for Leadership

Philosophy Intrinsically Neither Good nor Bad. Most contemporary philosophy started in attempts to specify a system of morality, about how we ought to treat one another and govern ourselves. John Locke started with the right to care for oneself. The social contract from Locke to Rawls has been understood as a human agreement intended to make it possible to take better care of ourselves. The contract is for us. Utilitarianism began as a means to identify how that might be done.

Philosophy does not have to have such goals. Much philosophy before Locke was designed to serve monarchies and justify slavery. Others more recent would put all of us under the control of a superman or aim at the production of a super race through eugenics or Darwinian selection. In that system, people now are just the means to super people later or for some to serve others now. Worse, all philosophy can be overdone, taking some proposition to an extreme that none of us would recognize as just. Indeed, what Edmund Burke objected to was the effort to engineer on the basis of a philosophy, taking ideas that sounded good into situations that were untested. He objected to the demand for consistency. In Emerson's words, "[C]onsistency is the hobgoblin of little minds, philosophers, statesmen and divines."

If one acts out of instinct or convention, philosophy will nevertheless play a role because none of us have grown up in a world insulated from philosophy. In that condition, however, we might harbor bits and pieces of several philosophies. Maybe that is good but it is not necessarily good; it depends what people strive for and do. Acting out of instinct or convention can lower the stakes because compromises among different ethical systems are much less clear guides. On the other hand, it can deepen the problems because of the lack of standards. Action out of prejudice is too easy a consequence.

Poles Apart. All of the members of the Court received their legal training after the great switch in 1937 from a Court that assessed the reasonableness of economic legislation to one much more concerned about democracy, equality, and personal freedom. Much of their language has been cast in terms of the categories developed in that struggle, categories shaped albeit in somewhat different ways by Justices Holmes, Brandeis, and Cardozo and championed in the academic world by then law professor Felix Frankfurter and political scientist Alpheus Mason, a protégé of Justice Brandeis who similarly championed the new understanding of judicial role.

Their deferential approach to economic regulation and their aggressive approach toward voting, discrimination, and the use of official force generated huge industries of scholarship, publication, and classroom exploration of how the judicial task should be undertaken, and even whether the courts had a proper role to play.

That debate focused on democratic and egalitarian issues but also obscured the contest among utilitarian, libertarian, and moralist worldviews that were central to the Court's resolution of these important problems. In the language of that period, it became possible for conservative critics to identify the liberal values of several of the justices and argue that by deciding constitutional cases in line with principles, liberal principles, they were importing their own values into the Constitution.

With the advent of a radically conservative Court, it has become evident that all justices import their own instincts into constitutional decision making and their instincts can be described as equally principled or unprincipled, equally their own, as are those of their liberal colleagues and predecessors. In fact, the conservatives also learned from the period of their own upbringing, as individuals and as lawyers. American conservatives have always hated "levelers," represented most objectionably in the twentieth century by the communists. The modern conservative movement, however, was reshaped and dramatically altered by World War II and the contest with totalitarian regimes. Conservatives came to perceive the subordination of the individual as the common failing of both Nazi and Communist forms of totalitarianism, but also had to learn to live with the dramatically enlarged and empowered state that the Cold War made necessary. For liberals, concern over the beatings that totalitarianism inflicted on individuals implied a need to protect liberty against governmental abuse. Conservatives feared the threat from within. They sought to constrain the individual morally.[12]

Conservatives complained that colleges and universities had become a vast liberal think tank and they fought back with their own intellectual institutions and efforts. Modern American conservatism is not merely a set of ad hoc feelings about current issues loosely strung together for political campaigns, although many voters certainly can be described that way. The more thoughtful and intellectual conservatives have been powerfully buffeted by these ideological winds. Those who are less theoretical in their conservatism but who travel in conservative circles nevertheless absorb the mind-set created by more theoretical conservatives, mimicking the process that takes place among liberals.

The members of the Court have grown up in an atmosphere in which conservative thinkers from Hayek to Rand and Strauss, reacting to twentieth-century totalitarianism in their own distinctively conservative ways, helped to shape the conservative agenda. It would be a small wonder if the justices' views could not be described ideologically in terms of these currents. Of the conservatives, only Rehnquist has resisted the pull of a consistent ideology and adopted a more ad hoc brand of radical conservatism.

In fact, the members of the Court do not fit any single conservative tradition, and it is clear that they are not committed as a group to any consistent set of values. That can be swept under the rug as eclecticism, evaluated as complacent or treated as reflecting politics, class attitudes, or interests rather than principle. It cannot result merely from a commitment to an interpretive procedure both because these justices are not committed to such a procedure and because such procedures are too porous to account for more than a small group of cases. Underlying attitudes and commitments show through.

On this Court even the "liberals" are conservatives. The principle conservative value for traditionalists like Justice Souter is a sense of caution, requiring slow movement, but not a fundamental rift with classical liberal values of individual autonomy. For Stevens, the primary conservative value has been public order, emphasizing guilt over procedure—but insisting nevertheless on the preeminence of factual accuracy. His use of order is within a basic utilitarian outlook that largely defers to legislative values and tries to bring about what he believes the legislators would have wanted.

For more radical conservatives like Justices O'Connor, Scalia, and Kennedy, the principal conservative value is moral character, although their treatment of it varies dramatically from O'Connor's concern with rewarding it, to Scalia's Darwinian sink-or-swim approach, and Kennedy's insistence on free will.

By contrast, the utilitarians on the Court, currently Stevens, Ginsburg, Breyer, and possibly Souter, have focused on the outcomes people may want and on giving people a fair start unimpeded by irrelevant factors of birth and circumstance. Law is about making it possible for all people to lead happy, productive lives. Their approach is much more Millian than the conservatives', placing equality and individual moral autonomy at the core.

These philosophic differences have important consequences on the Court. Each of the justices has absorbed an outlook or worldview, either formal and trained or instinctive and from the "gut." All of them show political and philosophic stripes and all of them necessarily interpret the Constitution in those terms.

The justices get along. They maintain friendships across philosophical divides. They can often agree on conclusions even when their premises differ. The utilitarianism of the "liberals" moderates some of the conflicts, but the differences in their premises are very sharp; they do not share a common starting point. It is no less a culture war because they agree on some outcomes.

Talk of a center on the Court is almost quixotic. Utilitarianism has no clear center. It is not clear what values we share or what we have to do to be happiest, and without that information utilitarians are somewhat lost.

Liberalism is to some extent at war with itself. Liberals want both freedom from government and for government to supply the conditions of freedom. They argue for both privacy and freedom of information. Conservatism does not inhabit the center either. The conservatives on the Court have taken a position that few Americans would recognize as moral.

There are many calls for a new way of looking at the world. What the justices see we will shortly feel.

Issues That Need Legal Leadership. Pluralism needs lots of leadership. Now. We are changing. We changed our immigration laws in the past and allowed many who had previously been excluded to enter. Others just came. Many of us moved, from south to north, farm to city, and now back south and west. We met one another in school, the factory, or the army. We gloried in the heritage of American pluralism, putting it on our coinage and inventing the vocabulary of the melting pot. Once we spoke of Americanization.

Now we are in a period of resentment and we speak of jealousy, opportunity, and equality as attacks on the many whose positions in society have been improving. Now many of us avoid meeting or meet across the divide between demonstrators and those who feel attacked. America continues to change. The faces of our politicians have changed, the mantel of power is being passed whether we who have it now will it or not.

The Court confronts angry battles over "affirmative action," "gay rights," and "official" English. Our battles over our pluralism lead to other battles about principle and speech and burned flags. These are battles that put our faith in our principles to the test. If the Court upheld traditional American legal principles of freedom and equality, would we learn to reject those principles as unfounded and hard to live with? It is not clear that we are learning to renew that faith. We need legal leadership, neither legal gridlock nor cultural war, from the fount of law.

Criminal law needs leadership. Many of us trust the police, though it is ironic how selective our trust is: police yes, politicians no; locals yes, nationals no; and so on. Despite the shortcomings that every lawyer confronts daily, to whatever degree we have developed a professional and reliable police, it has not always been this way. The country has had its share of kangaroo courts, police out of control, corrupt and dangerous. In the thirst for the blood of murderers, we are tearing apart the very protections that we have long celebrated. Perhaps the vast majority of those sentenced to die deserved it, despite the small but steady pace of injustices that condemn the innocent. Still, our handling of the death penalty has not been a model of caution or fairness. We need legal leadership, not legal posturing.

Yet this Court cannot lead, follow, or calm. We cannot shout across the angry divide when we have no confidence in the moral integrity of those on the other side. We cannot follow when the justices cannot agree. We cannot follow when the justices insist on dividing instead of uniting, not just themselves but us. We pick sides and line up.

When the Court decided *Brown v. Board of Education*, all the members understood the importance of unanimity. On major issues, unanimity conveys a great deal. The last holdout in that struggle bargained with his colleagues: I'll join if the Court does not insist on instant integration. In the event, the Court waited seventeen years between *Brown* and the beginning of strong measures to integrate schools.

It is not just unanimity that matters. Unanimity in the face of injustice is hypocrisy. So we still anxiously await the next appointment.

The Need for Choice

The stakes are about our lives. At issue is the security of our persons, faiths, property, and opportunity. The security of our persons is at stake because the Court plays a large role in deciding the standards of behavior for those armed individuals we call the police. Can they act on their prejudices, their whims, their egos? In many parts of the world, they do. Our Court has played a large part in changing the way they behave. Do we abandon those protections because some of us have forgotten what it was like for our parents and haven't noticed or understood what it is like for our neighbors?

Our faiths are at stake because the Court determines the cost of believing. As we become increasingly diverse, do we have to learn to kowtow to a national religion, determined by pop culture, not sophisticated clergy?

Our finances and opportunities are at stake because the Court determines what is reasonable when an employee objects to mistreatment, and whether business can discriminate for and against the new and the old, the light and the dark, keeping alive kinds of barriers few of us have seen since World War II made prejudice unattractive and concealed.

What shows is not pleasant. The Court has clearly been rejecting the sense of judicial restraint that emerged in 1937 after a long struggle with another activist Court. The Rehnquist Court is no more restrained than its predecessors, and its concept of its role has lost its moorings in the democratic values that had been familiar to the American bench and bar for most of the past half century.

There are no liberals on this Court. Those who have been described as liberal are better described as conservative. Those we have described as conservative are better described as radicals; they do not seek to conserve but to change.

The conservative majority often portrays its decisions as rectifying the "mistakes" of the Warren Court, returning us a mere three decades to set law right again. But there is also a similarity to *Lochner v. New York*, the discredited decision of 1905, when the conservative majority turns eighteenth-century common law into late-twentieth-century constitutional rules. And one must be willing to notice that the claim of a right to state nullification of federal law, which made its original sustained appearance in the slavery controversy before the Civil War, has echoes in this Court's treatment of the Eleventh Amendment.[13]

Most of us don't accept putting innocent people to death. We don't accept inflicting great punishments on people who have not hurt others. We do expect adherence to the fundamental value of equality. We have fought wars for those values. This Court has planted its ideological feet against them. Many of the rhetorical theories the conservative majority claims also have deep roots in many American hearts. But the majority's behavior belies the reasons it has claimed. It has not acted for interpretive reasons nor for democratic ones. The conservative majority is determined to move the country toward its nonconsequentialist conception of law.

Conservative members of the Court have rejected liberal tolerance, realism, and functionalism. What unites a portion of the conservative group on the Court has been a focus not on the consequences of law but on the purity of official motives. It is more important to these justices that people have the opportunity to prove their worth to their maker than that the lives of ordinary citizens improve. What unites the core of the conservative group on the Court has been a skepticism about law and government and a hostility toward the underdogs who seek their protection. But they can't say that.

Notes

NOTES TO THE PREFACE

1. *See, e.g.,* Alden v. Maine, 527 U.S. 706 (1999) (Congress cannot override state immunity from damages in suits by private parties when states violate rights in areas committed to the exclusive jurisdiction of Congress by U.S. Const., Art. I).

2. For a brief description of the realist movement, *see* John Monahan and Laurens Walker, *Social Science in Law: Cases and Materials* (Westbury, N.Y.: Foundation Press, University Casebook Series, 3d ed., 1994) at 17–30. *See also* Joan Williams, "The Constitutional Vulnerability of American Local Government: The Politics of City Status in American Law," 1986 *Wis. L. Rev.* 83, 101 (describing the realist attention to the divergence between announced doctrinal claims and the underlying political vision that animates the justices' conclusion with particular reference to the Burger Court).

3. *See* Glenn A. Phelps and John B. Gates, "The Myth of Jurisprudence: Interpretive Theory in the Constitutional Opinions of Justices Rehnquist and Brennan," 31 *Santa Clara L. Rev.* 567 (1991); Glenn A. Phelps and Timothy A. Martinez, "Brennan v. Rehnquist: The Politics of Constitutional Jurisprudence," 22 *Gonz. L. Rev.* 307, 314–25 (1987).

4. *See* Daniel A. Farber, William N. Eskridge, Jr., and Philip P. Frickey, *Cases and Materials on Constitutional Law: Themes for the Constitution's Third Century* (St. Paul, Minn.: West, 1993) at 125–28; and *see generally* Margaret Jane Radin and Frank I. Michelman, "Pragmatist and Poststructuralist Critical Legal Practice," 139 *U. Pa. L. Rev.* 1019 (1991).

5. Including, *e.g.,* theories of liberty, *see e.g.,* John Locke, *The Second Treatise of Government* (1690, reprint, New York: Macmillan, Thomas P. Peardon ed., 1952), Immanuel Kant, *Foundations of the Metaphysics of Morals* (New York: Macmillan, Lewis White Beck trans., 1985) (1785), John Stuart Mill, *On Liberty* (New York: Liberal Arts Press, Currin V. Shields ed., 1956) (1859), John Rawls, *A Theory of Justice* (Cambridge: Belknap Press of Harvard University Press, 1971), Robert Nozick, *Anarchy, State and Utopia* (New York: Basic Books, 1974); utility, *see* Jeremy Bentham, *The Principles of Morals and Legislation* (1789, reprint, New York: Macmillan, J. H. Burns and H. L. A. Hart eds., 1970); and positivism, *see* H. L. A. Hart, "Positivism and the Separation of Law and Morals," 71 *Harv. L. Rev.* 593 (1958).

6. *See* Robin West, "Progressive and Conservative Constitutionalism," 88 *Mich. L. Rev.* 641, 649 (1990) (commenting upon the internal differences informing conservative and progressive theories). Moral conservatives are particularly concerned about a group of religious issues but may not have much common ground with economic, social, or traditional conservatives, *see ibid.* at 654–58 (dividing American conservatives into moral, legal, and free-market conservatives). Their point is that abortion and smut should be banned and prayer encouraged for religious reasons. For them, the degree of moral autonomy embraced by liberals is unacceptable; the primary curse of liberalism, in their view, is its greater relativism, *see ibid.* at 652–54, 659–60.

Economic conservatives need not reject a relatively broad definition of moral autonomy at all, *see ibid.* at 657–58. Indeed, classical market economics both glories in, and justifies itself in terms of, individual moral autonomy, *see* Jules L. Coleman, *Markets, Morals and the Law* (New York: Cambridge University Press, 1988) at 95–132; West, *supra*, at 657–58 (explaining that free-market conservatives believe the state should defer the source of social authority to forces within private economic markets). Thus economic conservatives need have no particular position with respect to issues regarding morality or schooling or other religious matters.

Traditional conservatives simply stress caution. *See* West, *supra*, at 652 (describing them as legal conservatives); *see also Dictionary of Conservative and Libertarian Thought* (New York: Routledge, Nigel Ashford and Stephen Davies eds., 1991) [hereinafter *Dictionary*] at 156–57, 178, 264; Robert A. Nisbet, *Conservatism: Dream and Reality* (Minneapolis: University of Minnesota Press, 1986) at 20, 26 (discussing the complexity of Burke's traditionalism). They are not necessarily wedded to any particular view of society but are relatively happy with the society they have inherited and relatively concerned about departures from existing arrangements. Included in that society, however, are principles that do push for changes. Traditionalists, partly as a result, are not always opposed to change. To the extent that the traditional principles they adopt reflect poorly on reality, they will seek to bring reality into line. What counts, therefore, are the particular principles blended with caution.

Finally, as developed more fully below, an important group of conservatives treat character as central.

7. *See, e.g.,* Jeffrey A. Segal and Harold J. Spaeth, *The Supreme Court and the Attitudinal Model* (New York: Cambridge University Press, 1993) at 299–332 (attempting to explain the Court's makeup on a liberal-conservative scale). For important exceptions, *see generally* Robert Devigne, *Recasting Conservatism: Oakeshott, Strauss, and the Response to Postmodernism* (New Haven: Yale University Press, 1994) (explaining how conservative theory is responding to postmodernism); Jerome L. Himmelstein, *To the Right: The Transformation of American Conservatism* (Berkeley: University of California Press, 1990) (discussing the rise of conservatism in America); Nisbet, *Conservatism*; West, "Progressive and Conservative" (dividing American conservatives into moral, legal, and free-market conservatives); Frank I.

Michelman, "Property, Federalism, and Jurisprudence: A Comment on *Lucas* and Judicial Conservatism," 35 *Wm. & Mary L. Rev.* 301 (1993).

8. *See, e.g.*, Segal and Spaeth, *The Supreme Court and the Attitudinal Model.*

NOTES TO CHAPTER 1

1. Except as otherwise noted, information about Chief Justice Rehnquist is drawn from Chris Henry, "William H. Rehnquist," in Leon Friedman and Fred L. Israel, eds., *The Justices of the United States Supreme Court, 1789–1978: Their Lives and Major Opinions*, vol. 5 (New York: Chelsea House, 1997) at 1663; David L. Shapiro, "William Hubbs Rehnquist," in Friedman and Israel, *Justices of the United States Supreme Court*, vol. 5 (1980 ed.) at 109. Basic biographical data about all of the sitting justices can also be found in Kenneth Jost, *The Supreme Court Yearbook, 1994–1995* (Washington, D.C.: Congressional Quarterly, 1995).

2. 347 U.S. 483 (1954).

3. Shapiro, "William Hubbs Rehnquist" at 109.

4. *Ibid.* at 110.

5. Sue Davis, *Justice Rehnquist and the Constitution* (Princeton: Princeton University Press, 1989) at 4; Committee on the Judiciary, *Nominations of William H. Rehnquist and Lewis F. Powell, Jr.: Hearings before the Committee on the Judiciary, United States Senate*, 92d Cong., 1st sess., November 3, 4, 8, 9, 10, (Washington, D.C.: G.P.O., 1971) [hereinafter *1971 Hearings*] at 139–40, 185, 313–15.

6. Henry, "Rehnquist" at 1669; Davis, *Justice Rehnquist* at 4; *1971 Hearings* at 43–48.

7. *See* Alan Freeman and Elizabeth Mensch, "Sandra Day O'Connor," in Friedman and Israel, *The Justices of the United States Supreme Court*, vol. 5 (1987 ed.) at 1759.

8. *Ibid.* at 1760.

9. For background on Justice Scalia, *see* George Kannar, "The Constitutional Catechism of Antonin Scalia," 99 *Yale L.J.* 1296 (1990); David A. Schultz and Christopher E. Smith, *The Jurisprudential Vision of Justice Antonin Scalia* (Lanham, Md.: Rowman and Littlefield, 1996) at xiii–xiv; Jost, *Supreme Court Yearbook, 1994–1995*; Jeffrey Rosen, "Antonin Scalia," in Friedman and Israel, *The Justices of the United States Supreme Court*, vol. 5 (1997 ed.) at 1715.

10. Kannar, "Catechism."

11. *Ibid.* at 1311.

12. *Ibid.* at 1313.

13. Antonin Scalia, "The Disease as Cure: In Order to Get Beyond Racism We Must First Take Account of Race," 1979 *Wash. U. L. Q.* 147; *and see* Kannar, "Catechism" at 1309; Rosen, "Scalia" at 1719.

14. *See* Theodore Eisenberg, "Anthony M. Kennedy," in Friedman and Israel, *The Justices of the United States Supreme Court*, vol. 5 (1997 ed.) at 1731.

15. Quoted in Douglas Jehl, "A Product of Two Sides of Town: Judge Kennedy's Roots in Sacramento Go Deep," *Los Angeles Times*, December 14, 1987 at 1.

16. Committee on the Judiciary, *On the Nomination of Anthony M. Kennedy to be Associate Justice of the Supreme Court of the United States, Hearings before the Committee on the Judiciary, United States Senate,* 100th Cong., 1st sess., December 14–16, 1987 (Washington, D. C.: G.P.O., 1989) (hereinafter *Kennedy Hearings*) at 754.

17. *Ibid.* at 750.

18. Jehl, "A Product of Two Sides of Town."

19. *Ibid.*

20. Aaron Freiwald, "Portrait of the Nominee as a Young Man," *Legal Times*, November 23, 1987 at 1.

21. Quoted in George J. Church, "Far More Judicious," *Time Magazine*, November 23, 1987 at 16.

22. *See* Scott Douglas Gerber, *First Principles: The Jurisprudence of Clarence Thomas* (New York: New York University Press, 1999); Jost, *Supreme Court Yearbook, 1994–1995* at 314; Susan N. Herman, "Clarence Thomas," in Friedman and Israel, *The Justices of the United States Supreme Court*, vol. 5 (1997 ed.) at 1829; Jane Mayer and Jill Abramson, *Strange Justice: The Selling of Clarence Thomas* (Boston: Houghton Mifflin, 1994); Timothy M. Phelps and Helen Winternitz, *Capitol Games: Clarence Thomas, Anita Hill, and the Story of a Supreme Court Nomination* (New York: Hyperion, 1992).

23. *See generally* Leonard Orland, "John Paul Stevens," in Friedman and Israel, *The Justices of the United States Supreme Court*, vol. 5 (1997 ed.) at 1691–1713.

24. Robert Judd Sickels, *John Paul Stevens and the Constitution* (University Park: Pennsylvania State University Press, 1988) at 37.

25. *See* H. Jefferson Powell, "The Original Understanding of Original Intent," 98 *Harv. L. Rev.* 885 (1985).

26. Sickels, *John Paul Stevens* at 1.

27. The nomination is described *ibid.* at 34–35.

28. *Ibid.* at 1.

29. *See* Jost, *Supreme Court Yearbook, 1994–1995* at 313; Edward De Grazia, "David Hackett Souter," in Friedman and Israel, *The Justices of the Supreme Court of the United States*, vol. 5 (1997 ed.) at 1806; Margaret Carlson, "An 18th Century Man," *Time Magazine*, August 6, 1990 at 19.

30. *See generally* Jost, *Supreme Court Yearbook, 1994–1995* at 316; Christopher Henry, "Ruth Bader Ginsburg," in Friedman and Israel, *The Justices of the United States Supreme Court*, vol. 5 (1997 ed.) at 1859, is helpful but unfortunately plagued with inaccuracies.

31. *See* Margaret Carlson, "The Law According to Ruth," *Time Magazine*, June 28, 1993 at 38.

32. *Ibid.*

33. *See generally* Jost, *Supreme Court Yearbook, 1994–1995* at 319; Leon Fried-man, "Stephen G. Breyer," in Friedman and Israel, *The Justices of the United States Supreme Court*, vol. 5 (1997 ed.) at 1874; good shorter biographies are in Clare Cushman, ed., *The Supreme Court Justices: Illustrated Biographies, 1789–1995* (Wash-ington, D.C.: Congressional Quarterly, 2d ed., 1995), and Joan Biskupic and Elder Witt, *The Supreme Court at Work* (Washington, D.C.: Congressional Quarterly, 2d ed., 1997).

34. Tony Mauro, "Lloyd's of London Haunts Breyer's High-Court Debut," *Legal Times*, October 10, 1994 at 8.

35. Jost, *Supreme Court Yearbook, 1994–1995* at 319.

NOTES TO CHAPTER 2

1. *See* George Kannar, "The Constitutional Catechism of Antonin Scalia," 99 *Yale L.J.* 1297 (1990); Richard A. Cordray and James T. Vradelis, Comment, "The Emerging Jurisprudence of Justice O'Connor," 52 *U. Chi. L. Rev.* 389, 403–8 (1985).

2. There is, of course, an argument over the word "moral" in this context. For conservatives, autonomy can exist only over areas where morality does not impose a duty. Hence, autonomy is relativist and amoral. But for liberals, autonomy de-pends on whether others are at risk, not on moral judgments. Thus there may be moral issues at stake.

3. The issue of what counts as injury and whether it can be demarcated is a complex philosophical problem. See the materials collected in Stephen E. Got-tlieb, *Jurisprudence: Cases and Materials* (Charlottesville, Va.: Michie, 1993) at 669–715. Liberals and conservatives tend to allow people a different set of choices, based on what appears to be, respectively, an injury or timeless values. For our purposes, it is enough that there is a common issue with different conclusions.

4. *See* Robert McCloskey, "Economic Due Process and the Supreme Court: An Exhumation and Reburial," 1962 *Sup. Ct. Rev.* 34, 38–44.

5. *See, e.g.,* Christopher E. Smith, "The Supreme Court's Emerging Majority: Restraining the High Court or Transforming Its Role?" 24 *Akron L. Rev.* 393 (1990). For a critical discussion, see Michael Stokes Paulsen, "The Many Faces of 'Judicial Restraint,'" 1993 *Pub. Interest L. Rev.* 3.

6. *See* Antonin Scalia, "The Rule of Law as a Law of Rules," 56 *U. Chi. L. Rev.* 1175 (1989); William H. Rehnquist, "The Notion of a Living Constitution," 54 *Tex. L. Rev.* 693 (1976). *See also* Robert H. Bork, "Neutral Principles and Some First Amendment Problems," 47 *Ind. L.J.* 1 (1971); Herbert Wechsler, "Toward Neutral Principles of Constitutional Law," 73 *Harv. L. Rev.* 9 (1959).

7. Robin West, "Progressive and Conservative Constitutionalism," 88 *Mich. L. Rev.* 641, 673 (1990).

8. *See* Rehnquist, "Living Constitution" at 706 (judicial creation of rights "is a

formula for an end run around popular government"); Antonin Scalia, "The Doctrine of Standing as an Essential Element of the Separation of Powers," 17 *Suffolk U. L. Rev.* 881, 894–96 (1983) (urging a narrow conception of standing in favor of democratic self-government).

9. *See, e.g.,* Erwin Chemerinsky, "The Vanishing Constitution," 103 *Harv. L. Rev.* 43 (1989).

10. *See* Stephen E. Gottlieb, "Introduction: Overriding Public Values," in *Public Values in Constitutional Law* (Ann Arbor: University of Michigan Press, Stephen E. Gottlieb ed., 1993) at 9; Stephen E. Gottlieb, "Compelling Governmental Interests: An Essential but Unanalyzed Term in Constitutional Adjudication," 68 *B.U. L. Rev.* 917, 941–62 (1988).

11. *See, e.g.,* Nollan v. California Coastal Comm'n, 483 U.S. 825 (1987); Lucas v. South Carolina Coastal Council, 505 U.S. 1003 (1992).

12. 489 U.S. 189 (1989).

13. West concludes, "The conservative approach to interpretation, in other words, seems to flow from *neither* a commitment to majoritarian democracy nor an adherence to strict constitutionalism." West, "Progressive and Conservative" at 673.

14. David Hume, *An Enquiry Concerning the Principles of Morals* (1777 ed., reprint, La Salle, Ill.: Open Court Press, 1966, App. I) at 125–36, essentially because the implementation of legal rules necessitates a moral decision.

15. *See, e.g.,* Karl N. Llewellyn, "Remarks on the Theory of Appellate Decision and the Rules or Canons about How Statutes Are to Be Construed," 3 *Vand. L. Rev.* 395 (1950). For contemporary discussions of the realist treatment of the issue of neutrality, *see* David Yassky, "Eras of the First Amendment," 91 *Colum. L. Rev.* 1699, 1753 (1991); Gary Peller, "The Classical Theory of Law," 73 *Cornell L. Rev.* 300, 304–5 (1988); Gary Peller, "The Metaphysics of American Law, Part 2," 73 *Cal. L. Rev.* 1151, 1225 (1985).

16. *See* Duncan Kennedy, "Form and Substance in Private Law Adjudication," 89 *Harv. L. Rev.* 1685 (1976); Paul Brest, "The Misconceived Quest for the Original Understanding," 60 *B.U. L. Rev.* 204 (1980).

17. Philip Bobbitt, *Constitutional Fate* (New York: Oxford University Press, 1982), explains that our notions of proper methods of interpretation are external to the Constitution and not determined by it. Hence interpretive methodology is not a "neutral" application of constitutional principles but an imposition on them. Nor are such choices ideologically neutral. A jurisprudence that depends on a search for original intentions, for example, can be described as complacent with respect to contemporary consequences.

18. *See* John Stuart Mill, *On Liberty* (New York: Liberal Arts Press, Currin V. Shields ed., 1956) (1859); Jeremy Bentham, *The Principles of Morals and Legislation* (Darien, Conn.: Hafner Press, 1948) (1789); *and see* Immanuel Kant, *Foundations of the Metaphysics of Morals* (New York: Macmillan, Lewis White Beck trans., 1985) (1785) at 39, 43.

19. Jerome L. Himmelstein, *To the Right: The Transformation of American Conservatism* (Berkeley: University of California Press, 1990) at 45–49.

20. *See* Bowers v. Hardwick, 478 U.S. 186 (1986) (White, J., wrote the majority opinion, joined by Chief Justice Burger and Justices Powell, Rehnquist, and O'Connor. Justices Blackmun and Stevens dissented, joined by Justices Brennan and Marshall); Barnes v. Glen Theatre, Inc., 501 U.S. 560 (1991) (Rehnquist, O'Connor, and Kennedy formed the plurality; Stevens alone remains of the dissenters; Scalia and Souter wrote separate concurrences). For an excellent discussion of the issue of moral autonomy in the context of *Barnes, see* Vincent Blasi, "Six Conservatives in Search of the First Amendment: The Revealing Case of Nude Dancing," 33 *Wm. & Mary L. Rev.* 611 (1992). For the contrary view, that Rehnquist is a moral relativist, *see* Sue Davis, *Justice Rehnquist and the Constitution* (Princeton: Princeton University Press 1989) at 26–28. Justice Thomas joined the Court after *Barnes* was decided, but his position in Romer v. Evans, 517 U.S. 620, 636 (Scalia, J., dissenting), and his dissent from the denial of certiorari in Swanner v. Anchorage Equal Rights Comm'n, 513 U.S. 979 (1994), discussed in chapter 5, indicate that he too denies individual moral autonomy.

21. 478 U.S. 186 (1986).

22. *Ibid.* at 196.

23. *See* Mill, *On Liberty* at 13, 91–93, 102–3. H. Jefferson Powell, *The Moral Tradition of American Constitutionalism* (Durham: Duke University Press, 1993) at 275, in a magnificent study of American constitutional traditions, recognizes somewhat ruefully the significance of utilitarianism in American legal thought.

24. 478 U.S. at 199.

25. *Ibid.* at 216.

26. His choice was reflected both in his opinion for the Court in *Bowers* and in his stand on voting rights.

27. *See* the discussion beginning at 38 below.

28. *But see* Rehnquist, "Living Constitution."

29. Barnes v. Glen Theatre, Inc., 501 U.S. 560 (1991).

30. *Ibid.* at 574.

31. *Ibid.* at 582.

32. *Ibid.* at 596. *See also* Bowers v. Hardwick, 478 U.S. 186, 199 (1986) (Blackmun, J., dissenting).

33. Romer v. Evans, 517 U.S. 620 (1996).

34. *Ibid.* at 636 (Scalia, J., dissenting).

35. *Ibid.* at 627–30.

36. *Ibid.* at 641, 645 (Scalia, J., dissenting) (italics in original).

37. *Ibid.* at 652–53.

38. *Ibid.* at 627–29.

39. *Ibid.* at 629.

40. *Ibid.* at 638.

41. *Ibid.* at 640–41.

42. In a subsequent case, Equality Foundation of Greater Cincinnati v. City of Cincinnati, 518 U.S. 1001 (1996), Scalia, Rehnquist, and Thomas dissented from a remand for consideration in light of Romer v. Evans. The Sixth Circuit then interpreted the Cincinnati charter as having "merely removed . . . special protection from gays and lesbians," which was consistent with the way Scalia, Rehnquist, and Thomas had described the Colorado amendment but unlike the description by the Colorado Supreme Court, which wrote of the repeal of protections against discrimination. *Compare* Equality Foundation of Greater Cincinnati v. City of Cincinnati, 525 U.S. 943 (1998) (opinion of Stevens, J., regarding the denial of certiorari) citing Equality Foundation of Greater Cincinnati v. City of Cincinnati, 128 F.3d 289, 301 (6 Cir. 1997) with Romer v. Evans, 517 U.S. at 626–27, quoting the Colorado Supreme Court in Evans v. Romer, 854 P.2d 1270, 1284–85 (1993).

43. Washington v. Glucksberg, 521 U.S. 702 (1997); Vacco v. Quill, 521 U.S. 793 (1997).

44. *Washington* at 738 (Stevens, J., concurring); ibid. at 752 (Souter, J., concurring in the judgment); ibid. at 789 (Ginsburg, J., concurring in the judgment); ibid. (Breyer, J., concurring in the judgment). Ginsburg in addition to her own opinion concurring in the judgment, also "substantially" joined Justice O'Connor's concurring opinion, *ibid.* at 736.

45. *Ibid.* at 736 (O'Connor, J., concurring).

46. Mill, *On Liberty*. *See also* Joel Feinberg, *The Moral Limits of the Criminal Law* (New York: Oxford University Press, 1984–88), a monumental study that includes separate volumes on harm and offense to oneself and others, plainly driven by derivatives of these liberal and utilitarian categories. On definitional problems, *see* Gottlieb, *Jurisprudence*, 669–715.

47. Mill, *On Liberty*.

48. Bentham, *Principles of Morals and Legislation*. Harm, however, is quite difficult to define and there is a degree of circularity in attempts to clarify the point. *See* Thomas Morawetz, "Persons Without History: Liberal Theory and Human Experience," 66 *B.U. L. Rev.* 1013 (1986).

49. The literature is reviewed in David Schultz, "Political Theory and Legal History: Conflicting Depictions of Property in the American Political Founding," 37 *Am. J. Legal Hist.* 464 (1993). *See also* Gordon S. Wood, *The Radicalism of the American Revolution* (New York: Knopf, 1992) at 6–7, 336; Gordon S. Wood, *Creation of the American Republic, 1776–1787* (New York: Norton, 1969) at 18–28; Clinton Rossiter, *Seedtime of the Republic: The Origin of the American Tradition of Political Liberty* (New York: Harcourt Brace, 1953).

50. Bentham, *Principles of Morals and Legislation*.

51. Mill, *On Liberty*.

52. *See* H. L. A. Hart, "Between Utility and Rights," 79 *Colum. L. Rev.* 828–31 (1979).

53. Benjamin N. Cardozo, *The Nature of the Judicial Process* (New Haven: Yale University Press, 1921) at 66.

54. Herrera v. Collins, 506 U.S. 390 (1993). One can argue that the Court was faithful to Townsend v. Sain, 372 U.S. 293 (1963), except that the Warren Court had and used other ways of dealing with problems with the reliability of the criminal system, both through a broad habeas corpus doctrine and a variety of substantive and procedural rulings, all of which have been choked off by the Rehnquist Court. *Compare* Suzanna Sherry, "All the Supreme Court Really Needs to Know It Learned from the Warren Court," 50 *Vand. L. Rev.* 459 (1997) (arguing that the Rehnquist Court has been truer to precedent than often believed) *with Herrera*, 506 U.S. at 437 (Blackmun, J., dissenting) (describing the language in *Townsend* as "distant dictum" and pointing out that the newly discovered evidence creates a new procedural posture not addressed by *Townsend*).

55. One might argue that cost-benefit analysis requires executions in order that capital punishment deter crime and that sacrifice of innocent lives is occasionally necessary. The inference that some lives should be sacrificed for community welfare has been consistently rejected by utilitarians. Essentially, there are three reasons. First, in pain, the individual cost of the innocent life is very large. Second, logically, the cost outweighs any but the most essential measures—to the extent that a system of capital punishment can be administered with a little more procedure, the extra effort does not compare to the loss of life in a utilitarian calculus. Third, it creates an instrumentalism toward people that undermines the utilitarian system itself; the justification is too dangerously cynical. *Compare* John Stuart Mill to William Thomas Thornton, Saint Véran (April 17, 1863) in 15 *The Collected Works of John Stuart Mill, The Later Letters, 1849–1873* (Toronto: University of Toronto Press, Francis E. Mineka and Dwight N. Lindley eds., 1972) at 854. Moreover, there is a conflict in the conservative bloc's willingness to trust district courts to dismiss frivolous *in forma pauperus* petitions in less vital circumstances, *see* Denton v. Hernandez, 504 U.S. 25 (1992), but not to allow them to consider whether matters of life and death were nonfrivolous, Herrera v. Collins, 506 U.S. 390 (1993); Schlup v. Delo, 513 U.S. 298, 334 (1995) (Rehnquist, C.J., dissenting).

56. 513 U.S. 298 (1995).

57. *Ibid.* at 334.

58. In another case in front of the Court at the time *Schlup* was being considered, Jesse Jacobs complained that he was about to be executed even though the same prosecutor had subsequently convicted someone else of precisely the same act for which he was sentenced to die. The prosecutor in Jacobs's trial had argued that Jacobs alone was responsible for the murder of Etta Urdiales and then argued in the later trial of Jacobs's sister both that Jacobs's sister had committed the murder and that Jacobs had neither shot Etta Urdiales nor realized that his sister was planning to kill her. The Court refused to hear the case. Justices Stevens, Ginsburg, and Breyer dissented. Jacobs v. Scott, 513 U.S. 1067 (1995). It must be pointed out,

however, that Jesse Jacobs was hardly a nice man. He had been convicted of another murder in a different state, committed several other crimes, and did not dispute that he had in fact abducted the victim. *See also* Ruth Bader Ginsburg, "Communicating and Commenting on the Court's Work," 83 *Geo. L.J.* 2119, 2128n (1995) (describing Jacobs's crimes and the press's misstatements).

See also M.L.B. v. S.L.J., 519 U.S. 102, 129 (1996) (Thomas, J., dissenting), in which Thomas, Rehnquist, and Scalia would have denied a transcript to an indigent women in a proceeding to terminate parental rights to two young children, and Thomas and Scalia would have reversed the seminal precedent requiring transcripts for indigent defendants in criminal proceedings.

59. For an example relating to personal safety, *see* DeShaney v. Winnebago County Dept. of Social Servs., 489 U.S. 189 (1989) (finding no state responsibility for returning and requiring a small boy to live with his abusive father). *Compare* William Blackstone, 1 *Commentaries on the Laws of England* 125 (1765, reprint, Chicago: University of Chicago Press, 1979), describing the right of personal security, which "consists in a person's legal and uninterrupted enjoyment of his life, his limbs, his health, and his reputation" as the primary right recognized by the laws of England. *See also* Richardson v. McKnight, 521 U.S. 399 (1997) (Scalia, J., dissenting) (arguing that private prison guards are entitled to qualified immunity for their misdeeds).

For an example relating to personal security, *see* County of Riverside v. McLaughlin, 500 U.S. 44 (1991), involving a dispute over the length of time people could be imprisoned before being arraigned before a magistrate. Scalia dissented from his conservative brethren, arguing that protection of the innocent was the irreducible minimum objective of the procedural protections of the Bill of Rights. Nevertheless, in Herrera v. Collins, 506 U.S. 390 (1993), he took an even stronger position against considering the possibility of entertaining the possibility of innocence. *Compare* Blackstone, *supra* at 125 (defining the ability to move about without restraint as the fundamental element of liberty).

For examples related to privacy, *see* Planned Parenthood of Southeastern Pennsylvania v. Casey, 505 U.S. 833 (1992); Webster v. Reproductive Health Servs., 492 U.S. 490 (1989).

With respect to personal moral choice, *see also* Bowers v. Hardwick, 478 U.S. 186 (1986) (private consensual behavior punishable); Barnes v. Glen Theatre, Inc., 501 U.S. 560 (1991) (no secondary effects necessary to proscribe consensual behavior).

60. John Locke, *The Second Treatise of Government* 17 (§ 27) (New York: Liberal Arts Press, Thomas P. Peardon ed., 1952) (1690).

61. *See* Himmelstein, *To the Right* at 31; West, "Progressive and Conservative" at 658.

62. *See, e.g.*, Robert Nozick, *Anarchy, State and Utopia* (New York: Basic Books, 1974); *and see* Antonin Scalia, "The Two Faces of Federalism," 6 *Harv. J.L. & Pub. Pol'y* 19, 20–21 (1982).

63. *See* Bowers v. Hardwick, 478 U.S. 186 (1986); Barnes v. Glen Theatre, Inc., 501 U.S. 560 (1991).

64. Herrera v. Collins, 506 U.S. 390 (1993); Schlup v. Delo, 513 U.S. 298, 334 (1995) (Rehnquist, C.J., dissenting). *See also* Kyles v. Whitley, 514 U.S. 419 (1995).

65. The use and rejection of general welfare arguments by the conservative justices is described in Gottlieb, "Overriding Public Values" at 2–4.

66. *See, e.g.,* Stone v. Powell, 428 U.S. 465 (1976).

67. Bendix Autolite Corp. v. Midwesco Enterprises, Inc., 486 U.S. 888, 897 (1988) (Scalia, J., concurring).

68. *See* Rehnquist, "Living Constitution"; Scalia, "Rule of Law."

69. *See, e.g.,* Bush v. Vera, 517 U.S. 952, 981–82 (1996); Miller v. Johnson, 515 U.S. 900 (1995); Shaw v. Hunt, 517 U.S. 899 (1996); Shaw v. Reno, 509 U.S. 630 (1993); City of Mobile v. Bolden, 446 U.S. 55 (1980).

70. 462 U.S. 835 (1985). The Court majority, which Justice Rehnquist joined, described that as a deviation from the average district size of 89 percent. Justice O'Connor wrote a concurring opinion, joined by Justice Stevens, in which they stressed the insignificance of the one county whose representation the Court chose to assess and their support for the Court's refusal to assess the broader issue of the large disparities in representation among the remaining counties in Wyoming. Despite joining the Court in *Brown,* Justice Stevens has frequently supported challenges to the adequacy of representation. *See for example,* Karcher v. Daggett, 462 U.S. 725, 744 (1985) (Stevens, J., concurring), decided the same day as Brown v. Thompson.

71. Salyer Land Co. v. Tulare Lake Basin Water Storage Dist., 410 U.S. 719 (1973) (*per* Rehnquist, J.); Ball v. James, 451 U.S. 355 (1981). Stevens and O'Connor joined the Court between those two decisions and both also joined the majority in *Ball,* though Stevens's voting pattern on issues related to democratic participation differs sharply in other respects that will be explored at greater length later in the book.

Rehnquist's conclusion in *Salyer* might be treated as unexceptional by comparison to older notions of property qualifications for voting. Property qualifications persisted for some time in the United States, although their elimination had begun by the Revolution and was greatly hastened by the Jacksonians. *See* Chilton Williamson, *American Suffrage from Property to Democracy, 1760–1860* (Princeton: Princeton University Press, 1960); James A. Henretta, "The Rise and Decline of 'Democratic-Republicanism': Political Rights in New York and the Several States, 1800–1915," in *Toward a Usable Past: Liberty Under State Constitutions* (Athens: University of Georgia Press, Paul Finkelman and Stephen E. Gottlieb eds., 1991) at 50. The civic republican approach to democracy stressed an attachment to the community that property seemed to secure. But the passing of the culture in which civic republicanism flourished left property claims to the vote dependent on a logically prior notion of who belonged in the polity, effectively placing some other entitlement, in most instances property, above democratic values. Modern democratic theory does not resolve the question of dividing membership among particular communities except that it tries to be inclusive by giving every adult that right in comparable communities defined by nations, states, legislative districts, and the like, and an equal vote within any polity. *See* Robert A. Dahl, *Dilemmas of Pluralist Democracy: Autonomy vs. Control* (New Haven: Yale University Press 1982) at 81–107. Thus the exclusion cases like *Salyer, and see also* Harper v. Virginia, 383 U.S. 663 (1966); Gomillion v. Lightfoot, 364 U.S. 339 (1960), are quite different from the districting cases like *Brown, and see also* Reynolds v. Sims, 377 U.S. 533 (1964); Wesberry v. Sanders, 376 U.S. 1 (1964). Rehnquist, the court's senior member, has not supported access in either situation, *see, e.g., Brown, Salyer, supra*. Other qualifications like membership on a board or tenured faculty are not analogous; they are not based on democratic theory at all but, rather, on a theory of administration. The justification for hierarchy in such structures is not democracy but effectiveness within a larger democratic sphere that controls the essential rights and structures. Thus it is hard to credit Rehnquist with any deference toward democracy rather than toward some other values that take precedence in his mind.

72. Bush v. Vera, 517 U.S. 952, 1005n (1996) (Stevens, J., dissenting); "House Membership in 104th Congress," 52 *Cong. Q.* 3299, 3300 (1994).

73. *See* Davis v. Bandemer, 478 U.S. 109, 144 (1986) (O'Connor, J., concurring).

74. 42 U.S.C. §§ 1973, 1973c.

75. Thornburg v. Gingles, 478 U.S. 30 at 96 (1986) (O'Connor, J., concurring in the judgment).

76. Bush v. Vera, 517 U.S. 952, 961–76 (1996).

77. Compare *ibid.* at 982 *with* Stephen E. Gottlieb, "Identifying Gerrymanders," 15 *St. Louis U. L.J.* 540, 544–46 (1971).

78. Bush v. Vera, 517 U.S. at 1001 (Thomas, J., concurring in the judgment); *and see ibid.* at 1009n (Stevens, J. dissenting); *but see* Hunt v. Cromartie, 526 U.S. 541 (1999) (*per* Thomas, J.) (conflicting racial and nonracial factors need to be sorted at trial, not summary judgment).

79. 509 U.S. 630 (1993).

80. Bush v. Vera, 517 U.S. at 1000 (Thomas, J., concurring in the judgment).

81. Holder v. Hall, 512 U.S. 874, 896–903 (1994) (Thomas, J., concurring in the judgment).

82. *Ibid.* at 945 (Thomas, J., concurring in the judgment).

83. *A Matter of Interpretation: Federal Courts and the Law* (Princeton: Princeton University Press, Amy Gutmann ed., 1997) at 144.

84. Scott Douglas Gerber, *First Principles: The Jurisprudence of Clarence Thomas* (New York: New York University Press, 1998).

85. *See, e.g.,* Bush v. Vera, 517 U.S. 952 (1996); *ibid.* at 990 (O'Connor, J., concurring); *ibid.* at 996 (Kennedy, J., concurring); Shaw v. Hunt, 517 U.S. 899 (1996); Miller v. Johnson, 515 U.S. 900 (1995); *ibid.* at 928–29 (O'Connor, J., con-

curring); Shaw v. Reno, 509 U.S. 630 (1993); City of Mobile v. Bolden, 446 U.S. 55 (1980).

86. *See, e.g.,* Bush v. Vera, 517 U.S. at 981–82; Miller v. Johnson, 515 U.S. 900 (1995); Shaw v. Hunt, 517 U.S. 899 (1996); Shaw v. Reno, 509 U.S. 630 (1993); City of Mobile v. Bolden, 446 U.S. 55 (1980).

87. Presley v. Etowah Co. Comm'n, 502 U.S. 491 (1992), *and see* Holder v. Hall, 512 U.S. 874 (1994).

88. *See, e.g.,* Dolan v. City of Tigard, 512 U.S. 374 (1994); Lucas v. South Carolina Coastal Council, 505 U.S. 1003 (1992); Nollan v. California Coastal Comm'n, 483 U.S. 825 (1987).

89. Lucas v. South Carolina Coastal Council, 505 U.S. 1003, 1014 (1992); *ibid.* at 1028 n.15 (declaring early history irrelevant).

90. Phillips v. Washington Legal Foundation, 524 U.S. 156 (1998).

91. Adarand Constructors, Inc. v. Pena, 515 U.S. 200 (1995) (barring federal affirmative action); City of Richmond v. J.A. Croson Co., 488 U.S. 469 (1989) (barring state affirmative action); Printz v. United States, 521 U.S. 898 (1997) (narrowing federal power over state firearms enforcement); United States v. Lopez, 514 U.S. 549 (1995) (narrowing congressional power over firearms under the commerce clause); New York v. United States, 505 U.S. 144 (1992) (restricting Congress's power to require state environmental compliance); Idaho v. Coeur d'Alene Tribe of Idaho, 521 U.S. 261 (1997) (expanding state immunity to actions based on federal law). *Compare* Lujan v. Defenders of Wildlife, 504 U.S. 555 (1992) (narrowing statutory standing for environmentalists according to its view of constitutional standards) *with* National Credit Union Admin. v. First National Bank and Trust Co., 522 U.S. 479 (1998) (commercial banks have standing to challenge regulation of federal credit unions).

92. Stephen E. Gottlieb, "Does Federalism Matter to Its Devotees on the Court?" 13 *Ohio N.U. L. Rev.* 1179 (1997). The recent cases may seem contrary to the assertion in the text, *see* Alden v. Maine, 527 U.S. 706 (1999). The Court has implemented federalism against Congress in areas related to gun control, *see* United States v. Lopez, 514 U.S. 549 (1995) and business regulation, *see Alden, supra,* and in favor of states in areas where they sought broad power to prosecute free of constitutional restraint, *see* Stone v. Powell, 428 U.S. 465 (1976), but has been hostile to state concerns in areas involving race, *see* City of Richmond v. J.A. Croson Co., 488 U.S. 469 (1989), and workers' claims, *see* Ingersoll-Rand Co. v. McClendon, 498 U.S. 133 (1990). We are surely entitled to ask which concern is driving the legal engine.

93. Parts of this story are nicely told in Harry Kalven, *The Negro and the First Amendment* (Chicago: University of Chicago Press, 1965).

94. International Society for Krishna Consciousness, Inc. v. Lee, 505 U.S. 672 (1992) (airports); United States v. Kokinda, 497 U.S. 720 (1990) (Postal Service sidewalks); PruneYard Shopping Center v. Robins, 447 U.S. 74 (1980) (shopping

centers); Members of the City Council of the City of Los Angeles v. Taxpayers for Vincent, 466 U.S. 789 (1984) (posters). *See also* Owen Fiss, "Silence on the Street Corner," in Gottlieb, *Public Values in Constitutional Law* at 199–204.

95. Forsyth County v. Nationalist Movement, 505 U.S. 123 (1992) (Rehnquist, C.J., dissenting) (discretionary demonstration fees).

96. Cornelius v. N.A.A.C.P. Legal Defense and Educ. Fund, 473 U.S. 788 (1985) (NAACP Legal Defense and Education Fund excluded from joint fundraising drive in federal offices).

97. Rust v. Sullivan, 500 U.S. 173 (1991); FCC v. League of Women Voters of California, 468 U.S. 364 (1984); Regan v. Taxation with Representation, 461 U.S. 540 (1983).

98. *See* R.A.V. v. City of St. Paul, 505 U.S. 377 (1992) (city may ban fighting words but only neutrally).

99. *See* Lechmere v. N.L.R.B., 502 U.S. 527 (1992) (union may not trespass to organize unless literally no other access); International Society for Krishna Consciousness v. Lee, 505 U.S. 672 (1992) (plurality concluding that airports are not public fora); Forsyth County v. Nationalist Movement, 505 U.S. 123, 137 (1992) (Rehnquist, C.J., dissenting) (small demonstration fees permissible); Burdick v. Takushi, 504 U.S. 428 (1992) (state may prohibit write-in votes); Cornelius v. N.A.A.C.P. Legal Defense and Educ. Fund, 473 U.S. 788 (1985) (activist organizations could be excluded from fund-raising drive in federal offices). The current Court's conservatives split in Texas v. Johnson, 491 U.S. 397 (1989) (Texas may not ban flag burning), where a conservative insistence on propriety in speech conflicted with the application of a bright-line rule of neutrality. Justices Scalia and Kennedy joined Justice Brennan's majority opinion, and Justice O'Connor joined Chief Justice Rehnquist's dissent along with Justice White. Justice Stevens also dissented.

100. *See* Owen Fiss, "Silence on the Street Corner," in Gottlieb, *Public Values in Constitutional Law* at 199–204. Two recent cases may seem to be counterexamples. But one, Reno v. ACLU, 521 U.S. 844 (1997), was unanimous in some of its basic holdings and only O'Connor and Rehnquist would have sustained any portion of the challenged provisions and then only in a narrow way. Unanimity is a good sign that the case is not debatable on technical doctrinal grounds, thus forcing justices to converge regardless of their own views. The other, Glickman v. Wileman Brothers and Elliott, Inc., 521 U.S. 457 (1997), has been described as an example of a crossover because three of the liberals, joined by O'Connor and Kennedy, voted against the speech claim and three of the conservatives, Rehnquist, Scalia, and Thomas, joining a dissenting opinion by Justice Souter, voted for it. Nevertheless, none of the justices treated this as a true free speech case. The majority, in an opinion by Justice Stevens, treated this essentially as a government speech case backed by taxes, and the dissenters argued that the government speech was motivated by partiality and "rent-seeking," a form of economic misuse of the democratic process. Although Souter cast that argument in traditional terms, his justifica-

tion would both make large inroads in governmental speech and have implications far beyond the confines of the speech cases.

101. 304 U.S. 144 (1938).

102. Alpheus T. Mason, protégé and biographer of Justice Louis Brandeis, championed the footnote as a major goal of his career, *see* Alpheus T. Mason, *The Supreme Court: Palladium of Freedom* (Ann Arbor: University of Michigan Press, 1962). In turn, a student of Mason's made an enormous mark with his own exegesis of the same footnote, *see* John Hart Ely, *Democracy and Distrust: A Theory of Judicial Review* (Cambridge: Harvard University Press, 1980). There has been an enormous amount of discussion of Ely's treatment of this note and the relevant legal and political science literature is huge. Some of the criticisms focus on difficulties in application and on questions about who, in a democracy, is truly disadvantaged. Some of the criticisms come from philosophical traditions different from those adopted by the justices.

103. *See* Bruce A. Ackerman, *Private Property and the Constitution* (New Haven: Yale University Press, 1977) at 71–87.

104. City of Richmond v. J.A. Croson Co., 488 U.S. 469, 494–96 (1989).

105. Compare generally Ackerman, *Private Property*.

106. 208 U.S. 412 (1908).

107. 198 U.S. 45 (1905).

108. *See* Howard Gillman, *The Constitution Besieged: The Rise and Demise of Lochner Era Police Powers Jurisprudence* (Durham: Duke University Press, 1993). The traditional explanations for the difference between *Muller* and *Carolene Products* are that the earlier judgment was political and the later was not, and that the earlier judgment invoked natural law and the later does not. These explanations are based on a misunderstanding. Both approaches are fundamentally political but make very different choices among values to uphold and both respect some overriding rights, whether called natural or otherwise.

109. Bowers v. Hardwick, 478 U.S. 186 (1986).

110. *Ibid.* at 191–94.

Roe, by contrast, is not *Lochner.* In *Roe* the central question whether there is injury to another, the fetus, or whether the fetus counts as another, is hotly contested. But the Court's activism stems from an extension of *Carolene Products*; women had historically although decreasingly been denied political power, and the Court's opinion gave women control over a matter that though primarily concerning themselves had been governed by men.

Lochner's view of judicial restraint had a very different relation to democratic politics. For the Court in *Lochner*, democratic politics was poisoned by legislation that took sides in the marketplace. Gillman, *The Constitution Besieged*. Intergroup neutrality rather than political access was the touchstone of the *Lochner* Court. Neutrality was measured largely by a common law baseline. Cass Sunstein, "Lochner's Legacy," 87 *Colum. L. Rev.* 873 (1987). The Court understood, however, that the common law could and often should be changed. It measured the appropriateness of those changes by what seemed rational to reasonable men. And that rationality defined the province of judicial restraint. *Roe* is not *Lochner* because their theories of judicial restraint are quite different.

111. *See above* pages 38–48.

112. *See* Himmelstein, *To the Right* at 61; Robert Devigne, *Recasting Conservatism: Oakeshott, Strauss, and the Response to Postmodernism* (New Haven: Yale University Press, 1994) at 53–64.

113. *See, e.g.,* County of Allegheny v. ACLU, Greater Pittsburgh Chapter, 492 U.S. 573, 623 (1989) (O'Connor, J., concurring); Lynch v. Donnelly, 465 U.S. 668, 687 (1984) (O'Connor, J., concurring).

114. Employment Division, Department of Human Resources of State of Oregon v. Smith, 494 U.S. 872 (1990); *ibid.* at 891 (O'Connor, J., concurring in the judgment). *See also* City of Boerne v. Flores, 521 U.S. 507, 544 (1997) (O'Connor, J., dissenting) (repeating her view that the rationale of *Smith* was wrongly constructed).

115. There are two additional reasons to believe that, despite their hostility to minority faiths, *Boerne* and *Smith* are not hostile to religion in general as the majority understands it. First, the decision might be understood as a decision about federalism—the Court held that Congress could not define state religious rights. Second, the decision tracks the rules of congressional power over the remedies available under the Fourteenth Amendment in the racial area. The decision thus holds a dagger to Congress's power in the racial area. Therefore, the possibility that the majority had nonreligious objectives in mind cannot be excluded. Both of these issues will be elaborated in chapter 4. For a decision supporting a minority faith's right to neutral laws, *see* Church of Lukumi Babalu Aye v. City of Hialeah, 508 U.S. 520 (1993).

116. *See, e.g.,* Agostini v. Felton, 521 U.S. 203 (1997) (overruling Aguilar v. Felton, 473 U.S. 402 (1985) and authorizing school board to send remedial teachers into parochial schools on a neutral basis); Rosenberger v. Rector and Visitors of the University of Virginia, 515 U.S. 819, 846 (1995) (O'Connor, J., concurring) (university must fund student religious newsletter); Lamb's Chapel v. Center Moriches Union Free Sch. Dist., 508 U.S. 384 (1993) (*per* White, J.) (church has equal right to use of school facilities); Board of Education of the Westside Community Schools v. Mergens, 496 U.S. 226, 248 (1990) (equal access to school facilities required for student religious club).

117. *See* Thomas James, "Rights of Conscience and State School Systems in Nineteenth-Century America," in Finkelman and Gottlieb, *Toward a Usable Past*, at 117, 122–26, 128–38; *and see* Peter S. Onuf, "State Politics and Republican Virtue: Religion, Education, and Morality in Early American Federalism," in *Toward a Usable Past* at 91.

118. *See* Stephen E. Gottlieb, "In the Name of Patriotism," 62 *N.Y.U. L. Rev.* 497, 502–3 (1987).

119. *See* Everson v. Board, 330 U.S. 1 (1947).

120. 465 U.S. 668 (1984).

121. *See* Stephen Bates, "Rule of Law: How Cries of 'Censorship' Stifle the Schools Debate," *Wall Street Journal*, December 22, 1993 at A11; Peter H. King, "A Debate Without End. Amen," *Los Angeles Times*, May 23, 1993 at 3; Irving Kristol, "The Coming 'Conservative Century,'" *Wall Street Journal*, February 1, 1993 at A10; Richard N. Ostling, "Jerry Falwell's crusade: Fundamentalist legions seek to remake church and society," *Time*, September 2, 1985 at 48.

122. *See* Melissa Healy, "End of 'Contract' Is Start of New Tests for GOP," *Los Angeles Times*, April 7, 1995, home ed., at A1; *see also* James Davison Hunter, "The Williamsburg Charter Survey: Methodology and Findings," 8 *J.L. & Religion* 257, 266 (1990) for data on the views of "evangelicals" on church/state issues.

123. County of Allegheny v. ACLU, Greater Pittsburgh Chapter, 492 U.S. 573, 623 (1989) (O'Connor, J., concurring); Lynch v. Donnelly, 465 U.S. 668, 687 (1984) (O'Connor, J., concurring).

124. 410 U.S. 113 (1973).

125. Planned Parenthood of Southeastern Pennsylvania v. Casey, 505 U.S. 833, 952 (1992) (Rehnquist, C.J., concurring in part and dissenting in part).

126. *See* Washington v. Davis, 426 U.S. 229 (1976).

127. *Ibid.*

128. Griggs v. Duke Power Co., 401 U.S. 424 (1971).

129. Palmer v. Thompson, 403 U.S. 217, 240 (1971) (White, J., dissenting). *See also* White v. Regester, 412 U.S 755 (1973).

130. *See* Washington v. Davis, 426 U.S. 229 (1976).

131. Justice White, never firmly in the conservative camp on the Court, dissented vigorously from the Court's rejection of intent in Palmer v. Thompson, 403 U.S. 217, 240 (1971) (White, J., dissenting) and its narrow constriction of intent in cases decided after Washington v. Davis. *See, e.g.,* City of Mobile v. Bolden, 446 U.S. 55, 94 (1980) (White, J., dissenting).

132. *See, e.g.,* Hernandez v. New York, 500 U.S. 352 (1991); Ward's Cove Packing Co., Inc. v. Atonio, 490 U.S. 642 (1989); City of Mobile v. Bolden, 446 U.S. 55 (1980).

133. *See* Police Dept. of Chicago v. Mosley, 408 U.S. 92 (1972).

134. Schneider v. State, 308 U.S. 147 (1939), *and see* Fiss, "Silence on the Street Corner" at 197–99.

135. *See, e.g.,* Regan v. Taxation with Representation, 461 U.S. 540 (1983) (effect on competing viewpoints unintended consequence of speaker subsidy); Stephen E. Gottlieb, "The Speech Clause and the Limits of Neutrality," 51 *Alb. L. Rev.* 19, 36–43 (1986). *But see* National Endowment for the Arts v. Finley, 524 U.S. 569, 599 (1998) (Scalia, J., concurring in the judgment) (arguing that the First Amendment does not apply to subsidies because they do not suppress speech).

136. *See, e.g.,* Hernandez v. New York, 500 U.S. 352 (1991); Patterson v.

McLean Credit Union, 491 U.S. 164 (1989); Ward's Cove Packing Co., Inc. v. Atonio, 490 U.S. 642 (1989). As noted above, the Civil Rights Act of 1991 overruled nine Supreme Court decisions regarding the definition of discrimination, *see* "Provisions: The Civil Rights Act of 1991," *Cong. Q.* December 7, 1991 at 3620.

137. Thomas would "not compel the elimination of all observed racial imbalance [or] the destruction of historically black colleges nor the severing of those institutions from their distinctive histories and traditions." United States v. Fordice, 505 U.S. 717, 745 (1992) (Thomas, J., concurring). Thomas believes that the courts should not focus on the imbalance itself but the justification for the policies that produce it. *Ibid.* at 746–47. He would "not foreclose the possibility that there exists 'sound educational justification' for maintaining historically black colleges *as such*" and would permit "a diverse assortment of institutions—including historically black institutions—open to all on a race-neutral basis, but with established traditions and programs that might disproportionately appeal to one race or another." *Ibid.* at 748, 749.

138. *See* Devigne, *Recasting Conservatism* at 95–96; William Schambra, "Progressive Liberalism and American Community," 80 *Pub. Interest* 31, 40 (Summer 1985); *see also* Robert A. Nisbet, *Conservatism: Dream and Reality* (Minneapolis: University of Minnesota Press, 1986) at 35–36, 50–52 (arguing that conservatives believe that liberalism weakens the social structure).

139. Madison's famous response is "The Federalist" No. 10, in Alexander Hamilton, James Madison, and John Jay, *The Federalist Papers* (New York: New American Library, Clinton Rossiter ed., 1961) at 77.

140. *See* Devigne, *Recasting Conservatism* at 95–96; Schambra, "Progressive Liberalism."

141. Pluralism has, however, changed somewhat in meaning from an older conception of contact and assimilation to a newer conception of separatism and continuation of separate traditions. For some thoughtful discussions of pluralism, *see* Sanford Levinson, "Some Reflections on Multiculturalism, 'Equal Concern and Respect,' and the Establishment Clause of the First Amendment," 27 *U. Rich. L. Rev.* 989 (1993); Bill Ong Hing, "Beyond the Rhetoric of Assimilation and Cultural Pluralism: Addressing the Tension of Separatism and Conflict in an Immigration-Driven Multiracial Society," 81 *Cal. L. Rev.* 863 (1993); Carl H. Esbeck, "A Restatement of the Supreme Court's Law of Religious Freedom: Coherence, Conflict, or Chaos?" 70 *Notre Dame L. Rev.* 581 (1995). An older understanding of pluralism as contact and cross-fertilization has deep roots. Horace Mann saw public schools for all children as a means to overcome the divisions in American society, *see* Lawrence A. Cremin, *Transformation of the School: Progressivism in American Education* (New York: Knopf, 1961) at 10. Cross-group contact has been treated as a means for eliminating discrimination, *see* Phyllis A. Katz and Dalmas A. Taylor, *Eliminating Racism: Profiles in Controversy* (New York: Pergamon Press, 1988) at 360 (describing the contact hypothesis); Mark A. Chesler, "Contemporary Sociological

Theories of Racism," in *Towards the Elimination of Racism* (New York: Pergamon Press, Phyllis A. Katz ed., 1976) at 36; Gordon Allport, *The Nature of Prejudice* (Cambridge, Mass.: Addison-Wesley, 1954) at 488–91; Samuel Stouffer et al., 4 *Studies in Social Psychology in World War II* (Princeton: Princeton University Press, 1950) (describing the impact of cultural and religious integration on servicemen). *See also* Donald S. Lutz, *Popular Consent and Popular Control: Whig Political Theory in the Early State Constitutions* (Baton Rouge: Louisiana State University Press, 1980) (describing the difference between "republican" thought, which praised homogeneity in the founding period, and "federalist" thought, which praised diversity).

142. *See* Devigne, *Recasting Conservatism* at 95–96; Schambra, "Progressive Liberalism."

143. Justice Scalia, in fact, has dismissed discrimination in capital sentencing as merely a fact of African-American life, *see* Dennis D. Dorin, "Far Right of the Mainstream: Racism, Rights, and Remedies from the Perspective of Justice Antonin Scalia's *McCleskey* Memorandum," 45 *Mercer L. Rev.* 1035, 1038 (1994); David A. Schultz and Christopher E. Smith, *The Jurisprudential Vision of Justice Antonin Scalia* (Lanham, Md.: Rowman and Littlefield, 1996) at 195.

144. *See, e.g.,* Hernandez v. New York, 500 U.S. 352 (1991); Patterson v. McLean, 491 U.S. 164 (1989); Ward's Cove Packing Co., Inc. v. Atonio, 490 U.S. 642 (1989). As noted above, the Civil Rights Act of 1991 overruled nine Supreme Court decisions regarding the definition of discrimination, *see* "Provisions: The Civil Rights Act of 1991," *Cong. Q.* December 7, 1991 at 3620.

The Court's rejection of utilitarianism and treatment of intentions also contribute to this result. The Court first announced that discrimination would be tested by the motives of the people in charge. Washington v. Davis, 426 U.S. 229 (1976). It applied that rule in both constitutional and statutory cases, although Congress has repeatedly overruled the Court regarding the latter. *See, e.g.,* The Civil Rights Act of 1991; The Voting Rights Act of 1982; *and see Cong. Q. supra* at 3620–22 (discussing the nine cases overruled by the 1991 act).

The Court then made it clear that even minimally rational claims would suffice to defeat a discrimination claim. *See, e.g.,* Hernandez v. New York, 500 U.S. 352 (1991). Even minimal differences among candidates for a position might produce more goods and services for less money so that those who argue for supposedly color-blind standards can argue that there are gains in efficiency with respect to wealth expressed in dollars.

Were the Court utilitarian in its approach, oriented toward the greatest social benefit, it would have had to weigh the reasons against the costs of the policies. The Court has consistently refused. Justice Stevens argued that equal protection claims should be evaluated on the basis of the social benefit to be expected. City of Richmond v. J.A. Croson Co., 488 U.S. 469, 511–13 (1989) (Stevens, J., concurring in part and concurring in the judgment). The Court has not done so.

The Court's approach, however, misses the injury to blacks and other minorities.

The nonmonetary costs of perpetuating discrimination and the greater nonmonetary cost to those with least prospects are not part of its calculus. Actually, minimum rationality could explain the Court's passivity only when examined from the perspective of the individual employer or other decision maker whose neutrality is questioned. Discrimination should be inefficient for the economy, regardless of the actor's good intentions, because it deprives the economy of the best use of the services of many people. Cass Sunstein, *After the Rights Revolution* (Cambridge: Harvard University Press, 1990) at 50–51, 62–63, 66–67, 80–81; *but see Discrimination, Affirmative Action, and Equal Opportunity: An Economic and Social Perspective* (Hillside, N.J.: Enslow, W. E. Block and M. A. Walker eds., 1982). The several contributors of the latter study assume that discrimination may be inefficient but argue that the market will eradicate discrimination wherever it is inefficient. Their economic attack on antidiscrimination laws is unjustifiably broad for five fundamental reasons. First, it assumes that individual preferences are independent of the preferences of other individuals so that the market will overcome racial preferences with financial ones. But stereotypes are social and systemic, thus corrupting the presumed self-corrective ability of the market. Second, the economic analysis ignores the time factor, among other transactions costs. Third, it ignores the resources problem, *see* Ian Shapiro, "Three Fallacies Concerning Majorities, Minorities and Democratic Practice," in *Nomos XXXII: Majorities and Minorities* (New York: New York University Press, John W. Chapman and Alan Wertheimer eds., 1990) at 86. Fourth, it ignores the uneconomic impact of a system that lowers expectations for future generations. Finally, despite systemic social inefficiency, discrimination may be an efficient response by a single firm in an economy dominated by prejudice since it can be costly to buck the tide, even an inefficient one. The conservative vision of Rehnquist and his most ideological colleagues thus falls far short of the general welfare.

145. *See, e.g.,* Charles H. Clarke, "Private Property, the Takings Clause and the Pursuit of Market Gain," 25 *Akron L. Rev.* 1 (1991).

146. Note more generally that no economic system brings consistent results under all circumstances for all goals. *See* Robert A. Dahl and Charles E. Lindblom, *Politics, Economics and Welfare: Planning and Politico-Economic Systems Resolved into Basic Social Processes* (New York: Harper, 1953). Hence faithful adherence to any economic method is likely to reflect a process–driven ideology rather than a realistic assessment of the effective achievement of social goals.

147. *See* John Rawls, *A Theory of Justice* (Cambridge: Belknap Press of Harvard University Press, 1971) at 76–80.

148. Richard A. Posner, "Utilitarianism, Economics, and Legal Theory," 8 *J. Legal Stud.* 103 (1979); *and see* Jules L. Coleman, *Markets, Morals and the Law* (New York: Cambridge University Press, 1988) at 96.

149. A third fundamental impetus for free market economics is libertarian. The market reflects a don't-tread-on-me attitude. Instead of defining markets for maximum shared gains, the market can be defined and manipulated to reflect

minimal responsibility for one another. Nozick's *Anarchy, State and Utopia* (1974) was in this tradition. He claimed no concern about material outcomes. For Nozick, only force and fraud justified intervention. Nozick treats the definition of property as nonintervention. (Hohfeldian and critical analysis, reflecting the completeness of the legal order, describe all private property rules as state intervention to define and defend who owns what. *See* Wesley N. Hohfeld, "Some Fundamental Legal Conceptions as Applied in Judicial Reasoning," 26 *Yale L.J.* 710 (1917); Wesley N. Hohfeld, "Some Fundamental Legal Conceptions as Applied in Judicial Reasoning," 23 *Yale L.J.* 16 (1913); James L. Kainen, "Nineteenth Century Interpretations of the Federal Contract Clause: The Transformation from Vested to Substantive Rights Against the State," 31 *Buff. L. Rev.* 381, 437–45 (1982).) Nozick's vision gave priority to the status quo and demanded individual consent for change. This tradition is profoundly conservative in terms of social and economic status: those who have, keep. Nevertheless, a universal emphasis on liberty would have results quite different from the Court's work, *see supra* at notes 9–12, 59–64.

Another group of conservatives make an argument about the moral goals of the market that emphasizes a "risk-taking orientation . . . that rewards the virtues of independence and creativity and discourages the vices of dependence and acquisitiveness." Devigne, *Recasting Conservatism* at 66. The market is measured in moral, not distributive, terms; it makes men out of boys. This can be associated with social Darwinism, in which people either do or should get what they deserve. *See* Eric Goldman, *Rendezvous with Destiny* (New York: Vintage Press, rev. ed., 1960) at 70–72, for a description of the history of this idea. Succeeding chapters suggest that some members of the Court are influenced by these ideas.

A third conservative approach to economic issues is based on order: people should defer to their "betters." Conservatives could just want to protect the status quo, regardless of what it includes, to protect the existing social hierarchy, or just their own crowd. Chief Justice Rehnquist has been described as following an essentially hierarchical model, *see* John Denvir, "Justice Brennan, Justice Rehnquist, and Free Speech," 80 *Nw. U. L. Rev.* 285, 298 (1985) (hostile to majoritarian efforts to limit the influence of powerful established institutions but otherwise largely nonactivist in the speech area); Stephen J. Massey, Note, "Justice Rehnquist's Theory of Property," 93 *Yale L.J.* 541, 546–59 (1984) (decisions favor those in charge of the most resources); the same description has been applied to the Rehnquist Court, *see* Theodore Y. Blumoff and Harold S. Lewis, Jr., "The Reagan Court and Title VII: A Common-Law Outlook on a Statutory Task," 69 *N.C. L. Rev.* 1, 68–69 (1990).

150. Lucas v. South Carolina Coastal Council, 505 U.S. 1003, 1014 (1992); *ibid.* at 1028 n.15 (declaring early history irrelevant); *and see* Dolan v. City of Tigard, 512 U.S. 374, 406–7 (1994) (Stevens, J., dissenting); Nollan v. California Coastal Comm'n, 483 U.S. 825 (1987).

151. *See* Margaret Jane Radin, "Government Interests and Takings: Cultural

Commitments of Property and the Role of Political Theory," in Gottlieb, *Public Values in Constitutional Law* at 69.

152. *See* Ackerman, *Private Property* at 31–39, 43–54, on activism within a utilitarian framework. In the effort to make them a bit more concrete, I have somewhat revised his categories.

153. 524 U.S. 156 (1998).

154. *See* District of Columbia v. Greater Washington Bd. of Trade, 506 U.S. 125 (1992); Ingersoll-Rand Co. v. McClendon, 498 U.S. 133 (1990); FMC Corp. v. Holliday, 498 U.S. 52 (1990).

NOTES TO CHAPTER 3

1. 489 U.S. 189, 213 (1989).

2. *See* Benjamin N. Cardozo, *Nature of the Judicial Process* (New Haven: Yale University Press, 1921); Felix Frankfurter, "Mr. Justice Cardozo and Public Law," 39 *Colum. L. Rev.* 88, 52 *Harv. L. Rev.* 440, 98 *Yale L.J.* 458 (1939).

3. Compare Bickel's remark: "No good society can be unprincipled; and no viable society can be principle-ridden." Alexander M. Bickel, "The Supreme Court, 1960 Term—Foreword: The Passive Virtues," 75 *Harv. L. Rev.* 40, 49 (1961).

4. William H. Rehnquist, "The Notion of a Living Constitution," 54 *Tex. L. Rev.* 693 (1976) (presenting himself as a positivist); Antonin Scalia, "The Rule of Law as a Law of Rules," 56 *U. Chi. L. Rev.* 1175 (1989); Robert Bork, *The Tempting of America: The Political Seduction of the Law* (New York: Free Press, 1990).

5. Rehnquist, "Living Constitution" at 706.

6. *See, e.g.,* John Hart Ely, *Democracy and Distrust* (Cambridge: Harvard University Press, 1980) at 1–41; Cardozo, *Nature of the Judicial Process* at 20–21. *See also* William Nelson, "History and Neutrality in Constitutional Adjudication," 72 *U. Va. L. Rev.* 1237, 1237–45 (1986), for criticism of "interpretivism" and "neutral principles." For a very insightful discussion of the extent and limitations of interpretivism, *see* Frederick Schauer, "Precedent," 39 *Stan. L. Rev.* 571 (1987), *and see* Frederick Schauer, *Playing by the Rules: A Philosophical Examination of Rule-Based Decision-Making in Law and in Life* (New York: Oxford University Press, 1991).

7. *See, e.g.,* U.S. Const., Amend V; Robert Nisbet, *History of the Idea of Progress* (New York: Basic Books, 1980) at 193–203; Arthur A. Ekirch, *The Idea of Progress in America, 1815–1860* (New York: AMS Press, 1969). On the founders' views of interpretation generally, *see* H. Jefferson Powell, "The Original Understanding of Original Intent," 98 *Harv. L. Rev.* 885 (1985); Donald O. Dewey, "James Madison Helps Clio Interpret the Constitution," 15 *Am. J. Legal Hist.* 38 (1971). *See also* Max Farrand, ed., 3 *Records of the Federal Convention of 1787* (New Haven: Yale University Press, 1966) [hereinafter Farrand, *Records*] at 371–75 (James Madison, March and April 1796) (the intentions of the delegates should not be referred to; the Constitution belongs to the people, not the convention); Farrand, 1 *Records* at

583 (July 11, 1787) (Gouverneur Morris) ("Surely those who come after us will judge better of things present, than we can of things future."). Madison later changed his views on some constitutional issues because of popular disagreement with his position, *see* Paul Brest and Sanford Levinson, *Processes of Constitutional Decisionmaking: Cases and Materials* (Boston: Little, Brown, 1992) at 18.

8. Rehnquist, "Living Constitution" at 699.

9. There are many aspects to the delegates' intent that the constitutional meaning not shrink with time, including their conviction that the courts would review statutes, and their concern to bind future generations. Space does not permit a full exposition of all these questions. It is worth noting, however, in light of the long-standing debate about whether the members of the convention intended that we have an institution that we would come to call judicial review, that all of the delegates who discussed the issue, including those in favor and those against, assumed that judicial review would be a fact under the new Constitution.

On June 4, the convention discussed whether the judiciary should be incorporated within a council of revision that would have the power to veto statutes passed by the legislature. Elbridge Gerry said that the courts "will have a sufficient check against encroachments on their own department by the exposition of the laws." Farrand, 1 *Records* at 97. He told the convention that defining exposition of the laws "involved a power of deciding on their constitutionality." *Ibid.* Legal scholars have argued at length whether the next statement Gerry made is correct, but his and his colleagues' perceptions are independently important—Gerry said, "In some states the judges had actually set aside laws as being against the Constitution." *Ibid.* No one disagreed with him. "With general approbation," added Gerry. *Ibid.* Gerry then distinguished that power of exposition, including constitutionality, from the power of determining on the policy of measures. *Ibid.* at 98. King responded that he wanted the judges "free" in expounding the law from any "bias of having participated in its formation," presumably as by inclusion within a council of revision. *Ibid.*

On July 21, Wilson returned to Gerry's point, that the courts would review the constitutionality of statutes as they arose in cases before the courts, but it struck Wilson as insufficient. Wilson continued: "Laws may be unjust, may be unwise, may be dangerous, may be destructive and yet not be so unconstitutional as to justify the judges in refusing to give them effect." Farrand, 2 *Records* at 73.

The convention returned to the courts on August 25. The report of the Committee of Detail had provided that the jurisdiction of the Supreme Court should extend to all cases arising under laws passed by the Congress. The convention then added "this constitution and the" before the word "laws." That change brought the language much closer to the present formula. Madison objected that was going too far. The jurisdiction of the Court should apply only to "matters of a Judiciary nature." The response that was made to Madison was that jurisdiction of cases arising under the Constitution would include only cases of a judicial nature. The vote apparently was based on that assumption, that the judicial power to handle constitutional cases would include only cases of a judicial nature. But the language "arising under the constitution" remained. Farrand, 2 *Records* at 430.

Several in the ratification debates wrote that the Court would perform that function, including, most famously, Alexander Hamilton in "The Federalist" No. 78, in Alexander Hamilton, James Madison, and John Jay, *The Federalist Papers* (New York: New American Library, Clinton Rossiter ed., 1961) at 466–70; James Wilson in Pennsylvania, and John Marshall and Patrick Henry in Virginia, all of whom claimed in their respective ratifying conventions that judicial review was intended, *see* George Lee Haskins and Herbert A. Johnson, *Foundations of Power: John Marshall, 1801–15* (New York: Macmillan, *The Oliver Wendell Holmes Devise History of the Supreme Court of the United States*, vol. 2, 1981) at 186–90. Robert Yates (N.Y.) and Luther Martin (Md.) opposed the Constitution in part because the term "arising under" implied judicial review. *Ibid.* And in the ratifying conventions there does not appear to have been other opposition to judicial review or to the interpretation that treated the Constitution as giving that power to the courts, *ibid.* at 188, but see Yates and Martin, *ibid.* at 186–87. The Judiciary Act of 1789, § 25, now codified at 28 U.S.C. 1257, passed by many of the same people who had participated in drafting and ratifying the Constitution, assumed judicial review by providing for Supreme Court jurisdiction to hear cases in which the constitutionality of either state or federal laws was challenged under provisions of the federal Constitution.

Thus it seems clear that the delegates and their contemporaries believed the courts had reviewed the constitutionality of statutes, that it was part of the power of the judges to declare laws void because they conflict with the Constitution, and that was one of the reasons that they didn't want to put the judicial nose into the tent of a council of revision. The judges should get only one opportunity to review laws and that on the issue of constitutionality.

The extent of the power is less clear than its existence. Madison's discussion of cases of a judiciary nature was not spelled out. It might have referred to cases and controversies or it might have referred to the substance of the controversies. Precedent is not entirely helpful since the delegates and their contemporaries were changing the role of courts radically and separating judicial powers from other powers in ways that were quite new.

10. Payne v. Tennessee, 501 U.S. 808, 827–30 (1991) (*per* Rehnquist, C.J.) (Supreme Court may overrule precedent where prior opinions appear poorly reasoned, especially in constitutional cases decided by narrow margins); *ibid.* at 844–45 (Marshall, J., dissenting) (criticizing the Court's willingness to overrule recent constitutional decisions decided by narrow margins). Rehnquist participated in thirty-one of the thirty-three cases he cited at 501 U.S. 828n and voted to overrule precedent in twenty-four, or 77 percent of them. Chief Justice Rehnquist elaborated his views on overturning precedent in Planned Parenthood of

Southeastern Pennsylvania v. Casey, 505 U.S. 833, 954–59 (1992) (Rehnquist, C.J., concurring in the judgment in part and dissenting in part). *See also* Carolyn D. Richmond, "The Rehnquist Court: What Is in Store for Constitutional Law Precedent?" 39 *N.Y.L. Sch. L. Rev.* 511, 542–45 (1994); Earl M. Maltz, "No Rules in a Knife Fight: Chief Justice Rehnquist and the Doctrine of Stare Decisis," 25 *Rutgers L.J.* 669 (1994) (Rehnquist prefers his own political agenda to application of precedent).

11. *See* Seminole Tribe of Florida v. Florida, 517 U.S. 44, 53–54 (1996) (applying Eleventh Amendment beyond its language); Nevada v. Hall, 440 U.S. 410, 433 (1979) (Rehnquist, J., dissenting) (declaring need to protect state sovereignty beyond express provisions of the Constitution); Fry v. United States, 421 U.S. 542, 557 (1975) (Rehnquist, J., dissenting) (Congress restrained above and beyond the wording of the Tenth and Eleventh Amendments).

12. *See* Lucas v. South Carolina Coastal Council, 505 U.S. 1003, 1014 (1992) (*per* Justice Scalia, joined by Chief Justice Rehnquist) (noting that the Court's current takings law reflects a change from historical understanding); *ibid.* at 505 U.S. 1028 n.15 (declaring early history irrelevant).

13. Glenn A. Phelps and Timothy A. Martinez, "Brennan v. Rehnquist: The Politics of Constitutional Jurisprudence," 22 *Gonz. L. Rev.* 307 (1987).

14. *See* Sue Davis, *Justice Rehnquist and the Constitution* (Princeton: Princeton University Press, 1989); Nancy Maveety, "The Populist of the Adversary Society: The Jurisprudence of Justice Rehnquist," 13 *J. Contemp. L.* 221 (1987). Frank H. Easterbrook, "William H. Rehnquist," in 3 *Encyclopedia of the American Constitution* (New York: Macmillan, Leonard W. Levy et al. eds., 1986) at 1533–35, describes Rehnquist at face value and notes that he separates his personal views, which oppose much economic regulation, from his judicial views, which require that he defer to economic regulation.

15. Rehnquist, "Living Constitution" at 706; Maveety, "The Populist of the Adversary Society." *See also* Texas v. Johnson, 491 U.S. 397, 421 (1989) (Rehnquist, C.J., dissenting) (public has right to ban burning of the flag).

16. Rehnquist, "Living Constitution" at 704, quoted in Davis, *Justice Rehnquist* at 26.

17. *See, e.g.,* Holt Civic Club v. City of Tuscaloosa, 439 U.S. 60 (1978) (*per* Rehnquist, J.) (holding that the extraterritorial extension of a municipality's police powers, judicial jurisdiction, and licensing powers to an unincorporated rural community outside the city limits does not require a concommitant extraterritorial extension of the franchise); Salyer Land Co. v. Tulare Lake Basin Water Storage Dist., 410 U.S. 719 (1973) (*per* Rehnquist, J.) (popular election "inapplicable" to a water district); Brown v. Thompson, 462 U.S. 835 (1983) (*per* Powell, J.) (89 percent population deviation permissible); Chisom v. Roemer, 501 U.S. 380, 404 (1991) (*per* Scalia, J., dissenting) and Houston Lawyers Ass'n v. Atty. Gen. of Texas, 501 U.S. 419, 428 (1991) (*per* Scalia, J., dissenting) (both arguing vote dilution

claims inapplicable to judicial elections); Davis v. Bandemer, 478 U.S. 109, 149 (1985) (*per* O'Connor, J., concurring) (refusing to apply one-person, one-vote principle to political gerrymandering); United States v. Sheffield Board of Comm'rs, 435 U.S. 110, 140 (1978) (*per* Stevens, J., dissenting) (arguing Section 5 of the Voting Rights Act does not apply to cities that do not register voters).

18. Bush v. Vera, 517 U.S. 952 (1996) (*per* O'Connor, J., plurality opinion), and Shaw v. Hunt, 517 U.S. 899 (1996) (Rehnquist, C.J.) (both voiding redistricting plans creating majority-minority districts for failing strict scrutiny); Miller v. Johnson, 515 U.S. 900 (1995) (*per* Kennedy, J.) and Shaw v. Reno, 509 U.S. 630 (1993) (*per* O'Connor, J.) (both ruling strict scrutiny test required for district schemes motivated by race, even if benign or remedial purpose).

19. *E.g.*, Rogers v. Lodge, 458 U.S. 613, 628 (1982) (*per* Powell, J., dissenting) (finding insufficient evidence of discriminatory intent); City of Mobile v. Bolden, 446 U.S. 55 (1980) (*per* Stewart, J., plurality opinion) (same and also finding Fifteenth Amendment limited to balloting and inapplicable to districting).

20. Hunter v. Underwood, 471 U.S. 222 (1985).

21. Ball v. James, 451 U.S. 355 (1981) (*per* Stewart, J.) (power district); Salyer Land Co. v. Tulare Lake Basin Water Storage District, 410 U.S. 719 (1973) (*per* Rehnquist, J.) (water district). Two footnotes in Ball v. James, 451 U.S. at 364–65 n.8 and *ibid.* at 371 n.20, also obliquely questioned the protection for voters in school district elections, an implication noted by both Justice Powell, concurring at 451 U.S. 373 n.2, and Justice White, dissenting at 451 U.S. 388 n.11.

22. *See supra* note 17.

23. Dolan v. City of Tigard, 512 U.S. 374 (1994); Lucas v. South Carolina Coastal Council, 505 U.S. 1003 (1992); Nollan v. California Coastal Comm'n, 483 U.S. 825 (1987).

24. *See, e.g.,* City of Richmond v. J.A. Croson Co., 488 U.S. 469 (1989) (Rehnquist, C.J., joining the majority finding city's affirmative action program in violation of equal protection). *See also infra* at notes 81ff.

25. Bowers v. Hardwick, 478 U.S. 186 (1986) (Rehnquist joined White's majority opinion).

26. Barnes v. Glen Theatre, Inc., 501 U.S. 560 (1991).

27. Roe v. Wade, 410 U.S. 113, 171 (1973) (Rehnquist, J., dissenting).

28. *See, e.g.,* Lee v. Weisman, 505 U.S. 577, 630 (1992) (Rehnquist joining Justice Scalia's dissenting opinion); Wallace v. Jaffrey, 472 U.S. 38, 106 (1985) (Rehnquist, J., dissenting) (arguing that government should be permitted to promote religion consistent with the First Amendment); Michael W. McConnell, "Religious Freedom at a Crossroads," 59 *U. Chi. L. Rev.* 115, 145–46 (1992).

29. *See* Bowers v. Hardwick, 478 U.S. at 208–9 (Blackmun, J., dissenting) (Court had no occasion to consider justifications because of procedural posture of the case, with the result that the privacy claim was denied without any claim of harm to others).

30. Barnes v. Glen Theatre, Inc., 501 U.S. at 562.

31. *Ibid.* at 582 (Souter, J., concurring). *See* Vincent Blasi, "Six Conservatives in Search of the First Amendment: The Revealing Case of Nude Dancing," 33 *Wm. & Mary L. Rev.* 611 (1992), for an excellent discussion of the role of moral autonomy in *Barnes*; whether the Court should adopt a relativist position is discussed in Steven Gey, "Is Moral Relativism a Constitutional Command?" 70 *Ind. L.J.* 331 (1995).

32. 410 U.S. at 172–77.

33. Wallace v. Jaffrey, 472 U.S. at 106 (Rehnquist, J., dissenting); McConnell, "Religious Freedom at a Crossroads" at 145–46.

34. Wallace v. Jaffrey, 472 U.S. at 106 (Rehnquist, J., dissenting).

35. Jeffrey A. Segal and Harold J. Spaeth, *The Supreme Court and the Attitudinal Model* (New York: Cambridge University Press 1993) at 320–22, document ninety-six cases through the 1989 term in which Rehnquist voted to overturn legislation. In percentage terms this is far less than his colleagues, but percentages are very misleading—the willingness to overturn legislation is greatly affected by the nature of the legislation brought before the Court and the impact of the other members of the Court in defining the Court's agenda. The prior question therefore is not the number of cases in which he has voted to overrule legislation but which kind of legislation he votes to overrule. Only if we could identify comparable types of legislation based on Rehnquist's value system and their prevalence in existing law could we begin to identify the extent of his actual restraint. The new majority on the Court has begun to reveal with greater clarity where Rehnquist would overrule legislation if given the opportunity, *see, e.g.,* three recent decisions finding state liability for "regulatory takings": Dolan v. City of Tigard, 512 U.S. 374 (1994) (*per* Rehnquist, C.J.); Lucas v. South Carolina Coastal Council, 505 U.S. 1003 (1992) (*per* Scalia, J.); Nollan v. California Coastal Comm'n, 483 U.S. 825 (1987) (*per* Scalia, J.).

36. Rehnquist, "Living Constitution" at 706; Stone v. Powell, 428 U.S. 465 (1976) (*per* Powell, J.); Bork, *Tempting of America* at 69–100.

37. David L. Shapiro, "William Hubbs Rehnquist," in *The Burger Court* (Leon Friedman ed., 1980), 5 *The Justices of the United States Supreme Court, 1789–1978* (New York: Chelsea House, Leon Friedman and Fred L. Israel eds., 1980) at 109, 111; David L. Shapiro, "Mr. Justice Rehnquist: A Preliminary View," 90 *Harv. L. Rev.* 293, 294 (1976).

38. In Codispoti v. Pennsylvania, 418 U.S. 506, 534 (1974) (Rehnquist, J., dissenting), Rehnquist noted the arguments against incorporation without further discussion:

Mr. Justice Harlan, in dissent, joined by Mr. Justice Stewart, forcefully argued that there was no indication that the drafters of the Fourteenth Amendment intended to make the Sixth Amendment applicable to the States. See Fairman, Does the Fourteenth Amendment Incorporate the Bill of Rights? The Original Understanding, 2 Stan. L. Rev. 5 (1949); Morrison, Does the Fourteenth Amendment Incorporate the Bill of Rights? The Judicial Interpretation, 2 Stan. L. Rev. 140 (1949).

Fairman's article served as the major academic attack on the incorporation doctrine.

Rehnquist apparently would replace selective incorporation with a "case-by-case approach to fundamental fairness," Herring v. New York, 422 U.S. 853, 868 (1975) (Rehnquist, J., dissenting), rather than treat fundamental fairness as a justification for a complete adoption of provisions of the Bill of Rights:

> However in some instances the Court has engaged in a process of "specific incorporation," whereby certain provisions of the Bill of Rights have been applied against the States. In making the decision whether or not a particular provision relating to the conduct of a trial should be incorporated, we have been guided by whether the right in question may be deemed essential to fundamental fairness—an analytical approach which is compelled if we are to remain true to the basic orientation of the Due Process Clause. But once we have determined that a particular right should be incorporated against the States, we have abandoned case-by-case considerations of fairness. Incorporation, in effect, results in the establishment of a strict prophylactic rule, one which is to be generally observed in every case regardless of its particular circumstances. . . .
>
> Beyond certain of the specified rights in the Bill of Rights, however, I do not understand the basis for abandoning the case-by-case approach to fundamental fairness.

Ibid. at 867–68 (citations omitted). In Buckley v. Valeo, 424 U.S. 1, 290 (1976) (Rehnquist, J., concurring in part and dissenting in part), he wrote: "[N]ot all of the strictures which the First Amendment imposes upon Congress are carried over against the States by the Fourteenth Amendment, but rather that it is only the 'general principle' of free speech . . . that the latter incorporates." *Ibid.* at 290.

He returned to the issue briefly in Middendorf v. Henry, 425 U.S. 25 (1976). Writing for the Court, Rehnquist suggested his own doubts by introducing a discussion of the Sixth Amendment with the unsettling words "Whatever may be the merits of 'selective incorporation'" and not returning to the issue. *Ibid.* at 34.

A few years later he referred to "[t]he mysterious process of transmogrification by which [a guarantee in the Bill of Rights] was held to be 'incorporated' and made applicable to the states by the Fourteenth Amendment." Carter v. Kentucky, 450 U.S. 288, 309 (1981) (Rehnquist, J., dissenting). And in Thomas v. Review Board of the Indiana Employment Security Division, 450 U.S. 707, 720 (1981) (Rehnquist, J., dissenting), he identified the incorporation doctrine as one of three causes for "'tension' between the Free Exercise and Establishment Clauses":

> Second, the decision by this Court that the First Amendment was "incorporated" into the Fourteenth Amendment and thereby made applicable

against the States, similarly multiplied the number of instances in which the "tension" might arise.

Ibid. at 721 (citations omitted) (Rehnquist, J., dissenting). And he added a suggestive appeal to originalism:

> [A]s originally enacted, the First Amendment applied only to the Federal Government, not the government of the States. Barron v. [Mayor and City Council of] Baltimore, 7 Pet. [32 U.S.] 243 (1833). The Framers could hardly anticipate *Barron* being superseded by the "selective incorporation" doctrine adopted by the Court, a decision which greatly expanded the number of statutes which would be subject to challenge under the First Amendment.

Ibid.

But see Lee v. Weisman, 505 U.S. 577, 620 n.4 (1992) (Souter, J., concurring) ("In *Everson v. Board of Educ. of Ewing,* we unanimously incorporated the Establishment Clause into the Due Process Clause of the Fourteenth Amendment and, by so doing, extended its reach to the actions of States. Since then not one Member of this Court has proposed disincorporating the Clause." [citations omitted]); *see also* TXO Prod. Corp. v. Alliance Resources Corp., 509 U.S. 443, 470 (1993) (Scalia, J., dissenting, joined by Justice Thomas), in which Justice Scalia suggested his acquiescence was not without some discomfort:

> I am willing to accept the proposition that the Due Process Clause of the Fourteenth Amendment, despite its textual limitation to procedure, incorporates certain substantive guarantees specified in the Bill of Rights.

39. Chicago, B. and Q. R.R. Co. v. City of Chicago, 166 U.S. 226, 239 (1897) (decided on substantive due process grounds); Gitlow v. New York, 268 U.S. 652 (1925) (assuming the First Amendment applies through the Fourteenth); and Palko v. Connecticut, 302 U.S. 319 (1937) (the Fourteenth Amendment includes provisions of the Bill of Rights "implicit in the concept of ordered liberty"). The historical basis for incorporation was developed at length by Justice Black in Adamson v. California, 332 U.S. 46, 68, 72–92 (1947) (Black, J., dissenting). At this time most of the Bill of Rights has been applied through the Fourteenth Amendment, *see* Laurence H. Tribe, *American Constitutional Law* (Mineola, N.Y.: Foundation Press, 2d ed., 1988) at 772–74.

40. Edelman v. Jordan, 415 U.S. 651, 673–74 (1974). *See* Davis, *Justice Rehnquist* at 154–59.

41. *See* Seminole Tribe of Florida v. Florida, 517 U.S. 44 (1996). Chief Justice Rehnquist, writing for the majority, asserted that federal laws could be enforced by other means, *ibid.* at 71 n.14, *but see ibid.* at 157 n.52 (Souter, J., dissenting) pointing to the limitations on the alternative remedies asserted by the majority.

42. Idaho v. Coeur d'Alene Tribe of Idaho, 521 U.S. 261 (1997).

43. Lujan v. Defenders of Wildlife, 504 U.S. 555 (1992) (*per* Scalia, J.); Valley

Forge Christian College v. Americans United for Separation of Church and State, Inc., 454 U.S. 464 (1982).

44. National Credit Union Admin. v. First National Bank and Trust Co., 522 U.S. 479 (1998).

45. *See, e.g.,* City of Richmond v. J.A. Croson Co., 488 U.S. 469 (1989) (Rehnquist, C.J., joining the majority finding city's affirmative action program in violation of equal protection). Much of Rehnquist's equal protection jurisprudence has involved narrowing the reach of legislation through restrictive interpretation. *See, e.g.,* Spallone v. United States, 493 U.S. 265 (1990) (construing equitable principles broadly to limit relief); Martin v. Wilks, 490 U.S. 755 (1989) (nonparties can sue to set aside consent decree); Local No. 93, International Association of Firefighters v. City of Cleveland, 478 U.S. 501, 535 (1986) (Rehnquist, J., dissenting) (arguing that relief should be limited to actual victims of discrimination); Local 28, Sheet Metal Workers' International Association v. E.E.O.C., 478 U.S. 421, 500 (1986) (Rehnquist, J., dissenting) (same); City Of Rome v. United States, 446 U.S. 156, 206 (1980) (Rehnquist, J., dissenting) (concluding that the Court had interpreted the Voting Rights Act in a way that exceeded Congress's powers under the Fourteenth Amendment). *See also* Patterson v. McLean Credit Union, 491 U.S. 164 (1989) (Rehnquist joining the majority excluding working conditions from the reach of Title VII).

46. *See, e.g.,* three recent eminent domain cases, Dolan v. City of Tigard, 512 U.S. 374 (1994) (*per* Rehnquist, C. J.); Lucas v. South Carolina Coastal Council, 505 U.S. 1003 (1992) (*per* Scalia, J.); Nollan v. California Coastal Comm'n, 483 U.S. 825 (1987) (*per* Scalia, J.).

47. *See* Ingersoll-Rand Co. v. McClendon, 498 U.S. 133, 145 (1990) (holding that ERISA preempted state prohibition of wrongful discharge that was based on imminent vesting of an employee's pension); F.M.C. Corp. v. Holliday, 498 U.S. 52, 65 (1990) (holding that ERISA preempted state regulation of self-insured pension plans not directly covered by ERISA).

48. *See, e.g.,* Charles H. Clarke, "Private Property, the Takings Clause and the Pursuit of Market Gain," 25 *Akron L. Rev.* 1 (1991); Robin West, "Progressive and Conservative Constitutionalism," 88 *Mich. L. Rev.* 641, 657–58 (1990).

49. Stephen J. Massey, Note, "Justice Rehnquist's Theory of Property," 93 *Yale L.J.* 541, 546–59 (1984); John Denvir, "Justice Brennan, Justice Rehnquist, and Free Speech," 80 *Nw. U. L. Rev.* 285, 295–99 (1985) (comparing Rehnquist with Brennan as opposite poles of the Court).

50. *See* United States v. Kokinda, 497 U.S. 720 (1990) (*per* O'Connor, J.); International Society for Krishna Consciousness, Inc. v. Lee, 505 U.S. 672 (1992) (*per* Rehnquist, C.J.); Forsyth County v. The Nationalist Movement, 505 U.S. 123, 136 (1992) (Rehnquist, C.J., dissenting); City of Cincinnati v. Discovery Network, Inc., 507 U.S. 410, 438 (1993) (Rehnquist, C.J., dissenting). *See generally* Owen Fiss, "Silence on the Street Corner," in *Public Values in Constitutional Law* (Ann

Arbor: University of Michigan Press, Stephen E. Gottlieb ed., 1993) at 195, 206–9.

51. *See* Alexander v. United States, 509 U.S. 544 (1993) (*per* Rehnquist, C.J.).

52. *See ibid.* at 560 (Kennedy, J., dissenting).

53. This flows naturally from the way that economics is a description of the interactions of subjective measures of value, whether described as utility functions or pleasure and pain. *See generally* Alfred Marshall, *Principles of Economics: An Introductory Volume* (New York: Macmillan, 9th ed., C. W. Guillebaud annot., 1961) at 92–93; George J. Stigler, *Essays in the History of Economics* (Chicago: University of Chicago Press 1965) at 67–75.

54. At least in the fashion of views Posner once espoused, *see* Richard A. Posner, "Utilitarianism, Economics, and Legal Theory," 8 *J. Legal Stud.* 103 (1979); Jules L. Coleman, *Markets, Morals and the Law* (New York: Cambridge University Press, 1988) at 96; *but see* Massey, "Justice Rehnquist's Theory of Property" at 557 n.93 (Rehnquist best explained by allocative efficiency).

55. Herrera v. Collins, 506 U.S. 390, 400 (1993) (*per* Rehnquist, C.J.).

56. Rehnquist's actual language is quite close to an economic argument. In *Herrera* he worried about paralyzing the judicial system with overwork, 506 U.S. at 399. And he joined the opinion in *Kyles*, in which Justice Scalia wrote that the burden of review would be far too great, 514 U.S. 419 at 457–58. Regardless of Rehnquist's explicit language, the question here is whether his conclusions are consistent with an economic approach.

57. *See supra* notes 50, 51.

58. Most recently in Felker v. Turpin, 518 U.S. 651 (1996) (Rehnquist, C.J.) (denying habeas and upholding limits on Court's authority to review petitions from state prisoners under the Effective Death Penalty Act of 1996, 28 U.S.C. 153 (1996)), Chief Justice Rehnquist wrote for a unanimous Court, but Justices Stevens, Souter, and Breyer concurred to make clear that more avenues of review remained than the Court identified in the opinion of Chief Justice Rehnquist. Gray v. Netherland, 518 U.S. 152 (1996) (Rehnquist, C.J.) (denying claim that prosecution gave inadequate notice of evidence used against petitioner at penalty phase of trial); Bowersox v. Williams, 517 U.S. 345 (1996) (*per curiam*) (vacating a stay of execution because court of appeals failed to give its reasons for the stay and district court's findings did not justify the stay); and Netherland v. Tuggle, 515 U.S. 951 (1995) (*per curiam*) (vacating stay of execution granted to allow petitioner to file petition for certiorari) were 5–4 decisions over the dissents of Stevens, Souter, Ginsburg, and Breyer. *See also* Anderson v. Buell, 516 U.S. 1100 (1996) (*per* Scalia, J., dissenting); Thompson v. Keohane, 516 U.S. 99, 116 (1995) (per Thomas, J., dissenting); Kyles v. Whitley, 514 U.S. 419, 458 (1995) (per Scalia, J. dissenting) ("We carefully consider whether the convictions and sentences in these cases had been obtained in reliance upon correct principles of federal law, but if we tried to consider, in addition, whether some of those correct principles had been applied, not

merely plausibly, but accurately, to the particular facts of each case, we could have done nothing else for the week."); and a particularly troubling result in Jacobs v. Scott, 513 U.S. 1067 (1995) (denying stay of execution of convicted murderer after prosecutors changed their mind and convicted another person for the same murder; the state "insist[ed] on the death penalty after repudiating the factual basis for that sentence," 513 U.S. at 1069 (Stevens, J., dissenting). *See also infra,* notes 90 and 96.

59. John 8:32 (New Testament).

60. One large group of such cases is in the First Amendment area. *See, e.g.,* Metromedia, Inc. v. City of San Diego, 453 U.S. 490, 569 (1981) (Rehnquist, J., dissenting) (aesthetic regulation of billboards permissible); Community Communications Co. v. City of Boulder, 455 U.S. 40, 60 (1982) (Rehnquist, J., dissenting) (regulation of CATV not preempted); First National Bank of Boston v. Bellotti, 435 U.S. 765, 822 (1978) (Rehnquist, J., dissenting) (regulation of corporate speech permissible); FEC v. National Right to Work Committee, 459 U.S. 197 (1983) (*per* Rehnquist, J.) (regulation of political action committees permissible); Buckley v. Valeo, 424 U.S. 1, 290 (1976) (Rehnquist, J., concurring in part and dissenting in part) (accepted most regulation of political speech by the Federal Election Campaign Act but dissented from treatment of minor parties and independent candidates); *but see* Federal Election Commission v. National Conservative PAC, 470 U.S. 480 (1985) (*per* Rehnquist, J.) (independent spending in presidential campaigns protected).

61. *Ibid. and see* Denvir, "Justice Brennan, Justice Rehnquist, and Free Speech" at 295–99.

62. In West Lynn Creamery, Inc. v. Healy, 512 U.S. 186, 212 (1994) (Rehnquist, C.J., dissenting), for example, he argued in favor of permitting state discrimination in favor of local dairies with funds raised from a tax on local and out-of-state dairy produce. For Rehnquist, rescuing the local farmer was more important than economic rationality, or, apparently, than rescuing various other social interests. Similarly, he voted against a national market in waste management, C and A Carbone, Inc. v. Town of Clarkstown, 511 U.S. 383, 410 (1994) (Souter, J., dissenting); Oregon Waste Systems, Inc. v. Oregon Department of Environmental Quality, 511 U.S. 93, 108 (1994) (Rehnquist, C.J., dissenting).

63. West, "Progressive and Conservative" at 655–57 (describing legal traditionalism's deference to the established legal system out of obedience to its power).

64. *See supra* note 10.

65. Kathleen M. Sullivan, "Foreword: The Justices of Rules and Standards," 106 *Harv. L. Rev.* 24, 115–17 (1992).

66. *See, e.g.,* United States v. Lopez, 514 U.S. 549 (1995); National League of Cities v. Usery, 426 U.S. 833 (1976).

67. *E.g.,* Wallace v. Jaffrey, 472 U.S. 38, 106, 113 (1985) (Rehnquist, J., dissenting); McConnell, "Religious Freedom at a Crossroads" at 145–46.

68. *See generally* Stephen E. Gottlieb, "Does Federalism Matter to Its Devotees on the Court?" 23 *Ohio N.U. L. Rev.* 1179 (1997).

69. On race, *see supra* note 45. On taking of property, *see supra* note 46. It has been suggested that some of the conservative justices may be responding to social choice theory. Social choice theory develops at length the ways that voting procedures and the resources available for competing positions can misrepresent majority preferences, and the ways that group decision-making processes can be skewed by individual calculations of advantage to the disadvantage of the general public, often termed rent-seeking behavior. *See* Samuel Issacharoff, "Polarized Voting and the Political Process: The Transformation of Voting Rights Jurisprudence," 90 *Mich. L. Rev.* 1833, 1884–90 (1992); Lynn A. Stout, *Strict Scrutiny and Social Choice: An Economic Inquiry into Fundamental Rights and Suspect Classifications,* 80 *Geo. L. J.* 1787, 1816–19 (1992). But it is hard to differentiate the groups these justices prefer from those they condemn in these terms. Social choice theory could explain misbehavior on the part of virtually all parties and indeed by the judiciary itself.

70. *See* Ingersoll-Rand Co. v. McClendon, 498 U.S. 133, 145 (1990) (holding that ERISA preempted state prohibition of wrongful discharge that was based on imminent vesting of an employee's pension); F.M.C. Corp. v. Holliday, 498 U.S. 52, 65 (1990) (holding that ERISA preempted state regulation of self-insured pension plans not directly covered by ERISA).

71. Rehnquist supported limitations on political parties in Buckley v. Valeo, 424 U.S. 1, 290 (1976) (approving contribution limitations, but Rehnquist opposed government funding and would have protected minor parties and independents). He joined the dissenters in Tashjian v. Republican Party, 479 U.S. 208, 234 (1986) (Scalia, J., dissenting), who would have denied autonomy to a party to select its own nomination procedures. Where the rights of the two major parties were in conflict, Rehnquist supported the traditional privileges of the controlling party over the rights of members of the minority party, *see* Branti v. Finkel, 445 U.S. 507, 522 (1980) (Powell, J., dissenting), in which Rehnquist joined the Powell dissent, which took the position that nonmembership in the controlling political party could be a basis for termination from certain public offices; Elrod v. Burns, 427 U.S. 347, 376 (1976) (Powell, J., dissenting) in which Rehnquist joined a very similar Powell dissent.

72. *See* First National Bank v. Bellotti, 435 U.S. 765, 822 (1978) (Rehnquist, J., dissenting) (advocating a restrictive approach toward corporate political expression); FEC v. National Right to Work Committee, 459 U.S. 197 (1983) (sustaining regulation of political action committees); *but see* Colorado Republican Federal Campaign Committee v. Federal Election Commission, 518 U.S. 604, 626 (1996) (Kennedy, J., concurring in the judgment and dissenting in part) (concluding that restriction of party spending in conjunction with the party's candidates is unconstitutional); ibid. at 631 (Thomas, J., concurring in the judgment and dissenting in part) (same); FEC v. National Conservative PAC, 470 U.S. 480 (1985) (opinion

permitting independent spending in presidential campaigns) *and see infra* note 133 on his respect for corporations generally.

73. *See* Robert Devigne, *Recasting Conservatism: Oakeshott, Strauss, and the Response to Postmodernism* (New Haven: Yale University Press, 1994) at 95–96; William Schambra, "Progressive Liberalism and American Community," 80 *Pub. Interest* 31, 40 (Summer 1985).

74. Madison's famous response is "The Federalist" No. 10.

75. *See* Devigne, *Recasting Conservatism* at 95–96; Schambra, "Progressive Liberalism."

76. For changes in the meaning of pluralism, see chapter 2, note 141.

77. *See* Devigne, *Recasting Conservatism* at 95–96; Schambra, "Progressive Liberalism."

78. Jack Greenberg, *Crusaders in the Courts* (New York: Basic Books, 1994); Mark V. Tushnet, *Making Civil Rights Law: Thurgood Marshall and the Supreme Court, 1936–1961* (New York: Oxford University Press, 1994) at 126–36.

79. *See* Greenberg, *Crusaders* at 85–87.

80. *See Desegregation from Brown to Alexander: An Exploration of Supreme Court Strategies* (Carbondale: Southern Illinois University Press, Stephen L. Wasby, *et al.*, 1977) at 137–38; Tushnet, *Making Civil Rights Law* at 367 n.2.

81. Jerome M. Culp, Jr., "Understanding the Racial Discourse of Justice Rehnquist," 25 *Rutgers L.J.* 597 (1994).

82. *See ibid.* at 609 n.40; Hunter v. Underwood, 471 U.S. 222 (1985) (finding statute intentionally discriminatory) (*per* Rehnquist, J.); Holder v. Hall, 512 U.S. 874 (1994) (denying relief under the Voting Rights Act without questioning the act itself. Rehnquist did not join Thomas's attack on the Voting Rights Act in *Holder,* 512 U.S. 891 (Thomas, J., concurring in the judgment), though he participated in many opinions eviscerating it. *See also* Lani Guinier, "The Supreme Court, 1993 Term: [E]Racing Democracy: The Voting Rights Cases," 108 *Harv. L. Rev.* 109, 118–25 (1994).

83. 505 U.S. 717 (1992) (*per* White, J.).

84. Freeman v. Pitts, 503 U.S. 467 (1992) (*per* Kennedy, J.); Board of Educ. of Oklahoma City v. Dowell, 498 U.S. 237 (1991) (*per* Rehnquist, C.J.).

85. Brown v. Board of Education, 347 U.S. 483 (1954).

86. The story of Rehnquist's work against the emerging civil rights movement and the controversies that surrounded the revelation of his efforts are told in Donald E. Boles, *Mr. Justice Rehnquist, Judicial Activist: The Early Years* (Ames: Iowa State University Press, 1987) at 75–104.

87. Ibid. at 99.

88. For example, Justice Rehnquist joined a pair of decisions in 1989 that divested Indian authorities of power over land transactions by non-Indians in fee-patented land on Indian reservations: Cotton Petroleum Corp. v. New Mexico, 490 U.S. 163 (1989) (state had authority to tax production of oil and gas by non-

Indian lessees on Indian reservation); Brendale v. Confederated Tribes and Bands of the Yakima Indian Nation, 492 U.S. 408 (1989) (White, J., plurality opinion) (tribe had no power to zone land held in fee by non-Indians on Indian reservation). The shift in power from the tribes to the states represented by those decisions is carefully described by Deborah A. Geier, "Power and Presumptions; Rules and Rhetoric; Institutions and Indian Law," 1994 *BYU L. Rev.* 451, 475–490. Rehnquist's skepticism toward Indian claims is also reflected in his own opinions: Oliphant v. Suquamish Indian Tribe, 435 U.S. 191 (1978) (tribe had no jurisdiction to try to punish non-Indians for crimes committed on Indian land without specific congressional authorization); United States v. Sioux Nation of Indians, 448 U.S. 371, 434–37 (1980) (Rehnquist, J., dissenting) (rejecting additional compensation for land taken in the wake of the campaign of General Custer and the decrease in tribal lands as based on history that is bad or unfair to the federal authorities). One of his most recent opinions is Seminole Tribe of Florida v. Florida, 517 U.S. 44 (1996) (first, holding that Congress had no power to abrogate state Eleventh Amendment immunity in favor of Indian tribes, thus removing a major enforcement tool from the tribes in their relations and legal disputes with the states and overruling Pennsylvania v. Union Gas Co., 491 U.S. 1 (1989), which had held that Congress does have that authority under the commerce clause, and second, declining to follow Ex parte Young, 209 U.S. 123 (1908) on the ground that Congress would not have intended such an action although it had authorized an action against the state). *See also* Employment Div. v. Smith, 494 U.S. 872 (1990) (*per* Scalia, J.) (Indian religious observance involving ceremonial use of peyote subject to state law).

89. West, "Progressive and Conservative" at 654–55 (Moral conservative defers to community's sense of morality defined by its moral commitments and traditions.).

90. *See* Davis, *Justice Rehnquist* at 167–71, describing Rehnquist's leading the Burger Court's "three pronged attack" on habeas corpus, barring many Fourth Amendment claims, requiring compliance with state procedures, and requiring explanation of difference from state factual determinations, all making it more difficult to resort to this form of relief. *See* Sumner v. Mata, 449 U.S. 539 (1981) (Rehnquist, J.) (courts must defer to state court factual determinations); Stone v. Powell, 428 U.S. 465 (1976) (*per* Powell, J.) (denying habeas jurisdiction over most Fourth Amendment claims); Davis v. United States, 411 U.S. 233 (1973) (Rehnquist, J.) (habeas may be waived by failure to comply with state procedures). *See also* Felker v. Turpin, 518 U.S. 651 (1996) (Rehnquist, C.J.) (denying habeas and upholding limits on Court's authority to review petitions from state prisoners under the Effective Death Penalty Act of 1996, 28 U.S.C. 153 (1996)).

91. One of the major barriers to relief was that the requirements of the Bill of Rights itself were only slowly becoming applicable to the states. For an excellent synopsis of the major points in the development of the doctrine of incorporation of the Bill of Rights by the Fourteenth Amendment, see Jerold H. Israel,

"Selective Incorporation: Revisited," 71 *Geo. L.J.* 253 (1982). In 1897, in Chicago, B. and Q. R.R. v. Chicago, 166 U.S. 226 (1897), the Court said that the Fourteenth Amendment prevented a state from taking property without paying compensation. The case, however, did not mention the Fifth Amendment. Two cases that followed addressed criminal procedure challenges raised under the Fourteenth Amendment. These cases, Maxwell v. Dow, 176 U.S. 581 (1900) and Twining v. New Jersey, 211 U.S. 78 (1908), rejected mechanical incorporation of the provisions of the Bill of Rights and adopted the more amorphous fundamental fairness conception of the Fourteenth Amendment. *See* Israel, "Selective Incorporation: Revisited" at 279–80. Using such a totality-of-the-circumstances approach, the Court found due process violations in Moore v. Dempsey, 261 U.S. 86 (1923) and Tumey v. Ohio, 273 U.S. 510 (1927), but in neither case did it make use of an explicitly enumerated protection from the Bill of Rights. Powell v. Alabama, 287 U.S. 45 (1932), was the first case to use the fundamental fairness approach to find that the Fourteenth Amendment protected a right specifically enumerated in the Bill of Rights.

92. 287 U.S. 45 (1932).

93. *See, e.g.,* Mapp v. Ohio, 367 U.S. 643 (1961); Miranda v. Arizona, 384 U.S. 436 (1966).

94. *See* Larry W. Yackle, "The Habeas Hagioscope," 66 *S. Cal. L. Rev.* 2331, 2348–49 (1993); Townsend v. Sain, 372 U.S. 293 (1963).

95. 428 U.S. 465 (1976) (*per* Powell, J.).

96. *See generally* Daniel H. Foote, "'The Door That Never Opens'?: Capital Punishment and Post-Conviction Review of Death Sentences in the United States and Japan," 19 *Brook. J. Int'l L.* 367, 393–411 (1993). Rehnquist joined in a series of 1986 decisions that developed the innocence requirement and lend support to Herrera's claim discussed in the text following this note. *See* Kuhlmann v. Wilson, 477 U.S. 436, 454 (1986) (plurality opinion) (*per* Powell, J.) ("We conclude that the 'ends of justice' require federal courts to entertain such petitions only where the prisoner supplements his constitutional claim with a colorable showing of factual innocence."); Murray v. Carrier, 477 U.S. 478, 496 (1986) (*per* O'Connor, J.) ("We think that in an extraordinary case, where a Constitutional violation has probably resulted in the conviction of one who is actually innocent, a federal habeas court may grant the writ even in the absence of a showing of cause for the procedural default."); and Smith v. Murray, 477 U.S. 527, 537 (1986) (O'Connor, J., quoting the language of Murray v. Carrier cited above). Although he joined the opinion in McCleskey v. Zant, 499 U.S. 467, 495 (1991) citing the *Kuhlmann* standard, the standard narrowed in Sawyer v. Whitley, 505 U.S. 333, 347 (1992) (Rehnquist, C.J.) (actual innocence "must focus on those elements [introduced at the original trial] that render a defendant eligible for the death penalty, and not on additional mitigating evidence that was prevented from being introduced as a result of a claimed constitutional error.").

97. Herrera v. Collins, 506 U.S. 390, 406–7 (1993) (*per* Rehnquist, C.J.).

98. *See supra* note 96.

99. 506 U.S. 404–5, 411.

100. For similar minimization of the right to life, see DeShaney v. Winnebago Co. Dep't of Social Servs., 489 U.S. 189 (1989) (*per* Rehnquist, C.J.). Only a self-regarding definition of moral obligations could treat the taking of life as trivial.

101. Rehnquist, O'Connor, Scalia, Kennedy, and Thomas joined in an opinion that assumed arguendo that actual innocence might give rise to relief—a right to a hearing on his evidence—but only if defendant met a very difficult burden of "truly persuasive" proof of innocence, *Herrera,* 506 U.S. at 417, 426–27. *See also* Schlup v. Delo, 513 U.S. 298 (1995); Kyles v. Whitley, 514 U.S. 419 (1995).

102. *Herrera,* 506 U.S. at 427–29 (Scalia, J., concurring).

103. Most of the majority opinion argued that habeas is unavailable except for procedural error.

104. *Herrera,* 506 U.S. at 442–43 (Blackmun, J., dissenting).

105. *Ibid.* at 417 ("We may assume, for the sake of argument in deciding this case, that in a capital case a truly persuasive demonstration of 'actual innocence' made after trial would render the execution of a defendant unconstitutional.")

106. Schlup v. Delo, 513 U.S. 298, 334(1995) (Rehnquist, C.J., dissenting). Chief Justice Rehnquist argued for a version of the standard adopted in Jackson v. Virginia, 443 U.S. 307 (1979), which considered only whether the original jury could have found the defendant guilty based on the evidence originally introduced at trial, thus effectively excluding after-acquired evidence from judicial consideration. *Schlup,* 513 U.S. at 340–41.

107. *Ibid.* at 332 (O'Connor, J., concurring).

108. Schlup v. Delo, *supra.*

109. *See supra* note 10.

110. *See supra* note 12.

111. *See* Scalia, "Rule of Law" at 1182–85.

112. *See* Bork, *Tempting of America* at 5–6.

113. *See* Ernest Young, "Rediscovering Conservatism: Burkean Political Theory and Constitutional Interpretation," 72 N.C. L. Rev. 619, 637–42 (1994) (discussing conservative preference for rules over standards).

114. Rehnquist, "Living Constitution."

115. Justice O'Connor has been quite candid by comparison, balancing and comparing important public values. *See* Sandra Day O'Connor, "Testing Government Action: The Promise of Federalism," in Gottlieb, *Public Values in Constitutional Law* at 35.

116. There is a complex debate about the logic and the likelihood of being able to follow rules. *See generally* Schauer, *Playing by the Rules*; Alan R. Madry, "Analytic Deconstructionism? The Intellectual Voyeurism of Anthony D'Amato," 63 *Fordham L. Rev.* 1033 (1995); Duncan Kennedy, "Form and Substance in Private

Law Adjudication," 89 *Harv. L. Rev.* 1685 (1976); Karl N. Llewellyn, "Remarks on the Theory of Appellate Decision and the Rules or Canons about How Statutes Are to Be Construed," 3 *Vand. L. Rev.* 395 (1950). For our purposes, it does not matter whether rules are hard to follow because of complexity or the nature of language. In either case, Rehnquist and his colleagues had acceptable choices.

117. 506 U.S. at 401 ("Few rulings would be more disruptive of our federal system than to provide for federal habeas review of free-standing claims of actual innocence."); *and see* Stephen E. Gottlieb, "The Paradox of Balancing Significant Interests," 45 *Hastings L.J.* 825, 831 (1994).

118. *See* Barnes v. Glen Theatre, Inc., 501 U.S. 560 (1991) (*per* Rehnquist, C.J., plurality opinion); Bowers v. Hardwick, 478 U.S. 714 (1986) (*per* White, J.); Roe v. Wade, 410 U.S. 113, 171 (1973) (Rehnquist, J., dissenting).

119. *See* Young v. American Mini Theatres, 427 U.S. 50, 58–60 (1976) (*per* Stevens, J.); Parker v. Levy, 417 U.S. 733, 756–59 (1974) (*per* Rehnquist, J.); Arnett v. Kennedy, 416 U.S. 134, 158–60 (1974) (Rehnquist, J., plurality opinion).

120. *See* Madsen v. Women's Health Center, Inc., 512 U.S. 753, 775–76 (1994); Parker v. Levy, 417 U.S. 733, 757–61 (1974); Arnett v. Kennedy, 416 U.S. 134, 158–60 (1974); Moose Lodge No. 107 v. Irvis, 407 U.S. 163, 167–68 (1972).

121. *Moose Lodge,* 407 U.S. at 167–68 (1972).

122. *See* Coates v. City of Cincinnati, 402 U.S. 611 (1971); Cox v. Louisiana, 379 U.S. 559 (1965) (Cox II); Cox v. Louisiana, 379 U.S. 536 (1965) (Cox I); Kunz v. New York, 340 U.S. 290 (1951); Niemotko v. Maryland, 340 U.S. 268 (1951); Cantwell v. Connecticut, 310 U.S. 296 (1940); Schneider v. State, 308 U.S. 147 (1939).

123. Scalia, "Rule of Law" at 1179.

124. Forsyth County v. The Nationalist Movement, 505 U.S. 123, 140–43 (1992) (Rehnquist, C.J., dissenting). Rehnquist cast his attack in procedural terms without explaining how a lower court could have found that "the county has a policy that precludes the administrator from arbitrarily imposing fees," *ibid.* at 141, based on the facts, and that, even if so, the ordinance would nevertheless not have been unconstitutional as it was applied.

125. Denvir, "Justice Brennan, Justice Rehnquist, and Free Speech" at 295–98, 309–10.

126. Dolan v. City of Tigard, 512 U.S. 374 (1994) (*per* Rehnquist, C.J.) (overturning local ordinances as uncompensated takings).

127. Lechmere, Inc. v. N.L.R.B., 502 U.S. 527 (1992) (*per* Thomas) (union organizers not protected if they trespass unless employees cannot be reached otherwise); Litton Financial Printing Div. v. N.L.R.B., 501 U.S. 190 (1991) (*per* Kennedy, J.) (arbitration rights do not survive contract); Air Courier Conf. v. American Postal Workers Union, 498 U.S. 517 (1991) (*per* Rehnquist, C.J.) (postal workers not protected by statute against competition by private express shippers nor permitted to challenge suspension of regulation); N.L.R.B. v. Retail Store

Employees Union, 447 U.S. 607 (1980) (*per* Powell, J.) (no First Amendment protection for picketing of firms doing business with employer); American Radio Ass'n v. Mobile S.S. Ass'n, 419 U.S. 215 (1974) (*per* Rehnquist, J.) (upholding an Alabama court's injunction against union picketing activities as not violating the First and Fourteenth Amendments); Windward Shipping (London) Ltd. v. American Radio Ass'n, 415 U.S. 104 (1974) (*per* Rehnquist, J.) (injunction proper to prevent union from picketing foreign-flag vessels in American ports paying substandard wages to foreign crewmen). The unions lost all their cases before the Supreme Court in the 1997 Term, and all with Rehnquist's vote, though a number were unanimous; for one that was not unanimous in which Rehnquist joined a dissent seeking an even more adverse decision than the Court reached, *see Allentown Mack Sales and Service, Inc. v. N.L.R.B.*, 522 U.S. 359, 380 (1998) (Rehnquist, C.J., dissenting).

128. *See, e.g.,* Air Courier Conf. v. American Postal Workers Union, 498 U.S. 517 (1991) (no standing for postal employees); E.E.O.C. v. Arabian American Oil Co., 499 U.S. 244 (1991) (*per* Rehnquist, C.J.) (no extraterritorial regulation of American corporate employment practices); Fort Halifax Packing Co. v. Coyne, 482 U.S. 1, 23 (1987) (White, J., dissenting) (arguing that federal law preempted state law requiring severance payments); United States R.R. Retirement Bd. v. Fritz, 449 U.S. 166 (1980) (*per* Rehnquist, J.) (sustaining discrimination among workers and denial of retirement benefits on insubstantial grounds).

129. *See supra* note 71.

130. *See supra* note 88.

131. *See, supra* text accompanying notes 18, 19, and 45, and Culp, "The Racial Discourse of Justice Rehnquist" at 600 n.8 (Rehnquist has the least liberal civil rights score of any justice in the Warren, Burger, and Rehnquist Courts (citing Segal and Spaeth, *The Attitudinal Model* at 242–60).

132. *See e.g.,* James G. March, *Decisions and Organizations* (New York: Blackwell, 1988); Richard Nisbett and Lee Ross, *Human Inference: Strategies and Shortcomings of Social Judgment* (Englewood Cliffs, N.J.: Prentice-Hall, 1980); Irving L. Janis and Leon Mann, *Decision Making: A Psychological Analysis of Conflict, Choice, and Commitment* (New York: Free Press, 1977); and *see generally* Daniel A. Farber and Philip P. Frickey, *Law and Public Choice: A Critical Introduction* (Chicago: University of Chicago Press, 1991).

133. On business entities and securities, for example, Rehnquist has participated in a significant narrowing of Rule 10b-5 of the Securities and Exchange Commission, thus limiting corporate liability for stock manipulation. *See, e.g.,* Santa Fe Industries, Inc. v. Green, 430 U.S. 462 (1977) (*per* White, J.); Ernst and Ernst v. Hochfelder, 425 U.S. 185 (1976) (*per* Powell, J.) (no action for negligence under Rule 10b-5); Blue Chip Stamps v. Manor Drug Stores, 421 U.S. 723 (1975) (*per* Rehnquist, J.) (plaintiffs defrauded into rejecting an offer of securities could not sue under Rule 10b-5 because neither a purchaser nor a seller). For a brief

history of the Supreme Court's treatment of implied causes of action generally and with respect to Rule 10b-5, *see* Thomas L. Hazen, 2 *Treatise on the Law of Securities Regulation* (St. Paul, Minn.: West, 3d ed. 1995) §§ 13.1-.2, at 446–53, 460. On discrimination, *see also* E.E.O.C. v. Arabian American Oil Co., 499 U.S. 244 (1991) (no extraterritorial application of discrimination laws against American corporation with respect to American workers). With respect to antitrust, Rehnquist participated in the substitution of the rule of reason for the more stringent per se rules previously applied, *see* Copperweld Corp. v. Independence Tube Corp. 467 U.S. 752 (1984) (*per* Burger, C.J.); *ibid.* 467 U.S. at 778 (Stevens, J., dissenting); Victor H. Kramer, "The Supreme Court and Tying Arrangements: Antitrust as History," 69 *Minn. L. Rev.* 1013, 1063–64 (1985) (Nixon appointees, Rehnquist included, together with Justice Stewart, reversed trend of antitrust law); *see also* Allen Redlich, "The Burger Court and the Per Se Rule," 44 *Alb. L. Rev.* 1 (1979) (the Burger Court abandoned noneconomic goals of antitrust law, specifically the effort to control the power of large business entities) (Prof. Redlich's article identified the specific contributions of other members of the Court, but he told me before his untimely death that Rehnquist had been part of that change in direction). *See also* J. Truett Payne Co. v. Chrysler Motors Corp., 451 U.S. 557 (1981) (*per* Rehnquist, J.) (deciding in favor of corporate defendant in the face of proof of violation of the Robinson–Patman antitrust act); Community Communications Co. v. City of Boulder, 455 U.S. 40, 60 (1982) (Rehnquist, J., dissenting) (municipality should be permitted to exclude competing cable operators); *but see* City of Los Angeles v. Preferred Communications, Inc., 476 U.S. 488 (1986) (*per* Rehnquist, J.) (complaint alleging First Amendment right to a competing franchise should not have been dismissed). With respect to regulation, *see* Connecticut v. Doehr, 501 U.S. 1, 26, 28 (1991) (Rehnquist, C.J., concurring in part and in the judgment) (would narrow requirement of prior hearing to those where the "plaintiff had no pre-existing interest in the real property which he sought to attach"); Jackson v. Metropolitan Edison Co., 419 U.S. 345 (1974) (*per* Rehnquist, J.) (utility cutoff without notice or prior hearing permissible; *and see* Mark V. Tushnet, "A Republican Chief Justice," 88 *Mich. L. Rev.* 1326, 1329 (1990) (reviewing Davis, *Justice Rehnquist* (1989)). Rehnquist's respect for corporations does not translate into favorable decisions in speech cases, however, *see supra* note 72, with respect to which he seems to think the bigger ones will happily take care of themselves.

134. Problems of public choice are in part problems of group dynamics. At one time it was common to argue that legislative deliberations were particularly affected by the pathologies of social choice. Frank Easterbrook, however, applied the theory to smaller bodies, like the Court, *see* Frank H. Easterbrook, "Ways of Criticizing the Court," 95 *Harv. L. Rev.* 802 (1982). And the irrationality of corporate choice has spawned a research industry, *see* sources cited *supra* note 132.

135. *Compare:*

Those who won our independence by revolution were not cowards. They did not fear political change. They did not exalt order at the cost of liberty. To courageous, self-reliant men, with confidence in the power of free and fearless reasoning applied through the processes of popular government, no danger flowing from speech can be deemed clear and present, unless the incidence of the evil apprehended is so imminent that it may befall before there is opportunity for full discussion.

Whitney v. California, 274 U.S. 357, 377 (1927) (Brandeis, J., concurring).

136. James S. Fishkin, *Tyranny and Legitimacy: A Critique of Political Theories* (Baltimore: Johns Hopkins University Press, 1979).

137. Robert A. Dahl and Charles Lindblom, *Politics, Economics and Welfare: Planning and Politico-Economic Systems Resolved into Basic Social Processes* (New York: Harper, 1953).

NOTES TO CHAPTER 4

1. *See* Gordon S. Wood, *The Creation of the American Republic, 1776–1787* (New York: Norton, 1969) at 107–14.

2. *See* Donald S. Lutz, *Popular Consent and Popular Control: Whig Political Theory in the Early State Constitutions* (Baton Rouge: Louisiana State University Press, 1980) at 9 (describing the view that a free government is possible only where equivalent fortunes transformed selfish concerns into zeal for the public good).

3. *See ibid.* at 205, 219–20 (discussing colonial requirement that local representatives own land to evince a "stake in the community"); 1 *Records of the Federal Convention of 1787* (New Haven: Yale University Press, Max Farrand ed., 1966) [hereinafter Farrand, *Records*] at 138 (Madison, June 6, 1787) at 138; *ibid.* at 450 (Sherman, June 28, 1787); 3 *ibid.* at 450 (Madison).

4. *See* Alexis de Tocqueville, 2 *Democracy in America* (New York: Knopf, Phillips Bradley ed., 1956) at 121–27.

5. *See* Farrand, 2 *Records* 207 (Gouvernour Morris, August 7, 1787).

6. *See Dictionary of Conservative and Libertarian Thought* (New York: Routledge, Nigel Ashford and Stephen Davies eds., 1991) at 2–3; Robert Devigne, *Recasting Conservatism: Oakeshott, Strauss, and the Response to Postmodernism* (New Haven: Yale University Press, 1994) at 118.

7. *See* the description in Robin West, "Progressive and Conservative Constitutionalism," 88 *Mich. L. Rev.* 641 (1990). Some conservatives argue that individuals will behave honorably in the absence of regulation. It can be difficult, however, to separate claims about individual rights and the economic benefits from the opportunity for individual gain from claims about the degree of responsibility that would be exercised by unregulated individuals. This difficulty arises because the two ideas are operationalized identically, at least in the short term, and partly because modern conservatism incorporates large elements of deterrence in its programs and thought. *See* Gary Orfield and Carole Ashkinase, *The Closing Door:*

Conservative Policy and Black Opportunity (Chicago: University of Chicago Press, 1991) at 206–7, 220.

8. *See* Devigne, *Recasting Conservatism* at 69; *Dictionary of Conservative and Libertarian Thought* at 89; Robert A. Nisbet, *Conservatism: Dream and Reality* (Minneapolis: University of Minnesota Press, 1986) at 34–46, 51 (discussing the conservative embrace of authoritative individuals); *see also* Tocqueville, 2 *Democracy in America*, 85–88 (arguing that aristocratic historians write about great men; democratic historians write about tides of history); Gordon S. Wood, *The Radicalism of the American Revolution* (New York: Knopf, 1992) at 11–92 (offering an excellent description of this socially hierarchal pattern in the Revolutionary era).

9. *See* Peter Westen, "'Freedom' and 'Coercion'—Virtue Words and Vice Words," 1985 *Duke L.J.* 541, 572 (explaining that both freedom and coercion must be defined by a baseline of proper behavior).

10. *See, e.g.,* Paul Brest, "State Action and Liberal Theory: A Casenote on Flagg Brothers v. Brooks," 130 *U. Pa. L. Rev.* 1296, 1301–2, 1324–30 (1982) (arguing that judges have improperly used the state action doctrine to protect business enterprises against the claims of consumers, minorities, and other relatively powerless citizens). *See also* Westen, "'Freedom' and 'Coercion'" at 577–78 (explaining how a state can influence an individual's free will through law enforcement that coerces compliance).

11. *See, e.g.,* Personnel Adm'r v. Feeney, 442 U.S. 256, 281 (1979) (Stevens, J., concurring) (asserting that adverse effects can be used to imply an intent to discriminate); *ibid.* at 283 (Marshall, J., dissenting) (arguing that the Massachusetts veterans' preference system discriminated against women based on unavoidable "resort to inference based on objective factors"). Though much more conservative than Justice Marshall, Justice White also felt the pull of this approach. *See* Palmer v. Thompson, 403 U.S. 217, 240–41 (1971) (White, J., dissenting) (arguing that closure of a swimming pool in Mississippi following an integration order was racially motivated and that the Court should have addressed that motivation).

12. *See* Stephen E. Gottlieb, "Reformulating the Motive/Effects Debate in Constitutional Adjudication," 33 *Wayne L. Rev.* 97, 105–6 (1986) (asserting that consequences are the most reliable indicia of intent).

13. *See* Kristin Luker, *Abortion and the Politics of Motherhood* (Berkeley: University of California Press, 1984) at 12–13, 186–88 (comparing pro-life advocates, who attribute childbirth decisions to God, with pro-choice advocates, who believe in personal choice).

14. *See Dictionary of Conservative and Libertarian Thought* at 46.

15. This was eloquently stated in an address by Ira Glasser, executive director of the ACLU, at the 1995 ACLU Biennial Meeting in New York City.

16. *See, e.g.,* Hernandez v. New York, 500 U.S. 352, 372 (1991) (holding that exclusion of bilingual jurors was not intentional discrimination against Hispanics because the prosecutor gave a race-neutral reason for the peremptory challenges);

Feeney, 442 U.S. at 280 (holding veterans' preference did not intentionally discriminate against women).

17. *See, e.g.,* Aaron Wildavsky, "Is Culture the Culprit?" 113 *Pub. Interest* 110, 113–14 (1993).

18. *Dictionary of Conservative and Libertarian Thought* at 45–46.

19. *See* Dolan v. City of Tigard, 512 U.S. 374 (1994) (holding that an exchange of a local zoning variance for an easement was a regulatory taking in violation of the eminent domain clause); Lucas v. South Carolina Coastal Council, 505 U.S. 1003, 1028–30 (1992) (holding that a landowner had suffered a "taking" when the state implemented a regulation that leaves the property void of any economic benefit unless previously restrained by nuisance law); Nollan v. California Coastal Comm'n, 483 U.S. 825, 837–39 (1987) (invalidating the exchange of a state land-use restriction for an easement as a regulatory taking); Eastern Enterprises v. Apfel, 524 U.S. 498 (1998) (invalidating required contribution to insufficiently funded pension plan after exit from operations).

20. *See* Jules L. Coleman, *Markets, Morals and the Law* (New York: Cambridge University Press 1988) at 95–132.

21. Utilitarianism adopted pleasure and pain as a principle of measurement and valuation as an alternative to the assumptions about natural and moral arguments in other philosophical systems. *See* Jeremy Bentham, *The Principles of Morals and Legislation* (Darien, Conn.: Hafner Press, 1948) (1789) at 13–20; Jeremy Bentham, "Anarchical Fallacies" in Jeremy Bentham, 2 *The Works of Jeremy Bentham* (New York: Russell and Russell, 1962, reprint of John Bowring ed., 1843) at 494–95. In turn, economics developed as a working out of the utility of transactions for individuals. *See* Alfred Marshall, *Principles of Economics: An Introductory Volume* (New York: Macmillan, 9th ed., C. W. Guillebaud annot., 1961) at 92–93; George J. Stigler, *Essays in the History of Economics* (Chicago: University of Chicago Press, 1965) at 67–75 (discussing the development of utilitarianism through the works of Adam Smith and Jeremy Bentham).

22. *See* chapter 1. Justice Scalia has had a great deal to say about property rights. *See generally* David A. Schultz and Christopher E. Smith, *The Jurisprudential Vision of Justice Antonin Scalia* (Lanham, Md.: Rowman and Littlefield, 1996) at 1–28. The question here, however, is the underlying moral agenda that informs those economic views.

23. 505 U.S. 833 (1992).

24. *See* Nisbet, *Conservatism* at 26 (clarifying that by appealing to tradition, conservatives are not endorsing every decision handed down from the past).

25. Indeed, *Casey* is an example of their willingness to make substantial changes.

26. *See* Sandra Day O'Connor, "Testing Government Action: The Promise of Federalism," in *Public Values in Constitutional Law* (Ann Arbor: University of Michigan Press, Stephen E. Gottlieb ed., 1993) at 35 (viewing federalism as beneficial

because competition between the federal and state governments ultimately benefits the people); Harold J. Spaeth, "Justice Sandra Day O'Connor: An Assessment," in *An Essential Safeguard: Essays on the United States Supreme Court and its Justices* (New York: Greenwood Press, D. Grier Stephenson, Jr. ed., 1991) at 94–95 (observing that in *Michigan v. Long*, 453 U.S. 1032 (1983), O'Connor subordinated her support of federalism to her conservativism); Richard A. Cordray and James T. Vradelis, Comment, "The Emerging Jurisprudence of Justice O'Connor," 52 *U. Chi. L. Rev.* 389, 423–36 (1985) (discussing O'Connor's effort to restrain federal action to enable state government operation with as much autonomy as possible).

27. 463 U.S. 1032 (1983).

28. *See* Ingersoll-Rand Co. v. McClendon, 498 U.S. 133, 145 (1990) (holding that ERISA preempted state prohibition of wrongful discharge that was based on imminent vesting of an employee's pension); F.M.C. Corp. v. Holliday, 498 U.S. 52, 65 (1990) (holding that ERISA preempted state regulation of self-insured pension plans not directly covered by ERISA).

29. *See* City of Richmond v. J.A. Croson Co., 488 U.S. 469, 498–500 (1989) (voiding as a violation of the Fourteenth Amendment a construction industry set-aside provision benefiting minority-owned subcontractors established in the capital of the Confederacy).

30. *See, e.g.*, Pacific Mutual Life Insurance Co. v. Haslip, 499 U.S. 1, 44 (1991), where Justice O'Connor attacked historical state common law punitive damages as unconstitutional for offering the jury insufficient guidance.

31. Dolan v. City of Tigard, 512 U.S. 374 (1994) (*per* Rehnquist, C.J.); Lucas v. South Carolina Coastal Council, 505 U.S. 1003 (1992) (*per* Scalia, J.); Nollan v. California Coastal Comm'n, 483 U.S. 825 (1987) (*per* Scalia, J.).

32. *See, e.g.*, Employment Division, Department of Human Resources of State of Oregon v. Smith, 494 U.S. 872, 878–82 (1990) (holding that a state could deny unemployment compensation benefits because of a plaintiff's drug use but that religious drug use was not protected under the free exercise clause).

33. *See* Spaeth, "O'Connor" at 94–95; Suzanna Sherry, "Civic Virtue and the Feminine Voice in Constitutional Adjudication," 72 *Va. L. Rev.* 543, 592–616 (1986) (exploring the feminine aspects of Justice O'Connor's jurisprudence); Cordray and Vradelis, "O'Connor."

34. *See, e.g., Employment Division v. Smith*, 494 U.S. at 903–7 (O'Connor, J., concurring) (balancing free exercise rights of Native Americans using peyote at religious ceremonies against uniform enforcement of drug laws).

35. O'Connor is concerned, for example, that trials reach firm conclusions about actual guilt but is unlikely to believe they have not. *Compare* Herrera v. Collins, 506 U.S. 390, 419–20 (1993) (O'Connor, J., concurring), *with* Schlup v. Delo, 513 U.S. 298, 333–34 (1995) (O'Connor, J., concurring) (stating that courts reserve traditional discretion to determine if new evidence of innocence might prove persuasive to a juror), *and* Mu'Min v. Virginia, 500 U.S. 415, 432–33 (1991)

(O'Connor, J., concurring) (agreeing that the trial judge has the discretion to determine if jurors' assurances of impartiality are credible).

36. *See infra* at notes 87, 132, 169, and 201 and the succeeding discussions.

37. Antonin Scalia, "Common-Law Courts in a Civil-Law System: The Role of United States Federal Courts in Interpreting the Constitution and Laws," in *A Matter of Interpretation: Federal Courts and the Law* (Princeton: Princeton University Press, Amy Gutmann ed., 1997) at 3.

38. *See* George Kannar, "Strenuous Virtues, Virtuous Lives: The Social Vision of Antonin Scalia," 12 *Cardozo L. Rev.* 1845, 1850 (1991). For a somewhat different view, *see* Schultz and Smith, *Scalia* at 208.

39. *See* Lucas v. South Carolina Coastal Council, 505 U.S. 1003, 1014 (1992) (noting that the Court's current interpretation of the takings clause reflects a change from historical understanding); *ibid.* at 1028 n.15 (declaring early history of the origins and use of the clause irrelevant to an interpretation of the takings clause). *See* Kannar, "Strenuous Virtues" at 1852 (stating that Scalia's views cannot be understood by a listing of judicial virtues); George Kannar, "The Constitutional Catechism of Antonin Scalia," 99 *Yale L.J.* 1297, 1305–7 (1990) (discussing Scalia as a "faint-hearted originalist" and considering the indeterminacy of language and history); *ibid.* at 1342 (stating that sources of Scalia's method do not have all the answers all the time" but explaining that "structuring constitutional analysis as though answers can be formalistically derived can frequently have outcome-determining effects.").

40. *See* Kannar, "Strenuous Virtues" at 1852–56.

41. *See* Antonin Scalia, "Morality, Pragmatism and the Legal Order," 9 *Harv. J.L. & Pub. Pol'y* 123, 124 (1986).

42. *See also* West, "Progressive and Conservative" at 658 (discussing the Darwinian strand in modern conservatism); Kannar, "Strenuous Virtues" at 1847 (noting Scalia's admiration for societies dominated by elites).

43. *See* Eric F. Goldman, *Rendezvous with Destiny* (New York: Vintage Press, rev. ed., 1960) at 70–72.

44. *See* Herbert Hovenkamp, "The Culture Crises of the Fuller Court," 104 *Yale L.J.* 2309, 2311–12, 2324–27 (1995) (reviewing Owen M. Fiss, *Troubled Beginnings of the Modern State, 1888–1910* (New York: Macmillan, 1994)) (describing social Darwinism in late-nineteenth- and early-twentieth-century thought, and explaining that social Darwinists believed government should avoid intervention and let nature take its course in order to avoid subsidizing its weakest members and burdening its strongest).

45. *See* Kannar, "Strenuous Virtues" at 1847–48 (discussing Scalia's interest in creating a "good society" through the law).

46. *See* Schlup v. Delo, 513 U.S. 298, 342 (1995) (Scalia, J., dissenting) (arguing that consideration of evidence of innocence of death row inmate was foreclosed); Herrera v. Collins, 506 U.S. 390, 427 (1993) (Scalia, J., concurring) (arguing no constitutional basis exists to consider new evidence after conviction).

47. *See* Employment Division v. Smith, 494 U.S. 872, 877–79 (1990) (holding that neutral laws prohibiting drug use foreclose free exercise claim to the use of peyote at Native American religious ceremony).

48. *See* Adarand Constructors, Inc. v. Pena, 515 U.S. 200, 239 (1995) (Scalia, J., concurring) (applying strict scrutiny to federal affirmative action program); City of Richmond v. J.A. Croson Co., 488 U.S. 469, 524–25 (1989) (Scalia, J., concurring) (agreeing that municipality's affirmative action program was void and urging that only prior de jure or official discrimination warrants official remediation).

49. *See* Lee v. International Soc'y for Krishna Consciousness, Inc., 505 U.S. 830, 831 (Rehnquist, dissenting) (arguing that leafletting as well as solicitation can be barred from airports).

50. *See* Dolan v. City of Tigard, 512 U.S. 374, 386–91 (1994) (*per* Rehnquist, C.J.) (invalidating contractual exchange of a local zoning variance for an easement as a regulatory taking in violation of the takings clause); Lucas v. South Carolina Coastal Council, 505 U.S. 1003, 1031 (1992) (invalidating restriction on construction in coastal plain because it deprived owner of all economically beneficial use of his land without identifying background principles of nuisance and property law); Nollan v. California Coastal Comm'n, 483 U.S. 825, 841–42 (1987) (invalidating contractual exchange of state land use restriction for easement as a regulatory taking). Scalia has been explicit in his desire to protect the powerful against the weak. *See* Austin v. Michigan Chamber of Commerce, 494 U.S. 652, 694 (1990) (Scalia, J., dissenting).

51. In addition to the cases referred to in the text just above, *see* Ward's Cove Packing Co., Inc. v. Atonio, 490 U.S. 642, 650 (1989) (Scalia joined the Court in reversing a finding of a court of appeals that a prima facie case of Title VII racial discrimination was made where nonwhites held a majority of unskilled labor positions, were recruited solely for unskilled positions, and were physically segregated from those recruited from other locations).

52. So, for example, *Adarand Constructors, Inc.* and *J.A. Croson Co.* were both suits by majority contractors.

53. *See* ABF Freight Sys., Inc. v. N.L.R.B., 510 U.S. 317, 326 (1994) (Scalia, J., concurring, joined by O'Connor, J.) (condemning the N.L.R.B. rule that provided relief against an employer for unfair labor practices despite employee misconduct in the procedures before the board). The employee's misconduct was clearly the focal point for Justice O'Connor. She is somewhat more willing, however, to credit employee claims than Scalia and other conservative colleagues. *See, e.g.,* Price Waterhouse v. Hopkins, 490 U.S. 228, 288 (1989). Scalia joined Kennedy's dissent, concluding that employee evidence of employer discrimination does not shift the burden of persuasion to the employer. In contrast, Justice O'Connor concluded that proof that discrimination is a necessary or "but for" cause of the employer's action requires shifting the burden of persuasion. *See ibid.* at 261.

54. *See Schlup*, 513 U.S. at 332 (O'Connor, J., concurring) (concluding that

district judge has discretion to order relief when there is a fundamental miscarriage of justice); *Herrera*, 506 U.S. at 427 (O'Connor, J., concurring) (leaving open, for a stronger case, question of constitutional implications in the event that death row inmate is actually innocent).

55. See Employment Division v. Smith, 494 U.S. at 899 (O'Connor, J., concurring in the judgment) (applying strict scrutiny but concluding that the state's interests outweighed the plaintiff's free exercise claim).

56. *See Adarand Constructors, Inc.*, 515 U.S. at 237–39 (plurality opinion) (O'Connor, J.) (remanding for consideration of whether the race-conscious set-asides were sufficiently narrowly tailored); *J.A. Croson Co.*, 488 U.S. at 520 (Scalia, J., concurring in the judgment) (opposing O'Connor's conclusion that government may discriminate on the basis of race to amend for past actions if narrowly tailored).

57. *See* International Society for Krishna Consciousness, Inc. v. Lee, 505 U.S. 672, 685 (1992) (O'Connor, J.) (concluding that it is unconstitutional to ban nondisruptive leafletting, but not soliciting, in airport).

58. *See* text *infra* at notes 90, 91.

59. *See* Peter B. Edelman, "Justice Scalia's Jurisprudence and the Good Society: Shades of Felix Frankfurter and the Harvard Hit Parade of the 1950s," 12 *Cardozo L. Rev.* 1799, 1800 (1991) (commenting that Scalia "would protect property rights of the 'haves' against government initiatives to protect the 'have nots'"); Toby Golick, "Justice Scalia, Poverty and the Good Society," 12 *Cardozo L. Rev.* 1817, 1817–18 (1991) (discussing Scalia's resistance to claims of the poor). Scalia has reached these results although he has differentiated welfare programs from programs that place disproportionate burdens on particular individuals. *See* Pennell v. San Jose, 485 U.S. 1, 22 (1988) (Scalia, J., dissenting in part) (concluding city was using rent regulation to establish a private welfare program funded by landlords); Schultz and Smith, *Scalia*, at 12 (discussing Scalia's reluctance to impose "public burdens" on private individuals instead of the public as a whole).

60. For example, in Barnes v. Glen Theatre, Inc., 501 U.S. 560, 569 (1991), where Kennedy joined the majority opinion.

61. *See infra* at notes 93–106, 138–57, 190–93, 207–9. *But see infra* note 212. For a strong and evocative description of Kennedy's view of character drawn largely from his speech cases, see Akhil Reed Amar, "Justice Kennedy and the Ideal of Equality," 28 *Pacific L.J.* 515 (1997).

62. *See* Lee v. Weisman, 505 U.S. 577, 588 (1992) (finding inclusion of benediction in graduation exercises coercive); County of Allegheny v. ACLU, 492 U.S. 573, 655 (1989) (Kennedy, J., concurring in the judgment in part and dissenting in part). On the difficulty of defining coercion, *see* Westen, "'Freedom' and 'Coercion.'"

63. *See Lee*, 505 U.S. at 592 (finding state has a duty to guard the sphere of personal conscience and belief). To protect private choice, Kennedy would also be expected to be hesitant to constrain private individuals by the constitutional standards applicable to public entities. In Edmonson v. Leesville Concrete Co., Inc.,

500 U.S. 614 (1991), however, Kennedy held the state responsible for peremptory challenges by private counsel for private parties and treated judicial dismissal of challenged jurors as an explicit and obvious use of state power. *See ibid.* at 624. This conclusion may be consistent with his view of individual responsibility, however, because the trial judge, jury, and courtroom are and appear official. *See ibid.* at 623–24.

64. *See, e.g.,* Washington v. Davis, 426 U.S. 229, 246 (1976) (holding that concerning facially neutral rules, discrimination is defined by intent).

65. *See infra* at notes 93–106.

66. *See, e.g.,* Herrera v. Collins, 506 U.S. 390, 419 (1993) (O'Connor, J., concurring, joined by Kennedy, J.) (declining to extend holding barring habeas corpus petitions based on claims of new evidence of innocence to cases where petitioner may present stronger case of actual innocence). Scalia prefers an absolute rule. *See Herrera,* 506 U.S. at 429.

67. *See* Farrand, 1 *Records* at 135 (recording Madison's remarks on June 6, 1787).

68. *See* Robert M. Cover, *Justice Accused: Antislavery and the Judicial Process* (New Haven:Yale University Press, 1975) at 8–30 (tracing opposition to slavery in the early to mid-eighteenth century).

69. *See Cong. Globe,* 39th Cong., 1st sess. 3148 (1866).

70. *See* Farrand, 2 *Records* at 370 (remarks of George Mason, August 22, 1787) (attacking the social, as well as political, consequences of slavery); David Hackett Fischer, *Albion's Seed: Four British Folkways in America* (New York: Oxford University Press, 1989) at 382–89 (describing the hierarchical culture of slaveholding society).

71. That idea harks back to the apologists of slavery and treats the relatively poor socioeconomic position of blacks as a reflection of their racial character. *See* Richard J. Herrnstein and Charles Murray, *The Bell Curve: Intelligence and Class Structure in American Life* (New York: Free Press, 1994).

72. *See* Wildavsky, "Is Culture the Culprit?" at 113–17 (discussing the belief that the public welfare system, and not race or class, is responsible for the plight of the poor).

73. City of Richmond v. J.A. Croson Co., 488 U.S. 469 (1989) (*per* O'Connor, J.) invalidated a racial set-aside, left a small area for possible "narrowly tailored" remedial programs, and envisioned consistent application of race-blind standards, *see ibid.* at 493–94. Justice Scalia concurred except to deny the possibility of narrowly tailored exceptions, *see ibid.* at 520. Marshall and Blackmun, dissenting, urged the need to take race into account in order to achieve equal opportunity.

74. Compare this conservative vision of equality with Dworkin's use of the term "equal respect." Ronald M. Dworkin, *Taking Rights Seriously* (Cambridge: Harvard University Press, 1977) at 272–78 (stating that all people should be treated as equal in worth). Dworkin uses the term "equal treatment" in a slightly different way. *See ibid.* at 227 ("the right to equal distribution of some opportu-

nity or resource or burden"). *See also* Ronald Dworkin, "What Is Equality? Part 1: Equality of Welfare," 10 *Phil. & Pub. Aff.* 185 (1981) (discussing equality in terms of welfare); Ronald Dworkin, "What Is Equality? Part 2: Equality of Resources," 10 *Phil. & Pub. Aff.* 283 (1981) (discussing equality in terms of resources).

75. Adarand Constructors, Inc. v. Pena, 515 U.S. 200, 237 (1995) ("As recently as" eight years prior "every Justice of this Court agreed that the Alabama Department of Public Safety's 'pervasive, systematic, and obstinate discriminatory conduct' justified a narrowly tailored race-based remedy," citing United States v. Paradise, 480 U.S. 149, 167 (1987)).

76. *See* Edmonson v. Leesville Concrete Co., 500 U.S. 614 (1991) (holding that a court could not allow a private litigant to discriminate on the basis of race in the selection of jurors); Batson v. Kentucky, 476 U.S. 79, 96 (1986) (holding that intent to discriminate could be proven with respect to individual cases rather than requiring petitioner to prove discrimination in a large group of cases).

77. 500 U.S. 352, 369–70 (1991) (plurality); *ibid.* at 372 (O'Connor, J., concurring in the judgment).

78. *See* United States v. Fordice, 505 U.S. 717, 731 (1992) (holding that abolishing legal requirements of separate education for blacks and whites alone does not satisfy the equal protection clause if the state perpetuates other segregative practices, provided such practices are without sound educational justification and can be practicably eliminated); *ibid.* at 743 (O'Connor, J., concurring); *ibid.* at 749 (Scalia, J., concurring in the judgment) (arguing Court imposed too great a burden on the state); Freeman v. Pitts, 503 U.S. 467, 489 (1992) (Kennedy, J.) (holding federal court could relinquish supervision and terminate a desegregation order selectively over different portions of school program); *ibid.* at 506 (Scalia, J., concurring) (arguing not the result of prior de jure segregation); *compare ibid.* at 509 (Blackmun, J., concurring in the judgment, joined by O'Connor, J.) (urging stronger standard for judging whether continued segregation was caused by illegal acts of school district, particularly whether district had contributed to residential segregation).

79. *See* City of Richmond v. J.A. Croson Co., 488 U.S. 469, 524 (1989) (Scalia, J., concurring in the judgment) (arguing that states should be prohibited from using race-conscious remedies unless they are necessary to eliminate de jure discrimination); *ibid.* at 518–19 (Kennedy, J., concurring) (indicating agreement with Justice Scalia's premises).

80. *See Freeman*, 503 U.S. at 506 (Scalia, J., concurring) (arguing that the Court should abandon the presumption that continuing segregation is the result of prior de jure segregation).

81. A case in a labor context is suggestive of their views, ABF Freight Sys., Inc. v. N.L.R.B., 510 U.S. 317, 325–27 (1994) (Scalia, J., dissenting, joined by O'Connor, J.) (stating that the discharged employee was a perjuror); *ibid.* at 325 (Kennedy, J., concurring) (expressing agreement with Scalia's position).

82. *See J.A. Croson Co.*, 488 U.S. at 507–8 (finding race-conscious remedies inappropriate); *Wygant*, 476 U.S. at 499 (O'Connor, J., concurring in part and in the judgment) (arguing that race-conscious remedies are inappropriate); Firefighters Local Union No. 1784 v. Stotts, 467 U.S. 561, 588 (1984) (O'Connor, J., concurring) (same).

83. *J.A. Croson Co.*, 488 U.S. at 524–25 (Scalia, J., concurring). *See also* Adarand Constructors, Inc. v. Pena, 515 U.S. 200, 239 (1995) (Scalia, J., concurring in part and in the judgment) ("In my view, government can never have a 'compelling interest' in discriminating on the basis of race in order to 'make up' for past racial discrimination in the opposite direction.").

84. This view is illustrated by Scalia's realization that race plays a significant part in capital sentencing, coupled with his casual dismissal of this realization as merely a fact of life with which African-Americans must live. *See* Schultz and Smith, *Scalia* at 195. Scalia's memo on which this characterization is based was excerpted and discussed in Dennis D. Dorin, "Far Right of the Mainstream: Racism, Rights, and Remedies from the Perspective of Justice Antonin Scalia's *McCleskey* Memorandum," 45 *Mercer L. Rev.* 1035, 1038 (1994).

85. *See* Wygant v. Jackson Bd. of Educ., 476 U.S. 267, 287 (1986) (O'Connor, J., concurring in part and in the judgment) (contending that unhired minorities are not victims where number of minorities in relevant labor pool does not substantially exceed those hired); Firefighters v. Stotts, 467 U.S. at 588 (O'Connor, J., concurring) (asserting that only identified victims of unlawful discrimination are entitled to relief).

86. *See, e.g., J.A. Croson Co.*, 488 U.S. at 498.

87. *See ibid.* at 498–99 (1989) (asserting generalized discrimination does not justify implementation of racial quota); *Wygant*, 476 U.S. at 294 (O'Connor, J., concurring in part and concurring in the judgment) (finding safeguard provision for minority teachers based on percentage of minority students did not satisfy "narrow tailoring" requirement).

88. *See J.A. Croson Co.*, 488 U.S. at 507 (finding race-conscious remedies inappropriate to relieve general discrimination instead of relief for a specific victim); *Wygant*, 476 U.S. at 288 (O'Connor, J., concurring in part and in the judgment) (arguing race-conscious remedies inappropriate to cure societal discrimination).

89. *See generally* Robert Nozick, *Anarchy, State and Utopia* (New York: Basic Books, 1974). Liberals vary considerably in defining the level playing field they seek and in their belief that the objective is obtainable. *See generally* Dworkin, "What Is Equality?" For present purposes, it suffices that liberals act as if they share some common definitional elements and that the goal is attainable.

90. In many instances Justice O'Connor has supported welfare claims. *See* Gardebring v. Jenkins, 485 U.S. 415, 432 (1988) (O'Connor, J., concurring in part and dissenting in part) (arguing that written notice of the applicable benefit rules should have been given to AFDC recipients); Lukhard v. Reed, 481 U.S. 368, 384

(1987) (O'Connor, J., joined Powell, J., dissenting) (objecting to the treatment of a personal injury award as income for AFDC purposes); Blum v. Bacon, 457 U.S. 132, 133 (1982) (holding that federal regulations require states to provide Emergency Assistance to AFDC and to permit recipients to use Emergency Assistance to replace stolen AFDC checks). *But see* Sullivan v. Stroop, 496 U.S. 478, 479–80 (1990) (rejecting statutory construction regarding calculation of benefits); Bowen v. Gilliard, 483 U.S. 587, 588 (1987) (holding that method of calculating benefits was permissible); Atkins v. Rivera, 477 U.S. 154, 155 (1986) (upholding denial of Medicaid benefits); Green v. Mansour, 474 U.S. 64, 65 (1985) (dismissing AFDC claimants' class action claims on jurisdictional grounds); Atkins v. Parker, 472 U.S. 115, 116 (1985) (refusing to accept food stamp recipients' claims of lack of notice after state reduced benefits without sending individualized notices); Heckler v. Turner, 470 U.S. 184, 185 (1985) (upholding state's determination of "income" for AFDC eligibility purposes); Blum v. Yaretsky, 457 U.S. 991, 992–93 (1982) (finding no state action where state-funded nursing homes decided to discharge patients or transfer them to lower levels of care).

Individuals sometimes bear disproportionate burdens, *e.g.*, layoffs, *see Wygant*, 476 U.S. at 283 (asserting that race-conscious layoffs would have placed burdens on employees with greater seniority), and public contracts, *see J.A. Croson Co.*, 488 U.S. at 493–94 (concluding that race-conscious set-asides would have imposed burdens on nonminority contractors). Substitution of the tax system can minimize those disproportions.

91. 470 U.S. 1018, 1021 (1985) (O'Connor, J., dissenting).

92. *See* Wygant v. Jackson Bd. of Educ., 476 U.S. 267, 289 (1986) (O'Connor, J., concurring in part) ("violation . . . arises when the wrong is committed"); *J.A. Croson Co.*, 488 U.S. at 506. *See also* Drew S. Days, III, "Fullilove," 96 *Yale L.J.* 453, 485 (1987) (arguing that the extent of remedies for discrimination should not be arbitrary).

93. 426 U.S. 229 (1976) (holding verbal skills test administered to black applicants not unconstitutional merely because of racially disproportionate impact).

94. *See* chapter 1 above; *see also* Palmer v. Thompson, 403 U.S. 217, 241–43, 247–61, 271 (1971) (White, J., dissenting).

95. *See, e.g.*, Hernandez v. New York, 500 U.S. 352, 360 (1991) (plurality) (concluding, "Unless discriminatory intent is inherent in the prosecutor's explanation, the reason [for excluding jurors] will be deemed race neutral."). Most members of the conservative bloc are reluctant even to question good intentions. *See* Mu'Min v. Virginia, 500 U.S. 415, 430–31 (1991) (finding it sufficient that jurors agreed to keep an open mind without specific or individual questioning). *But see ibid.* at 450 (Kennedy, J., dissenting) (concluding individual questioning of jurors for possible bias required).

96. 500 U.S. 352, 355–58 (1991) (plurality).

97. *See* Edmonson v. Leesville Concrete Co., 500 U.S. 614 (1991) (holding

private litigants may not use peremptory challenges to exclude jurors on account of their race).

98. *See Hernandez*, 500 U.S. at 372 (O'Connor, J., with whom Scalia, J., joined, concurring). Chief Justice Rehnquist and Justices White and Souter joined Kennedy's opinion for the Court.

99. *See J.A. Croson, Co.*, 488 U.S. at 516 (Kennedy, J., concurring).

100. *Compare Mu'Min*, 500 U.S. at 425–29 (no need for questions because no precedent for requiring exclusions), *with ibid.* at 450 (Kennedy, J., dissenting) ("a juror's acknowledgment of exposure to pretrial publicity initiates a duty to assess the juror's ability to be impartial.").

101. *Hernandez*, 500 U.S. at 363 ("In the context of this trial, the prosecutor's frank admission that his ground for excusing these jurors . . . raised a plausible, though not a necessary, inference that language might be a pretext for what in fact were race-based peremptory challenges.").

102. *Compare Mu'Min*, 500 U.S. at 432 (O'Connor, J., concurring), *with ibid.* at 451–52 (Kennedy, J., dissenting); *Hernandez,* 500 U.S. at 372–75 (O'Connor, J., concurring in the judgment, joined by Scalia, J.). Many would have deduced at least unconscious intent, *see* Charles Lawrence III, "The Id, the Ego, and Equal Protection: Reckoning with Unconscious Racism," 39 *Stan. L. Rev.* 317 (1987).

103. *See also* Ward's Cove Packing Co., Inc. v. Atonio, 490 U.S. 642 (1989) (finding no intentional discrimination where white–collar plant was recruited from, and staffed by, a largely white California-based workforce and adjacent canning plant was recruited from and staffed by largely Alaskan Inuit population despite supervisor explanations that the two population groups would not mix well).

104. *See, e.g.,* Edmonson v. Leesville Concrete Co., 500 U.S. 614 (1991); *Mu'Min*, 500 U.S. at 448 (Kennedy, J., dissenting).

105. *J.A. Croson Co.*, 488 U.S. 469, 518 (Kennedy, J., concurring in part and in the judgment).

106. *See* Lee v. Weisman, 505 U.S. 577, 589 (1992) (enjoining officially arranged prayer at public high school graduation ceremony as coercive).

107. *See* Vincent Blasi, *Milton's* Areopagitica *and the Modern First Amendment* (New Haven: Yale Law School occasional papers 1995) at 13–19; John Locke, "A Letter Concerning Toleration," in John Locke, *Treatise of Civil Government and a Letter Concerning Toleration* (New York: D. Appleton, Charles L. Sherman ed., 1965) at 173, 192; Timothy L. Hall, "Roger Williams and the Foundations of Religious Liberty," 71 *B.U. L. Rev.* 455, 490–91 (1991).

108. *See* Charles Teague, "Freedom of Religion: The Freedom to Draw Circles," in *Religious Traditions and the Limits of Tolerance* (Chambersburg, Pa.: Anima Books, Louis J. Hammann and Harry M. Buck eds., 1988) at 18 (describing American Baptist tradition eschewing governmental interference in the exercise of religious practice); Scott W. Gustafson, "The Scandal of Particularity and the Universality of Grace," in *Religious Traditions* at 28; Clinton Rossiter, *Seedtime of the Re-*

public (New York: Harcourt Brace, 1953) at 40, 54 (describing the individualism at the core of Protestantism, generally, and Puritanism, in particular, as leading toward a belief in "right of private judgment" later formalized in the Virginia Declaration of Rights).

109. *See* Blasi, *Milton's* Areopagitica at 13–14.

110. *See* Thomas James, "Rights of Conscience and State School Systems in Nineteenth-Century America," in *Toward a Usable Past: Liberty Under State Constitutions* (Athens: University of Georgia Press, Paul Finkelman and Stephen E. Gottlieb, eds., 1991) at 126; *see also* Peter S. Onuf, "State Politics and Republican Virtue: Religion, Education, and Morality in Early American Federalism," in *Toward a Usable Past* at 92–97; Devigne, *Recasting Conservatism* at 111; *Dictionary of Conservative and Libertarian Thought* at 212–13; Rossiter, *Seedtime of the Republic* at 432–33 (asserting that the practice of Christianity was understood "as essential to virtue as was virtue to freedom").

111. *See* James, "Rights of Conscience and State School Systems"; Onuf, "State Politics and Republican Virtue"; Wood, *The Creation of the American Republic* at 414–15, 427–28; Michael W. McConnell, "Religious Freedom at a Crossroads," 59 *U. Chi. L. Rev.* 115, 191 n.329 (1992).

112. *See* Onuf, "State Politics and Republican Virtue" at 93–94; McConnell, "Religious Freedom at a Crossroads" at 183.

113. *See* Stephen E. Gottlieb, "In the Name of Patriotism: The Constitutionality of 'Bending' History in Public Secondary Schools," 62 *N.Y.U. L. Rev.* 497, 502–3 (1987).

114. *See* James, "Rights of Conscience and State School Systems" at 117, 124–35 (describing the resistance Catholic immigrants encountered trying to introduce versions of the Bible other than King James into state-sponsored schools); *see also* Onuf, "State Politics and Republican Virtue" at 91.

115. *See* Everson v. Board of Educ., 330 U.S. 1, 18 (1947) (announcing that "the First Amendment has erected a wall between church and state" and deciding nondiscriminatory school-bus-fare program had not breached that wall).

116. *See* McConnell, "Religious Freedom at a Crossroads" at 117–20 (discussing inconsistency and confusion of religion clause jurisprudence).

117. *See* McConnell, "Religious Freedom at a Crossroads" at 120–27, 134–37. McConnell argues wall of separation hostile toward religion, particularly as applied, and Rehnquist Court is, in part, redressing balance, treating recent accommodationist cases as generally appropriate but insufficient to redress Court's privileging of secular purposes. McConnell is quite critical of the non-neutrality of some accommodationist cases, *see ibid.* at 146–47. There is room for argument whether the justices are motivated by an attempt to "correct" the balance, support religion without breaking with too much precedent, or a less clearly articulated purpose. Conservative understandings of the role of religion in public life, however, should contribute to our understanding of the justices' treatment of the religion clauses.

118. *See* Edwards v. Aguillard, 482 U.S. 578, 592 (1987) (finding statute requiring that if evolution were taught, then creation science had to be taught violated the establishment clause); *see also* McConnell, "Religious Freedom at a Crossroads" at 134–35 (observing Burger Court promoted "secular liberalism" by weak support of the religion clauses).

119. *See* Melissa Healy, "End of 'Contract' Is Start of New Tests for GOP," *Los Angeles Times*, April 7, 1995, home ed., at A1; *see also* James Davison Hunter, "The Williamsburg Charter Survey: Methodology and Findings," 8 *J.L. & Religion* 257, 266 (1990) (providing data on the views of "evangelicals" on church and state issues).

120. *See* County of Allegheny v. ACLU, 492 U.S. 573, 601–2, 616–21 (1989) (holding solo creche on courthouse grounds violated establishment clause, but display of menorah together with Christmas tree outside a government building did not); Lynch v. Donnelly, 465 U.S. 668, 685–87 (1984) (holding display of creche on public grounds surrounded by likenesses of admiring people and barn animals did not violate establishment clause).

121. 494 U.S. 872, 890–91 (1990) (holding free exercise clause did not protect Native American use of peyote at religious ceremony).

122. *See ibid.*; Hernandez v. Commissioner, 490 U.S. 680, 699–700 (1989) (upholding denial of tax deduction for contributions to Church of Scientology though given for more traditional faiths).

123. *See, e.g.*, Zobrest v. Catalina Foothills Sch. Dist., 509 U.S. 1, 13–14 (1993) (Rehnquist, C.J.) (holding that a state's provision of sign language interpreter to a deaf student in religious school was not in violation of the establishment clause); *Lynch*, 465 U.S. at 673–79, 685, 687 (holding a Christmas display including Nativity scene permissible).

124. 521 U.S. 507 (1997).

125. Chief Justice Rehnquist has been particularly explicit in this regard. *See* Wallace v. Jaffree, 472 U.S. 38, 106 (1985) (Rehnquist, C.J., dissenting) ("The Establishment Clause did not require government neutrality between religion and irreligion nor did it prohibit the Federal Government from providing nondiscriminatory aid to religion.").

126. County of Allegheny v. ACLU, 492 U.S. 573, 655 (1989) (Kennedy, J., concurring in part and dissenting in part, joined by Rehnquist, C.J., Scalia and White, JJ.).

127. *Ibid.* at 670.

128. *See ibid.*

129. *See ibid.* Kennedy also objects that the endorsement test involves the Court in triviality: "A reviewing court must consider whether the city has included Santas, talking wishing wells, reindeer, or other secular symbols as 'a center of attention separate from the crèche,'" *ibid.* at 674.

130. *See* Board of Education v. Mergens, 496 U.S. 226, 261–62 (1990)

(Kennedy, J., concurring) (asserting literal application of the endorsement test "may result in neutrality in name, but hostility in fact").

131. *See, e.g., County of Allegheny*, 492 U.S. at 628 (O'Connor, J., concurring) ("[T]he endorsement test asks the right question about governmental practices challenged on Establishment Clause grounds.").

132. *See* Rosenberger v. Rector and Visitors of the University of Virginia, 515 U.S. 819, 846 (1995) (O'Connor, J., concurring) (agreeing that university must fund student religious newsletter); Lamb's Chapel v. Center Moriches Union Free Sch. Dist., 508 U.S. 384 (1993) (O'Connor, J., joined White, J., writing for majority) (holding church has equal right to use of school facilities); *Mergens*, 496 U.S. at 248 (holding equal access to school facilities required for student religious club). O'Connor would also permit public displays of religious symbols on public property so long as they are unaccompanied by apparent government approval or condemnation. *See County of Allegheny*, 492 U.S. at 623 (O'Connor, J., concurring); *Lynch*, 465 U.S. at 687.

133. *See Lynch*, 465 U.S. at 687 (O'Connor, J., concurring) (arguing that the overall setting of the holiday display negates any message of religious endorsement).

134. Employment Division v. Smith, 494 U.S. 872, 894–901, 905 (1990) (O'Connor, J., concurring).

135. *See Mergens*, 496 U.S. at 261; Rosenberger, note 132 above.

136. Agostini v. Felton, 521 U.S. 203 (1997).

137. *See ibid.* at 662–64 (stating that while individuals are free "to turn their backs" on religious displays, coercive government action violates the establishment clause).

138. 492 U.S. 573 (1989).

139. *See ibid.* at 659. Kennedy has reiterated the views he expressed in *County of Allegheny*, in *Mergens*, 496 U.S. at 260 (Kennedy, J., concurring), *and see* Lamb's Chapel v. Center Moriches Union Free School District, 508 U.S. 384, 394–96 (1993) (Kennedy, J., concurring).

140. 505 U.S. 577 (1992).

141. *See ibid.* at 587.

142. *See ibid.* at 586–89.

143. *See ibid.* at 590.

144. *See ibid.* at 590–97. *See also* Board of Educ. v. Grumet, 512 U.S. 687, 730 (1994) (Kennedy, J., concurring in the judgment) (objecting to "forced separation" of religious communities).

145. 508 U.S. 520 (1993).

146. *See ibid.* at 532 (invalidating ban on ritual slaughter).

147. *See ibid.* at 540–41.

148. *See Church of Lukumi Babalu Aye*, 508 U.S. at 558.

149. *See ibid.* (criticizing the Court's consideration of legislative motivation).

Souter, by contrast to both Kennedy and Scalia, called for a reexamination of the rule that neutrality of form and intent are insufficient to satisfy the establishment clause. *See ibid.* at 564 (Souter, J., concurring). Blackmun aligned much more with Souter than with either Kennedy or Scalia, and concurred with O'Connor in the judgment to emphasize the compelling interest test. *Ibid.* at 577–78.

150. 512 U.S. 687 (1994).

151. *See ibid.* at 702–4.

152. *See ibid.*

153. *Grumet,* 512 U.S. at 732.

154. *Ibid.* at 722 (Kennedy, J., concurring).

155. *Ibid.* at 730.

156. *See ibid.* at 730. Note that O'Connor, in *Board of Education v. Grumet,* 512 U.S. at 719, has separated herself from the coercion rationale of *Lee v. Weisman,* 505 U.S. 577 (1992).

157. *See Grumet,* 512 U.S. at 730 (Kennedy, J., concurring).

158. A realist might balk that government is essential to the resulting incorporation as well as school districting, and that government action coerces those who object. Kennedy might respond to the realists that in order to respect free will, it is necessary to protect a sphere of action not subject to the rules and standards applicable to government action. Therefore, he might argue that it is important to establish a rule that delegates village incorporation to individual choice. Private action exists under our constitutional system because it should and must exist. Formal rules respect, indeed allow, private individual free will. Thus, the vice in *Grumet* was not the segregation itself, as a realist might argue, but the government locus of the decision to segregate the districts. It was bad because it was explicit, not merely permissive.

159. *See* Zobrest v. Catalina Foothills Sch. Dist., 509 U.S. 1, 10 (1993) (Rehnquist, C.J.) (stating that because interpreters would be available in every school, the state was not causing parents to choose the sectarian school).

160. *See ibid.* (arguing government subsidy of interpreters permissible since law imparted benefit to sectarian schools only as a result of parental choice).

161. Agostini v. Felton, 521 U.S. 203 (1997).

162. Rosenberger, 515 U.S. at 847.

163. *See* Board of Educ. v. Mergens, 496 U.S. 226, 261 (1990) (arguing that a facially neutral rule is impermissible when its effect is hostile).

164. On neutrality regarding government-funded speech, *compare* Rust v. Sullivan, 500 U.S. 173, 223 (1991) (dissenting from restriction on the speech of personnel in government-funded health clinics), *with* Regan v. Taxation with Representation, 461 U.S. 540, 550–51 (1983) (joining majority upholding tax exemption for lobbying by veterans' organizations, but not other nonprofit organizations, as government speech). Regarding speaker bias, *compare* Leathers v. Medlock, 499 U.S. 439, 453 (1991) (concluding an extension of a generally ap-

plicable sales tax to cable, but exemption for the print media, did not violate the First Amendment) *and* R.A.V. v. City of St. Paul, 505 U.S. 377, 399 (1992) (joining Justice White's concurring opinion that would have permitted discrimination against hate speech) *with* Minneapolis Star and Tribune Co. v. Minnesota Comm'r of Revenue, 460 U.S. 575, 576–93 (1983) (invalidating tax that discriminated against the print press, and particularly against larger concerns). O'Connor, nonetheless, supports freedom of speech in traditional areas by conventional methods, *see* International Society for Krishna Consciousness, Inc. v. Lee, 505 U.S. 672, 685 (1992) (O'Connor, J., concurring) (concerning books and leaflets); Forsyth County v. The Nationalist Movement, 505 U.S. 123, 130 (1992) (parades); some in areas that have been abandoned or ignored by some of her colleagues, *see* R.A.V., 505 U.S. at 399 (overbreadth); Cable News Network, Inc. v. Noriega, 498 U.S. 976, 976–77 (1990) (O'Connor, J., joined Marshall, J., dissenting from denial of certiorari) (prior restraint).

165. *See Leathers*, 499 U.S. at 448 (finding sales tax permissible because of size of media group subject to the tax).

166. *See Rust*, 500 U.S. at 223 (O'Connor, J., dissenting) (finding impermissible restriction on speech of medical staff regarding abortion at government-funded health clinics); Capital Area Right To Life v. Downtown Frankfort, Inc., 511 U.S. 1135 (1994) (O'Connor, J., dissenting from denial of certiorari) (objecting to restriction of controversial speech at state fair as not content-neutral and noting that neutrality requirement not limited to viewpoint).

167. *See* City of Ladue v. Gilleo, 512 U.S. 43. 59 (1994) (O'Connor, J., concurring) (preferring to decide as not neutral regarding content but agreeing ban on residential signs overly burdensome).

168. *See* Cable News Network, Inc. v. Noriega, 498 U.S. 976, 976 (O'Connor, J., joined Marshall, J., dissenting from denial of certiorari) (arguing certiorari should have been granted to determine constitutionality of injunction against "publication of information alleged to threaten a criminal defendant's right to a fair trial without any threshold showing that the information will indeed cause such harm").

169. *See* Gentile v. State Bar, 501 U.S. 1030, 1081 (1991) (O'Connor, J., concurring) (arguing First Amendment does not bar state from disciplining attorney for making statements to press alleging official corruption); Ibanez v. Florida Dep't of Bus. and Prof'l Regulation, 512 U.S. 136, 149 (1994) (O'Connor, J., concurring in part and dissenting in part) (arguing First Amendment does not bar state from disciplining attorney for truthful listing as certified financial planner); Edenfield v. Fane, 507 U.S. 761, 778 (1993) (O'Connor, J., dissenting) ("[T]he States have the broader authority to prohibit commercial speech that, albeit not directly harmful to the listener, is inconsistent with the speaker's membership in a learned profession and therefore damaging to the profession and society at large."); Shapero v. Kentucky Bar Ass'n, 486 U.S. 466, 480 (1988) (O'Connor, J.,

dissenting) (arguing First Amendment does not bar state from prohibiting truthful personal solicitations by attorneys triggered by specific events); Zauderer v. Office of Disciplinary Counsel, 471 U.S. 626, 676–67 (1985) (O'Connor, J., concurring in part and dissenting in part) (arguing First Amendment does not prevent state from barring unsolicited legal advertisements from printed ads).

170. *See* International Society for Krishna Consciousness, Inc. v. Lee, 505 U.S. 672, 686–92 (1992) (O'Connor, J., concurring) (arguing prohibition of leafletting in airport is unconstitutional but agreeing prohibition of solicitations permissible); United States v. Kokinda, 497 U.S. 720, 725 (1990) (arguing same relating to grounds of Postal Service).

171. 497 U.S. 720 (1990).

172. 505 U.S. 672 (1992).

173. *See Kokinda*, 497 U.S. at 732–33 (concluding ban on sidewalk solicitations in front of post office was reasonable); Lee v. International Society for Krishna Consciousness, Inc. 505 U.S. 830, 831 (1992) (Rehnquist, C.J., dissenting); *see also* Forsyth County v. The Nationalist Movement, 505 U.S. 123, 129–37 (1992) (both O'Connor and Kennedy joined the majority barring sliding fees for demonstrations, while Scalia dissented); *Ibanez*, 512 U.S. at 149 (O'Connor, J., concurring in part and dissenting in part) (arguing attorney regulation proper); *Ladue*, 512 U.S. at 60 (O'Connor, J., concurring) (arguing regulation of residential signs unconstitutional); *Capital Area Right To Life*, 511 U.S. 1135 (O'Connor, J., dissenting from denial of certiorari) (arguing restriction of controversial speech at state fair unconstitutional).

174. *See, e.g., Lee*, 505 U.S. at 685 (arguing solicitor interrupts the activities of audience); *Kokinda*, 497 U.S. at 734 (observing solicitors are "more intrusive and intimidating").

175. City of Lakewood v. Plain Dealer Publ'g Co., 486 U.S. 750, 772 (1988) (White, J., dissenting) (supporting ban on news racks for advertisers); Members of the City Council of the City of Los Angeles v. Taxpayers for Vincent, 466 U.S. 789, 796–803 (1984) (*per* Stevens, J.) (supporting ban of flyers on utility poles).

176. *See Ibanez*, 512 U.S. at 149 (O'Connor, J., concurring in part and dissenting in part) (arguing attorney advertising may be regulated); Edenfield v. Fane, 507 U.S. 761, 778 (1993) (O'Connor, J., dissenting) (asserting states have broad authority to regulate speech of licensed professionals); *Gentile*, 501 U.S. at 1081 (O'Connor, J., concurring) (agreeing state may regulate speech by lawyers). O'Connor also has little patience for advertising, *see* Board of Trustees of SUNY v. Fox, 492 U.S. 469, 475 (1989), and she gives considerable, though not full, leeway to government employers over employee speech, *see* Waters v. Churchill, 511 U.S. 661 (1994).

177. *See* William J. Brennan, Jr., "The Supreme Court and the Meiklejohn Interpretation of the First Amendment," 79 *Harv. L. Rev.* 1 (1965).

178. For example, O'Connor expressed considerable concern about the shaping of the broadcast media, even for possibly good reasons, on content grounds.

See Turner Broadcasting System, Inc. v. Federal Communications Commission, 512 U.S. 622, 674 (1994) (O'Connor, J., concurring in part and dissenting in part) (urging strict scrutiny for must-carry provisions of cable television statute). O'Connor, in *Turner Broadcasting System, Inc.*, states:

> Preferences for diversity of viewpoints, for localism, for educational programming, and for news and public affairs all make reference to content. They may not reflect hostility to particular points of view, or a desire to suppress certain subjects because they are controversial or offensive. They may be quite benignly motivated. But benign motivation, we have consistently held, is not enough to avoid the need for strict scrutiny of content-based justifications.

Ibid. at 677.

179. Cohen v. California, 403 U.S. 15, 26 (1971) (invalidating plaintiff's conviction for wearing a shirt with an obscene word directed against the draft).

180. FCC v. Pacifica Found., 438 U.S. 726, 762 (1978) (Brennan, J., dissenting) (objecting to sanction of radio station for broadcasting satiric monologue on seven "dirty" and, theretofore, unmentionable words on radio).

181. Gentile v. State Bar, 501 U.S. 1030 (1991).

182. *See ibid.* at 1034 (classifying the attorney's comments, which were critical of the government and its officials, as political speech).

183. *See ibid.* at 1081 (O'Connor, J., concurring) (commenting that attorney's speech alleging official frame-up violated Rules of Professional Conduct). *See also* Florida Bar v. Went For It, Inc., 515 U.S. 618 (1995) (*per* O'Connor, J.) (sustaining prohibition of targeted solicitation). It may also be the case that O'Connor does not view many types of speech, including commercial speech, as important. *See, e.g.,* Shapero v. Kentucky Bar Ass'n, 486 U.S. 466, 480 (1988) (O'Connor, J., dissenting) (arguing First Amendment does not bar state from prohibiting truthful personal solicitations by attorneys triggered by specific events); *Board of Trustees of SUNY*, 492 U.S. at 480 (Scalia, J.) (commenting that a vendor could be prohibited from demonstrating and proposing commercial transaction in college dormitory); Peel v. Attorney Registration and Disciplinary Comm'n, 496 U.S. 91, 119 (1990) (O'Connor, J., dissenting) (arguing attorney should be subject to discipline for truthfully asserting certification as a civil trial specialist by a private organization that set standards).

184. *See* United States v. Eichman, 496 U.S. 310 (1990) (Scalia, J., joined Brennan, J.) (invalidating flag burning statute because intended to censor speech); Texas v. Johnson, 491 U.S. 397 (1989) (Scalia, J., joined Brennan, J.) (invalidating flag desecration statute as not neutral).

185. *See, e.g.,* R.A.V. v. City of St. Paul, 505 U.S. 377 (1992) (concluding hate speech rule not neutral); *Gentile*, 501 U.S. at 1076 (*per* Rehnquist, C.J., dissenting in part) (arguing that neutral rule is sufficient basis for prosecuting attorney for public statement).

186. *See* National Endowment for the Arts v. Finley, 524 U.S. 569, 595–99 (1998) (Scalia, J., concurring in the judgment) (subsidies should not be treated as suppression of speech or subjected to strictures of First Amendment); Arkansas Writers' Project, Inc. v. Ragland, 481 U.S. 221, 235 (1987) (Scalia, J., dissenting) (arguing rule of neutrality should not apply to government subsidies).

187. *See* International Society for Krishna Consciousness, Inc. v. Lee, 505 U.S. 672, 677–84 (1992) (remarking that when government acts as proprietor, rather than lawmaker, its actions are not subject to heightened review); Owen Fiss, "Silence on the Street Corner," in *Public Values in Constitutional Law* (Ann Arbor: University of Michigan Press, Stephen E. Gottlieb ed., 1993) at 206–7.

188. 497 U.S. 62 (1990).

189. *See* Rutan v. Republican Party, 497 U.S. 62, 94 (1990) (Scalia, J., dissenting) (claiming constitutional restrictions apply to government as lawmaker, not as employer). Justices O'Connor and Kennedy joined Scalia's dissent in *Rutan*, but have subsequently abandoned that position in Board of County Commissioners v. Umbehr, 518 U.S. 668, 680–83 (1996). Scalia's admiration for power is also reflected in his consistent support for the executive branch. *See* Daniel N. Reisman, "Deconstructing Justice Scalia's Separation of Powers Jurisprudence: The Preeminent Executive," 53 *Alb. L. Rev.* 49 (1988).

190. *See, e.g.,* Masson v. New Yorker Magazine, Inc., 501 U.S. 496, 517 (1991) ("[A] deliberate alteration of the words uttered by a plaintiff does not equate with knowledge of falsity . . . unless the alteration results in a material change in the meaning conveyed by the statement."); *Gentile*, 501 U.S. at 1034–35 (concluding attorney's pretrial remarks alleging client being prosecuted to cover official corruption was core political speech entitled to substantial protection); Alexander v. United States, 509 U.S. 544, 560 (1993) (Kennedy, J., dissenting) (objecting to "destruction of a book and film business and its entire inventory . . . as punishment for a single past speech offense"). *See also Johnson*, 491 U.S. at 420 (Kennedy, J., concurring) (asserting flag burning is protected speech), and Amar, "Justice Kennnedy."

191. *See Gentile*, 501 U.S. at 1034–35 (commenting that in suppressing attorney's comments, Nevada is punishing the dissemination of information regarding alleged governmental misconduct, which previously received First Amendment protection).

192. *Masson*, 501 U.S. at 514–16.

193. *See ibid.*

194. *See* H. Jefferson Powell, "The Original Understanding of Original Intent," 98 *Harv. L. Rev.* 885, 889 (1985) (describing the scriptual interpretation derived from Protestant theology).

195. *See* Richard Hofstadter, *The Age of Reform from Bryan to F.D.R.* (New York: Knopf, 1955) at 149–53 (examining the role of the clergy in the populist and Progressive movements). The clergy played major roles in both abolition, *see* William G. McLoughlin, "Charles Grandison Finney," in *Ante-Bellum Reform*

(New York: Harper and Row, David Brion Davis ed., 1967) at 103; Lee Benson, "Religious Group and Political Parties" in *Ante-Bellum Reform* at 118, and temperance, Hofstadter, *The Age of Reform* at 287. William Jennings Bryan is well known both for his populism and his prosecution of the Scopes trial. *See ibid.* at 286–87.

196. *See* Wildavsky, "Is Culture the Culprit?" at 111 (discussing the sexual revolution); Jessica Gress-Wright, "The Contraception Paradox," 113 *Pub. Interest* 15 (Fall 1993) (evaluating the moral argument concerning unwed teenagers, premarital sex, and contraception, and suggesting an economic explanation).

197. *See, e.g.,* Planned Parenthood v. Casey, 505 U.S. 833, 850 (1992) (stating there will always be disagreement about the moral and spiritual implications of abortion); Webster v. Reproductive Health Servs., 492 U.S. 490 (1989) (determining preamble to Missouri statute regulating abortions can be read as expressing a value judgment).

198. *See* Roe v. Wade, 410 U.S. 113, 129–47 (1973) (describing the history of abortion rules and various organizational positions).

199. *See* Luker, *Abortion* at 12–13, 186–88. Luker argues that the historical Judeo-Christian position was quite close to *Roe,* treating early-term abortions as permissible and later-term abortions as punishable, but that contemporary views of abortion activists are closely related to their current religious views.

200. *See* Kannar, "The Constitutional Catechism of Antonin Scalia" at 1309–20 (describing Scalia's religious training and its impact on his thinking).

201. O'Connor's view of the moral priority of the public has been somewhat inconsistent. She has been one of the most vocal justices about the importance of overriding state or government purposes in constitutional adjudication. *See* Leathers v. Medlock, 499 U.S. 439, 447, 455 (1991) (asserting that overriding public purposes would be needed to merit a burden on speech); United States v. Kokinda, 497 U.S. 720, 734 (1990) (finding that solicitation causes problems that justify the ban); Metro Broadcasting, Inc. v. FCC, 497 U.S. 547, 611 (1990) (O'Connor, J., dissenting) (stating that congressional action endorsed an FCC policy with purposes insufficiently important); City of Richmond v. J.A. Croson Co., 488 U.S. 469, 493 (1989) (judging city's plan by the strength of its interest in eradicating discrimination). O'Connor's conclusions in *J.A. Croson Co.* and *Metro,* and in the eminent domain cases reflect a judgment that private values are either consistent with or outweigh public ones. *See* Lucas v. South Carolina Coastal Council, 505 U.S. 1003 (1992); Nollan v. California Coastal Comm'n, 483 U.S. 825 (1987).

202. *See* Planned Parenthood v. Casey, 505 U.S. 833, 846 (1992) (holding state has certain interests in the life of an unborn fetus but not sufficient to prohibit all abortions).

203. *See* Stephen E. Gottlieb, "Introduction: Overriding Public Values," in *Public Values in Constitutional Law* at 21.

204. *See Planned Parenthood*, 505 U.S. at 950–53 (Scalia, J., joined Rehnquist, C.J., concurring in part and dissenting in part) (asserting that there is no fundamental right to an abortion); *ibid.* at 979–80 (Scalia, J., concurring in the judgment in part and dissenting in part) (same); Webster v. Reproductive Health Servs., 492 U.S. 490, 532 (1989) (Scalia, J., concurring in part) (opposing O'Connor's view that *Roe* mandated right to abortion may not be reconsidered); *see also* Edelman, "Justice Scalia's Jurisprudence" at 1810 (offering that Scalia is unenthusiastic about fundamental personal rights).

205. *See* Barnes v. Glen Theatre, Inc., 501 U.S. 560, 579–81 (1991) (Scalia, J., concurring in the judgment); Bendix Autolite Corp. v. Midwesco Enters., Inc., 486 U.S. 888, 897–98 (1988) (Scalia, J., concurring) (espousing view that balancing is not part of a court's essential function).

206. *Compare Planned Parenthood*, 505 U.S. at 979–80 (Scalia denying any fundamental right to abort), *with* Dolan v. City of Tigard, 512 U.S. 374 (1994) (*per* Rehnquist, C.J.) (defending property rights against exchanges forced by zoning rules), *and* Lucas v. South Carolina Coastal Council, 505 U.S. 1003, 1022–28 (1992) (defending property rights as defined by nuisance law).

207. Webster v. Reproductive Health Servs., 492 U.S. 490, 517–20 (1989).

208. 505 U.S. 833 (1992).

209. *See Planned Parenthood*, 505 U.S. at 843–901.

210. 506 U.S. 390 (1993).

211. *See ibid.* at 419–20 (Kennedy, J., joined O'Connor, J., concurring).

212. *See* Schlup v. Delo, 513 U.S. 298, 334 (1995) (Kennedy, J., joined Rehnquist, C.J., dissenting). The Court of Appeals in *Schlup* held that Sawyer v. Whitley, 505 U.S. 333, 336 (1992), "foreclosed consideration" of Schlup's evidence of innocence because evidence sufficient to convict was introduced at the original trial. *See Schlup*, 513 U.S. at 311–12. The Rehnquist dissent adopted the *Sawyer* test and urged that, in the absence of *Sawyer*, the appropriate standard is that no reasonable juror would have convicted. *See ibid.* at 341. On that basis the dissenters would have foreclosed trial court discretion to grant relief.

213. *See Schlup*, 513 U.S. 298 at 332–34 (O'Connor, J., concurring) (agreeing that the district judge had discretion to consider evidence of actual innocence). *Schlup* posed a narrower legal question than *Herrera*. In *Schlup*, the evidence of actual innocence was brought to enable the court to look at another otherwise barred constitutional claim. *See ibid.* at 301. In *Herrera*, however, the evidence of actual innocence was brought as an independent ground and the constitutional claim was that Texas's law, which barred consideration of such evidence from a period shortly after the original trial, was constitutional error. *See Herrera*, 506 U.S. at 393.

214. 500 U.S. 44 (1991).

215. *See ibid.* at 70–71 (Scalia, J., dissenting) (arguing arraignment must take place within twenty-four hours of arrest).

216. *Ibid.* at 71 (Scalia, J., dissenting).

217. 506 U.S. at 428–29 (Scalia, J., concurring).

218. *See ibid.* at 393.

219. *See ibid.* at 427–28.

220. 513 U.S. at 310–09.

221. *See* chapter 2 above.

222. United States v. Carolene Products Co., 304 U.S. 144 (1938).

223. *Compare Carolene Products* at 152–53 n.4 (explaining Court will defer to popularly elected branches of government except where they interfere with the democratic process itself, or where the democratic process is so corrupted by "prejudice against discrete and insular minorities" that it cannot function properly) *with* City of Richmond v. J.A. Croson Co., 488 U.S. 469, 494–96 (1989) (O'Connor, J.) (explicitly refusing to vary the level of scrutiny according to the group's status as a discrete and insular minority).

224. *See* Presley v. Etowah County Comm'n., 502 U.S. 491, 509–10 (1992) (Kennedy, J.) (holding that changing the form of government so that newly elected black officials would not exercise the power of their white predecessors is permissible under the Voting Rights Act); Chisom v. Roemer, 501 U.S. 380, 384 (1991) (holding that judicial elections are covered by the Voting Rights Act) (O'Connor, J., joined the majority while Justices Scalia, Rehnquist, and Kennedy dissented); Brown v. Thomson, 462 U.S. 835, 847–48 (1983) (Justices Rehnquist and O'Connor joined a majority upholding apportionment with 89 percent population deviation); *see also* City of Mobile v. Bolden, 446 U.S. 55, 65–66 (1980) (Justice Rehnquist joined opinion refusing to find racial motivation in districting); Holt Civic Club v. City of Tuscaloosa, 439 U.S. 60, 63 (1978) (*per* Rehnquist, J.) (holding extraterritorial extension of a municipality's police powers, judicial jurisdiction, and licensing powers to an unincorporated rural community outside the city limits does not require a concomitant extraterritorial extension of the franchise); Salyer Land Co. v. Tulare Lake Basin Water Storage Dist., 410 U.S. 719, 728–35 (1973) (*per* Rehnquist, J.) (holding residents who do not own land can be excluded from voting in water district elections).

While refusing to find discrimination against minorities, the conservative justices have found discrimination in favor of minorities, not on the ground that they were "overrepresented," as in the apportionment cases, but on the ground that "race-conscious" districting designed to enable their representation was improper. *See* Miller v. Johnson, 515 U.S. 900 (1995) (*per* Kennedy, J.) (holding it improper to use Voting Rights Act as justification for homogeneous districting and roughly proportional representation); Shaw v. Reno, 509 U.S. 630, 647–48 (1993) (O'Connor, J.) (holding irregular shapes and homogeneous districting without sufficient justification in reapportionment scheme suffices as a claim under the equal protection clause).

225. *See* chapter 2 above.

226. *See* Pacific Mut. Life Ins. Co. v. Haslip, 499 U.S. 1, 24–40 (1991) (Scalia,

J., concurring in the judgment) (reaffirming that traditional treatment of punitive damages is permissible).

227. *See* Rutan v. Republican Party, 497 U.S. 62, 92–115 (1990) (Scalia, J., dissenting) (arguing Constitution does not invalidate patronage in public employment regardless of effect on individual freedom); Tashjian v. Republican Party of Connecticut, 479 U.S. 208, 234 (1986) (Scalia, J., dissenting) (supporting protection of political parties from independent voters).

228. *See* Brown v. Thompson, 462 U.S. 835, 848–50 (1983) (O'Connor, J., concurring) (upholding apportionment scheme characterized by 89 percent population deviation).

229. *See* Miller v. Johnson, 515 U.S. 900, 928 (1995) (O'Connor, J., concurring) (quoting from majority opinion to effect that race may be considered as long as it does not "'subordinate[] traditional race-neutral districting principles'"). Unfortunately, her position may actually require a racial gerrymander because it requires "stacking" minority voters into some homogenous districts to satisfy the Voting Rights Act but "cracking" the remainder to satisfy her and the Court's scruples about racial line drawing. "Stacking" and "cracking," in combination, are the tools of gerrymandering that may result in the worst possible combination for minority voters. On gerrymandering, in general, see Stephen E. Gottlieb, "Fashioning a Test for Gerrymandering," 15 *J. Legis.* 1 (1988).

230. Kennedy sidestepped the issue of multimember districts in Chisom v. Roemer, 501 U.S. 380, 418 (1991) (Kennedy, J., dissenting) but suggested that he would reconsider Thornburg v. Gingles, 478 U.S. 30 (1986). Kennedy also concluded in *Chisom* that judges were not covered by the Voting Rights Act. *See Chisom,* 501 U.S. at 416–18.

Multimember districts reflect gerrymandered inequality, i.e., we benefit from a close relation with our representatives in small districts where we can and swamp you in our multimember territory elsewhere. Thus, it involves a failure to come to grips with the inequalities that multimember districts create in combination with single-member districts. The Court, however, has not understood gerrymandering in any of its forms. *See generally* Gottlieb, "Test for Gerrymandering"; *see also* Stephen E. Gottlieb, "Identifying Gerrymanders," 15 *St. Louis U. L.J.* 540 (1971).

More crucial to assessing his treatment of the relationship between districting and democracy would be his view on justiciability. Kennedy, however, had not been appointed when the Court decided Davis v. Bandemer, 478 U.S. 109 (1986) (holding that political gerrymandering cases are justiciable under the equal protection clause).

The Voting Rights Act cases were discussed at length in chapter 2. Kennedy joined the majority in Shaw v. Reno, 509 U.S. 630 (1993) and subsequent cases, concluding that racial gerrymandering required close scrutiny even for remedial purposes, *ibid.* at 643–44. Kennedy's conclusion that it is permissible to change the power of elected officials in order to exclude probable black elected officials from power despite the Voting Rights Act, Presley v. Etowah County Comm'n,

502 U.S. 491 (1992), may indicate antipathy toward equality of democratic rights but can be rationalized as majoritarian.

231. Kennedy's basic support for people to express their political will is reflected in Burdick v. Takushi, 504 U.S. 428 (1992), in which Kennedy dissented from a decision upholding Hawaii's ban on write-in votes because it prevented voters from casting a meaningful vote. *See ibid.* at 442. In a similar but less revealing vein, Kennedy joined a unanimous (8–0) Court in Eu v. San Francisco County Democratic Central Committee, 489 U.S. 214 (1989), striking down provisions that interfered with political expression. *See ibid.* at 233.

232. 497 U.S. 62, 92–115 (1990) (Scalia, J., dissenting) (arguing that the Constitution does not invalidate patronage considerations in public employment decisions regardless of the effect they may have on individual freedom to make political judgments).

233. *Umbehr,* 518 U.S. 668 at 680–83.

234. *See, e.g.,* Cordray and Vradelis, "O'Connor" (commenting on Justice O'Connor's view of federalism).

235. *See* Miller v. Johnson, 515 U.S. 900 (1995) (rejecting redistricting plan); City of Richmond v. J.A. Croson Co., 488 U.S. 469, 524–25 (1989) (overruling racial set-asides); Michigan v. Long, 463 U.S. 1032 (1983) (requiring explicit statement of independent state grounds).

236. *See* Devigne, *Recasting Conservatism* at 68.

237. *See ibid.* at 96.

238. *See, e.g.,* Barnes v. Glen Theatre, Inc., 501 U.S. 560, 567–69 (1991) (upholding a state's interest in morality as sufficient to ban nude dancing); Webster v. Reproductive Health Servs., 492 U.S. 490 (1989) (upholding state restrictions on abortion); Bowers v. Hardwick, 478 U.S. 186 (1986) (upholding state sodomy statute); Board of Education, Island Trees Union Free School District v. Pico, 457 U.S. 853, 885 (1982) (Rehnquist and O'Connor, JJ., joined Burger, C.J., dissenting) (arguing that local school boards have authority to censor school libraries in an "area traditionally left to the states").

239. *See, e.g., J.A. Croson Co.,* 488 U.S. at 470 (overruling local set-aside for minority construction contractors); Michigan v. Long, 463 U.S. 1032 (1983) (overruling state court suppression of evidence in a criminal case).

240. *See* Coleman v. Thompson, 501 U.S. 722, 759 (1991) (Blackmun, J., dissenting). Kennedy quoted Blackmun to explain the import of federalism in United States v. Lopez, 514 U.S. 549, 576 (1995).

241. *See e.g.,* Barnes v. Glen Theatre, Inc., 501 U.S. 560 (1991) (regulating nudity); Webster v. Reproductive Health Servs., 492 U.S. 490 (1989) (abortion regulations); Bowers v. Hardwick, 478 U.S. 186 (1986) (punishing sodomy); Board of Education v. Pico, 457 U.S. 853 (pruning of a school library).

242. *See, e.g.,* Linda Greenhouse, "High Court Voids a Law Expanding Religious Rights," *New York Times,* June 26, 1997 at A1, D24.

243. In *Boerne*, 521 U.S. at 527–33, Kennedy compared the structure of RFRA to the structure of the Voting Rights Act under Congress's power pursuant to §5 of the Fourteenth Amendment and discussed several of the examples in the text.

244. *See, e.g.*, Antonin Scalia, "The Rule of Law as a Law of Rules," 56 *U. Chi. L. Rev.* 1175 (1989) (exploring the dichotomy between "general rule of law" and "personal discretion").

NOTES TO CHAPTER 5

1. Scott Douglas Gerber, *First Principles: The Jurisprudence of Clarence Thomas* (New York: New York University Press, 1999).

2. Clarence Thomas, "Toward a 'Plain Reading' of the Constitution—The Declaration of Independence in Constitutional Interpretation," 30 *Howard L.J.* 983, 988–989 (1987). He often takes an originalist position with no presumption that the draftsmen had good intentions or high purposes.

Thomas's recent writings in the criminal area reiterate his insistence on formal rather than instrumental jurisprudence. For example, in Shannon v. United States, 512 U.S. 573 (1994), Thomas, writing for the Court, held that a federal district court does not have to explain to the jury that a defendant, after acquittal by reason of insanity, is then bound over for hearing on the danger to himself or others because of his mental state, and may be committed until he is no longer thought dangerous. In doing so, Thomas argued that the legislative history in Congress is too meager to give guidance, and that the federal statute does not track the language of the District of Columbia statute under which that practice had been thought proper. He concluded that the instruction is not required and may not do any good anyway. There is no discussion in his opinion, however, of which rule would produce the better outcome, what the jury would actually do under the circumstances, and why. Thomas wrote:

> Whether the instruction works to the advantage or disadvantage of a defendant is of course, somewhat beside the point. Our central concern here is that the inevitable result of such an instruction would be to draw the jury's attention toward the very thing—the possible consequences of its verdict— it should ignore.

512 U.S. at 586. Language has "inevitable" consequences and comparisons about actual behavior are useless. Given the conclusion that many have drawn, that the jury does pay attention and does make such assumptions, his conclusion has to be read as a formal one—we assume it does not consider consequences or punishment simply because it should not. 512 U.S. at 585. On those assumptions, no instruction could be helpful.

3. *See* United States v. Lopez, 514 U.S. 549, 585–94 (1995) (Thomas, J., concurring), in which Thomas argued for a very narrow definition of the commerce that Congress can regulate that would include trade but not include manufactur-

ing or agriculture or, as laid down by Chief Justice Marshall in the early nineteenth century, what affects commerce. Sanford Levinson, "Raoul Berger Pleads for Judicial Activism: A Comment," 74 *Tex. L. Rev.* 773, 775 (1996), notes that Thomas's argument mimics an argument first made in Richard Epstein, "The Proper Scope of the Commerce Power," 73 *Va. L. Rev.* (1987), and comments caustically on Thomas's failure to cite the Epstein article.

4. "The Supreme Court, 1993 Term: IV. The Statistics," 108 *Harv. L. Rev.* 373 (1994/95); "The Supreme Court, 1992 Term: IV. The Statistics," 107 *Harv. L. Rev.* 373 (1993/94); "The Supreme Court, 1991 Term: IV. The Statistics," 106 *Harv. L. Rev.* 379 (1992/93); Christopher E. Smith and Scott Patrick Johnson, "The First-Term Performance of Justice Clarence Thomas," 76 *Judicature* 173, 175 (1992–93).

5. It may be significant that Thomas was not prepared, to the same extent as Rehnquist and Kennedy, to reduce the availability of suits in federal courts against state officials to require compliance with federal law, a major weapon in the effort to enforce the various constitutional guarantees, Idaho v. Coeur d'Alene Tribe of Idaho, 521 U.S. 261, 288 (1997) (O'Connor, J., concurring). *But see* Alden v. Maine, 527 U.S. 706 (1999); College Savings Bank v. Florida Prepaid Postsecondary Educ. Expense Bd., 527 U.S. 666, 119 S. Ct. 2219, 144 L. Ed. 2d 605 (1999); Florida Prepaid Postsecondary Educ. Expense Bd. v. College Savings Bank, 527 U.S. 627, 119 S. Ct. 2199, 144 L. Ed. 2d 575 (1999).

6. *See infra* text at notes 43–53.

7. *See, e.g.,* Cass County, Minn. v. Leech Lake Band of Chippewa Indians, 524 U.S. 103 (1998); Montana v. Crow Tribe of Indians, 523 U.S. 696 (1998); Kiowa Tribe of Okla. v. Manufacturing Technologies, Inc., 523 U.S. 751, 760 (1998) (Stevens, J., concurring); Idaho v. Coeur d'Alene Tribe of Idaho, 521 U.S. 261, 288 (1997) (O'Connor, J., concurring). My point, of course, as it is through most of this work, is the pattern, not the rationale.

8. 513 U.S. 979 (1994) (Thomas, J., dissenting from denial of certiorari).

9. The landlord attacked the statute, claiming that rental to an unmarried and cohabiting couple violated his religious principles. That raised the issue whether the statute was permissible under the free exercise clause and the Religious Freedom Restoration Act. RFRA has subsequently been held unconstitutional, *see* City of Boerne v. Flores, 521 U.S. 507 (1997). Under RFRA as it then applied, religious practices were protected from governmental burdens unless there was a compelling government interest in favor of the burden. Thomas wrote that privacy of marital status is not a compelling government interest that government can assert to defend the statute. Thus Alaska could not bar discrimination against unmarried couples where any contrary rights were asserted and the Alaska antidiscrimination statute was unconstitutional at least as applied in this context. Thomas wrote that he was "at a loss to know what asserted government interests are [less] compelling." 513 U.S. at 982.

10. 517 U.S. 620 (1996). Similarly in *Romer*, the breadth of the amendment in-

volved went well beyond what are arguably the competing rights of those who frown on homosexual relationships.

11. *See, e.g.,* Agostini v. Felton, 521 U.S. 203 (1997) (overruling Aguilar v. Felton, 473 U.S. 402 (1985) and authorizing school board to send remedial teachers into parochial schools on a neutral basis); Rosenberger v. Rector and Visitors of the University of Virginia, 515 U.S. 819, 852 (1995) (Thomas, J., concurring) (university must fund student religious newsletter); Lamb's Chapel v. Center Moriches Union Free Sch. Dist., 508 U.S. 384 (1993) (Scalia, J., concurring in the judgment) (nondiscriminatory church access to school facilities does not violate establishment clause).

12. *Rosenberger* 515 U.S. at 855–56; *Lamb's Chapel,* 508 U.S. at 401 (Scalia, J., concurring in the judgment).

13. 505 U.S. 377 (1992).

14. 514 U.S. 334, 358 (1995).

15. 44 Liquormart, Inc. v. State of Rhode Island, 517 U.S. 484, 518 (1996) (Thomas, J., concurring in part and in the judgment) (arguing that there is no justification for keeping consumers ignorant).

16. *See* Lechmere v. N.L.R.B., 502 U.S. 527 (1992) (nonemployee union organizers may not trespass to organize unless literally no other access); International Society for Krishna Consciousness, Inc. v. Lee, 505 U.S. 672 (1992) (joining Rehnquist plurality concluding that airports are not public fora).

17. Forsyth County v. Nationalist Movement, 505 U.S. 123, 137 (1992) (Rehnquist, C.J., dissenting).

18. National Endowment for the Arts v. Finley, 524 U.S. 569, 595–99 (1998) (Scalia, J., concurring in the judgment). For another indication of his relaxed treatment of the First Amendment, *see* Dawson v. Delaware, 503 U.S. 159, 169 (1992) (Thomas, J., dissenting) (jury could have deduced bad character from evidence of membership in gang without examination of tenets in the specific unit).

19. Thomas is willing to execute those who are probably innocent, *see* Herrera v. Collins, 506 U.S. 390 (1993); Schlup v. Delo, 513 U.S. 298, 334 (1995). He argues that the cruel and unusual punishment clause has no application to abuse in prison, Hudson v. McMillian, 503 U.S. 1, 17 (1992) (Thomas, J., dissenting); Helling v. McKinney, 509 U.S. 25, 37 (Thomas, J., dissenting); Farmer v. Brennan, 511 U.S. 825, 858 (Thomas, J., concurring in the judgment), *and see* Richardson v. McKnight, 521 U.S. 399 (1997) reaching the same result based on 42 U.S.C. § 1983. He would defer to state court findings of fact, thus largely giving up one of the major tools of federal enforcement of the Bill of Rights, Wright v. West, 505 U.S. 277 (1992) (Thomas, J., plurality opinion).

20. United States v. Lopez, 514 U.S. 549, 584 (1995). *See also* Printz v. United States, 521 U.S. 898, 936 (1997) (Thomas, J., concurring); U.S. Term Limits, Inc. v. Thornton, 514 U.S. 779, 845 (1995) (Thomas, J., dissenting).

21. Idaho v. Coeur d'Alene Tribe of Idaho, 521 U.S. 261, 288 (1997) (O'Con-

nor, J., concurring in part and in the judgment); Seminole Tribe of Florida v. Florida, 517 U.S. 44 (1996).

22. The Civil Rights Cases, 109 U.S. 3 (1883).

23. In Adarand Constructors, Inc. v. Pena, 515 U.S. 200 (1995), the Court decided that the same standard, strict scrutiny, applied to race-based classifications by federal agencies that applied to state and local decisions in City of Richmond v. J.A. Croson Co. 488 U.S. 469 (1989) and vice versa. Thomas concurred in that portion of the opinion. The more deferential approach to the affirmative action cases was stated in Marshall's dissenting opinion in *J.A. Croson Co.* at 535. All of the takings cases involved state and local decisions. *See, e.g.,* Lucas v. South Carolina Coastal Council, 505 U.S. 1003 (1992). Justice Blackmun provided one formulation of the more restrained approach to takings cases in *ibid.* at 1045–46 (Blackmun, J., dissenting) *and see ibid.* at 1062 (Stevens, J., dissenting).

24. Clarence Thomas, "The Higher Law Background of the Privileges or Immunities Clause of the Fourteenth Amendment," 12 *Harv. J.L. & Pub. Pol'y* 63, 67–68 (1989).

25. *See* Thomas position in *Casey* and his attack on the use of the Ninth Amendment in a 1988 book chapter, discussed in NAACP Legal Defense and Education Fund, "An Analysis of the Views of Judge Clarence Thomas" (August 13, 1991) at 13, but the "Analysis" does not consider the conflict with his article on unenumerated rights. *See also* his criticism of Moore v. City of East Cleveland, 431 U.S. 494 (1977) (grandmother can have son and grandchildren by different children in same house) as an attack on the family—despite the fact that Thomas himself was raised by grandparents, Legal Defense Fund, "Judge Clarence Thomas" at 14–16.

26. He opposed opportunity for factual development, Keeney v. Tamayo-Reyes, 504 U.S. 1 (1992) (White, J.) (no factual development in habeas beyond state proceeding unless cause and prejudice); opposed consideration of mercy on habeas, Sawyer v. Whitley, 505 U.S. 333 (1992) (Rehnquist, C.J.) (mitigating evidence in capital sentencing hearing not within miscarriage of justice standard); Morgan v. Illinois, 504 U.S. 719, 739 (1992) (Scalia, J., dissenting) (no voir dire needed on mercy because no constitutional right); Sochor v. Florida, 504 U.S. 527, 541 (1992) (joined Rehnquist and White dissenting in part—weighing invalid aggravating factor harmless error since there were no mitigating factors); questioned review in general, Wright v. West, 505 U.S. 277 (1992) (Thomas, J., plurality, joined by Rehnquist and Scalia) (questioned federal de novo review of state application of constitutional law to fact). He made an exception, applying the rule of lenity, in Caron v. United States, 524 U.S. 308, 319–20 (1998) (Thomas, J., dissenting).

27. *See* Richardson v. McKnight, 521 U.S. 399 (1997).

28. Kansas v. Hendricks, 521 U.S. 346, 360–61, 364–66 (1997).

29. 506 U.S. 390 (Rehnquist, C.J.); *ibid.* at 427 (Scalia, J., concurring).

30. Schlup v. Delo, 513 U.S. 298, 334 (1995) (Rehnquist, C.J., dissenting). Thomas recently joined Scalia's dissenting opinion in which they concluded that the actual innocence exception should not be available after a guilty plea, Bousley v. United States, 523 U.S. 614, 629 (1998) (Scalia, J., dissenting).

31. 505 U.S. 277 (1992) (Thomas, J., plurality).

32. The specific issue was de novo review of the factual basis of state conclusions about the application of federal law. Despite the history in which the federal courts developed factual review to prevent state disregard of federal guarantees, Thomas would apply deferential review to state determinations of federal law on both the law and the facts. More recently, in McFarland v. Scott, 512 U.S. 849, 864 (1994) (dissenting), Thomas objected that an inmate had no right either to the appointment of counsel or to a stay of execution to allow time for the appointment of counsel prior to the filing of a petition for habeas corpus. *See also* Stewart v. Martinez-Villareal, 523 U.S. 637, 646–47 (1998) (Scalia, J., dissenting) (state court determinations need not always be reviewable in federal court); *ibid.* at 523 U.S. 652 (Thomas, J., dissenting).

33. Plessy v. Ferguson, 163 U.S. 537, 552 (1896) (Harlan, J., dissenting).

34. Thomas, "The Higher Law."

35. *See* Thomas, "Plain Reading" at 991.

36. *See ibid.*

37. *See ibid.* at 992.

38. 402 U.S. 1 (1971).

39. 391 U.S. 430 (1968).

40. Legal Defense Fund, "Judge Clarence Thomas" at 12.

41. Green v. County School Board of New Kent County, 391 U.S. 430 (1968).

42. Missouri v. Jenkins, 515 at 125 (Thomas, J., concurring). Thomas also argued on historical grounds against the expansion of equitable powers to structural injunctions and continued supervision of public institutions, *ibid.* at 126–33.

43. 505 U.S. 717, 745 (1992).

44. *Ibid.* at 745.

45. *Ibid.* at 745.

46. *Ibid.* at 746–47.

47. *Ibid.* at 748, 749.

48. 515 U.S. 70, 114 (1995) (Thomas, J., concurring).

49. *Ibid.* at 116.

50. *Ibid.* at 120.

51. *Ibid.* at 121.

52. *Ibid.*

53. Green v. County School Board of New Kent County, 391 U.S. 430, 437–38 (1968).

54. *See* Adarand Constructors, Inc. v. Pena, 515 U.S. 200 (1995).

55. In *Adarand* at 240 (1995) (Thomas, J., concurring in part and in the

judgment), involving racial set-asides in the construction business, Thomas wrote that paternalism or equality of results "is at war with the principle of inherent equality that underlies and infuses our Constitution," citing the Declaration of Independence.

56. *See* Peter Westen, "The Empty Idea of Equality," 95 *Harv. L. Rev.* 537 (1982) (demonstrating that equality is insufficient to determine cases without another premise, although Westen goes on to argue that the second premise makes the equality principle unnecessary).

57. *See* United States v. Fordice, 505 U.S. 717, 747 (1992) (Thomas, J., concurring). *But see* Adarand Constructors, Inc. v. Pena, 515 U.S. at 241n (Thomas, J., concurring in part and concurring in the judgment) (since "every racial classification helps, in a narrow sense, some races and hurts others," the difference would depend "on 'whose ox is gored,' . . . or on distinctions found only in the eye of the beholder").

58. *See Adarand Constructors, Inc.,* 515 U.S. at 240; United States v. Fordice, 505 U.S. at 746.

59. Legal Defense Fund, "Judge Clarence Thomas" at 5–6.

60. Clarence Thomas, Commentary, "Affirmative Action Goals and Time Tables: Too Tough? Not Tough Enough!" 5 *Yale L. & Pol'y Rev.* 402 (1987).

61. 510 U.S. 317 (1994).

62. *See* Bush v. Vera, 517 U.S. 952, 1000 (1996) (Thomas, J., concurring) and the discussion of the districting cases in chapter 2.

63. 512 U.S. 874, 891 (1994) (Thomas, J., concurring in the judgment, in an opinion in which Scalia joined).

64. Thomas's treatment of the text is plausible though arguable, but his argument that Congress did not intend the 1982 amendments to overrule City of Mobile v. Bolden, 446 U.S. 55 (1980), is not plausible. *See* Holder v. Hall, 512 U.S. at 921. City of Mobile v. Bolden rejected inferential proof of racial discrimination in a plan involving at-large districting, a class of vote dilution cases that Thomas argued were not governed by the statute. The 1982 Amendments to the Voting Rights Act were explicitly aimed at overruling it. *See* 1982 U.S. Code Cong. Adm. News 179, 193. Almost concurrently the Court reversed its position, *see* Rogers v. Lodge, 458 U.S. 613, 618–22 (1982), and the statute has consistently been applied in districting cases since, *see* Thornburg v. Gingles, 478 U.S. 30 (1986) and *Holder* itself.

65. 512 U.S. at 892.

66. *Ibid.* at 898–99, citing Allen v. State Board of Education, 393 U.S. 544, 586 (1969) (Harlan, J., concurring and dissenting).

67. *Allen,* 393 U.S. at 586.

68. *See* 512 U.S. at 902–3. That is what the concept of symmetry is designed to measure. See Stephen E. Gottlieb, "Fashioning a Test for Gerrymandering," 15 *J. Legis.* 1 (1988); Richard G. Niemi, "The Relationship Between Votes and Seats:

The Ultimate Question in Political Gerrymandering," 33 *UCLA L. Rev.* 185, 191–201 (1985).

69. *See* 512 U.S. at 905.

70. *Ibid.* at 906–7 quoting Wright v. Rockefeller, 376 U.S. 52, 67 (1964) (Douglas, J., dissenting).

71. 369 U.S. 186 (1962).

72. *See* 512 U.S. at 896, 897.

73. *Ibid.* at 913. Thomas's decision not to protect a voter's right to write in the name of a candidate on a primary or general election ballot may stem either from refusal to choose among political theories, in this case ordered versus participatory democracy, or disapproval of the latter, Burdick v. Takushi, 504 U.S. 428 (1992).

74. *See* Thomas, "The Higher Law" at 69.

75. *See, e.g.*, Lucas v. South Carolina Coastal Council, 505 U.S. 1003 (1992); Phillips v. Washington Legal Foundation, 524 U.S. 156 (1998). Thomas joined the majority in Yee v. City of Escondido, 503 U.S. 519 (1992), holding that rent control is not a taking, rather than the objections to discussion of regulatory takings raised by Blackmun and Souter, concurring.

76. 512 U.S. 532 (1994).

77. *Ibid.* at 554.

78. *Ibid.* at 547–48.

79. *Ibid.* at 557, quoting Cameron v. Pepin, 610 A.2d 279, 283 (Me. 1992).

80. 512 U.S. at 557.

81. *Ibid.*

82. 512 U.S. 504, 518 (1994) (Thomas, J., dissenting). Thomas's conclusions were based on a textual examination of the statute and an examination of the history of interpretation by prior Secretaries.

83. 512 U.S. 477, 490 (1994) (Thomas, J., concurring).

84. *Ibid.* at 494–95.

85. *Ibid.* at 495–96 (Souter, J., concurring in the judgment).

86. *Ibid. and see* William L. Prosser, *Handbook of the Law of Torts* (St. Paul: West, 3d ed., 1964) at 873, taking a position that no doubt helped to solidify the modern elements of malicious prosecution.

87. *See* 512 U.S. at 501–2 (discussing policy considerations). Souter, joined by Stevens, O'Connor, and Ginsburg, would have required exhaustion of state process first, which would have the same results for state prisoners as the Court's ruling, but would allow those not in custody to gain access to federal courts via § 1983, which the Court's ruling bars because they have no way to reach the federal courts without a prior ruling on the merits—the absence of which they are trying to challenge. *Ibid.* at 501.

88. *But see* Jacobson v. United States, 503 U.S. 540 (1992) (*per* White, J.) (endorsing the entrapment defense of a man charged with purchase of obscene material).

NOTES TO CHAPTER 6

1. Melvin I. Urofsky, *A March of Liberty: A Constitutional History of the United States* (New York: Knopf, 1988) at 705–6, 712–13.

2. 304 U.S. 144, 152 n.4 (1938).

3. *See* Rogers v. Lodge, 458 U.S. 613 (1981) (White, J.); City of Mobile v. Bolden, 446 U.S. 55, 94 (1980) (White, J., dissenting); White v. Regester, 412 U.S. 755 (1973) (White, J.).

4. *See* Roe v. Wade, 410 U.S. 113, 221 (1973) (White, J., dissenting) ("The up-shot [of this decision] is that the people and the legislatures of the fifty states are constitutionally disentitled to weigh the relative importance of the continued existence and development of the fetus on one hand, against a spectrum of possible impacts on the mother, on the other hand." *Ibid.* at 222); Bowers v. Hardwick, 478 U.S. 186 (1986) (*per* White, J.).

5. 410 U.S. 113 (1973).

6. 478 U.S. 186 (1986).

7. *Ibid.* at 192–94.

8. *Compare Bowers*, 478 U.S. at 196 (*per* White, J.) (acknowledging that Georgia sodomy law is based on morality) *with ibid.* (Burger, J., concurring) ("[C]ondemnation of those practices is firmly rooted in Judeo-Christian moral and ethical standards.") *and* 478 U.S. at 212 (Blackmun, J., dissenting) ("'Mere public intolerance or animosity cannot constitutionally justify the deprivation of a person's physical liberty,'" quoting O'Connor v. Donaldson, 422 U.S. 563, 575 [1975]) and 478 U.S. at 218–20 [Stevens, J., dissenting]).

9. 478 U.S. at 199 (Blackmun, J., dissenting) and *ibid.* at 214 (Stevens, J., dissenting).

10. *Roe*, 410 U.S. at 153 (Blackmun, J.).

11. *See* Guido Calabresi, "Foreword: Antidiscrimination and Constitutional Accountability (What the Bork-Brennan Debate Ignores)," 105 *Harv. L. Rev.* 80 (1991).

12. See John Stuart Mill, *Utilitarianism* (Buffalo: Prometheus Books, 1987) (1863) and *On Liberty* (New York: Liberal Arts Press, Currin V. Shields ed., 1956) (1859); Jeremy Bentham, *The Principles of Morals and Legislation* (Darien, Conn.: Hafner Press, 1948) (1789) at 13–20.

13. See Thomas Paine, "The Rights of Man," in Thomas Paine, *Collected Writings* (New York: Library of America, Eric Foner ed., 1995) at 464–65 (describing natural rights of the mind and the pursuit of happiness).

14. For discussions of utilitarianism *see, e.g.*, David Lyons, *Rights, Welfare, and Mill's Moral Theory* (New York: Oxford University Press, 1994); and Richard B. Brandt, *Morality, Utilitarianism, and Rights* (New York: Cambridge University Press, 1992); Donald Regan, *Utilitarianism and Cooperation* (New York: Oxford University Press, 1980); H. L. A. Hart, "Between Utility and Rights," 79 *Colum. L. Rev.* 828–31 (1979).

15. See John Stuart Mill to William Thomas Thornton, Saint Véran (April 17, 1863) in 15 *The Collected Works of John Stuart Mill, The Later Letters, 1849–1873* (Toronto: University of Toronto Press, Francis E. Mineka and Dwight N. Lindley eds., 1972) at 854.

16. John Rawls, *A Theory of Justice* (Cambridge: Belknap Press of Harvard University Press, 1971); Ronald Dworkin, *Taking Rights Seriously* (Cambridge: Harvard University Press, 1977).

17. 304 U.S. 144, 152 n.4 (1938).

18. John Locke, *An Essay Concerning Human Understanding* (London: William Tegg, 38th ed., 1894) (1690); *and see* Dworkin, *Taking Rights Seriously* at 173, 177–81 (describing contract theories as based on equality).

19. Anatole France, *Le Lys Rouge* (1894), quoted in John Bartlett, *Familiar Quotations* (Boston: Little, Brown, Emily Morison Beck ed., 15th ed., 1980) at 655.

20. Herrera v. Collins, 506 U.S. 390 (1993).

21. *Ibid.* at 400.

22. *Ibid.* at 393 (*per* Rehnquist, C.J.).

23. *Ibid.* at 430 (Blackmun, J., dissenting).

24. 513 U.S. 298 (1995). In another death penalty case, Kyles v. Whitley, 514 U.S. 419 (1995), Justice O'Connor joined the liberal bloc, refusing to find error harmless.

25. 513 U.S. at 332 (O'Connor, J., concurring).

26. In Vernonia School Dist. 47J v. Acton, 515 U.S. 646, 666 (1995) (O'Connor, J., dissenting), Stevens and Souter joined O'Connor's dissent, splitting the liberal bloc over warrantless random urinalysis without suspicion of school athletes. In United States v. Mezzanatto, 513 U.S. 196, 211 (1995) (Ginsburg, J., concurring); *ibid.* (Souter, J., dissenting), the liberal bloc split over waiver of confidentiality of plea negotiations. In Arizona v. Evans, 514 U.S. 1 (1995) the liberal bloc split over the abandonment of the exclusionary rule for clerical error. *See also* Jaffee v. Redmond, 518 U.S. 1 (1996) (adopting a psychotherapist privilege despite the possibility of releasing a guilty person).

27. *See, e.g.*, Bush v. Vera, 517 U.S. 952, 1003 (1996) (Stevens, J., dissenting); *ibid.* at 1045 (Souter, J., dissenting); Shaw v. Hunt, 517 U.S. 899, 918 (1996) (Stevens, J., dissenting); Miller v. Johnson, 515 U.S. 900, 934 (1996) (Ginsburg, J., dissenting).

28. Restricted by citizenship but on nondiscriminatory terms, *see* U.S. Const., Amend. XIV, §1.

29. *See* Bush v. Vera, 517 U.S. at 1013 (Stevens, J., dissenting).

30. These complexities are described in Charles Cameron, David Epstein, and Sharyn O'Halloran, "Do Majority-Minority Districts Maximize Substantive Black Representation in Congress?" 90 *Am. Pol. Sci. Rev.* 794 (1996); Charles S. Bullock III, "The South and the 1996 Elections," 29 *PS: Pol. Sci. & Pol.* 450 (1996); Richard E. Cohen, "Changing the Rules of Redistricting," *Nat'l J.*, June

22, 1996, at 1383; "Southern Comfort (Republicans' Advantage in Southern States)," *New Republic*, January 8, 1996, at 4. Stevens, joined by Ginsburg and Breyer, objected that political, not racial, gerrymandering was the real problem before the Court; *see* Bush v. Vera, 517 U.S. at 1039.

31. *See* Lani Guinier, "The Triumph of Tokenism: The Voting Rights Act and the Theory of Black Electoral Success," 89 *Mich. L. Rev.* 1077 (1991); T. Alexander Aleinikoff and Samuel Issacharoff, "Race and Redistricting: Drawing Constitutional Lines after Shaw v. Reno," 92 *Mich. L. Rev.* 588, 634–38 (1993); Pamela S. Karlan, "The Rights to Vote: Some Pessimism after Formalism," 71 *Tex. L. Rev.* 1705, 1740 (1993); Stephen E. Gottlieb, "Fashioning a Test for Gerrymandering," 15 *J. Legis.* 1 (1988); Stephen E. Gottlieb, "Identifying Gerrymanders," 15 *St. Louis U. L.J.* 540 (1971).

32. Bush v. Vera, 517 U.S. at 1008–11 (Stevens, J., dissenting).

33. *Ibid.* at 1054–55 (Souter, J., dissenting).

34. *Ibid.* at 1010–11 (Stevens, J., dissenting); *ibid.* at 1053–54 (Souter, J., dissenting).

35. *Ibid.* at 1071–77 (Souter, J., dissenting).

36. *See ibid.* at 1018–20 (Stevens, J., dissenting).

37. *See ibid.* at 952; *ibid.* at 1009 (Stevens, J., dissenting) *and see* Stevens's description of the districts involved, *ibid.* at 1018–22.

38. See Stevens's description of several majority-white districts in the same districting plan, *ibid.* at 1018–22 (dissenting). Conservative objections to so-called majority-minority districts leave majority-majority districts as the only alternative.

39. Justice Souter wrote, "It is difficult to see how the consideration of race that *Shaw* condemns (but cannot avoid) is essentially different from the consideration of ethnicity that entered American politics from the moment that immigration began to temper regional homogeneity. . . . The result has been . . . ethnic participation and even a moderation of ethnicity's divisive effect in political practice." *Ibid.* at 1074. *See also ibid.* at 1036 (Stevens, J., dissenting); *ibid.* at 1055, 1071–72 (Souter, J., dissenting).

40. *Ibid.* at 1011, 1033 (Stevens, J., dissenting). *See also ibid.* at 1066–69 (Souter, J., dissenting); Shaw v. Hunt, 517 U.S. at 930 (Stevens, J., dissenting) (discussing majority requirement that race not "predomin[ate]"); *ibid.* at 945 (discussing Court's refusal to permit drawing any more majority-minority districts than required by Voting Rights Act as interpreted in Thornburgh v. Gingles, 478 U.S. 30 (1986)).

41. For the Court's incoherent treatment of districting, *see generally*, Pamela S. Karlan and Daryl J. Levinson, "Why Voting Is Different," 84 *Cal. L. Rev.* 1201 (1996); Binny Miller, "Who Shall Rule and Govern? Local Legislative Delegations, Racial Politics, and the Voting Rights Act," 102 *Yale L.J.* 105 (1992).

42. Bush v. Vera, 517 U.S. at 1005.

43. Shaw v. Hunt, 517 U.S. at 933–39 (1996) (Stevens, J., dissenting); Bush v. Vera, 517 U.S. at 1005–8, 1014–32 (1996) (Stevens, J.); *and see* Stephen E. Gottlieb,

"Reformulating the Motive/Effects Debate in Constitutional Adjudication," 33 *Wayne L. Rev.* 97 (1986) (describing the weakness of the Court's motive test in discrimination cases). Justice Souter noted that racial motives cannot be distinguished from "neutral" ones because the evidence is so hopelessly entangled, Bush v. Vera, 517 U.S. at 1059–61 (dissenting). *Compare* Hernandez v. New York, 500 U.S. 352 (1991) (finding no discrimination in explanation that jurors were dismissed because bilingual although all bilingual jurors were also Hispanic).

44. *See* Gottlieb, "A Test for Gerrymandering"; Gottlieb, "Identifying Gerrymanders."

45. *See* Presley v. Etowah Co. Comm., 502 U.S. 491, 510 (1992) (Stevens, J., dissenting). Note, however, that Justice Souter joined the majority opinion.

46. Holder v. Hall, 512 U.S. 874, 956 (1994).

47. *See* Joseph Schumpeter, *Capitalism, Socialism and Democracy* (New York: Harper, 3d ed., 1950) at 269–73.

48. *See* John Denvir, "Justice Brennan, Justice Rehnquist and Free Speech," 80 *Nw. U. L. Rev.* 285 (1985).

49. *See* Donald S. Lutz, *Popular Consent and Popular Control* (Baton Rouge: Louisiana State University Press, 1980).

50. *See, e.g.*, McIntyre v. Ohio Elections Commission, 514 U.S. 334 (1995) (*per* Stevens, J.) (supporting the right to distribute anonymous political literature); United States v. National Treasury Employees Union, 513 U.S. 454 (1995) (*per* Stevens, J.) (finding prohibition on honoraria for federal government employees below upper echelons unnecessarily broad).

51. Reno v. ACLU, 521 U.S. 844 (1997).

52. *Compare* Florida Bar v. Went For It, Inc., 515 U.S. 618 (1995) (*per* O'Connor, J., joined by Breyer, J.); *with ibid.* at 635 (Kennedy, J., dissenting, joined by Stevens, Souter, and Ginsburg, JJ.).

53. 512 U.S. 622, 674 (1994) (O'Connor, J., concurring and dissenting in part); *ibid.* at 685 (Ginsburg concurring and dissenting in part).

54. *Ibid.* at 685.

55. *Ibid.* at 677.

56. Glickman v. Wileman Brothers and Elliot, Inc., 521 U.S. 457 (1997).

57. For the conservative position, *see, e.g.*, Rust v. Sullivan, 500 U.S. 173 (1991); Regan v. Taxation with Representation, 461 U.S. 540 (1983); Branti v. Finkel, 445 U.S. 507 (1980); Elrod v. Burns, 427 U.S. 347 (1976), although only Scalia and Thomas seem to remain faithful to that line of dissenting views, *see* Board of County Commissioners v. Umbehr, 518 U.S. 668, 686 (1996) (Scalia, J., dissenting, joined by Thomas, J.). What actually concerned Justice Souter in his opinion was what looked like rent-seeking behavior—that is, instead of the assessments being used in a way that was hostile to the growers, it was actually used by the growers to reduce their collective advertising budget. In other words, he pro-

vided a dissent that focused on a regulatory issue that is far broader than the issue of speech rights.

58. This is similar to the difference principle in the famous work of Rawls, *A Theory of Justice.*

59. *See* Robert A. Dahl and Charles Lindblom, *Politics, Economics and Welfare: Planning and Politico-Economic Systems Resolved into Basic Social Processes* (New York: Harper, 1953).

60. *See* Shaw v. Hunt, 517 U.S. at 918 (Stevens, J., dissenting); *ibid.* at 950 (Souter, J., dissenting); Bush v. Vera, 517 U.S. at 1003 (Stevens, J., dissenting); *ibid.* at 1045 (Souter, J., dissenting); Adarand Constructors, Inc. v. Pena, 515 U.S. 200, 245 (1995) (Stevens, J., dissenting); *ibid.* at 274 (Ginsburg, J., dissenting) (supporting affirmative action as needed to end racism); *ibid.* at 270 (Souter, J., dissenting) (affirmative action may be reasonable); Missouri v. Jenkins, 515 U.S. 70, 138 (1995) (Souter, J., dissenting); *ibid.* at 175 (Ginsburg, J., dissenting). *See also* Regents of the University of California v. Bakke, 438 U.S. 265, 407 (1977) (Blackmun, J., separate opinion) ("In order to get beyond racism, we must first take account of race. There is no other way.")

61. *See, e.g.*, Church of the Lukumi Babalu Aye, Inc. v. City of Hialeah, 508 U.S. 520, 561 (1993) (Souter, J., concurring) ("A law that is religion neutral on its face or in its purpose may lack neutrality in its effect"); Ward's Cove Packing Co., Inc. v. Atonio, 490 U.S. 642, 662 (1989) (Stevens, J., dissenting) (regretting the Court's retreat from Griggs v. Duke Power Co., 401 U.S. 424 (1971), which barred employment practices that had discriminatory effects).

62. Regents of the University of California v. Bakke, 438 U.S. 265, 407 (1978) (Blackmun, J.).

63. *Adarand*, 515 U.S. at 245.

64. Frontiero v. Richardson, 411 U.S. 677 (1973) (Ginsburg argued for military health and housing benefits for husbands of military wives); Weinberger v. Wiesenfeld, 420 U.S. 636 (1975) (Ginsburg argued men equally entitled to Social Security survivors' benefits); Orr v. Orr, 440 U.S. 268 (1979) (Ginsburg opposed rule requiring husbands, but not wives, to pay alimony); Craig v. Boren, 429 U.S. 190 (1976) (Ginsburg opposed different ages for the purchase of beer).

65. Ruth Bader Ginsburg, "Speaking in a Judicial Voice," 67 *N.Y.U. L. Rev.* 1185, 1199 (1992).

66. She has urged a practice of "measured motion," Ginsburg, "Judicial Voice" at 1198, in which "without taking giant strides and thereby risking a backlash too forceful to contain, the Court, through constitutional adjudication, can reinforce or signal a green light for a social change," *ibid.* at 1208.

67. *Ibid.* at 1202.

68. Calabresi, "Antidiscrimination and Constitutional Accountability" at 91–92.

69. Benjamin Franklin, *The Autobiography of Benjamin Franklin* (New York: Pocket Books, 1955) at 142–44.

70. Michael W. McConnell, "Religious Freedom at a Crossroads," 59 *U. Chi. L. Rev.* 115, 145–46 (1992).

71. Board of Education of Kiryas Joel Village School District v. Grumet, 512 U.S. 687 (1994).

72. *Ibid.* at 732.

73. *See generally* Stephen E. Gottlieb, "Districting and the Meanings of Pluralism: The Courts' Futile Search for Standards in *Kiryas Joel*," in *The U.S. Supreme Court and the Electoral Process* (Washington, D.C.: Georgetown University Press, David K. Ryden ed., 2000).

74. 512 U.S. 687, 711 (1994).

75. *Ibid.*

76. Arnett v. Kennedy, 416 U.S. 134, 154 (1974) (opinion of Rehnquist, J.).

77. *See* Texaco, Inc. v. Short, 454 U.S. 516, 525 (1982) ("Property interests, of course, are not created by the Constitution. Rather, they are created and their dimensions are defined by existing rules or understandings that stem from an independent source such as state law—rules or understandings that secure certain benefits and that support claims of entitlement to those benefits," quoting Board of Regents v. Roth, 408 U.S. 564, 577 [1972]); Bishop v. Wood, 426 U.S. 341, 345 (1976) (same).

78. *See* Bishop v. Wood, 426 U.S. at 350 (Brennan, J., dissenting); *ibid.* at 355 (White, J., dissenting); *ibid.* at 361 (Blackmun, J., dissenting); Fuentes v. Shevin, 407 U.S. 67 (1972); Snaidach v. Family Finance Corp., 395 U.S. 337 (1972).

79. Treating a building ban as likely barring all "economically beneficial uses," Lucas v. South Carolina Coastal Council, 505 U.S. 1003, 1019, 1030–32 (1992).

80. Dolan v. City of Tigard, 512 U.S. 374 (1994); Nollan v. California Coastal Com'n, 483 U.S. 825, 829–30 (1987).

81. *Dolan*, 512 U.S. at 411 (Stevens, J., dissenting) (criticizing the changing burden of proof from claimant to government); *ibid.* at 413–14 (Souter, J., dissenting) (same). Justice Breyer joined the Court after the major takings cases were decided. *But see* Suitum v. Tahoe Regional Planning Agency, 520 U.S. 725, 749–50 (1997) (Scalia, J., concurring in part) (asserting that the majority opinion, written by Souter and joined by Rehnquist, Stevens, Kennedy, Ginsburg, and Breyer, threatened to gut the Court's takings jurisprudence). Breyer has not been willing to impose the entire risk of legal changes involving government contractual obligations on private parties, *see* United States v. Winstar Corp., 518 U.S. 839, 910–11 (1996) (Breyer, J., concurring).

82. These implications are worked out extensively in C. Edwin Baker, "Property and Its Relation to Constitutionally Protected Liberty," 134 *U. Pa. L. Rev.* 741 (1986).

83. Lucas v. South Carolina Coastal Council, 505 U.S. 1003 (1992).

84. David A. Schultz, *Property, Power, and American Democracy* (New Brunswick, N.J.: Transaction, 1992) at 27–28; William J. Novak, *Intellectual Origins of the State Police Power: The Common Law Vision of a Well-Regulated Society* (Madison: Institute for Legal Studies, University of Wisconsin-Madison Law School, 1989) at 63–66, 107; William J. Novak, "Public Safety: Fire!" (paper presented to the annual meeting of the American Society for Legal History, Chicago, October 19, 1990); William Michael Treanor, "The Original Understanding of the Takings Clause and the Political Process," 95 *Colum. L. Rev.* 782 (1995). *See also* Jennifer Nedelsky, *Private Property and the Limits of American Constitutionalism* (Chicago: University of Chicago Press, 1990); James W. Ely, Jr., "'That Due Satisfaction May Be Made': The Fifth Amendment and the Origins of the Compensation Principle," 36 *Am. J. Legal Hist.* 1 (1992). On the conceptual and historical relationships between property, vested rights, the pervasiveness of law, and fairness, *see* James L. Kainen, "Nineteenth Century Interpretations of the Federal Contract Clause: The Transformation from Vested to Substantive Rights against the State," 31 *Buff. L. Rev.* 381 (1982). On the takings clause generally, *see* Frank I. Michelman, "Property, Utility, and Fairness: Comments on the Ethical Foundations of 'Just Compensation' Law," 80 *Harv. L. Rev.* 1165 (1967); William A. Fischel, *Regulatory Takings: Law, Economics, and Politics* (Cambridge: Harvard University Press, 1995); Bruce A. Ackerman, *Private Property and the Constitution* (New Haven: Yale University Press, 1977).

85. U.S. Const., Art. I, secs. 9, 10; Max Farrand ed., 2 *The Records of the Federal Convention of 1787* (New Haven: Yale University Press, 1966) at 439–40; *and see* Steven R. Boyd, "The Contract Clause and the Evolution of American Federalism, 1789–1815," 44 *Wm. & Mary Q.* 529 (3d ser. 1987) (describing the original interpretation of the obligation of contracts clause, which similarly allowed significant government regulation).

86. Nollan v. California Coastal Com'n, 483 U.S. 825 (1987).

87. *See* Ackerman, *Private Property and the Constitution* at 49–54 (describing factors that would lead the decision makers to miscalculate).

88. *But see* Fischel, *Regulatory Takings*. Fischel argues that the background facts not discussed in the Court opinions are actually more appealing than the cases as presented.

NOTES TO CHAPTER 7

1. *See* Ian Shapiro, "Three Fallacies Concerning Majorities, Minorities and Democratic Practice," in *Nomos XXXII: Majorities and Minorities* (New York: New York University Press, John W. Chapman and Alan Wertheimer eds., 1990) at 86; Ian Shapiro, "Notes Toward a Conditional Theory of Rights and Obligations in Property," in Stephen E. Gottlieb, *Jurisprudence: Cases and Materials* (Charlottesville, Va: Michie, 1993) at 379.

2. The seminal work is Immanuel Kant, *Foundations of the Metaphysics of Morals* (New York: Macmillan, Lewis White Beck trans., 1985) (1785) at 39, 42–50.

3. John Rawls, *A Theory of Justice* (Cambridge: Belknap Press of Harvard University Press, 1971) at 11–17, 136–42.

4. Ronald Dworkin, "Will Clinton's Plan Be Fair?" *New York Review*, January 13, 1994, at 20, 23–24.

5. 304 U.S. 144 (1938).

6. *Ibid.* at 152.

7. Stephen E. Gottlieb, ed., *Public Values in Constitutional Law* (Ann Arbor: University of Michigan Press, 1993) at 7–11; Stephen E. Gottlieb, "Compelling Government Interests: An Essential but Unanalyzed Term in Constitutional Adjudication," 68 *B.U. L. Rev.* 917, 932–40 (1988).

8. *See* John Stuart Mill to William Thomas Thornton, Saint Véran (April 17, 1863) in 15 *The Collected Works of John Stuart Mill, The Later Letters, 1849–1873* (Toronto: University of Toronto Press, Francis E. Mineka and Dwight N. Lindley eds., 1972) at 854.

9. "[T]he misguided notion that a good end is a sufficient justification for the existence and exercise of power . . . should invite far more exacting scrutiny." Celotex Corp. v. Edwards, 514 U.S. 300, 331–32(1995) (Stevens, J., dissenting, joined by Ginsburg).

10. *See, e.g.,* Joan Biskupic, "Clinton Has Chance to Change Face of U.S. Judiciary," *Portland Oregonian*, November 24, 1996 at A14; Delma Houghton, "Appointing Judges a Presidential Prize," *Tulsa World*, November 3, 1996 at G2; Laurie Asseo, "Balance: O'Connor, Kennedy Tip Scales," *Orange County Register,* October 5, 1996; Lyle Denniston, "Court's Workload Low, But Cases Were Significant," *Baltimore Sun*, July 3, 1996 at 1A; Terry Eastland, "Rule of Law: If Clinton Wins, Here's What the Courts Will Look Like," *Wall Street Journal*, February 28, 1996 at A15; Editorial, "Term Limits for Justices?" *Wall Street Journal*, May 24, 1995 at A14; "Justice Stevens Raises Question of Death Penalty," *Chicago Tribune*, March 27, 1995 at 1; Joan Biskupic, "At Long Last, Seniority: 'Quirky' Stevens Takes Helm of Court's Liberal Wing," *Washington Post*, March 20, 1995 at A15.

11. *See* William D. Popkin, "A Common Law Lawyer on the Supreme Court: The Opinions of Justice Stevens," 1989 *Duke L.J.* 1087, 1121–22.

12. *See* "The Supreme Court, 1988 Term: IV. The Statistics," 103 *Harv. L. Rev.* 394, 395 (1989); "The Supreme Court, 1982 Term: IV. The Statistics," 97 *Harv. L. Rev.* 295, 296 (1983) (covering the 1978 through 1982 terms of Court).

13. *See, e.g.,* Bishop v. Wood, 426 U.S. 341 (1976) (no process due); DeShaney v. Winnebago County Dep't of Social Servs., 489 U.S. 189 (1989) (no municipal responsibility absent policy or deliberate indifference); City of Canton v. Harris, 489 U.S. 378 (1989) (same); *but see* Edmonson v. Leesville Concrete Co., Inc., 500 U.S. 614 (1991) (juror exclusion by private attorney was state action) and Owen v.

City of Independence, 445 U.S. 622 (1980) (no qualified immunity for municipalities), in which Stevens joined the majorities.

14. Popkin, "Common Law Lawyer." *See also* R.A.V. v. City of St. Paul, 505 U.S. 377, 416 (1992) (Stevens, J., concurring) ("The quest for doctrinal certainty through the definition of categories and subcategories is, in my opinion, destined to fail."); Note, "Justice Stevens's Equal Protection Jurisprudence," 100 *Harv. L. Rev.* 1146, 1146, 1154 (1987). Stevens version of equal protection analysis "both pushes toward discussion of what is really at stake in deciding whether a statute denies equal protection and moves away from the idea of mechanistic, purportedly neutral, abstract categorization of legislative and administrative classifications," *ibid.* at 1161; and suggests a sliding scale of scrutiny, Kathleen M. Sullivan, "Foreword: The Justices of Rules and Standards," 106 *Harv. L. Rev.* 22, 88–90 (1992). *But see* Owen M. Fiss, "Silence on the Street Corner" in Gottlieb, *Public Values in Constitutional Law* at 199–204.

15. Hewitt v. Helms, 459 U.S. 460, 485 (1983); *and see* William D. Popkin, "A Common Law Lawyer on the Supreme Court: The Opinions of Justice Stevens," 1989 *Duke L.J.* 1087, 1121–22.

16. *See* Thomas Scanlon, "A Theory of Freedom of Expression," 1 *Phil. & Pub. Aff.* 204 (1972). Stevens urged stronger protection for First Amendment rights than the Court granted in United States v. Kokinda, 497 U.S. 720 (1990) (Stevens joined Brennan, J., dissenting) (arguing ban on solicitation on Postal Service sidewalks unconstitutional); Central Hudson v. Public Serv. Comm'n, 447 U.S. 557, 579 (1980) (Stevens, J., concurring) (insufficient justification for commercial regulation); Dun and Bradstreet, Inc. v. Greenmoss Builders, 472 U.S. 749 (1985) (seeking greater protection for commercial speech); *and see* Rust v. Sullivan, 500 U.S. 173, 220 (1991) (Stevens, J., dissenting) (arguing statute did not authorize restriction on employees' speech); *ibid.* at 207 (Stevens joined Blackmun, J., objecting to viewpoint-based suppression of speech as unconstitutional condition). Stevens, however, is not doctrinaire in this area. *See, e.g.,* Members of the City Council of the City of Los Angeles v. Taxpayers for Vincent, 466 U.S. 789 (1984) (political signs may be banned from utility poles); City of Lakewood v. Plain Dealer Pub. Co., 486 U.S. 750, 772 (1988) (Stevens joined White, J., dissenting) (arguing city could ban some news racks on city streets); Texas v. Johnson, 491 U.S. 397, 436 (1989) (Stevens, J., dissenting) (arguing state could ban flag burning); R.A.V. v. City of St. Paul, 505 U.S. 377, 416 (1992) (Stevens, J., concurring in the judgment) (arguing state may ban hate speech); Federal Communications Comm'n v. League of Women Voters of California, 468 U.S. 364, 408 (1984) (Stevens, J., dissenting) (arguing government may ban editorializing by public broadcasters).

17. *See, e.g.,* Catharine A. MacKinnon, *Toward a Feminist Theory of the State* (Cambridge: Harvard University Press, 1989) at 45–47, 115–16, 161–70; Clare

Dalton, "An Essay in the Deconstruction of Contract Doctrine," 94 *Yale L.J.* 997 (1985).

18. *See* H. L. A. Hart, "Between Utility and Rights," 79 *Colum. L. Rev.* 828 (1979).

19. *See* Harold D. Lasswell and Myres S. McDougal, *Jurisprudence for a Free Society: Studies in Law, Science and Policy* (New Haven: New Haven Press, 1992).

20. John Paul Stevens, "Commentary," 49 *U. Pitt. L. Rev.* 723, 728 (1988).

21. *Ibid.* and *see also* Michael H. v. Gerald D., 491 U.S. 110, 135–36 (1989) (Stevens, J., concurring in the judgment) (finding family rights based on precedent). Stevens has subsequently written for a 7–2 majority finding some of those previously unwritten rights in the privileges and immunities clauses of the Constitution, *see* Saenz v. Roe, 526 U.S. 489 (1999).

22. *See, e.g.,* DeShaney v. Winnebago County Department of Social Services, 489 U.S. 189 (1989) (Rehnquist, C.J.); Members of the City Council of the City of Los Angeles v. Taxpayers for Vincent, 466 U.S. 789 (1984); Bishop v. Wood, 426 U.S. 341 (1976). For utilitarians, great individual harms may outweigh more minor generalized social benefits. Therefore, some utilitarian decisions may be indistinguishable from decisions that could have been reached on libertarian grounds, *see, e.g.,* Washington v. Harper, 494 U.S. 210, 237 (1990) (Stevens, J., concurring and dissenting).

23. Texas v. Johnson, 491 U.S. 397, 436 (1989) (Stevens, J. dissenting).

24. *Ibid.* at 399.

25. 488 U.S. 469 (1989).

26. *Ibid.* at 512n (1989) (Stevens, J., concurring in part and in the judgment).

27. *See, e.g.,* Jeremy Bentham, "Anarchical Fallacies," in 2 *The Works of Jeremy Bentham* (New York: Russell and Russell, 1962, reprint of John Bowring ed., 1843) at 494–95.

28. Popkin, "Common Law Lawyer" at 1128.

29. *See generally* Jules L. Coleman, *Markets, Morals and the Law* (New York: Cambridge University Press, 1988) at 95–132.

30. *See, e.g.,* the 1991 ERISA cases, FMC Corp. v. Holliday, 498 U.S. 52, 65 (1990) (Stevens, J., dissenting); United States v. R. Enterprises, Inc., 498 U.S. 292, 305–6 (1991) (Stevens, J., concurring in part and concurring in the judgment).

31. Bruce A. Ackerman, *Private Property and the Constitution* (New Haven: Yale University Press, 1977) at 44–70.

32. Popkin, "Common Law Lawyer" at 1149–51.

33. Herrera v. Collins, 506 U.S. 390 (1993).

34. Stevens recently criticized the death penalty, saying, "'The recent development of reliable scientific evidentiary methods has made it possible to establish conclusively that a disturbing number of persons who had been sentenced to death were actually innocent.'" Such mistakes, he said, "make it 'appropriate to raise the question whether either the deterrent value of the death penalty or its

therapeutic effect on the community outraged by a vicious crime justifies its continued popular support.'" "Justice Stevens Criticizes Election of Judges," *Washington Post*, August 4, 1996 at A14.

35. *See* Akhil Reed Amar, "The Bill of Rights as a Constitution," 100 *Yale L.J.* 1131 (1991).

36. Kant, *Foundations* at 46–49.

37. *See* Hart, "Utility" at 828–31.

38. It may be difficult to avoid, however, when rights conflict. To avoid interpersonal comparisons, one might take an individual perspective. For example, Dworkin argues that health care legislation should provide what we would prudently buy for ourselves as insurance; and then argued on the basis of equality that it should be for everyone. Dworkin, "Will Clinton's Plan Be Fair?" at 20, 23–24.

39. Because it would encourage other abusive demands. Mill to Thornton at 854. Sacrificing an individual for the benefit of others would also be an "acknowledged injustice," John Stuart Mill, "Utilitarianism," in 10 *The Collected Works of John Stuart Mill, Essays on Ethics, Religion and Society* (Toronto: University of Toronto Press, J. M. Robson ed., 1969) at 252.

40. See Ronald M. Dworkin, *Taking Rights Seriously* (Cambridge: Harvard University Press, 1977).

41. *See generally,* Stephen E. Gottlieb, "Overriding Public Values," in Gottlieb, *Public Values in Constitutional Law*; Richard H. Fallon, Jr., "Individual Rights and the Powers of Government," 27 *Ga. L. Rev.* 343 (1993); Dworkin, *Taking Rights Seriously*; and *compare* U.S. Const., Art. VI.

42. Jaffee v. Redmond, 518 U.S. 1 (1996).

43. John Paul Stevens, "Commentary," 49 *U. Pitt. L. Rev.* 723, 725–26 (1988); *and see, e.g.,* Michigan v. Long, 463 U.S. 1032, 1067 (1983) (Stevens, J., dissenting).

44. Stevens supported unions in Litton Financial Printing Div. v. N.L.R.B., 501 U.S. 190, 218 (1991) (Stevens, J., dissenting); Norfolk and Western Ry. Co., v. American Train Dispatchers Assn., 499 U.S. 117, 134 (1991) (Stevens, J., dissenting); employees in Gilmer v. Interstate/Johnson Lane Corp., 500 U.S. 20, 36 (1991) (Stevens, J., dissenting); and Groves v. Ring Screw Works, 498 U.S. 168 (1990); union members in Int'l Org. of Masters, Mates and Pilots v. Brown, 498 U.S. 466 (1991) *but see* Airline Pilots Ass'n. Int'l. v. O'Neill, 499 U.S. 65 (1991) (supporting the union against its members); pensioners against self-insured pension plans in FMC Corp. v. Holliday, 498 U.S. 52, 65 (1990) (Stevens, J., dissenting); and individuals against later delivered corporate contracts of adhesion, Carnival Cruise Lines, Inc. v. Shute, 499 U.S. 585, 597 (1991) (Stevens, J., dissenting).

Stevens favored federal economic regulation in Arcadia v. Ohio Power Co., 498 U.S. 73, 86 (1990) (Stevens, J., concurring), but where individual injury is apparent, stands ready to overturn sovereign immunity, and interpret statutes to preserve remedies, United States v. Smith, 499 U.S. 160, 175 (1991) (Stevens, J., dissenting); apply antitrust rules against local government in City of Columbia v. Omni Outdoor Adv.,

Inc., 499 U.S. 365, 385 (1991) (Stevens, J., dissenting); and Summit Health, Ltd. v. Pinhas, 500 U.S. 322 (1991).

45. *See e.g.,* Lucas v. South Carolina Coastal Council, 505 U.S. 1003, 1061 (1992) (Stevens, J., dissenting).

46. *See* West Virginia University Hospitals, Inc. v. Casey, 499 U.S. 83, 103 (1991) (Stevens, J., dissenting).

47. *See* Washington v. Davis, 426 U.S. 229, 254 (1976) (Stevens, J., concurring) (motive inferred from natural and probable consequences); Davis v. Bandemer, 478 U.S. 109, 161 (1986) (Powell, J., concurring in part and dissenting in part, joined by Stevens); Karcher v. Daggett, 462 U.S. 725, 753–54 (1983) (Stevens, J., separate opinion). *But see* City of Mobile v. Bolden, 446 U.S. 55, 90 (1980) (Stevens, J., concurring) (distinction between objective effects and subjective motives). Stevens's treatment of motive is discussed in Stephen E. Gottlieb, "Fashioning a Test for Gerrymandering," 15 *J. Legis.* 1, 4–5 (1988); Stephen E. Gottlieb, "Reformulating the Motive/Effects Debate in Constitutional Adjudication," 33 *Wayne L. Rev.* 97, 100, 103n, 111–12 (1986). Stevens failed again to get the Court to take a realistic approach to motive in *Hernandez v. New York,* 500 U.S. 352, 375–77 (1991) (Stevens, J., dissenting). By contrast, Stevens has sometimes been the advocate of a fairly formal version of the rule of neutrality in First Amendment interpretation. *See* Fiss, "Silence on the Street Corner."

48. *Compare, e.g.,* City of Canton v. Harris, 489 U.S. 378 (1989) (requiring proof of policy or deliberate indifference for municipal liability), *with* Owen v. City of Independence, 445 U.S. 622 (1980) (refusing to find immunity).

49. 499 U.S. 621, 629 (1991) (Stevens, J., dissenting).

50. McNeil v. Wisconsin, 501 U.S. 171, 183 (1991) (Stevens, J., dissenting).

51. Michigan v. Lucas, 500 U.S. 145, 157–58 (1991) (Stevens, J., dissenting).

52. 500 U.S. 352, 379 (1991) (Stevens, J., dissenting).

53. See, e.g., Keeney v. Tamayo-Reyes, 504 U.S. 1, 12 (1992) (O'Connor, J., dissenting); Sawyer v. Whitley, 505 U.S. 333, 360 (1992) (Stevens, J., concurring in the judgment); Stringer v. Black, 503 U.S. 222 (1992) (Kennedy, J.); Wright v. West, 505 U.S. 277, 297 (1992) (O'Connor, J., concurring); Estelle v. McGuire, 502 U.S. 62, 75 (1991) (O'Connor, J., concurring in part and dissenting in part); Morgan v. Illinois, 504 U.S. 719 (1992) (*per* White, J.); Sochor v. Florida, 504 U.S. 527, 545 (1992) (Stevens, J., concurring in part and dissenting in part).

54. Forsyth County v. Nationalist Movement, 505 U.S. 123, 133 (1992).

55. 512 U.S. 821, 844 (1994) (concurring in part and in the judgment).

56. Ruth Bader Ginsburg, "Speaking in a Judicial Voice," 67 *N.Y.U. L. Rev.* 1185, 1191 (1992).

57. 512 U.S. 477, 484 (1994) (*per* Scalia, J.).

58. *Ibid.* at 484–90.

59. 512 U.S. 415 (1994).

60. *Ibid.* at 435.

61. *Ibid.* at 421–26.

62. *Ibid.* at 446–49.

63. 510 U.S. 443 (1994).

64. 244 U.S. 205 (1917).

65. *Ibid.* at 222 (Holmes, J., dissenting). See *American Dredging,* 510 U.S. at 458 (Stevens, J., concurring in part and in the judgment).

66. *See, e.g.,* Consolidated Rail Corp. v. Gottshall, 512 U.S. 532, 563–66 (1994).

67. Ginsburg, "Judicial Voice" at 1187–88.

68. Ruth Bader Ginsburg, "Some Thoughts on Autonomy and Equality in Relation to *Roe v. Wade,*" 63 *N.C. L. Rev.* 375, 378 (1985).

69. One well-known version of this distinction is in Ronald Dworkin, "The Model of Rules," 35 *U. Chi. L. Rev.* 14, 22–29 (1967).

70. Stephen Breyer, *Regulation and Its Reform* (Cambridge: Harvard University Press, 1982) at 8.

71. *Ibid.* at 7.

72. *See ibid.* at 5; Stephen Breyer, *Breaking the Vicious Circle: Toward Effective Risk Regulation* (Cambridge: Harvard University Press, 1993) at 33–35.

73. See Breyer, *Vicious Circle* at 11, 56.

74. *See* Breyer, *Regulation* at 27–28, 34. Breyer distinguished difficulties evaluating information from pure paternalistic government substitution of judgment, questioned whether "the brand of paternalism based on mistrust of consumer rationality is consistent with the notions of freedom of choice that underlie the free market" at 34, but found the latter a legitimate part of policy analysis because many support it. Much has been written about Justice Breyer's approach to interpretation, which similarly rejects the skepticism of public-choice theory and argues that much legislation should be understood as driven by conceptions of the public interest. *See* Sidney Shapiro, "Keeping the Baby and Throwing Out the Bathwater: Justice Breyer's Critique of Regulation," 8 *Admin. L.J. of Am. U.* 721 (1995); Stephen Breyer, "On the Uses of Legislative History in Interpreting Statutes," 65 *S. Cal. L. Rev.* 845 (1992). *But see* Edward A. Fallone, "The Clinton Court Is Open for Business: The Business Law Jurisprudence of Justice Stephen Breyer," 59 *Mo. L. Rev.* 857 (1994) (describing Breyer's work before joining the Court as based on a fairly conservative approach to business issues).

75. There are several other approaches that could produce similar results in most cases. To avoid the infamous pitfalls of utilitarianism, *see* Jules L. Coleman, *Markets, Morals and the Law* (New York: Cambridge University Press, 1988) at 95–132, one might explore intrapersonal instead of interpersonal comparisons, *see* Dworkin, "Will Clinton's Plan Be Fair?" Or temper utilitarianism with competing approaches, following James Fishkin, *Tyranny and Legitimacy: A Critique of Political Theories* (Baltimore: Johns Hopkins University Press, 1979), that no philosophy untempered by competing systems of value is just.

76. Breyer, *Vicious Circle* at 17, 33–35, comparing reactions to risks from voluntary activities like driving with involuntary ones like environmental poisons.

77. *See ibid.* at 14, 33.

78. *See ibid.* at 20. *See also* Adarand Constructors, Inc. v. Pena, 515 U.S. 200, 273–74 (1995) (Ginsburg, J., dissenting) (regulation justified to secure equality); Schlup v. Delo, 513 U.S. 298 (1995) (*per* Stevens, J.) (innocence mattered more than judicial efficiency); Kyles v. Whitley, 514 U.S. 419 (1995) (*per* Souter, J.) (error not harmless); United States v. Lopez, 514 U.S. 549, 615 (1995) (Breyer, J., dissenting) (federal regulation of gun possession legitimate and public impact determinative under the commerce clause).

79. Babbitt v. Sweet Home Chapter of Communities for a Great Oregon, 515 U.S. 687 (1995) (joined also by O'Connor and Kennedy, JJ., finding harm to species includes harm to their habitat).

80. *See* McCulloch v. Maryland, 17 U.S. (4 Wheat.) 316 (1819) (*per* Marshall, C.J.).

81. United States v. Lopez, 514 U.S. 549, 602 (1995) (Stevens, J., dissenting); *ibid.* at 603 (Souter, J., dissenting); *ibid.* at 615 (Breyer, J., dissenting).

82. *Ibid.* at 615. *See also* Allied-Bruce Terminix Companies, Inc. v. Dobson, 513 U.S. 265 (1995) (*per* Breyer, J.) (broad interpretation of national arbitration statute preempting contrary state legislation); American Airlines, Inc. v. Wolens, 513 U.S. 219 (1995) (*per* Ginsburg, J.) (determining preemption based on efficiency of enforcement).

83. Their position on federalism in the 1994–95 term was strikingly consistent. *See* United States v. Lopez, 514 U.S. 549, 602 (1995) (Stevens, J., dissenting) (would sustain the federal Gun-Free Schools Act under the commerce clause); *ibid.* at 603 (Souter, J., dissenting) (same); *ibid.* at 615 (Breyer, J., dissenting) (same); National Private Truck Council, Inc. v. Oklahoma Tax Comm., 515 U.S. 582 (1995) (unanimous) (no federal court relief under section 1983 from state tax where state legal remedy exists); Oklahoma Tax Comm. v. Chickasaw Nation, 515 U.S. 450, 468 (1995) (Breyer, J., concurring and dissenting in part) (would have barred the states from taxing Indians living off the reservation but working on the reservation for the tribe and commuting to work); Oklahoma Tax Comm. v. Jefferson Lines, Inc., 514 U.S. 175 (1995) (*per* Souter, J.) (permitting state taxation); U.S. Term Limits, Inc. v. Thornton, 514 U.S. 779 (1995) (*per* Stevens, J.) (states barred from imposing term limits on state representatives to federal Congress); Freightliner Corp. v. Myrick, 514 U.S. 280 (1995) (unanimous but for concurrence in the judgment without opinion by Scalia, J.) (no preemption because federal standards on which preemption had been based had been suspended by court order by lower court in separate proceeding); Allied-Bruce Terminix Companies, Inc. v. Dobson, 513 U.S. 265 (1995) (*per* Breyer, J.) (national arbitration statute preempts contrary state legislation); American Airlines, Inc. v. Wolens, 513 U.S. 219 (1995) (*per* Ginsburg) (airline deregulation act preempts state fraud legislation, though it does not preempt enforcement of contracts by state law);

Hess v. Port Authority Trans-Hudson Corp., 513 U.S. 30 (1994) (*per* Ginsburg, J.) (no Eleventh Amendment immunity for the Port Authority of New York); *but see* Oklahoma Tax Comm. v. Jefferson Lines, Inc., 514 U.S. at 201 (Breyer, J., dissenting) (would have invalidated state tax because risk of double taxation by different taxes remains); Oklahoma Tax Comm. v. Chickasaw Nation, 515 U.S. at 452 (Ginsburg, J., majority opinion) (permitting state taxation of Indians); New York State Conf. of Blue Cross and Blue Shield Plans v. Travelers Ins. Co., 514 U.S. 645 (1995) (unanimous) (no preemption of incidental effect of state regulation); Wolens, 513 U.S. at 235 (Stevens, J., concurring and dissenting in part).

84. Seminole Tribe of Florida v. Florida, 517 U.S. 44, 76 (1996) (Stevens, J., dissenting); *ibid.* at 100 (Souter, J., dissenting).

85. *See, e.g.,* Metro-North Commuter RR Co. v. Buckley, 521 U.S. 424 (1997) (*per* Breyer, J., joined by Souter, J., among others) (railroad workers removing asbestos under Grand Central Terminal without proper protections who had not yet become symptomatic may not receive compensation under the Federal Employees' Liability Act either for emotional injuries or for the costs of medical testing). Compare *ibid.* at 445 (Ginsburg, J., dissenting in part, joined by Stevens, J.) (expenses of medical examinations should be covered).

86. Gustafson v. Alloyd Co., Inc., 513 U.S. 561, 596, 604n (1995) (Ginsburg, J., dissenting, joined by Breyer, J.) (the statutory regulation of prospectuses became more important because the Court had limited the meaning of the fraud provisions of section 10(b)(5) and despite the problems created by the coverage of negligent misrepresentations in the provisions regarding prospectuses, the issue should be left for Congress to determine). *See also ibid.* at 584 (Thomas, J., dissenting, joined by Scalia, Ginsburg, and Breyer, JJ.). Justices Stevens and Souter joined the majority, declining to extend the securities laws to negligent misrepresentations in a private sale and not part of a prospectus.

87. Celotex Corp. v. Edwards, 514 U.S. 300 (1995) (*per* Rehnquist, C.J., with Souter and Breyer in the majority and Ginsburg, joined by Stevens, dissenting) (holding bankruptcy judges had power over all of bankrupt's affairs, even those determined by regular courts).

88. Gutierrez de Martinez v. Lamagno, 515 U.S. 417 (1995) (*per* Ginsburg, joined by Stevens, and Breyer, JJ., among others) (holding attorney general's certification of the scope of employment reviewable). Souter dissented.

89. *See* Chandris, Inc. v. Latsis, 515 U.S. 347, 377 (1995) (Stevens, J., concurring in the judgment, joined by Thomas and Breyer, JJ.) (seaman should be covered by Jones Act at least while on duty at sea) (Ginsburg and Souter, JJ., joined the majority).

NOTES TO CHAPTER 8

1. *See* James L. Kainen, "Nineteenth Century Interpretations of the Federal

Contract Clause: The Transformation from Vested to Substantive Rights against the State," 31 *Buff. L. Rev.* 381 (1982); Max Farrand, ed., 2 *The Records of the Federal Convention of 1787* (New Haven:Yale University Press, 1966) [hereinafter Farrand, *Records*] at 439–40 (discussion of the obligation of contracts clause, August 28, 1787).

2. Farrand, 2 *Records* at 448 (remarks of Dickenson, August 29, 1787).

3. Charles S. Hyneman and George W. Carey, *A Second Federalist: Congress Creates a Government* (New York: Appleton-Century Crofts, 1967) at 268 citing 1 *The Debates and Proceedings in the Congress of the United States* (Washington: Gales and Seaton, 1834–56) (*The Annals of Congress*) at 437 (speech of James Madison, April 8, 1789, 1st Cong., 1st sess.).

4. 514 U.S. 499, 514 (1995) (Stevens, J., dissenting, joined by Souter, J.).

5. Donald S. Lutz, *Popular Consent and Popular Control: Whig Political Theory in the Early State Constitutions* (Baton Rouge: Louisiana State University Press, 1980).

6. Peter Westen, "'Freedom' and 'Coercion'—Virtue Words and Vice Words," 1985 *Duke L.J.* 541; Robert A. Dahl, *Dilemmas of Pluralist Democracy: Autonomy vs. Control*, 81–107 (New Haven:Yale University Press, 1982); David Hume, "Of the Original Contract" (1748), reprinted in *Social Contract* (Westport, Conn.: Greenwood Press, Ernest Barker ed., 1980) at 147–66.

7. BMW of North America, Inc. v. Gore, 517 U.S. 559 (1996). In Honda Motor Co., Ltd. v. Oberg, 512 U.S. 415 (1994), Justice Stevens, joined by Blackmun, O'Connor, Scalia, Kennedy, Souter, and Thomas, in an earlier opinion for the Court that also crossed ideological boundaries, held that the removal of postverdict review for reasonableness of punitive damage awards resulted in the denial of due process. Justice Ginsburg dissented, joined by Chief Justice Rehnquist, 512 U.S. at 436. She argued that the Oregon procedure provided more protection than the two states whose procedures had been found sufficient in prior cases. Oregon had provided more extensive criteria to juries than other states, 512 U.S. at 438–43. Thus Ginsburg would not subject the state regulation to a heavy gauntlet of judicial scrutiny.

8. 516 U.S. 442 (1996).

9. 518 U.S. 37 (1996).

10. *Ibid.* at 56 (Ginsburg, J., concurring); *ibid.* at 61 (O'Connor, J., dissenting); *ibid.* at 77–79 (Souter, J., dissenting). Breyer and Stevens would have reserved the question whether a statute could redefine the intent element, 518 U.S. at 80.

11. Jaffee v. Redmond, 518 U.S. 1, 10–12 (1996). Justice Scalia and Chief Justice Rehnquist responded in a balancing mode that psychotherapists are not so important. 518 U.S. at 18.

12. *See* Vernonia School District 47J v. Acton, 515 U.S. 646 (1995) (*per* Scalia, J.); *ibid.* at 666 (Ginsburg, J., concurring); *ibid.* at 666 (O'Connor, J., dissenting).

13. Arizona v. Evans, 514 U.S. 1 (1995) (*per* Rehnquist, C.J.); *ibid.* at 16 (O'Connor, J., concurring).

14. 513 U.S. 150 (1995).

15. 514 U.S. 386 (1995).

16. This practice has been challenged in United States v. Singleton, 144 F.3d 1343 (10 Cir. 1998), rev'd 165 F.3d 1297 (1999, *en banc*), cert. filed 1999, no. 98-8758. A panel of the Tenth Circuit found that the offer of leniency to a codefendant in exchange for favorable testimony essentially bribed that witness and threatened the truthfulness of the testimony. Undoubtedly because the practice is so common, the original *Singleton* decision was widely condemned and the full Court eventually reversed. The panel clearly did have a point, however, and similar inducements in a federal trial by anyone other than a United States attorney are clearly prohibited precisely because of the impact on the testimony.

17. United States v. Mezzanatto, 513 U.S. 196 (1995); *ibid.* at 211 (Ginsburg, J., concurring); *ibid.* (Souter, J., dissenting).

18. Schlup v. Delo, 513 U.S. 298 (1995).

19. O'Neal v. McAninch, 513 U.S. 432 (1995).

20. Sandin v. Conner, 515 U.S. 472, 491 (1995) (Breyer, J., dissenting); *ibid.* at 488 (Ginsburg, J., dissenting); *but see* Tome v. United States, 513 U.S. 150, 169 (1995) (Breyer, J., dissenting) (prior consistent statement, made after motive arose to make statement, is admissible).

21. Harris v. Alabama, 513 U.S. 504 (1995); *ibid.* at 515 (Stevens, J., dissenting).

22. Arizona v. Evans, 514 U.S. 1 (1995); *ibid.* at 18 (Stevens, J., dissenting); *and see ibid.* at 23 (Ginsburg, J., dissenting).

23. United States v. Mezzanatto, 513 U.S. 196 (1995); *ibid.* at 211 (Souter, J., dissenting, joined by Stevens, J.); *and see ibid.* (Ginsburg, J., concurring).

24. Vernonia School District 47J v. Acton, 515 U.S. 646 (1995); *and see ibid.* at 666 (Ginsburg, J., concurring); *ibid.* (O'Connor, J., dissenting joined by Stevens and Souter, JJ.).

25. *See ibid.* at 646 (Ginsburg and Breyer, JJ., joining the majority and finding drug search of school athletes permissible). *But see ibid.* at 666 (O'Connor, J., dissenting, joined by Stevens and Souter, JJ.) (objecting that mass searches are constitutionally proscribed and individualized searches required).

26. For Stevens, on the opposite side from both Ginsburg and Breyer, *see*: United States v. Mezzanatto, 513 U.S. 196, 211 (1995) (Breyer, J., joined Ginsburg, J., concurring); *ibid.* (Stevens, J., joined Souter, J., dissenting); Vernonia School District 47J v. Acton, 515 U.S. 646 (1995); *ibid.* at 666 (Ginsburg, J., concurring); *ibid.* at 666 (O'Connor, J., dissenting); United States v. Aguilar, 515 U.S. 593, 606 (1995) (Stevens, J., concurring in part and dissenting in part); California v. Morales, 514 U.S. 499, 514 (1995) (Stevens, J., dissenting); Gustafson v. Alloyd Co., Inc., 513 U.S. 561 (1995); *ibid.* at 584 (Ginsburg and Breyer, JJ., joined Thomas, J., dissenting); *ibid.* at 596 (Ginsburg, J., dissenting, joined by Breyer, J.); Harris v. Alabama, 513 U.S. 504, 515 (1995) (Stevens, J., dissenting); Asgrow Seed v. Winterboer, 513 U.S. 179, 193 (1995) (Stevens, J., dissenting).

For Stevens and Breyer supporting the individual against the government and opposite Ginsburg, *see* Bennis v. Michigan, 516 U.S. 442, 457 (1996) (Ginsburg, J., concurring); *ibid.* at 458 (Stevens, J., dissenting, joined by Souter and Breyer, JJ.); Oklahoma Tax Comm. v. Chickasaw Nation, 515 U.S. 450 (1995) (*per* Ginsburg, J.); *ibid.* at 468 (Stevens and Souter, JJ., joined Breyer, J., concurring and dissenting in part).

For Breyer supporting government against the individual and opposed to both Stevens and Ginsburg, *see* Arizona v. Evans, 514 U.S. 1, 16 (1995) (O'Connor, J., concurring, joined by Souter and Breyer, JJ.) (exclusionary rule appropriately not applied to record keeping error); *ibid.* at 18 (Souter, J., concurring) (same); Florida Bar v. Went For It, 515 U.S. 618 (1995) (*per* O'Connor, J., joined by Breyer, J.) (supporting delay before solicitation of accident clients); *ibid.* at 635 (Kennedy, J., dissenting, joined by Stevens, Souter, and Ginsburg, JJ.); Celotex Corp. v. Edwards, 514 U.S. 300 (1995) (supporting the power of the bankruptcy judge); *ibid.* at 313 (Stevens, J., dissenting, joined by Ginsburg, J.); Plaut v. Spendthrift Farm, Inc., 514 U.S. 211, 240 (1995) (Breyer, J., concurring in the judgment) (opposing Congress's attempt to restore rights cut off by a surprising Court interpretation of a statute of limitations).

There are, of course, some exceptions. For Breyer supporting the individual against the government and opposed to both Stevens and Ginsburg, *see* Oklahoma Tax Comm. v. Jefferson Lines, Inc., 514 U.S. 175, 201 (1995) (Breyer, J., dissenting) (concluding that state tax law invited double taxation); Stone v. Immigration and Naturalization Service, 514 U.S. 386, 406 (1995) (Breyer, J., dissenting) (fearing that the procedural decision would be a trap for the unwary).

Breyer also departed from both Stevens and Ginsburg in Tome v. United States, 513 U.S. 150, 169 (1995) (Breyer, J., dissenting) in which he argued for greater admissibility of evidence.

27. Idaho v. Coeur d'Alene Tribe of Idaho, 521 U.S. 261, 297 (1997) (Souter, J., dissenting); Seminole Tribe of Florida v. Florida, 517 U.S. 44, 76 (1996) (Stevens, J., dissenting); *ibid.* at 100 (Souter, J., dissenting).

28. Stone v. Immigration and Naturalization Service, 514 U.S. 386 (1995).

29. Oklahoma Tax Comm. v. Chickasaw Nation, 515 U.S. 450 (1995) (*per* Ginsburg) (authorizing taxation of Indians working for the tribe on the reservation but living off it); *ibid.* at 468 (Breyer, J., concurring and dissenting in part); Cass County, Minn. v. Leech Lake Band of Chippewa Indians, 524 U.S. 103 (1998) (making once alienable reservation land repurchased by tribe taxable by state); Montana v. Crow Tribe of Indians, 523 U.S. 696 (1998) (*per* Ginsburg) (denying tribe taxes state collected illegally on Indian land); *ibid.* at 719 (Souter, J., concurring and dissenting in part).

30. 517 U.S. 620 (1996).

31. 516 U.S. 442, 452 (1996).

32. *Ibid.* at 458 (Stevens, J., dissenting).

33. United States v. Armstrong, 517 U.S. 456 (1996); *ibid.* at 476 (Stevens, J., dissenting). Some police officials agree with Stevens and offer very different excuses for the disparity in arrests, *see* Harvy Lipman, "Albany's War on Drugs Ignores Whites," [Albany, N.Y.] *Times Union,* December 22, 1991 at A1; Editorial, "Blacks Dealt with Harder," [Albany, N.Y.] *Times Union,* December 28, 1991 at A8.

34. *E.g.,* in Thomas Jefferson University v. Shalala, 512 U.S. 504, 518 (1994) Justice Kennedy, joined by Chief Justice Rehnquist, and Justices Blackmun, Scalia, and Souter, concluded that the regulations properly denied the teaching university reimbursement. Based on a textual examination of the statute and an examination of the history of interpretation by prior secretaries, Justice Thomas, dissenting, joined by Justices Stevens, O'Connor, and Ginsburg, argued that the secretary improperly shifted the allocation of some eligible costs from Medicaid to medical education.

35. 512 U.S. 532, 559 (1994) (Ginsburg, J., dissenting). It is noteworthy that when she joined the Court, she was described, not as liberal, but as "moderate to conservative" at least on matters related to business. Edward A. Fallone, "Neither Liberal nor Laissez Faire: A Prediction of Justice Ginsburg's Approach to Business Law Issues," 1993 *Colum. Business L. Rev.* 279.

36. 510 U.S. 317 (1994) (*per* Stevens, J.); *compare ibid.* at 326 (Scalia, J., concurring in the judgment, joined by O'Connor, J.).

37. Department of Revenue of Oregon v. ACF Industries, Inc., 510 U.S. 332 (1994) (*per* Kennedy, J.).

38. Chandris, Inc. v. Latsis, 515 U.S. 347, 377 (1995) (Stevens, J., concurring in the judgment).

39. BMW of North America, Inc. v. Gore, 517 U.S. 559 (1996).

40. 515 U.S. 687 (1995); *compare ibid.* at 714 (Scalia, J., dissenting).

41. Asgrow Seed v. Winterboer, 513 U.S. 179, 193 (1995) (Stevens, J., dissenting).

42. Brown v. Pro Football, 518 U.S. 231, 252 (1996) (Stevens, J., dissenting).

43. Another example is Plaut v. Spendthrift Farm, Inc., 514 U.S. 211, 246 (1995) (Stevens, J., dissenting) in which Stevens and Ginsburg but not Breyer supported Congress's attempt to restore rights cut off by a surprising Court interpretation of a statute of limitations. On the other hand, there are instances in which Stevens does not support regulation. He and Souter would not subject securities dealers to the penalties of the securities laws for misdescribing transactions in conversations. Gustafson v. Alloyd Co. Inc., 513 U.S. 561 (1995) (*per* Kennedy, J.). Ginsburg and Breyer would have interpreted Congress to punish communications other than formal written prospectuses, *ibid.* at 596 (Ginsburg, J., dissenting); *and see ibid.* at 584 (Thomas, J., dissenting).

44. See "The Federalist" Nos. 47–48 (Madison), in Alexander Hamilton, James Madison, and John Jay, *The Federalist Papers* (New York: New American Library, Clinton Rossiter ed., 1961).

45. Plaut v. Spendthrift Farm, Inc., 514 U.S. 211 (1995); *ibid.* at 240 (Breyer, J., concurring); *ibid.* at 246 (Stevens, J., dissenting).

46. Federal Election Commission v. NRA Political Victory Fund, 513 U.S. 88 (1994); *ibid.* at 100 (Stevens, J., dissenting). Ginsburg took no part in the decision.

47. Clinton v. New York, 524 U.S. 417 (1998); *ibid.* at 453 (Scalia, J., concurring and dissenting in part); *ibid.* at 469 (Breyer, J., dissenting).

48. *See* "The Federalist" No. 10 (Madison).

49. McCulloch v. Maryland, 17 U.S. (4 Wheat.) 316, 428 (1819).

50. *See* Jonathan D. Varat, "Justice White and the Breadth and Allocation of Federal Authority," 58 *U. Colo. L. Rev.* 371 (1987).

51. *See* Coleman v. Thompson, 501 U.S. 722, 759 (1991) (Blackmun, J., dissenting). Kennedy quoted Blackmun to explain the import of federalism in United States v. Lopez, 514 U.S. 549, 576 (1995) (Kennedy, J., concurring). *See also ibid.* at 552 (*per* Rehnquist, C.J.) (noting original purpose of federalism for the protection of liberty).

52. Printz v. United States, 521 U.S. 898, 939 (1997) (Stevens, J., dissenting).

53. Idaho v. Coeur d'Alene Tribe of Idaho, 521 U.S. 261, 297 (1997) (Souter, J., dissenting); Seminole Tribe of Florida v. Florida, 517 U.S. at 76 (Stevens, J., dissenting); *ibid.* at 100 (Souter, J., dissenting, joined by Ginsburg and Breyer, JJ.).

54. BMW of North America, Inc. v. Gore, 517 U.S. 559 (1996) (*per* Stevens, J.); *ibid.* at 607 (Ginsburg, J., dissenting).

55. West Lynn Creamery, Inc. v. Healy, 512 U.S. 186 (1994) (milk subsidy) (*per* Stevens, J.); Associated Industries of Missouri v. Lohman, 511 U.S. 641 (1994) (statewide use tax that did not mirror local variations) (*per* Thomas, J.); Oregon Waste Systems, Inc. v. Oregon Department of Environmental Quality, 511 U.S. 93 (1994) (*per* Thomas, J.) (Oregon could not regulate by requiring use of facility and differentiate by charging out-of-state companies the full cost of service and instate companies the tax-subsidized price).

56. C and A Carbone, Inc. v. Town of Clarkstown, 511 U.S. 383 (1994) (*per* Kennedy, J.) (law improperly required all local waste processing at town facility); *compare ibid.* at 410 (Souter, J., dissenting).

57. Idaho v. Coeur d'Alene Tribe of Idaho, 521 U.S. 261, 297 (1997) (Souter, J., dissenting); Seminole Tribe of Florida v. Florida, 517 U.S. 44, 100 (1996) (Souter, J., dissenting).

58. American Dredging Co. v. Miller, 510 U.S. 443 (1994) (*per* Scalia, J.); *and see ibid.* at 457 (Souter, J., concurring); *ibid.* at 458 (Stevens, J., concurring in part and in the judgment).

59. National Organization for Women, Inc. v. Scheidler, 510 U.S. 249 (1994) (Rehnquist, C.J., for a unanimous Court); *see also ibid.* at 263 (Souter, J., concurring).

60. United States v. Lopez, 514 U.S. 549, 615 (1995) (Breyer, J., dissenting); *see also ibid.* at 602 (Stevens, J., dissenting); *ibid.* at 603 (Souter, J., dissenting).

61. American Airlines, Inc. v. Wolens, 513 U.S. 219 (1995); *see also ibid.* at 235 (Stevens, J., concurring and dissenting in part).

62. Oklahoma Tax Comm. v. Chickasaw Nation, 515 U.S. 450 (1995) (tax on

Indians living off the reservation but working for the tribe on the reservation); *see ibid.* at 468 (Breyer, J., concurring and dissenting in part); Oklahoma Tax Comm. v. Jefferson Lines, Inc., 514 U.S. 175 (1995) (*per* Souter, J.) (sales tax on interstate tickets), *but see ibid.* at 201 (Breyer, J., dissenting); Department of Revenue of Oregon v. ACF Industries, Inc., 510 U.S. 332 (1994) (*per* Kennedy, J.) (railroad tax), *but see ibid.* at 348 (Stevens, J., dissenting).

In *Barclay's Bank v. Franchise Tax Board of California*, 512 U.S. 298 (1994), Justice Ginsburg wrote for the majority consisting of Chief Justice Rehnquist, and Justices Blackmun, Stevens, Kennedy, and Souter (Scalia joined all but the section on federal uniformity in foreign affairs and concurred separately), that it was permissible to tax a percentage of income based on the California proportion of the wages, property, and sales done by the company's worldwide business, including the combined entities of which the taxpayers were part—though California has since retreated from its tax law. Precedent cleared the precise taxing statute at issue with respect to American companies. With respect to foreign companies and foreign affairs, Congress could but has not changed the rules, and the executive, despite a history of objections, is not the branch to which the power over domestic and foreign commerce has been given by the Constitution. The fundamental problem is that all systems of taxation are likely to produce double taxation. Breyer but not Stevens, Souter, or Ginsburg would have found that a sales tax on interstate tickets risked double taxation and was unconstitutional. Oklahoma Tax Comm. v. Jefferson Lines, Inc., 514 U.S. 175 (1995) (*per* Souter, J.); *ibid.* at 201 (Breyer, J., dissenting).

63. Hawaiian Airlines, Inc. v. Norris, 512 U.S. 246 (1994) (unanimous).

64. *See* BFP v. Resolution Trust Corp., 511 U.S. 531, 549 (1994) (Souter, J., dissenting).

65. *See* Custis v. United States, 511 U.S. 485 (1994) (*per* Rehnquist, C.J.); *compare ibid.* at 498 (Souter, J., dissenting).

66. BMW of North America, Inc. v. Gore, 517 U.S. 559 (1996).

67. Brown v. Pro Football, 518 U.S. 231 (1996).

68. 515 U.S. 347 (1995).

69. Gustafson v. Alloyd Co., Inc., 513 U.S. 561, 596 (1995) (Breyer, J., dissenting).

70. Kansas v. Hendricks, 521 U.S. 346, 373 (1997) (Breyer, J., dissenting).

71. Richardson v. McKnight, 521 U.S. 399 (1997).

72. Federal Election Commission v. NRA Political Victory Fund, 513 U.S. 88 (1994) (*per* Rehnquist, C.J., joined by Souter and Breyer, JJ., among others). Stevens dissented, *ibid.* at 100. Ginsburg took no part in the decision.

73. Tome v. United States, 513 U.S. 150, 169 (1995) (Breyer, J., dissenting). *See also* Williamson v. United States, 512 U.S. 594, 607 (1994) (Ginsburg, J., concurring in part and in the judgment).

74. Federal Election Commission v. NRA Political Victory Fund, 513 U.S. 88, 100 (1994) (Stevens, J., dissenting).

NOTES TO CHAPTER 9

1. Planned Parenthood v. Casey, 505 U.S. 833 (1992).

2. 505 U.S. 577, 609 (1992) (Souter, J., concurring) (blessings at graduation coerce religious observance).

3. Holder v. Hall, 512 U.S. 874, 896 (1994) (Thomas, J., concurring in the judgment) citing Allen v. State Board of Education, 393 U.S. 544, 586 (1969) (Harlan, J., concurring and dissenting).

4. Washington v. Glucksberg, 521 U.S. 702, 762–72 (1997) (Souter, J., concurring in the judgment) citing Poe v. Ullman, 367 U.S. 497, 542 (1961) (Harlan, J., dissenting).

5. *See, e.g.,* "The Supreme Court, 1993 Term: IV. The Statistics," 108 *Harv. L. Rev.* 372 (1994); Linda Greenhouse, "The Nation: Gavel Rousers; Farewell to the Old Order in the Court," *New York Times,* July 2, 1995, sec. 4, at 1.

6. 512 U.S. 532, 559 (1994).

7. *Ibid.* at 563–67.

8. *Ibid.* at 559 (Souter, J., concurring), quoting *Kernan v. American Dredging Co.,* 355 U.S. 426, 432 (1958).

9. 501 U.S. 560 (1991).

10. *Ibid.* at 582 (Souter, J., concurring).

11. He does not appear to be a rationalist/originalist conservative. *See* Kathleen M. Sullivan, "Foreword: Justices of Rules and Standards," 106 *Harv. L. Rev.* 22, 115–17 (1992) (comparing Burkean conservatism with discontinuous rationalist conservatism).

12. *Ibid.* at 115–17.

13. McFarland v. Scott, 512 U.S. 849 (1994).

14. United States v. James Daniel Good Real Property, 510 U.S. 43 (1993).

15. *See* United States v. Alvarez-Machan, 504 U.S. 655 (1992) (cross-border abduction permissible).

16. His initial decisions in the criminal area were quite tough, as they had been in New Hampshire, *see* Keeney v. Tamayo-Reyes, 504 U.S. 1 (1992); Stringer v. Black, 503 U.S. 222, 238 (1992) (Souter, J., dissenting); Wright v. West, 505 U.S. 277, 310 (1992) (Souter, J., concurring in the judgment); Estelle v. McGuire, 502 U.S. 62 (1991); Wilson v. Seiter, 501 U.S. 294 (1991); Harmelin v. Michigan, 501 U.S. 957 (1991); *but see* Morgan v. Illinois, 504 U.S. 719 (1992); Sochor v. Florida, 504 U.S. 527 (1992); Doggett v. United States, 505 U.S. 647 (1992). He found no double jeopardy on capital punishment eligibility in Schiro v. Farley, 510 U.S. 222 (1994). In Herrera v. Collins, 506 U.S. 390, 443 (1993), Souter joined Blackmun's opinion, urging a standard of probable innocence as sufficient for substantive habeas relief. Since Justice Souter had agreed earlier that a constitutional error separate from innocence was necessary, *see* Sawyer v. Whitley, 505 U.S. 333 (1992), *Herrera* does suggest some growth or change on Souter's part.

17. Sullivan, "Rules and Standards" at 113, 115, 122.

18. *See* Campbell v. Acuff-Rose Music, Inc., 510 U.S. 569 (1994). Souter speaking for an almost unanimous Court examined the purposes of parody and the value it adds, *ibid.* at 574 and 579, examining purpose historically. No comment on the quality of the parody would be appropriate, *ibid.* 582–83, according to Souter.

19. Sullivan, "Rules and Standards" at 115. Sullivan comments, "Standards are thus the tool not only of political moderates, but also of post-realist progressives. Standards better accommodate a world in which the formerly clear boundaries of public/private and speech/conduct have been relativized or dissolved." *Ibid.* at 107.

20. 512 U.S. 452, 466 (1994) (Souter, J., concurring).

21. *Ibid.* at 466, 469–75.

22. *Ibid.* at 468–69, quoting Connecticut v. Barrett, 479 U.S. 523, 528 (1987), quoting in turn Miranda v. Arizona, 384 U.S. 436, 469 (1966).

23. *Compare* Arizona v. Evans, 514 U.S. 1 (1995) (clerical errors in police files as not worth the costs of deterrence via the exclusionary rule despite significant individual consequences); *ibid.* at 16 (O'Connor, J., concurring) (same); *ibid.* at 18 (Souter, J., concurring) (same); *with* United States v. Mezzanatto, 513 U.S. 196, 211 (1995) (Souter, J., dissenting) (confidentiality of plea negotiations should not be waivable) and Vernonia School District 47J v. Acton, 515 U.S. 646, 666 (1995) (O'Connor, J., dissenting) (random urinalysis of school athletes should not be permissible).

24. Dolan v. City of Tigard, 512 U.S. 374, 411 (Souter, J., dissenting); Lucas v. South Carolina Coastal Council, 505 U.S. 1003, 1076 (1992) (Souter, J., separate opinion) (case not ready on the facts).

25. Glickman v. Wileman Bros. and Elliott, Inc., 521 U.S. 457, 477 (1997) (Souter, J., dissenting).

26. *See, e.g.,* Robert A. Dahl, *A Preface to Democratic Theory* (Chicago: University of Chicago Press, 1970), one of the seminal works.

27. *See, e.g.,* William Riker, *Liberalism against Populism* (San Francisco: W. H. Freeman, 1982).

28. *See, e.g.,* Donald P. Green and Ian Shapiro, *Pathologies of Rational Choice Theory: A Critique of Applications in Political Science* (New Haven: Yale University Press, 1994) at 13–17; Mark G. Kelman, "On Democracy Bashing: A Skeptical Look at the Theoretical and 'Empirical' Practice of the Public Choice Movement," 74 *Va. L. Rev.* 199 (1988); *and see* Daniel A. Farber, "Positive Theory as Normative Critique," 68 *S. Cal. L. Rev.* 1565, 1569–73 (1995).

29. *See* "The Supreme Court, 1991 Term: IV. The Statistics," 106 *Harv. L. Rev.* 378 (1992/93); "The Supreme Court, 1990 Term: IV. The Statistics," 105 *Harv. L. Rev.* 420 (1991/92).

30. *See* Cohen v. Cowles Media, 501 U.S. 663, 676 (1991) (Souter, J., dissenting); Simon and Schuster v. New York State Crime Victim Board, 502 U.S. 105

(1991); Forsyth County v. Nationalist Movement, 505 U.S. 123 (1992); R.A.V. v. City of St. Paul, 505 U.S. 377 (1992); International Society for Krishna Consciousness v. Lee, 505 U.S. 672, 709 (1992) (Souter, J., concurring and dissenting); and Burson v. Freeman, 504 U.S. 191, 217 (1991) (Stevens, J., dissenting); *but see* Barnes v. Glen Theatre, Inc., 501 U.S. 560, 581 (1991) (Souter, J., concurring); Burdick v. Takushi, 504 U.S. 428 (1992).

More recently, Souter joined Stevens's opinion for a unanimous Court in City of Ladue v. Gilleo, 512 U.S. 43 (1994) (can't ban for-sale signs); and Souter wrote *Campbell,* 510 U.S. 569 (1994) (parody is not infringement but fair use).

31. Lee v. Weisman, 505 U.S. 577, 609 (1992) (Souter, J., concurring); *and see* Board of Education of Kiryas Joel v. Grumet, 512 U.S. 687 (1994). With respect to the broader issue of autonomy, he also accepts some aspects of women's autonomy. In addition to his participation in the plurality in *Casey,* 505 U.S. 833, *see also* Madsen v. Women's Health Center, 512 U.S. 753 (1994) (Souter joined Rehnquist majority finding the 36' buffer zone proper) and agreed with a unanimous Court that RICO applies, National Organization for Women, Inc. v. Scheidler, 510 U.S. 249, 263 (1994) (Souter, J., concurring).

32. 512 U.S. 997 (1994).

33. 512 U.S. 874, 946 (1994).

34. *See also, e.g.*, Bush v. Vera, 517 U.S. 952, 1045 (1996) (Souter, J., dissenting).

35. *Ibid.* at 1045, 1053–54, 1062, 1071–77 (1996).

36. *See, e.g.*, J.E.B. v. Alabama *ex rel* T.B., 511 U.S. 127 (1994), in which Souter joined Blackmun in a 6–3 opinion, extending prohibition to gender-based peremptories.

37. *See* Lucas v. South Carolina Coastal Council, 505 U.S. 1003, 1076 (1992) (Souter, J., separate opinion) (urging that the factual posture of the case was not sufficiently developed).

38. 512 U.S. 374, 411 (1994).

39. 483 U.S. 825 (1987).

40. *Dolan,* 512 U.S. at 413–14.

41. 198 U.S. 45, 65 (1905) (Harlan, J., dissenting).

42. 512 U.S. at 407–9.

43. *Ibid.* at 414 citing *Lucas,* 505 U.S. at 1076.

44. Souter's views in the related areas of federalism and the environment also seem relatively fluid, *see* Oregon Waste Systems, Inc. v. Oregon Department of Environmental Quality, 511 U.S. 93 (1994) (*per* Thomas, J.) (holding that states can't charge actual costs to out-of-state shippers to compensate for in-state taxation; general revenues don't qualify; and Oregon had to charge identical costs or take over the premises itself instead of functioning as a regulator); C and A Carbone, Inc. v. Town of Clarkstown, 511 U.S. 383, 410 (1994) (Souter, J., dissenting) (urging that states should be allowed to direct recycling to a local facility); PUD No. 1

of Jefferson Co. v. Washington Dept. of Ecology, 511 U.S. 700 (1994) (*per* O'Connor, J.) (holding that states can regulate the quantity of water flowing through hydroelectric projects to protect fish).

45. *See* Cohen v. Cowles Media, 501 U.S. 663, 676 (1991) (Souter, J., dissenting); Simon and Schuster v. New York State Crime Victim Board, 502 U.S. 105 (1991); Forsyth County v. Nationalist Movement, 505 U.S. 123 (1992); R.A.V. v. City of St. Paul, 505 U.S. 377 (1992); International Society for Krishna Consciousness v. Lee, 505 U.S. 672, 709 (1992) (Souter, J., concurring and dissenting); and Burson v. Freeman, 504 U.S. 191, 217 (1991) (Stevens, J., dissenting); *but see* Barnes v. Glen Theatre, Inc., 501 U.S. 560, 581 (1991) (Souter, J., concurring); Burdick v. Takushi, 504 U.S. 428 (1992).

More recently Souter joined Stevens's opinion for a unanimous Court in City of Ladue v. Gilleo, 512 U.S. 43 (1994) (can't ban for-sale signs); and Souter wrote *Campbell,* 510 U.S. 569 (1994) (parody is not infringement but fair use).

46. Printz v. United States, 521 U.S. 898, 970 (1997) (Souter, J., dissenting).

47. Washington v. Glucksberg, 521 U.S. 702, 752 (1997) (Souter, J., concurring in the judgment).

48. Raines v. Byrd, 521 U.S. 811, 830 (1997) (Souter, J., concurring in the judgment).

49. Agostini v. Felton, 521 U.S. 203, 240 (1997) (Souter, J., dissenting).

50. Idaho v. Coeur d'Alene Tribe of Idaho, 521 U.S. 261, 297 (1997) (Souter, J., dissenting).

51. Boerne v. Flores, 521 U.S. 507, 565 (1997) (Souter, J., dissenting).

NOTES TO CHAPTER 10

1. H. Jefferson Powell, *The Moral Tradition of American Constitutionalism* (Durham: Duke University Press, 1993) at 182–259.

2. *See* Guido Calabresi, "Foreword: Antidiscrimination and Constitutional Accountability (What the Bork-Brennan Debate Ignores)," 105 *Harv. L. Rev.* 80 (1991); Committee on the Judiciary, *On the Nomination of Anthony M. Kennedy to be Associate Justice of the Supreme Court of the United States, Hearings before the Committee on the Judiciary, United States Senate, 100th Cong., 1st sess., Dec. 14–16, 1987* (Washington, D.C.: G.P.O., 1989); Symposium: "The Bork Nomination: Essays and Reports," 9 *Cardozo L. Rev.* 1–530 (1987); "Excerpts from Senate's Hearings on the Souter Nomination," *New York Times*, nat'l ed., September 15, 1990 at 10.

3. Thurgood Marshall, "The Constitution's Bicentennial: Commemorating the Wrong Document?" 40 *Vand. L. Rev.* 1337 (1987); William J. Brennan, Jr., "The Constitution of the United States: Contemporary Ratification," 43 *National Lawyers Guild Practitioner* 1 (1986).

4. Seminole Tribe of Florida v. Florida, 517 U.S. 44, 76 (1996) (Stevens, J.,

dissenting) (disputing Eleventh Amendment immunity); *ibid.* at 100 (Souter, J., dissenting) (same); Lee v. Weisman, 505 U.S. 577, 609 (1992) (Souter, J., concurring) (blessings at graduation coerce religious observance).

5. *See* Planned Parenthood v. Casey, 505 U.S. 833, 847–50 (1992) criticizing Michael H. v. Gerald D., 491 U.S. 110, 127n (1989) (opinion of Scalia, J.); *Casey*, 505 U.S. at 981 (Scalia, J., dissenting) (explaining his remarks in *Michael H.*). Chief Justice Rehnquist joined Justice Scalia's opinion in *Michael H.* but Justices O'Connor and Kennedy specifically disclaimed concurrence in that note. Chief Justice Rehnquist and Justices White and Thomas joined Justice Scalia's opinion in *Casey.* The earlier note by Scalia makes it clear that specific traditions govern when they are available and it is appropriate to consult more general principles only when more specific ones are not available.

6. *See generally* Donald S. Lutz, *Popular Consent and Popular Control* (Baton Rouge: Louisiana State University Press, 1980), for a discussion of competing ideologies in the constitution-building period.

7. The relevant history is described in Regents of the University of California v. Bakke, 438 U.S. 265, 397–98 (1978) (Marshall, J., dissenting).

8. *See* Lutz, *Popular Consent and Popular Control.*

9. Powell, *The Moral Tradition* at 52–66.

10. U.S. Const., Preamble.

11. This provision was included in the Virginia Plan submitted to the Convention on May 29, 1787, and was submitted in that form to the Committee of Detail. *See* Max Farrand, ed., 1 *The Records of the Federal Convention of 1787* (New Haven: Yale University Press, 1966) at 21, 47, 225; 2 *ibid.* at 17, 21, 131.

12. *See* Robert Devigne, *Recasting Conservatism: Oakeshott, Strauss, and the Response to Postmodernism* (New Haven: Yale University Press 1994) at 123–31.

13. *See, e.g.,* Alden v. Maine, 527 U.S. 706 (1999). In dicta in *Alden*, the Court stated that the federal government could enforce federal law directly through a federal bureaucracy but could not permit a private party to sue a state on a federal claim. Curiously, the Court's explanation was that this would substitute political judgments for the rule of law, which had been the hallmark of the conservative objection to liberal jurisprudence.

Bibliography

CASES

ABF Freight System, Inc. v. N.L.R.B., 510 U.S. 317
Adamson v. California, 332 U.S. 46
Adarand Constructors, Inc. v. Pena, 515 U.S. 200
Agostini v. Felton, 521 U.S. 203
Aguilar v. Felton, 473 U.S. 402
Air Courier Conf. v. American Postal Workers Union, 498 U.S. 517
Air Line Pilots Association International v. O'Neill, 499 U.S. 65
Alden v. Maine, 527 U.S. 706, 119 S. Ct. 2240, 144 L. Ed. 2d 636
Alexander v. United States, 509 U.S. 544
Allen v. State Board of Education, 393 U.S. 544
Allentown Mack Sales and Service, Inc. v. N.L.R.B., 522 U.S. 359. 128
Allied-Bruce Terminix Companies, Inc. v. Dobson, 513 U.S. 265
American Airlines, Inc. v. Wolens, 513 U.S. 219
American Dredging Co. v. Miller, 510 U.S. 443
American Radio Association v. Mobile Steamship Association, Inc., 419 U.S. 215
Anderson v. Buell, 516 U.S. 1100
Arcadia v. Ohio Power Co., 498 U.S. 73
Arizona v. Evans, 514 U.S. 1
Arkansas Writers' Project, Inc. v. Ragland, 481 U.S. 221
Arnett v. Kennedy, 416 U.S. 134
Asgrow Seed v. Winterboer, 513 U.S. 179
Associated Industries of Missouri v. Lohman, 511 U.S. 641
Atkins v. Parker, 472 U.S. 115
Atkins v. Rivera, 477 U.S. 154
Austin v. Michigan Chamber of Commerce, 494 U.S. 652
Babbitt v. Sweet Home Chapter of Communities for a Great Oregon, 515 U.S. 687
Baker v. Carr, 369 U.S. 186
Ball v. James, 451 U.S. 355
Barclay's Bank v. Franchise Tax Board of California, 512 U.S. 298
Barnes v. Glen Theatre, Inc., 501 U.S. 560
Barron v. Mayor and City Council of Baltimore, 7 Pet. (32 U.S.) 243

Batson v. Kentucky, 476 U.S. 79

Bendix Autolite Corp. v. Midwesco Enterprises, Inc., 486 U.S. 888

Bennis v. Michigan, 516 U.S. 442

BFP v. Resolution Trust Corp., 511 U.S. 531

Bishop v. Wood, 426 U.S. 341

Blue Chip Stamps v. Manor Drug Stores, 421 U.S. 723

Blum v. Bacon, 457 U.S. 132

Blum v. Yaretsky, 457 U.S. 991

BMW of North America, Inc. v. Gore, 517 U.S. 559

Board of County Commissioners v. Umbehr, 518 U.S. 668

Board of Education, Island Trees Union Free School District v. Pico, 457 U.S. 853

Board of Education of Kiryas Joel Village School District v. Grumet, 512 U.S. 687

Board of Education of Oklahoma City v. Dowell, 498 U.S. 237

Board of Education of the Westside Community Schools v. Mergens, 496 U.S. 226

Board of Regents v. Roth, 408 U.S. 564

Board of Trustees of SUNY v. Fox, 492 U.S. 469

Bousley v. United States, 523 U.S. 614

Bowen v. Gilliard, 483 U.S. 587

Bowers v. Hardwick, 478 U.S. 186

Bowersox v. Williams, 517 U.S. 345

Branti v. Finkel, 445 U.S. 507

Brendale v. Confederated Tribes and Bands of the Yakima Indian Nation, 492 U.S. 408

Brown v. Board of Education, 347 U.S. 483

Brown v. Pro Football, 518 U.S. 231

Brown v. Thompson, 462 U.S. 835

Buckley v. Valeo, 424 U.S. 1

Burdick v. Takushi, 504 U.S. 428

Burson v. Freeman, 504 U.S. 191

Bush v. Vera, 517 U.S. 952

C and A Carbone, Inc. v. Town of Clarkstown, 511 U.S. 383

Cable News Network, Inc. v. Noriega, 498 U.S. 976

California v. Hodari D., 499 U.S. 621

California Department of Corrections v. Morales, 514 U.S. 499

Cameron v. Pepin, 610 A.2d 279

Campbell v. Acuff-Rose Music, Inc., 510 U.S. 569

Cantwell v. Connecticut, 310 U.S. 296

Capital Area Right To Life v. Downtown Frankfort, Inc., 511 U.S. 1135

Carnival Cruise Lines, Inc. v. Shute, 499 U.S. 585

Caron v. United States, 524 U.S. 308

Carter v. Kentucky, 450 U.S. 288

Cass County, Minnesota v. Leech Lake Band of Chippewa Indians, 524 U.S. 103

Celotex Corp. v. Edwards, 514 U.S. 300

Central Hudson Gas & Electric Corp. v. Public Service Commission, 447 U.S. 557

Chandris, Inc. v. Latsis, 515 U.S. 347

Chicago, B. and Q. R.R. Co. v. City of Chicago, 166 U.S. 226

Chisom v. Roemer, 501 U.S. 380

Church of the Lukumi Babalu Aye, Inc. v. City of Hialeah, 508 U.S. 520

City of Boerne v. Flores, 521 U.S. 507

City of Canton v. Harris, 489 U.S. 378

City of Cincinnati v. Discovery Network, Inc., 507 U.S. 410

City of Columbia v. Omni Outdoor Adv., Inc., 499 U.S. 365

City of Ladue v. Gilleo, 512 U.S. 43

City of Lakewood v. Plain Dealer Publishing Co., 486 U.S. 750

City of Los Angeles v. Preferred Communications, Inc., 476 U.S. 488

City of Mobile v. Bolden, 446 U.S. 55

City of Richmond v. J.A. Croson Co., 488 U.S. 469

City of Rome v. United States, 446 U.S. 156

Civil Rights Cases, 109 U.S. 3

Clinton v. New York, 524 U.S. 417

Coates v. City of Cincinnati, 402 U.S. 611

Codispoti v. Pennsylvania, 418 U.S. 506

Cohen v. California, 403 U.S. 15

Cohen v. Cowles Media, 501 U.S. 663

Coleman v. Thompson, 501 U.S. 722

College Savings Bank v. Florida Prepaid Postsecondary Educ. Expense Bd., 527 U.S. 666

Colorado Republican Federal Campaign Committee v. Federal Election Commission, 518 U.S. 604

Community Communications Co. v. City of Boulder, 455 U.S. 40

Connecticut v. Barrett, 479 U.S. 523

Connecticut v. Doehr, 501 U.S. 1

Consolidated Rail Corp. v. Gottshall, [Conrail] 512 U.S. 532

Copperweld Corp. v. Independence Tube Corp., 467 U.S. 752

Cornelius v. NAACP Legal Defense and Education Fund, 473 U.S. 788

Cotton Petroleum Corp. v. New Mexico, 490 U.S. 163

County of Allegheny v. ACLU, Greater Pittsburgh Chapter, 492 U.S. 573

County of Riverside v. McLaughlin, 500 U.S. 44

Cox v. Louisiana, 379 U.S. 536 (Cox I)

Cox v. Louisiana, 379 U.S. 559 (Cox II)

Craig v. Boren, 429 U.S. 190

Custis v. United States, 511 U.S. 485

Davis v. Bandemer, 478 U.S. 109

Davis v. United States, 411 U.S. 233

Davis v. United States, 512 U.S. 452

Dawson v. Delaware, 503 U.S. 159

Denton v. Hernandez, 504 U.S. 25

Department of Revenue of Oregon v. ACF Industries, Inc., 510 U.S. 332

DeShaney v. Winnebago County Department of Social Services, 489 U.S. 189

District of Columbia v. Greater Washington Board of Trade, 506 U.S. 125

Doggett v. United States, 505 U.S. 647

Dolan v. City of Tigard, 512 U.S. 374

Dun and Bradstreet, Inc. v. Greenmoss Builders, 472 U.S. 749

E.E.O.C. v. Arabian American Oil Co., 499 U.S. 244

Eastern Enterprises v. Apfel, 524 U.S. 498

Edelman v. Jordan, 415 U.S. 651

Edenfield v. Fane, 507 U.S. 761

Edmonson v. Leesville Concrete Co., Inc., 500 U.S. 614

Edwards v. Aguillard, 482 U.S. 578

Elrod v. Burns, 427 U.S. 347

Employment Division, Department of Human Resources of State of Oregon v. Smith, 494 U.S. 872

Equality Foundation of Greater Cincinnati v. City of Cincinnati, 518 U.S. 1001

Equality Foundation of Greater Cincinnati v. City of Cincinnati, 525 U.S. 943, 119 S. Ct. 365, 142 L. Ed. 2d 302

Equality Foundation of Greater Cincinnati v. City of Cincinnati, 128 F.3d 289, 301 (6 Cir. 1997)

Ernst and Ernst v. Hochfelder, 425 U.S. 185

Estelle v. McGuire, 502 U.S. 62

Eu v. San Francisco County Democratic Central Committee, 489 U.S. 214

Evans v. Romer, 854 P.2d 1270 (Colo. 1993)

Everson v. Board of Education, 330 U.S. 1

Ex parte Young, 209 U.S. 123

Farmer v. Brennan, 511 U.S. 825

Federal Communications Commission v. League of Women Voters of California, 468 U.S. 364

Federal Communications Commission v. Pacifica Foundation, 438 U.S. 726

Federal Election Commission v. National Conservative PAC, 470 U.S. 480

Federal Election Commission v. National Right to Work Committee, 459 U.S. 197

Federal Election Commission v. NRA Political Victory Fund, 513 U.S. 88

Felker v. Turpin, 518 U.S. 651

Firefighters Local Union No. 1784 v. Stotts, 467 U.S. 561

First National Bank of Boston v. Bellotti, 435 U.S. 765

Florida Bar v. Went For It, Inc., 515 U.S. 618

Florida Prepaid Postsecondary Educ. Expense Bd. v. College Savings Bank, 527 U.S. 627, 119 S. Ct. 2199, 144 L. Ed. 2d 575 (1999)

FMC Corp. v. Holliday, 498 U.S. 52

Forsyth County v. Nationalist Movement, 505 U.S. 123

Fort Halifax Packing Co. v. Coyne, 482 U.S. 1

44 Liquormart, Inc. v. State of Rhode Island, 517 U.S. 484

Freeman v. Pitts, 503 U.S. 467

Freightliner Corp. v. Myrick, 514 U.S. 280

Frontiero v. Richardson, 411 U.S. 677

Fry v. United States, 421 U.S. 542

Fuentes v. Shevin, 407 U.S. 67

Gardebring v. Jenkins, 485 U.S. 415

Gentile v. State Bar, 501 U.S. 1030

Gilmer v. Interstate/Johnson Lane Corp., 500 U.S. 20

Gitlow v. New York, 268 U.S. 652

Glickman v. Wileman Brothers and Elliott, Inc., 521 U.S. 457

Gomillion v. Lightfoot, 364 U.S. 339

Gray v. Netherland, 518 U.S. 152

Green v. County School Board of New Kent County, 391 U.S. 430

Green v. Mansour, 474 U.S. 64

Gregory v. Town of Pittsfield, 470 U.S. 1018

Griggs v. Duke Power Co., 401 U.S. 424

Griswold v. Connecticut, 381 U.S. 479

Groves v. Ring Screw Works, 498 U.S. 168

Gustafson v. Alloyd Co., Inc., 513 U.S. 561

Gutierrez de Martinez v. Lamagno, 515 U.S. 417

Harmelin v. Michigan, 501 U.S. 957

Harper v. Virginia, 383 U.S. 663

Harris v. Alabama, 513 U.S. 504

Hawaiian Airlines, Inc. v. Norris, 512 U.S. 246

Heck v. Humphrey, 512 U.S. 477

Heckler v. Turner, 470 U.S. 184

Helling v. McKinney, 509 U.S. 25

Hernandez v. Commissioner, 490 U.S. 680

Hernandez v. New York, 500 U.S. 352

Herrera v. Collins, 506 U.S. 390

Herring v. New York, 422 U.S. 853

Hess v. Port Authority Trans-Hudson Corp., 513 U.S. 30

Hewitt v. Helms, 459 U.S. 460

Holder v. Hall, 512 U.S. 874

Holt Civic Club v. City of Tuscaloosa, 439 U.S. 60

Honda Motor Co., Ltd. v. Oberg, 512 U.S. 415

Houston Lawyers' Association v Attorney General of Texas, 501 U.S. 419

Hudson v. McMillian, 503 U.S. 1

Hunt v. Cromartie, 526 U.S. 541

Hunter v. Underwood, 471 U.S. 222

Ibanez v. Florida Department of Business and Professional Regulation, 512 U.S. 13

Idaho v. Coeur d'Alene Tribe of Idaho, 521 U.S. 261

Ingersoll-Rand Co. v. McClendon, 498 U.S. 133

International Organization of Masters, Mates and Pilots v. Brown, 498 U.S. 466

International Society for Krishna Consciousness, Inc. v. Lee, 505 U.S. 672

International Union, UMWA v. Bagwell, 512 U.S. 821

J. Truett Payne Co. v. Chrysler Motors Corp., 451 U.S. 557

J.E.B. v. Alabama ex rel T.B., 511 U.S. 127

Jackson v. Metropolitan Edison Co., 419 U.S. 345

Jackson v. Virginia, 443 U.S. 307

Jacobs v. Scott, 513 U.S. 1067

Jacobson v. United States, 503 U.S. 540

Jaffee v. Redmond, 518 U.S. 1

Johnson v. DeGrandy, 512 U.S. 997

Kansas v. Hendricks, 521 U.S. 346

Karcher v. Daggett, 462 U.S. 725

Keeney v. Tamayo-Reyes, 504 U.S. 1

Kernan v. American Dredging Co., 355 U.S. 426

Kiowa Tribe of Oklahoma v. Manufacturing Technologies, Inc., 523 U.S. 751

Kuhlmann v. Wilson, 477 U.S. 436

Kunz v. New York, 340 U.S. 290

Kyles v. Whitley, 514 U.S. 419

Lamb's Chapel v. Center Moriches Union Free School District, 508 U.S. 384

Leathers v. Medlock, 499 U.S. 439

Lechmere v. N.L.R.B., 502 U.S. 527

Lee v. International Society for Krishna Consciousness, Inc. 505 U.S. 830

Lee v. Weisman, 505 U.S. 577

Litton Financial Printing Division v. N.L.R.B., 501 U.S. 190

Local 28, Sheet Metal Workers' International Association v. E.E.O.C., 478 U.S. 421

Local No. 93, International Association of Firefighters v. City of Cleveland, 478 U.S. 501

Lochner v. New York, 198 U.S. 45

Lucas v. South Carolina Coastal Council, 505 U.S. 1003

Lujan v. Defenders of Wildlife, 504 U.S. 555

Lukhard v. Reed, 481 U.S. 368

Lynch v. Donnelly, 465 U.S. 668

M.L.B. v. S.L.J., 519 U.S. 102

Madsen v. Women's Health Center, Inc., 512 U.S. 753

Mapp v. Ohio, 367 U.S. 643

Martin v. Wilks, 490 U.S. 755

Masson v. New Yorker Magazine, Inc., 501 U.S. 496

Maxwell v. Dow, 176 U.S. 581

McCleskey v. Zant, 499 U.S. 467

McCulloch v. Maryland, 17 U.S. (4 Wheat.) 316

McFarland v. Scott, 512 U.S. 849

McIntyre v. Ohio Elections Commission, 514 U.S. 334

McNeil v. Wisconsin, 501 U.S. 171

Members of the City Council of the City of Los Angeles v. Taxpayers for Vincent, 466 U.S. 789

Metromedia, Inc. v. City of San Diego, 453 U.S. 490

Metro Broadcasting, Inc. v. Federal Communications Commission, 497 U.S. 547

Metro-North Commuter RR Co. v. Buckley, 521 U.S. 424

Michael H. v. Gerald D., 491 U.S. 110

Michigan v. Long, 463 U.S. 1032

Michigan v. Lucas, 500 U.S. 145

Middendorf v. Henry, 425 U.S. 25

Miller v. Johnson, 515 U.S. 900

Minneapolis Star and Tribune Co. v. Minnesota Commissioner of Revenue, 460 U.S. 57

Miranda v. Arizona, 384 U.S. 436

Missouri v. Jenkins, 515 U.S. 70

Montana v. Crow Tribe of Indians, 523 U.S. 696

Montana v. Egelhoff, 518 U.S. 37

Moore v. City of East Cleveland, 431 U.S. 494

Moore v. Dempsey, 261 U.S. 86

Moose Lodge No. 107 v. Irvis, 407 U.S. 163

Morgan v. Illinois, 504 U.S. 719

Mu'Min v. Virginia, 500 U.S. 415

Muller v. Oregon, 208 U.S. 412

Murray v. Carrier, 477 U.S. 478

National Credit Union Admin. v. First National Bank and Trust Co., 522 U.S. 479

National Endowment for the Arts v. Finley, 524 U.S. 569

National League of Cities v. Usery, 426 U.S. 833

National Organization for Women, Inc. v. Scheidler, 510 U.S. 249

National Private Truck Council, Inc. v. Oklahoma Tax Commission, 515 U.S. 582

Netherland v. Tuggle, 515 U.S. 951

Nevada v. Hall, 440 U.S. 410

New York v. United States, 505 U.S. 144

New York State Conf. of Blue Cross and Blue Shield Plans v. Travelers Insurance Co., 514 U.S. 645

Niemotko v. Maryland, 340 U.S. 268

N.L.R.B. v. Retail Store Employees Union, 447 U.S. 607

Nollan v. California Coastal Commission, 483 U.S. 825

Norfolk and Western Railway Co. v. American Train Dispatchers Association, 499 U.S. 117

O'Connor v. Donaldson, 422 U.S. 563

O'Neal v. McAninch, 513 U.S. 432

Oklahoma Tax Commission v. Chickasaw Nation, 515 U.S. 450

Oklahoma Tax Commission v. Jefferson Lines, Inc., 514 U.S. 175

Oliphant v. Suquamish Indian Tribe, 435 U.S. 191

Oregon Waste Systems, Inc. v. Oregon Department of Environmental Quality, 511 U.S. 93

Orr v. Orr, 440 U.S. 268

Owen v. City of Independence, 445 U.S. 622

Pacific Mutual Life Insurance Co. v. Haslip, 499 U.S. 1

Palko v. Connecticut, 302 U.S. 319

Palmer v. Thompson, 403 U.S. 217

Parker v. Levy, 417 U.S. 733

Patterson v. McLean Credit Union, 491 U.S. 164

Payne v. Tennessee, 501 U.S. 808

Peel v. Attorney Registration and Disciplinary Commission, 496 U.S. 91

Pennell v. San Jose, 485 U.S. 1

Pennsylvania v. Union Gas Co., 491 U.S. 1

Personnel Administrator v. Feeney, 442 U.S. 256

Phillips v. Washington Legal Foundation, 524 U.S. 156

Planned Parenthood of Southeastern Pennsylvania v. Casey, 505 U.S. 833

Plaut v. Spendthrift Farm, Inc., 514 U.S. 211

Plessy v. Ferguson, 163 U.S. 537

Poe v. Ullman, 367 U.S. 497

Police Department of Chicago v. Mosley, 408 U.S. 92

Powell v. Alabama, 287 U.S. 45

Presley v. Etowah County Commission, 502 U.S. 491

Price Waterhouse v. Hopkins, 490 U.S. 228

Printz v. United States, 521 U.S. 898

PruneYard Shopping Center v. Robins, 447 U.S. 74

PUD No. 1 of Jefferson Co. v. Washington Department of Ecology, 511 U.S. 700

R.A.V. v. City of St. Paul, 505 U.S. 377

Raines v. Byrd, 521 U.S. 811

Regan v. Taxation with Representation, 461 U.S. 540

Regents of the University of California v. Bakke, 438 U.S. 265

Reno v. ACLU, 521 U.S. 844

Reynolds v. Sims, 377 U.S. 533

Richardson v. McKnight, 521 U.S. 399

Roe v. Wade, 410 U.S. 113

Rogers v. Lodge, 458 U.S. 613

Romer v. Evans, 517 U.S. 620

Rosenberger v. Rector and Visitors of the University of Virginia, 515 U.S. 819

Rust v. Sullivan, 500 U.S. 173

Rutan v. Republican Party, 497 U.S. 62

Saenz v. Roe, 526 U.S. 489

Salyer Land Co. v. Tulare Lake Basin Water Storage District, 410 U.S. 719

Sandin v. Conner, 515 U.S. 472

Santa Fe Industries, Inc. v. Green, 430 U.S. 462

Sawyer v. Whitley, 505 U.S. 333

Schiro v. Farley, 510 U.S. 222

Schlup v. Delo, 513 U.S. 298

Schneider v. State, 308 U.S. 147

Seminole Tribe of Florida v. Florida, 517 U.S. 44

Shannon v. United States, 512 U.S. 573

Shapero v. Kentucky Bar Association, 486 U.S. 466

Shaw v. Hunt, 517 U.S. 899

Shaw v. Reno, 509 U.S. 630

Simon & Schuster v. New York State Crime Victims Board, 502 U.S. 105

Smith v. Murray, 477 U.S. 527

Snaidach v. Family Finance Corp., 395 U.S. 337

Sochor v. Florida, 504 U.S. 527

Southern Pacific Co. v. Jensen, 244 U.S. 205

Spallone v. United States, 493 U.S. 265

Stewart v. Martinez-Villareal, 523 U.S. 637

Stone v. Immigration and Naturalization Service, 514 U.S. 386

Stone v. Powell, 428 U.S. 465

Stringer v. Black, 503 U.S. 222

Suitum v. Tahoe Regional Planning Agency, 520 U.S. 725

Sullivan v. Stroop, 496 U.S. 478

Summit Health, Ltd. v. Pinhas, 500 U.S. 322

Sumner v. Mata, 449 U.S. 539

Swann v. Charlotte-Mecklenburg Bd. of Ed., 402 U.S. 1

Swanner v. Anchorage Equal Rights Commission, 513 U.S. 979

Tashjian v. Republican Party of Connecticut, 479 U.S. 208

Texaco, Inc. v. Short, 454 U.S. 516

Texas v. Johnson, 491 U.S. 397

Thomas Jefferson University v. Shalala, 512 U.S. 504

Thomas v. Review Board of the Indiana Employment Security Division, 450 U.S. 707

Thompson v. Keohane, 516 U.S. 99

Thornburg v. Gingles, 478 U.S. 30

Tome v. United States, 513 U.S. 150

Townsend v. Sain, 372 U.S. 293

Tumey v. Ohio, 273 U.S. 510

Turner Broadcasting System, Inc. v. Federal Communications Commission, 512 U.S. 622

Twining v. New Jersey, 211 U.S. 78

TXO Production Corp. v. Alliance Resources Corp., 509 U.S. 443

U.S. Term Limits, Inc. v. Thornton, 514 U.S. 779

United States R.R. Retirement Board v. Fritz, 449 U.S. 166

United States v. Aguilar, 515 U.S. 593

United States v. Alvarez-Machan, 504 U.S. 655

United States v. Armstrong, 517 U.S. 456

United States v. Carolene Products Co., 304 U.S. 144

United States v. Eichman, 496 U.S. 310

United States v. Fordice, 505 U.S. 717

United States v. James Daniel Good Real Property, 510 U.S. 43

United States v. Kokinda, 497 U.S. 720

United States v. Lopez, 514 U.S. 549

United States v. Mezzanatto, 513 U.S. 196

United States v. National Treasury Employees Union, 513 U.S. 454

United States v. Paradise, 480 U.S. 149

United States v. R. Enterprises, Inc., 498 U.S. 292

United States v. Sheffield Board of Comm'rs, 435 U.S. 110

United States v. Singleton, 144 F.3d 1343

United States v. Singleton, 165 F.3d 1297

United States v. Sioux Nation of Indians, 448 U.S. 371

United States v. Smith, 499 U.S. 160

United States v. Winstar Corp., 518 U.S. 839

Vacco v. Quill, 521 U.S. 793

Valley Forge Christian College v. Americans United for Separation of Church and State, Inc., 454 U.S. 464

Vernonia School District 47J v. Acton, 515 U.S. 646

Wallace v. Jaffrey, 472 U.S. 38

Ward's Cove Packing Co., Inc. v. Atonio, 490 U.S. 642

Washington v. Davis, 426 U.S. 229

Washington v. Glucksberg, 521 U.S. 702

Washington v. Harper, 494 U.S. 210

Waters v. Churchill, 511 U.S. 661

Webster v. Reproductive Health Services, 492 U.S. 490

Weinberger v. Wiesenfeld, 420 U.S. 636

Wesberry v. Sanders, 376 U.S. 1

West Lynn Creamery, Inc. v. Healy, 512 U.S. 186

West Virginia University Hospitals, Inc. v. Casey, 499 U.S. 83
White v. Regester, 412 U.S. 755
Whitney v. California, 274 U.S. 357
Williamson v. United States, 512 U.S. 594
Wilson v. Seiter, 501 U.S. 294
Windward Shipping (London) Ltd. v. American Radio Association, 415 U.S. 104
Wright v. Rockefeller, 376 U.S. 52
Wright v. West, 505 U.S. 277
Wygant v. Jackson Board of Education, 476 U.S. 267
Yee v. City of Escondido, 503 U.S. 519
Young v. American Mini Theatres, 427 U.S. 50
Zauderer v. Office of Disciplinary Counsel, 471 U.S. 626
Zobrest v. Catalina Foothills School District, 509 U.S. 1

DOCUMENTS

Committee on the Judiciary, *Nominations of William H. Rehnquist and Lewis F. Powell, Jr.: Hearings before the Committee on the Judiciary,* 92d Cong., 1st sess., November 3, 4, 8, 9, 10 (Washington, D.C.: G.P.O., 1971) [*1971 Hearings*]
Committee on the Judiciary, *On the Nomination of Anthony M. Kennedy to Be Associate Justice of the Supreme Court of the United States, Hearings before the Committee on the Judiciary, United States Senate, 100th Cong., 1st sess., Dec. 14–16, 1987* (Washington, D.C.: G.P.O. 1989) at 754 [*Kennedy Hearings*]
Congressional Globe, 39th Cong., 1st sess. (1866)
The Debates and Proceedings in the Congress of the United States (Washington, D.C.: Gales and Seaton, 1834–56 (*The Annals of Congress*)
Max Farrand, ed., *Records of the Federal Convention of 1787* (New Haven: Yale University Press, 1966) [Farrand, *Records*]
U.S. Code Congressional and Administrative News [1982]

BOOKS

Ackerman, Bruce A., *Private Property and the Constitution* (New Haven: Yale University Press, 1977)
Allport, Gordon, *The Nature of Prejudice* (Cambridge, Mass.: Addison–Wesley, 1954)
Ante-Bellum Reform (New York: Harper & Row, David Brion Davis ed., 1967)
Bartlett, John, *Familiar Quotations* (Boston: Little, Brown, Emily Morison Beck ed., 15th ed., 1980)
Bentham, Jeremy, *The Principles of Morals and Legislation* (Darien, Conn.: Hafner Press, 1948) (1789)
Biskupic, Joan and Elder Witt, *The Supreme Court at Work* (Washington, D.C.: Congressional Quarterly, 2d ed., 1997)

Blackstone, William, *Commentaries on the Laws of England* (1765, reprint, Chicago: University of Chicago Press, 1979)

Blasi, Vincent, *Milton's Areopagitica and the Modern First Amendment* (New Haven: Yale Law School occasional papers, 1995)

Boles, Donald E., *Mr. Justice Rehnquist, Judicial Activist: The Early Years* (Ames: Iowa State University Press, 1987)

Brandt, Richard B., *Morality, Utilitarianism, and Rights* (New York: Cambridge University Press, 1992)

Brest, Paul, and Sanford Levinson, *Processes of Constitutional Decisionmaking: Cases and Materials* (Boston: Little, Brown, 1992)

Breyer, Stephen, *Breaking the Vicious Circle: Toward Effective Risk Regulation* (Cambridge: Harvard University Press, 1993)

Breyer, Stephen, *Regulation and Its Reform* (Cambridge: Harvard University Press, 1982)

Cardozo, Benjamin N., *The Nature of the Judicial Process* (New Haven: Yale University Press, 1921)

Coleman, Jules L., *Markets, Morals and the Law* (New York: Cambridge University Press, 1988)

Cover, Robert M., *Justice Accused: Antislavery and the Judicial Process* (New Haven: Yale University Press, 1975)

Cremin, Lawrence A., *Transformation of the School: Progressivism in American Education* (New York: Knopf, 1961)

Dahl, Robert A., *Dilemmas of Pluralist Democracy: Autonomy vs. Control* (New Haven: Yale University Press, 1982)

Dahl, Robert A., and Charles E. Lindblom, *Politics, Economics, and Welfare: Planning and Politico-Economic Systems Resolved into Basic Social Processes* (New York: Harper, 1953)

Davis, Sue, *Justice Rehnquist and the Constitution* (Princeton: Princeton University Press, 1989)

De Tocqueville, Alexis, *Democracy in America* (New York: Knopf, Phillips Bradley ed., 1956)

Desegregation from Brown to Alexander: An Exploration of Supreme Court Strategies (Carbondale: Southern Illinois University Press, Stephen L. Wasby et al., 1977)

Devigne, Robert, *Recasting Conservatism: Oakeshott, Strauss, and the Response to Postmodernism* (New Haven: Yale University Press, 1994)

Dictionary of Conservative and Libertarian Thought (New York: Routledge, Nigel Ashford and Stephen Davies eds., 1991)

Discrimination, Affirmative Action, and Equal Opportunity: An Economic and Social Perspective (Hillside, N.J.: Enslow, W. E. Block and M. A. Walker eds., 1982)

Dworkin, Ronald M., *Taking Rights Seriously* (Cambridge: Harvard University Press, 1977)

Ekirch, Arthur A., *The Idea of Progress in America, 1815-1860* (New York: AMS Press, 1969)

Eliminating Racism: Profiles in Controversy (New York: Plenum Press, Phyllis A. Katz and Dalmas A. Taylor eds., 1988)

Ely, John Hart, *Democracy and Distrust* (Cambridge: Harvard University Press, 1980)

Farber, Daniel A., William N. Eskridge, Jr., and Philip P. Frickey, *Cases and Materials on Constitutional Law: Themes for the Constitution's Third Century* (St. Paul: West, 1993)

Feinberg, Joel, *The Moral Limits of the Criminal Law* (New York: Oxford University Press, 1984–88)

Fischel, William A., *Regulatory Takings: Law, Economics, and Politics* (Cambridge: Harvard University Press, 1995)

Fischer, David Hackett, *Albion's Seed: Four British Folkways in America* (New York: Oxford University Press, 1989)

Fishkin, James S., *Tyranny and Legitimacy: A Critique of Political Theories* (Baltimore: Johns Hopkins University Press, 1979)

Fiss, Owen M., *Troubled Beginnings of the Modern State, 1888–1910* (New York: Macmillan, 1994)

France, Anatole, *Le Lys Rouge* (1894)

Franklin, Benjamin, *The Autobiography of Benjamin Franklin* (New York: Pocket Books, 1955)

Gerber, Scott Douglas, *First Principles: The Jurisprudence of Clarence Thomas* (New York: New York University Press, 1998)

Gillman, Howard, *The Constitution Besieged: The Rise and Demise of Lochner Era Police Powers Jurisprudence* (Durham: Duke University Press, 1993)

Goldman, Eric F., *Rendezvous with Destiny* (New York: Vintage Press, rev. ed., 1960)

Gottlieb, Stephen E., *Jurisprudence: Cases and Materials* (Charlottesville, Va.: Michie, 1993)

Green, Donald P., and Ian Shapiro, *Pathologies of Rational Choice Theory: A Critique of Applications in Political Science* (New Haven: Yale University Press, 1994)

Greenberg, Jack, *Crusaders in the Courts* (New York: Basic Books, 1994)

Hamilton, Alexander, James Madison, and John Jay, *The Federalist Papers* (New York: New American Library, Clinton Rossiter ed., 1961)

Haskins, George Lee, and Herbert A. Johnson, *Foundations of Power: John Marshall, 1801–15* (New York: Macmillan, *The Oliver Wendell Holmes Devise History of the Supreme Court of the United States*, vol. 2, 1981)

Hazen, Thomas L., *Treatise on the Law of Securities Regulation* (St. Paul, Minn.: West, 3d ed., 1995)

Herrnstein, Richard J., and Charles Murray, *The Bell Curve: Intelligence and Class Structure in American Life* (New York: Free Press, 1994)

Himmelstein, Jerome L., *To the Right: The Transformation of American Conservatism* (Berkeley: University of California Press, 1990)

Hofstadter, Richard, *The Age of Reform from Bryan to F.D.R.* (New York: Knopf, 1955)

Hume, David, *An Enquiry Concerning the Principles of Morals* (1777 ed., reprint, La Salle, Ill.: Open Court Press, 1966)

Hyneman, Charles S., and George W. Carey, *A Second Federalist: Congress Creates a Government* (New York: Appleton-Century Crofts, 1967)

Janis, Irving L., and Leon Mann, *Decision Making: A Psychological Analysis of Conflict, Choice, and Commitment* (New York: Free Press, 1977)

John, Book of (New Testament)

Johnson, Herbert A., *Foundations of Power: John Marshall, 1801–15* (New York: Macmillan, *The Oliver Wendell Holmes Devise History of the Supreme Court of the United States*, vol. 2, 1981)

Jost, Kenneth, *Supreme Court Yearbook, 1994–1995* (Washington, D.C.: Congressional Quarterly, 1995)

Justices of the United States Supreme Court, 1789–1978: Their Lives and Major Opinions (New York: Chelsea House, Leon Friedman and Fred L. Israel eds., 1980)

Justices of the United States Supreme Court: Their Lives and Major Opinions, vol. 5 (New York: Chelsea House, Leon Friedman and Fred L. Israel eds., 1997)

Kalven, Harry, *The Negro and the First Amendment* (Chicago: University of Chicago Press, 1965)

Kant, Immanuel, *Foundations of the Metaphysics of Morals* (New York: Macmillan, Lewis White Beck trans., 1985) (1785)

Katz, Phyllis A. and Dalmas A. Taylor, *Eliminating Racism: Profiles in Controversy* (New York: Pergamon Press, 1988)

Lasswell, Harold D., and Myres S. McDougal, *Jurisprudence for a Free Society: Studies in Law, Science, and Policy* (New Haven: New Haven Press, 1992)

Locke, John, *The Second Treatise of Government* (New York: Liberal Arts Press, Thomas P. Peardon ed., 1952) (1690)

Luker, Kristin, *Abortion and the Politics of Motherhood* (Berkeley: University of California Press, 1984)

Lutz, Donald S., *Popular Consent and Popular Control: Whig Political Theory in the Early State Constitutions* (Baton Rouge: Louisiana State University Press, 1980)

Lyons, David, *Rights, Welfare, and Mill's Moral Theory* (New York: Oxford University Press, 1994)

MacKinnon, Catharine A., *Toward a Feminist Theory of the State* (Cambridge: Harvard University Press, 1989)

March, James G., *Decisions and Organizations* (New York: Blackwell, 1988)

Marshall, Alfred, *Principles of Economics: An Introductory Volume* (New York: Macmillan, 9th ed., C. W. Guillebaud annot., 1961)

Mason, Alpheus T., *The Supreme Court: Palladium of Freedom* (Ann Arbor: University of Michigan Press, 1962)

A Matter of Interpretation: Federal Courts and the Law (Princeton: Princeton University Press, Amy Gutmann ed., 1997)

Mayer, Jane, and Jill Abramson, *Strange Justice: The Selling of Clarence Thomas* (Boston: Houghton Mifflin, 1994)

Mill, John Stuart, *On Liberty* (New York: Liberal Arts Press, Currin V. Shields ed., 1956) (1859)

Mill, John Stuart, *Utilitarianism* (Buffalo: Prometheus Books, 1987) (1863)

Monahan, John, and Laurens Walker, *Social Science in Law: Cases and Materials* (Westbury, N.Y.: Foundation Press, University Casebook Series, 3d ed., 1994)

Nedelsky, Jennifer, *Private Property and the Limits of American Constitutionalism* (Chicago: University of Chicago Press, 1990)

Nisbet, Robert A., *Conservatism: Dream and Reality* (Minneapolis: University of Minnesota Press, 1986)

Nisbett, Richard, and Lee Ross, *Human Inference: Strategies and Shortcomings of Social Judgment* (Englewood Cliffs, N.J.: Prentice-Hall, 1980)

Nisbet, Robert, *History of the Idea of Progress* (New York: Basic Books, 1980)

Novak, William J., *Intellectual Origins of the State Police Power: The Common Law Vision of a Well-Regulated Society* (Madison: Institute for Legal Studies, University of Wisconsin-Madison Law School, 1989)

Nozick, Robert, *Anarchy, State and Utopia* (New York: Basic Books, 1974)

Orfield, Gary, and Carole Ashkinase, *The Closing Door: Conservative Policy and Black Opportunity* (Chicago: University of Chicago Press, 1991)

Phelps, Timothy M., and Helen Winternitz, *Capitol Games: Clarence Thomas, Anita Hill, and the Story of a Supreme Court Nomination* (New York: Hyperion, 1992)

Powell, H. Jefferson, *The Moral Tradition of American Constitutionalism* (Durham: Duke University Press, 1993)

Prosser, William L., *Handbook of the Law of Torts* (St. Paul: West, 3d ed., 1964)

Public Values in Constitutional Law (Ann Arbor: University of Michigan Press, Stephen E. Gottlieb ed., 1993)

Rawls, John, *A Theory of Justice* (Cambridge: Belknap Press of Harvard University Press, 1971)

Regan, Donald, *Utilitarianism and Cooperation* (New York: Oxford University Press, 1980)

Rossiter, Clinton, *Seedtime of the Republic* (New York: Harcourt Brace, 1953)

Schauer, Frederick, *Playing by the Rules: A Philosophical Examination of Rule-Based Decision-Making in Law and in Life* (New York: Oxford University Press, 1991)

Schultz, David A., *Property, Power, and American Democracy* (New Brunswick, N.J.: Transaction, 1992)

Schultz, David A., and Christopher E. Smith, *The Jurisprudential Vision of Justice Antonin Scalia* (Lanham, Md.: Rowman and Littlefield, 1996)

Schumpeter, Joseph, *Capitalism, Socialism and Democracy* (New York: Harper, 3d ed., 1950)

Segal, Jeffrey A., and Harold J. Spaeth, *The Supreme Court and the Attitudinal Model* (New York: Cambridge University Press, 1993)

Sickels, Robert Judd, *John Paul Stevens and the Constitution* (University Park: Pennsylvania State University Press, 1988)

Stigler, George J., *Essays in the History of Economics* (Chicago: University of Chicago Press, 1965)

Stouffer, Samuel et al., 4 *Studies in Social Psychology in World War II* (Princeton: Princeton University Press, 1950)

Sunstein, Cass, *After the Rights Revolution* (Cambridge: Harvard University Press, 1990)

Toward a Usable Past: Liberty under State Constitutions (Athens: University of Georgia Press, Paul Finkelman and Stephen E. Gottlieb eds., 1991)

Tribe, Laurence H., *American Constitutional Law* (Mineola, N.Y.: Foundation Press, 2d ed., 1988)

Tushnet, Mark V., *Making Civil Rights Law: Thurgood Marshall and the Supreme Court, 1936–1961* (New York: Oxford University Press, 1994)

Urofsky, Melvin I., *A March of Liberty: A Constitutional History of the United States* (New York: Knopf, 1988)

Williamson, Chilton, *American Suffrage from Property to Democracy, 1760–1860* (Princeton: Princeton University Press, 1960)

Wood, Gordon S., *The Creation of the American Republic, 1776–1787* (New York: Norton, 1969)

Wood, Gordon S., *The Radicalism of the American Revolution* (New York: Knopf, 1992)

ARTICLES

Aleinikoff, Alexander T., and Samuel Issacharoff, "Race and Redistricting: Drawing Constitutional Lines After Shaw v. Reno," 92 *Mich. L. Rev.* 588 (1993)

Amar, Akhil Reed, "The Bill of Rights as a Constitution," 100 *Yale L.J.* 1131 (1991)

Amar, Akhil Reed, "Justice Kennedy and the Ideal of Equality," 28 *Pacific L.J.* 515 (1997)

Asseo, Laurie, "Balance: O'Connor, Kennedy Tip Scales," *Orange County Register,* October 5, 1996

Baker, C. Edwin, "Property and Its Relation to Constitutionally Protected Liberty," 134 *U. Pa. L. Rev.* 741 (1986)

Bates, Stephen, "Rule of Law: How Cries of 'Censorship' Stifle the Schools Debate," *Wall Street Journal,* December 22, 1993, at A11

Benson, Lee, "Religious Group and Political Parties" in *Ante-Bellum Reform* (this bibliography) at 11

Bickel, Alexander M., "The Supreme Court, 1960 Term—Foreword: The Passive Virtues," 75 *Harv. L. Rev.* 40 (1961)

Blasi, Vincent, "Six Conservatives in Search of the First Amendment: The Revealing Case of Nude Dancing," 33 *Wm. & Mary L. Rev.* 611 (1992)

Blumoff, Theodore Y., and Harold S. Lewis, Jr., "The Reagan Court and Title VII: A Common-Law Outlook on a Statutory Task," 69 *N.C. L. Rev.* 1 (1990)

Bork, Robert H., "Neutral Principles and Some First Amendment Problems," 47 *Ind. L.J.* 1 (1971)

Boyd, Steven R., "The Contract Clause and the Evolution of American Federalism, 1789–1815," 44 *Wm. & Mary Q.* 529 (3d ser. 1987)

Brennan, Jr., William J., "The Constitution of the United States: Contemporary Ratification," 43 *Nat'l Lawyers Guild Prac.* 1 (1986)

Brennan, Jr., William J., "The Supreme Court and the Meiklejohn Interpretation of the First Amendment," 79 *Harv. L. Rev.* 1 (1965)

Brest, Paul, "The Misconceived Quest for the Original Understanding," 60 *B.U. L. Rev.* 204 (1980)

Brest, Paul, "State Action and Liberal Theory: A Casenote on Flagg Brothers v. Brooks," 130 *U. Pa. L. Rev.* 1296 (1982)

Breyer, Stephen, "On the Uses of Legislative History in Interpreting Statutes," 65 *S. Cal. L. Rev.* (1992)

Bullock III, Charles S., "The South and the 1996 Elections," 29 *PS: Pol. Sci. & Pol.* 450 (1996)

Calabresi, Guido, "Foreword: Antidiscrimination and Constitutional Accountability (What the Bork-Brennan Debate Ignores)," 105 *Harv. L. Rev.* 80 (1991)

Cameron, Charles, David Epstein, and Sharyn O'Halloran, "Do Majority-Minority Districts Maximize Substantive Black Representation in Congress?" 90 *Am. Pol. Sci. Rev.* 794 (1996)

Carlson, Margaret, "An Eighteenth Century Man," *Time Magazine*, August 6, 1990, at 19

Carlson, Margaret, "The Law According to Ruth," *Time Magazine*, June 28, 1993, at 38

Chemerinsky, Erwin, "The Vanishing Constitution," 103 *Harv. L. Rev.* 43 (1989)

Chesler, Mark A., "Contemporary Sociological Theories of Racism" in *Towards the Elimination of Racism* (New York: Pergamon Press, Phyllis A. Katz ed., 1976)

Church, George J., "Far More Judicious," *Time Magazine*, November 23, 1987, at 16

Clarke, Charles H., "Private Property, the Takings Clause and the Pursuit of Market Gain," 25 *Akron L. Rev.* 1 (1991)

Cohen, Richard E., "Changing The Rules of Redistricting," *Nat'l J.* at 1383 (June 22, 1996)

Cordray, Richard A., and James T. Vradelis, Comment, "The Emerging Jurisprudence of Justice O'Connor," 52 *U. Chi. L. Rev.* 389 (1985)

Culp, Jr., Jerome M., "Understanding the Racial Discourse of Justice Rehnquist," 25 *Rutgers L. J.* 597 (1994)

Dalton, Clare, "An Essay in the Deconstruction of Contract Doctrine," 94 *Yale L.J.* 997 (1985)

Days, III, Drew S., "Fullilove," 96 Yale L.J. 453 (1987)

de Grazia, Edward, "David Hackett Souter" in *Justices of the Supreme Court of the United States*, vol. 5 (Friedman and Israel eds., 1997) (this bibliography) at 1806

Denvir, John, "Justice Brennan, Justice Rehnquist and Free Speech," 80 *Nw. U. L. Rev.* 285 (1985)

Dewey, Donald O., "James Madison Helps Clio Interpret the Constitution," 15 *Am. J. Legal Hist.* 38 (1971)

Dorin, Dennis D., "Far Right of the Mainstream: Racism, Rights, and Remedies from the Perspective of Justice Antonin Scalia's *McCleskey* Memorandum," 45 *Mercer L. Rev.* 1035 (1994)

Dworkin, Ronald, "The Model of Rules," 35 *U. Chi. L. Rev.* 14 (1967)

Dworkin, Ronald, "What Is Equality? Part 1: Equality of Welfare," 10 *Phil. & Pub. Aff.* 185 (1981)

Dworkin, Ronald, "What Is Equality? Part 2: Equality of Resources," 10 *Phil. & Pub. Aff.* 283 (1981)

Easterbrook, Frank H., "Ways of Criticizing the Court," 95 *Harv. L. Rev.* 802 (1982)

Easterbrook, Frank H., "William H. Rehnquist" in 3 *Encyclopedia of the American Constitution* 1533 (New York: Macmillan, Leonard W. Levy et al. eds., 1986)

Eastland, Terry, "Rule of Law: If Clinton Wins, Here's What the Courts Will Look Like," *Wall Street Journal*, February 28, 1996, at A15

Edelman, Peter B., "Justice Scalia's Jurisprudence and the Good Society: Shades of Felix Frankfurter and the Harvard Hit Parade of the 1950s," 12 *Cardozo L. Rev.* 1799 (1991)

Eisenberg, Theodore, "Anthony M. Kennedy" in *Justices of the United States Supreme Court*, vol. 5 (Friedman and Israel eds., 1997) (this bibliography) at 1731

Ely, James W., Jr., "'That Due Satisfaction May Be Made': The Fifth Amendment and the Origins of the Compensation Principle," 36 *Am. J. Legal Hist.* 1 (1992)

Epstein, Richard, "The Proper Scope of the Commerce Power," 73 *Va. L. Rev.* 1387 (1987)

Esbeck, Carl H., "A Restatement of the Supreme Court's Law of Religious Freedom: Coherence, Conflict, or Chaos?" 70 *Notre Dame L. Rev.* 581 (1995)

Fairman, Charles, "Does the Fourteenth Amendment Incorporate the Bill of Rights? The Original Understanding," 2 *Stan. L. Rev.* 5 (1949)

Fallon, Jr., Richard H., "Individual Rights and the Powers of Government," 27 *Ga. L. Rev.* 343 (1993)

Fallone, Edward A., "The Clinton Court Is Open for Business: The Business Law Jurisprudence of Justice Stephen Breyer," 59 *Mo. L. Rev.* 857 (1994)

Fallone, Edward A., "Neither Liberal nor Laissez Faire: A Prediction of Justice Ginsburg's Approach to Business Law Issues," 1993 *Colum. Bus. L. Rev.* 279

Farber, Daniel A., "Positive Theory as Normative Critique," 68 *S. Cal. L. Rev.* 1565 (1995)

Fiss, Owen M., "Silence on the Street Corner" in *Public Values in Constitutional Law* (this bibliography) at 195

Foote, Daniel H., "'The Door That Never Opens'? Capital Punishment and Post-Conviction Review of Death Sentences in the United States and Japan," 19 *Brook. J. Int'l L.* 367 (1993)

Frankfurter, Felix, "Mr. Justice Cardozo and Public Law," 39 *Colum. L. Rev.* 88, 52 *Harv. L. Rev.* 440, 98 *Yale L.J.* 458 (1939)

Freeman, Alan, and Elizabeth Mensch, "Sandra Day O'Connor" in *Justices of the United States Supreme Court*, vol. 5 (Friedman and Israel eds., 1997) (this bibliography) at 1758

Freiwald, Aaron, "Portrait of the Nominee as a Young Man," *Legal Times*, November 23, 1987, at 1

Friedman, Leon, "Stephen G. Breyer" in *Justices of the United States Supreme Court*, vol. 5 (Friedman and Israel eds., 1997) (this bibliography) at 1874

Geier, Deborah A., "Power and Presumptions; Rules and Rhetoric; Institutions and Indian Law," 1994 *BYU L. Rev.* 451

Gey, Steven, "Is Moral Relativism a Constitutional Command?" 70 *Ind. L.J.* 331 (1995)

Ginsburg, Ruth Bader, "Communicating and Commenting on the Court's Work," 83 *Geo. L.J.* 2119 (1995)

Ginsburg, Ruth Bader, "Some Thoughts on Autonomy and Equality in Relation to *Roe v. Wade*," 63 *N.C. L. Rev.* 375 (1985)

Ginsburg, Ruth Bader, "Speaking in a Judicial Voice," 67 *N.Y.U. L. Rev.* 1185 (1992)

Golick, Toby, "Justice Scalia, Poverty and the Good Society," 12 *Cardozo L. Rev.* 1817 (1991)

Gottlieb, Stephen E., "Compelling Government Interests: An Essential But Unanalyzed Term in Constitutional Adjudication," 68 *B.U. L. Rev.* 917 (1988)

Gottlieb, Stephen E., "Does Federalism Matter to Its Devotees on the Court?" 23 *Ohio N.U. L. Rev.* 1179 (1997)

Gottlieb, Stephen E., "Fashioning a Test for Gerrymandering," 15 *J. Legis.* 1 (1988)

Gottlieb, Stephen E., "Identifying Gerrymanders," 15 *St. Louis U. L.J.* 540 (1971)

Gottlieb, Stephen E., "In the Name of Patriotism: The Constitutionality of "Bending" History in Public Secondary Schools," 62 *N.Y.U. L. Rev.* 497 (1987)

Gottlieb, Stephen E., "Introduction: Overriding Public Values" in *Public Values in Constitutional Law* (this bibliography) at 1

Gottlieb, Stephen E., "The Paradox of Balancing Significant Interests," 45 *Hastings L.J.* 825 (1994)

Gottlieb, Stephen E., "Reformulating the Motive/Effects Debate in Constitutional Adjudication," 33 *Wayne L. Rev.* 97 (1986)

Gottlieb, Stephen E., "The Speech Clause and the Limits of Neutrality," 51 *Alb. L. Rev.* 19 (1986)

Greenhouse, Linda, "The Nation: Gavel Rousers; Farewell to the Old Order in the Court," *New York Times*, July 2, 1995, §4, p. 1

Gress-Wright, Jessica, "The Contraception Paradox," 113 *Pub. Interest* 15 (Fall 1993)

Guinier, Lani, "The Supreme Court, 1993 Term: [E]Racing Democracy: The Voting Rights Cases," 108 *Harv. L. Rev.* 109 (1994)

Guinier, Lani, "The Triumph of Tokenism: The Voting Rights Act and the Theory of Black Electoral Success," 89 *Mich. L. Rev.* 1077 (1991)

Gustafson, Scott W., "The Scandal of Particularity and the Universality of Grace" in *Religious Traditions and the Limits of Tolerance* (Chambersburg, Pa.: Anima Books, Louis J. Hammann and Harry M. Buck eds., 1988) at 28

Hall, Timothy L., "Roger Williams and the Foundations of Religious Liberty," 71 *B.U. L. Rev.* 455 (1991)

Hart, H. L. A., "Between Utility and Rights," 79 *Colum. L. Rev.* 828 (1979)

Hart, H. L. A., "Positivism and the Separation of Law and Morals," 71 *Harv. L. Rev.* 593 (1958)

Healy, Melissa, "End of 'Contract' Is Start of New Tests for GOP," *Los Angeles Times*, April 7, 1995, home ed., at A1

Henretta, James A., "The Rise and Decline of 'Democratic-Republicanism': Political Rights in New York and the Several States, 1800–1915" in *Toward a Usable Past* (this bibliography) at 50

Henry, Chris, "William H. Rehnquist" in *Justices of the United States Supreme Court*, vol. 5 (Friedman and Israel eds., 1997) (this bibliography) at 1663

Henry, Christopher, "Ruth Bader Ginsburg" in *Justices of the United States Supreme Court*, vol. 5 (Friedman and Israel eds., 1997) (this bibliography) at 1859

Herman, Susan N., "Clarence Thomas" in *The Justices of the United States Supreme Court*, vol. 5 (Friedman and Israel eds., 1997) (this bibliography) at 1829

Hing, Bill Ong, "Beyond the Rhetoric of Assimilation and Cultural Pluralism: Addressing the Tension of Separatism and Conflict in an Immigration-Driven Multiracial Society," 81 *Cal. L. Rev.* 863 (1993)

Hohfeld, Wesley N., "Some Fundamental Legal Conceptions as Applied in Judicial Reasoning," 23 *Yale L.J.* 16 (1913)

Hohfeld, Wesley N., "Some Fundamental Legal Conceptions as Applied in Judicial Reasoning," 26 *Yale L.J.* 710 (1917)

Houghton, Delma, "Appointing Judges a Presidential Prize," *Tulsa World*, November 3, 1996 at G2

Hovenkamp, Herbert, "The Culture Crises of the Fuller Court," 104 *Yale L.J.* 2309 (1995)

Hunter, James Davison, "The Williamsburg Charter Survey: Methodology and Findings," 8 *J. L. & Religion* 257 (1990)

Israel, Jerold H., "Selective Incorporation: Revisited," 71 *Geo. L.J.* 253 (1982)

Issacharoff, Samuel, "Polarized Voting and the Political Process: The Transformation of Voting Rights Jurisprudence," 90 *Mich. L. Rev.* 1833 (1992)

James, Thomas, "Rights of Conscience and State School Systems in Nineteenth-Century America" in *Toward a Usable Past* (this bibliography) at 117

Jehl, Douglas, "A Product of Two Sides of Town: Judge Kennedy's Roots in Sacramento Go Deep," *Los Angeles Times*, December 14, 1987, at 1

Kainen, James L., "Nineteenth Century Interpretations of the Federal Contract Clause: The Transformation from Vested to Substantive Rights against the State," 31 *Buff. L. Rev.* 381 (1982)

Kannar, George, "The Constitutional Catechism of Antonin Scalia," 99 *Yale L.J.* 1296 (1990)

Kannar, George, "Strenuous Virtues, Virtuous Lives: The Social Vision of Antonin Scalia," 12 *Cardozo L. Rev.* 1845 (1991)

Karlan, Pamela, and Daryl J. Levinson, "Why Voting Is Different," 84 *Cal. L. Rev.* 1201 (1996)

Karlan, Pamela S., "The Rights to Vote: Some Pessimism after Formalism," 71 *Tex. L. Rev.* 1705 (1993)

Kelman, Mark G., "On Democracy Bashing: A Skeptical Look at the Theoretical and 'Empirical' Practice of the Public Choice Movement," 74 *Va. L. Rev.* 199 (1988)

Kennedy, Duncan, "Form and Substance in Private Law Adjudication," 89 *Harv. L. Rev.* 1685 (1976)

King, Peter H., "A Debate without End. Amen," *Los Angeles Times*, May 23, 1993, at 3

Kramer, Victor H., "The Supreme Court and Tying Arrangements: Antitrust as History," 69 *Minn. L. Rev.* 1013 (1985)

Kristol, Irving, "The Coming 'Conservative Century,'" *Wall Street Journal*, February 1, 1993, at A10

Lawrence III, Charles, "The Id, the Ego, and Equal Protection: Reckoning with Unconscious Racism," 39 *Stan. L. Rev.* 317 (1987)

Levinson, Sanford, "Raoul Berger Pleads for Judicial Activism: A Comment," 74 *Tex. L. Rev.* 773 (1996)

Levinson, Sanford, "Some Reflections on Multiculturalism, 'Equal Concern and Respect,' and the Establishment Clause of the First Amendment," 27 *U. Rich. L. Rev.* 989 (1993)

Lipman, Harvy, "Albany's War on Drugs Ignores Whites," [Albany, N.Y.] *Times Union*, December 22, 1991 at A1

Llewellyn, Karl N., "Remarks on the Theory of Appellate Decision and the Rules or Canons about How Statutes Are to Be Construed," 3 *Vand. L. Rev.* 395 (1950)

Locke, John, "A Letter Concerning Toleration" in John Locke, *Treatise of Civil Government and a Letter Concerning Toleration* (New York: D. Appleton, Charles L. Sherman ed., 1965) at 17

Madry, Alan R., "Analytic Deconstructionism? The Intellectual Voyeurism of Anthony D'Amato," 63 *Fordham L. Rev.* 1033 (1995)

Maltz, Earl M., "No Rules in a Knife Fight: Chief Justice Rehnquist and the Doctrine of Stare Decisis," 25 *Rutgers L.J.* 669 (1994)

Marshall, Thurgood, "The Constitution's Bicentennial: Commemorating the Wrong Document?" 40 *Vand. L. Rev.* 1337 (1987)

Massey, Steven J., Note, "Justice Rehnquist's Theory of Property," 93 *Yale L.J.* 541 (1984)

Mauro, Tony, "Lloyd's of London Haunts Breyer's High-Court Debut," *Legal Times*, October 10, 1994, at 8

Maveety, Nancy, "The Populist of the Adversary Society: The Jurisprudence of Justice Rehnquist," 13 *J. Contemp. L.* 221 (1987)

McCloskey, Robert, "Economic Due Process and the Supreme Court: An Exhumation and Reburial," 1962 *Sup. Ct. Rev.* 34

McConnell, Michael W., "Religious Freedom at a Crossroads," 59 *U. Chi. L. Rev.* 115 (1992)

McLoughlin, William G., "Charles Grandison Finney" in *Ante-Bellum Reform* (this bibliography) at 103

Michelman, Frank I., "Property, Utility, and Fairness: Comments on the Ethical Foundations of 'Just Compensation' Law," 80 *Harv. L. Rev.* 1165 (1967)

Michelman, Frank I., "Property, Federalism, and Jurisprudence: A Comment on *Lucas* and Judicial Conservatism," 35 *Wm. & Mary L. Rev.* 301 (1993)

Mill, John Stuart, to William Thomas Thornton, Saint Vran (April 17, 1863) in 15 *The Collected Works of John Stuart Mill, The Later Letters, 1849–1873* (Toronto: University of Toronto Press, Francis E. Mineka and Dwight N. Lindley eds., 1972) at 854

Miller, Binny, "Who Shall Rule and Govern? Local Legislative Delegations, Racial Politics, and the Voting Rights Act," 102 *Yale L.J.* 105 (1992)

Morawetz, Thomas, "Persons Without History: Liberal Theory and Human Experience," 66 *B.U. L. Rev.* 1013 (1986)

Morrison, Stanley, "Does the Fourteenth Amendment Incorporate the Bill of Rights? The Judicial Interpretation," 2 *Stan. L. Rev.* 140 (1949)

Nelson, William, "History and Neutrality in Constitutional Adjudication," 72 *U. Va. L. Rev.* 1237 (1986)

Niemi, Richard G., "The Relationship Between Votes and Seats: The Ultimate Question in Political Gerrymandering," 33 *UCLA L. Rev.* 185 (1985)

Note, "Justice Stevens' Equal Protection Jurisprudence," 100 *Harv. L. Rev.* 1146 (1987)

O'Connor, Sandra Day, "Testing Government Action: The Promise of Federalism" in *Public Values in Constitutional Law* (this bibliography) at 35

Onuf, Peter S., "State Politics and Republican Virtue: Religion, Education, and Morality in Early American Federalism" in *Toward a Usable Past* (this bibliography) at 91

Orland, Leonard, "John Paul Stevens" in *The Justices of the United States Supreme Court*, vol. 5 (Friedman and Israel eds., 1997) (this bibliography) at 1690

Ostling, Richard N., "Jerry Falwell's Crusade: Fundamentalist Legions Seek to Remake Church and Society," *Time Magazine*, September 2, 1985, at 48

Paine, Thomas, "The Rights of Man" in Thomas Paine, *Collected Writings* (New York: Library of America, Eric Foner ed., 1995) at 464–65

Paulsen, Michael Stokes, "The Many Faces of 'Judicial Restraint,'" 1993 *Pub. Interest L. Rev.* 3

Peller, Gary, "The Classical Theory of Law," 73 *Cornell L. Rev.* 300 (1988)

Peller, Gary, "The Metaphysics of American Law, Part 2," 73 *Cal. L. Rev.* 1151 (1985)

Phelps, Glenn A., and John B. Gates, "The Myth of Jurisprudence: Interpretive Theory in the Constitutional Opinions of Justices Rehnquist and Brennan," 31 *Santa Clara L. Rev.* 567 (1991)

Phelps, Glenn A., and Timothy A. Martinez, "Brennan v. Rehnquist: The Politics of Constitutional Jurisprudence," 22 *Gonz. L. Review* 307 (1987)

Popkin, William D., "A Common Law Lawyer on the Supreme Court: The Opinions of Justice Stevens," 1989 *Duke L.J.* 1087

Posner, Richard A., "Utilitarianism, Economics, and Legal Theory," 8 *J. Legal Stud.* 103 (1979)

Powell, H. Jefferson, "The Original Understanding of Original Intent," 98 *Harv. L. Rev.* 885 (1985)

"Provisions: The Civil Rights Act of 1991," *Cong. Q.* 3620 (December 7, 1991)

Radin, Margaret Jane, and Frank I. Michelman, "Pragmatist and Poststructuralist Critical Legal Practice," 139 *U. Pa. L. Rev.* 1019 (1991)

Radin, Margaret Jane, "Government Interests and Takings: Cultural Commitments of Property and the Role of Political Theory" in *Public Values in Constitutional Law* (this bibliography) at 69

Redlich, Allen, "The Burger Court and the Per Se Rule," 44 *Alb. L. Rev.* 1 (1979)

Rehnquist, William H., "The Notion of a Living Constitution," 54 *Tex. L. Rev.* 693 (1976)

Reisman, Daniel N., "Deconstructing Justice Scalia's Separation of Powers Jurisprudence: The Preeminent Executive," 53 *Alb. L. Rev.* 49 (1988)

Richmond, Carolyn D., "The Rehnquist Court: What Is in Store for Constitutional Law Precedent?" 39 *N.Y.L. Sch. L. Rev.* 511 (1994)

Rosen, Jeffrey, "Antonin Scalia" in *Justices of the United States Supreme Court*, vol. 5 (Friedman and Israel eds., 1997) (this bibliography) at 1714

Scalia, Antonin, "The Two Faces of Federalism," 6 *Harv. J.L. & Pub. Pol'y* 19 (1982)

Scalia, Antonin, "The Disease as Cure: In Order to Get Beyond Racism We Must First Take Account of Race," 1979 *Wash. U. L. Q.* 147

Scalia, Antonin, "Morality, Pragmatism and the Legal Order," 9 *Harv. J.L. & Pub. Pol'y* 123, 124 (1986)

Scalia, Antonin, "The Doctrine of Standing as an Essential Element of the Separation of Powers," 17 *Suffolk U. L. Rev.* 881 (1983)

Scalia, Antonin, "The Rule of Law as a Law of Rules," 56 *U. Chi. L. Rev.* 1175 (1989)

Scanlon, Thomas, "A Theory of Freedom of Expression," 1 *Phil. & Pub. Aff.* 204 (1972)

Schambra, William, "Progressive Liberalism and American Community," 80 *Pub. Interest* 31 (Summer 1985)

Schauer, Frederick, "Precedent," 39 *Stan. L. Rev.* 571 (1987)

Schultz, David, "Political Theory and Legal History: Conflicting Depictions of Property in the American Political Founding," 37 *Am. J. Legal Hist.* 464 (1993)

Shapiro, David L., "Mr. Justice Rehnquist: A Preliminary View," 90 *Harv. L. Rev.* 293 (1976)

Shapiro, David L., "William Hubbs Rehnquist" in *The Burger Court* (Leon Friedman ed., 1980) (5 *The Justices of the United States Supreme Court, 1789–1978* (New York: Chelsea House, Leon Friedman and Fred L. Israel eds., 1980))

Shapiro, Ian, "Notes Toward a Conditional Theory of Rights and Obligations in Property" in Gottlieb, *Jurisprudence: Cases and Materials* (this bibliography) at 379

Shapiro, Ian, "Three Fallacies Concerning Majorities, Minorities and Democratic Practice" in *Nomos XXXII: Majorities and Minorities* (New York: New York University Press, John W. Chapman and Alan Wertheimer eds., 1990) at 86

Shapiro, Sidney, "Keeping the Baby and Throwing Out the Bathwater: Justice Breyer's Critique of Regulation," 8 *Admin. L.J. of Am. U.* 721 (1995)

Sherry, Suzanna, "All the Supreme Court Really Needs to Know It Learned from the Warren Court," 50 *Vand. L. Rev.* 459 (1997)

Sherry, Suzanna, "Civic Virtue and the Feminine Voice in Constitutional Adjudication," 72 *Va. L. Rev.* 543 (1986)

Smith, Christopher E., "The Supreme Court's Emerging Majority: Restraining the High Court or Transforming Its Role?" 24 *Akron L. Rev.* 393 (1990)

Smith, Christopher E., and Scott Patrick Johnson, "The First-Term Performance of Justice Clarence Thomas," 76 *Judicature* 173 (1992-93)

Stevens, John Paul, "Commentary," 49 *U. Pitt. L. Rev.* 723, 728 (1988)

Stout, Lynn A., "Strict Scrutiny and Social Choice: An Economic Inquiry into Fundamental Rights and Suspect Classifications," 80 *Geo. L.J.* 1787 (1992)

Sullivan, Kathleen M., "Foreword: The Justices of Rules and Standards," 106 *Harv. L. Rev.* 22 (1992)

Sunstein, Cass, "Lochner's Legacy," 87 *Colum. L. Rev.* 873 (1987)

"The Supreme Court, 1982 Term: IV. The Statistics," 97 *Harv. L. Rev.* 295 (1983)

"The Supreme Court, 1988 Term: IV. The Statistics," 103 *Harv. L. Rev.* 394 (1989)

"The Supreme Court, 1990 Term: IV. The Statistics," 105 *Harv. L. Rev.* 420 (1991/92)

"The Supreme Court, 1991 Term: IV. The Statistics," 106 *Harv. L. Rev.* 378 (1992/93)

"The Supreme Court, 1992 Term: IV. The Statistics," 107 *Harv. L. Rev.* 373 (1993/94)

"The Supreme Court, 1993 Term: IV. The Statistics," 108 *Harv. L. Rev.* 372 (1994/95)

Symposium: "The Bork Nomination: Essays and Reports," 9 *Cardozo L. Rev.* 1–530 (1987)

Teague, Charles, "Freedom of Religion: The Freedom to Draw Circles," in *Religious Traditions and the Limits of Tolerance* (Chambersburg, Pa.: Anima Books, Louis J. Hammann and Harry M. Buck eds., 1988)

Thomas, Clarence, Commentary, "Affirmative Action Goals and Time Tables: Too Tough? Not Tough Enough!" 5 *Yale L. & Pol'y Rev.* 402 (1987)

Thomas, Clarence, "The Higher Law Background of the Privileges or Immunities Clause of the Fourteenth Amendment," 12 *Harv. J. L. & Pub. Pol'y* 63 (1989)

Thomas, Clarence, "Toward a 'Plain Reading' of the Constitution—The Declaration of Independence in Constitutional Interpretation," 30 *Howard L.J.* 983 (1987)

Treanor, William Michael, "The Original Understanding of the Takings Clause and the Political Process," 95 *Colum. L. Rev.* 782 (1995)

Tushnet, Mark V., "A Republican Chief Justice," 88 *Mich. L. Rev.* 1326 (1990)

Varat, Jonathan D., "Justice White and the Breadth and Allocation of Federal Authority," 58 *U. Colo. L. Rev.* 371 (1987)

Wechsler, Herbert, "Toward Neutral Principles of Constitutional Law," 73 *Harv. L. Rev.* 9 (1959)

West, Robin, "Progressive and Conservative Constitutionalism," 88 *Mich. L. Rev.* 641 (1990)

Westen, Peter, "'Freedom' and 'Coercion'—Virtue Words and Vice Words," 1985 *Duke L.J.* 541

Westen, Peter, "The Empty Idea of Equality," 95 *Harv. L. Rev.* 537 (1982)

Wildavsky, Aaron, "Is Culture the Culprit?" 113 *Pub. Interest* 110 (1993)

Williams, Joan, "The Constitutional Vulnerability of American Local Government: The Politics of City Status in American Law," 1986 *Wis. L. Rev.* 83

Yackle, Larry W., "The Habeas Hagioscope," 66 *S. Cal. L. Rev.* 2331 (1993)

Yassky, David, "Eras of the First Amendment," 91 *Colum. L. Rev.* 1699 (1991)

Young, Ernest, "Rediscovering Conservatism: Burkean Political Theory and Constitutional Interpretation," 72 *N.C. L. Rev.* 619 (1994)

Index

About the Author

Stephen E. Gottlieb is Professor of Law at Albany Law School. He has also been Joseph C. Hostetler-Baker and Hostetler Visiting Chair in Law at Cleveland-Marshall College of Law, and Robert F. Boden Distinguished Visiting Chair at Marquette University Law School. He has written or edited several books in the fields of constitutional law and jurisprudence and is also widely known for his work on the Supreme Court, constitutional theory, and election campaign law. His articles have appeared in *New York University Law Review, Yale Law and Policy Review, Hastings Law Journal,* and *Boston University Law Review* among many others.

Professor Gottlieb is a "veteran" of the legal services program, the Peace Corps, and corporate practice in New York City. Educated at Princeton and Yale Law School, he is active on the board of the New York Civil Liberties Union, is a member of the New York Advisory Committee to the United States Commission on Civil Rights, and once founded and ran a political action committee, but still makes time to practice both the piano and the harpsichord. He is married to the former Jeanette Grayson, another former Peace Corps volunteer. They met in Iran, courted in India and Kashmir, and have two grown children, BettyAnne and Eli.